# ALINE

# ÆLINE

## by Carole Klein

Harper & Row, Publishers
New York, Hagerstown, San Francisco, London

FIRST EDITION

*Designed by Gloria Adelson*

Library of Congress Cataloging in Publication Data

Klein, Carole.
  Aline.

  1. Bernstein, Aline Frankau, 1881–1955—Biography. 2.
Wolfe, Thomas, 1900–1938—Relationship with women—
Aline Frankau Bernstein. 3. New York (City)—Intellectual
life. 4. Set designers—United States—Biography. 5. Novel-
ists, American—20th century—Biography.
PS3503.E727Z75      792'.025'0924 [B]      76–26239
ISBN 0–06–012423–7

79 80 81 82 83 10 9 8 7 6 5 4 3 2 1

*Gratefully, to Ted,*
*who believes, encourages and sustains*

# Contents

*A section of photographs follows page 210*

# Acknowledgments

"It makes me happy to remember Aline," someone said to me in the course of my interviews, and to a large degree this sentiment was widely shared. It was my good fortune as a biographer that Aline Bernstein left such a lasting impression on the scores of people whose lives her own touched. It is impossible for me to thank all those people by name—indeed, some would rather remain anonymous. However, I shall single out a few to thank publicly, knowing that my private thank-yous extend to all those others who so thoroughly contributed to my research.

My thanks then to Herman Shumlin, Clara Weiss, Alice Beer, Emaline Roche, Andrew Goodman, Helen Walker, Mr. and Mrs. John Loeb, Mrs. E. Willard Loeb, Ruth Warner, Josephine Hutchinson, Gerstle Mack, William Koshland, Helen Gahagan Douglas, Irvene Drutman, Jimmy Amster and the late Russell Wright. Also, to David Forsberg, who brought me the important memories of Aline's old friend, Dan Totheroh. To Alfred Knopf, who shared verbal and physical photographs of Aline with me. To John Brinnin, who patiently answered far too many questions than one should have to on a fall weekend. To Mr. and Mrs. Pare Lorentz, who allowed me to visit their home in Armonk —the home that was once Aline's treasured retreat, and who carefully recreated for me what it was like when the Bernsteins lived there. A special thank-you, as well, to Ceil Blau, Aline's old friend, who vividly brought back experiences the two had lovingly shared. Similarly special thank-yous to Helen Hayes and Eva Le Gallienne, who took so much time away from their busy lives to help me form a true portrait of their friend Aline Bernstein. I am deeply grateful for their cooperation.

Singular words of gratitude to Bella Spewack, whose friendship with Aline was long and lasting, and who, to my delight, saved many of Aline's letters, to which she gave me full access.

I would like to single out, as well, Peggy Murphy, Aline's housekeeper for the last decade of her life. Her association with Aline was intimate and important, and she willingly and tirelessly shared it with me.

I also give special thanks to Melville Cane, both for his memories of Aline and Thomas Wolfe, and for his arranging for me to have access to the correspondence between Aline and Wolfe, which is now housed in the Thomas Wolfe Collection at Harvard University. On that note, my gratitude to Paul Gitlin, executor of the Wolfe estate, whose letter of permission opened up that collection to me, and to Ms. Marte Shaw, curator of the Reading Room at Harvard's Houghton Library, for allowing me to work there. Other people and institutions I am indebted to are Ms. Stella Blum of the Costume Museum in New York City and William F. Rothwell, Jr., of Vassar College, who greatly contributed to my understanding of Aline's association with both places. I also found much valuable information at the Carl Jung Foundation in New York and the Library of Princeton University, where the Maxwell Perkins correspondence is housed. The hours I spent at the Library and Museum of the Performing Arts at Lincoln Center were many, and I thank Paul Myers, Curator of the Theater Collection, for this important resource. A particular expression of thanks to Ms. Dorothy Swerdlove, First Assistant at the Theater Collection, for her informed attention to my quest for photographs of Aline's designs.

A number of people whose professional or personal lives involve Thomas Wolfe were extremely helpful to me, and also completely objective about Tom's treatment of Aline. To name only a few, Professor Richard Kennedy of Temple University; H. G. Jones, Curator of the North Carolina Collection at Chapel Hill; Clayton and Kitty Hoagland;

and most especially, Professor Richard Walser, Professor John Phillip-son and Aldo Maggi. Their vast knowledge of Wolfe and their generosity about sharing it with me contributed to my attempts to present a fair and accurate picture of Thomas Wolfe.

Two people to whom I owe particular thanks again are Dr. Michael Barton of Drake University and Dr. Donald Stowell, Jr., of Florida State University. Both men did their doctoral dissertations on the work of Aline Bernstein in costume and scenic design, and their research vastly aided my own. In addition to having access to their theses, Dr. Barton shared several of his sources with me, while Don Stowell literally dropped years of his own painstaking investigations into my lap, making me far more sophisticated about the history of theater design than I would have been able to be without his help. I am forever in his debt and applaud both his impressive scholarship and his willingness to share it with other serious researchers.

Finally, I pay the most grateful acknowledgment of all to Mrs. Edla Cusick. When I first told her I wanted to do a book about her mother, she promised me her cooperation and was unfailing in giving it to me during all our written and personal meetings. Her intelligence, wit and warmth made these meetings memorable for me, and made Aline Bernstein come alive in ways no person other than her daughter could have made happen. Mrs. Cusick opened up the doors to so many other peoples' memories that I can never attempt to count them. That I was able to say she had suggested an interview made that interview happen time and time again. I know that some of our talks were painful ones, and I was continuously struck by her determination to be fair and open and not to influence my research in any way. It is my great pleasure to be able to pay public tribute to her participation in this biography. I can only wish for other writers the same kind of integrity and generosity in their primary sources. More than any other person, Mrs. Cusick inspired me to write the most accurate and concrete biography of Aline Bernstein that I could. Once again, then, my deep and lasting appreciation.

*"She was fair, she had dove's eyes, and in all the world, there was no one like her."*
—Thomas Wolfe

# August 25, 1925

---
❧❧

*It had been a wonderful summer, Aline was thinking as she sat on the promenade deck watching the horizon while the* Olympic *moved closer to home. She thought back to the recent weeks of architectural research for her work on* The Dybbuk. *She was already picturing the sets and costumes in her mind. Then she let her thoughts wander over the many interludes with loving friends: the magnificent meals they'd shared, and the wine they'd drunk, their leisurely motoring through ancient villages. She'd dressed up in her loveliest clothes and been admired by interesting strangers. She smiled to herself at her delight in such admiration. And she thought of her family, who would be at the dock, waiting to take her back to her lovely house and her cool, shaded bedroom. Was she moving to a quieter time of her life? One less filled with emotional peaks? Would she be able to accept life on such a placid plane?*

*She sighed and shook her head, and smiled now at her traveling companion, Mina Curtiss, who was waking from a nap in the adjoining chair. They had met in London this summer, and both women immediately knew their friendship would be an enduring one, although Mina was still a very young* woman, many years younger than Aline. Of course, that wasn't so uncommon lately, Aline thought wryly. Although she knew she had never looked better, she was forty-four years old, and many of the people she knew personally and professionally were no older than her own children.

Just as she was thinking this, a young architect approached, a man whom she and Mina had come to know during the voyage. Though traveling tourist class, he had learned how to sneak up to first, and Aline and Mina greeted him warmly.

"I've been telling my friends about you two ladies," the young man said shyly. "and they'd like to meet you before we land." He went on to speak of his friends, one a bookseller and the other a young playwright, who was, he said, a particularly interesting fellow. When Aline heard the writer's name, she started. He must be the person whose manuscript she had carried overseas to Alice Lewisohn, whom she was still trying to talk into staging it at the Neighborhood Playhouse. She started to say something about the coincidence, but suddenly thought better of it. Happily, she accepted the invitation to meet in the first class lounge after dinner.

Thomas Wolfe was uncomfortable as he and his architect friend waited for the ladies they were meeting. The familiar feeling of not belonging, quickly followed by contempt for those who did, engulfed him. Turning to say something to his companion, he saw two women coming through the door, and was as startled as Aline had been at the sound of his name. For here was the woman whom he had sighted at Cherbourg, when he stood on deck looking down on the passengers joining the ship. He had been thinking about the hidden stories each man and woman might tell when suddenly he had caught sight of one particular face, rosily flushed, uplifted, concentrating deeply on something known only to her. In a moment, the face was gone, lost in the confusion. But during the voyage he had often thought of her, and it was almost shocking to see her standing now in front of him.

Aline felt the intensity of the writer's gaze even from his great height. She felt pinned by his eyes as she might pin a piece of fabric to her drawing board. There was something smoldering and violent in the meeting, and it exhilarated her and frightened her, and she turned quickly to greet the bookseller, shaking his hand with enthusiasm. But the touch of the writer's hand remained on her own. It was absurdly melodramatic, she said to herself. But it was also true.

As drink followed drink in the handsome wood-paneled lounge, she told him only that she was a theatrical designer. One by one the other passengers left to join the party they could hear going on in the ballroom. When the young men said they had promised to join friends in tourist, Aline gathered up her things. But as she turned to say good night, Wolfe beckoned her aside. The others did not hear him beg her to meet him later in the evening and did not hear her agree.

"How foolish of me to say I'd come," Aline thought, as she danced with one portly first class passenger after another. To ease her inexplicable nervousness, she'd drunk far too much champagne and her head was spinning faster than her feet. Excusing herself, she went out on deck to clear her head. There was nothing attractive about a woman her age getting ill from drinking too much, she thought ruefully.

So she stood very still, letting the cool air restore her, and then made her way down the stairs to the second class deck. This was not like her at all. Despite her pleasure in being admired and her eagerness for new experience, she had no patience with casual encounters. If she now looked to Theo more for peace than passion, she did not spend her passions lightly elsewhere. Like her father she was a romantic, who gloried in the sensual, but like her mother she took pride in ordering her instincts. Most of all, however, she prided herself in midlife on her autonomy, on still "having her pack on her back" and being her own "instrument for living," remaining gratefully, as she was now, "intact, calm," and her "own mistress."

She thought all this as she moved to meet the strange young man who seemed to have willed her to appear. She prayed he would not be there, that she could turn quietly around and go back to her safe, luxurious world. She prayed that he had not changed his mind.

There he was, looking up the stairs at her as she descended, looking so hard and steadily that she felt shy and awkward. She wanted to say something light-hearted, but she could not find the words. Indeed, she could not find any words of any kind. So in silence, she moved to his side, and, as though by agreement, they turned to the railing together in one joined motion and stood looking into the black waters. Ahead of them, the lights of the waiting city flickered, welcoming them home. Their eyes traveled to the lights and then back again to the sea. They did not look at each other.

And still neither of them spoke. The party noises began to recede. Each moment now seemed to come to her separately, pause to be savored and then move on for another to take its place. Her head felt crystally clear again, and a rush of joy suddenly flooded through her.

In the morning they would both reenter that world of lights, pick up their lives, follow their old routines. But for now, while night still covered them,

3

that other world seemed as distant as the Europe they had left behind and less real than a fairy tale told to a child. Reality was only here—in each separate, jewel-like moment.

She needed to look at him, to drink in that magnificence of size and being. She glanced quickly toward him, and marveled again at what she saw. But once again she felt nervous, and so she started to speak, to say anything that would bridge the silence between them. She began to talk about the city. She told him she had been born there, raised there. "I love every stone of it, stone on stone on stone," she said.

How could she know how divided he was about this home city of hers? Not knowing, she was shocked by the anger that moved across his face. Suddenly he lunged toward her and caught her by the arms and shook her back and forth so that her head rolled and her teeth clicked together. She would write later of the unchecked fury that was so much a part of this man's nature. But on this first night of witnessing it, she was strangely unafraid. His hands on her body filled her with such joy that any pain seemed a small price to pay.

He switched to verbal attack, rage deepening his voice and accentuating the stammer she had noticed earlier.

"Where did you get your face, raised in that dung heap of the theater, among evil and rotten people, strutting and showing their bodies! Answer me! Where did you get your eyes of love, your mouth of love, your flower face!"

The words flew around her head, but she said nothing, fascinated by his gaze, his eyes shining with a light that seemed to illuminate her entire life. She felt that until now she had been a proud flame "burning alone," and that now "another flame, a great roaring, leaping flame," had joined itself to hers.

Perhaps he sensed her thoughts, for he stopped shaking her, although his arms still held her tightly encircled. She must speak, she thought, must move beyond this ocean of feeling to a safer place. And so she twisted her head impatiently and told him his diatribe was absurd.

"You like the theater yourself, you want to be part of it; you wrote a play. I've read it, you didn't know I had read it, did you?" And then she told him about his play being tucked inside her suitcase, and traveling with her all summer. The play was far too long, she informed him, but she still believed in it and would continue to try and convince her colleagues to produce it. The animation that was so characteristic of her speech fascinated Wolfe.

He burst into laughter, his arms loose around her now. How extraordinary this was. He could scarcely believe it. He had a million questions to ask her. It was too amazing that she should be who she was, and that he should have felt as he did about her without knowing. God, he wished he had some brandy, but all the bars were closed by now.

"Listen," he said. "Do you have any brandy in your stateroom?"

A bottle of fine brandy lay unopened in her cabin, the gift of a man who had fallen in love with her in Paris, a small sad token of his feeling after she had turned down far more costly gifts, and the greatest one of all, himself. She told Wolfe about the bottle, and he dropped his arms from her body, and she felt like a little girl pushed from her parents' embrace. The air turned cold and the night grew darker. How could she leave him even to go to her cabin?

"If you promise not to move," she said seriously, "if you promise faithfully you will not leave while I'm away, I'll bring it to you."

They asked a deckhand who was busy folding chairs to find them a corkscrew and glasses, and soon they were sipping brandy together, resting their drinks on the rail when they turned to embrace each other. Holding her, or standing at her side, he talked. He never stopped talking, telling her about his life, demanding details of her own.

Suddenly there was a lull in his talk. Perhaps he had paused to take a long breath. His last question repeated itself in her mind: could she make a good salad dressing? Quickly she shouted, "I can make the best salad dressing in the world!" And as she said this, laughter bubbled inside her throat; she shrieked with laughter, gasping for air. But within minutes she was crying. Crying as though she would never stop, and indeed she worried that she might never be able to.

He stopped her tears with kisses. His hands were gentle but in their power still bruising as they explored her body, running frantically over every inch of her, clutching, tearing at her clothes until she felt that if she could pull herself away she would have to jump into the ocean, for the feelings released tonight would make every other night of her life a diminished thing.

But when somehow she did find the strength to protest his torrential passion, she did not jump into the ocean. Instead, she also found the strength to deny his urgent pleading that she take him to her cabin. Characteristically, the demands of reality took precedence over her own desire. The ship's steward was stationed right outside her cabin; it would be impossible to enter her room without being seen. More importantly, she did not want to bring Wolfe into that room and that bed. Suffused with longing as

5

*she was, the inner sovereignty of her nature said no, wait, decide with a quieter mind and heart.*

*He accepted her decision, but begged her to stay with him, not to leave him yet. And so, spent with emotion, they watched the sky begin to lighten. Then, with a final gathering of strength, she turned from him and walked quickly along the deck.*

*Years later, Thomas Wolfe would write of this meeting and their parting —would write that he was never able from this night on to see her as she undoubtedly looked to countless others: "a matronly figure of middle age, a creature with a warm and jolly little face, a wholesome and indomitable energy for every day, a shrewd, able and immensely talented creature of action, able to hold her own in a man's world." These things he knew or found out about her later, but this picture of her, which was perhaps the one by which the world best knew her, was gone forever. . . .*

*She became the most beautiful woman that ever lived—and not in any symbolic or idealistic sense—but with all the blazing, literal and mad concreteness of his imagination. She became the creature of incomparable loveliness to whom all the other women in the world must be compared, the creature with whose image he would for years walk the city's swarming streets, looking into the faces of every woman he passed with a feeling of disgust, muttering: "No, no good. Bad . . . coarse . . . meager . . . thin . . . sterile. There's not one like her—no one in the whole world who can touch her!"*

*And elsewhere in that recollection he would say, "After all the blind tormented wanderings of his youth, that woman would become his heart's center and the target of his life."*

# Part One

1880–1898

I

It was important to Aline Bernstein to know the details of the night she was born, for all her life she would talk about the joy of having a "head full of pictures." A sudden breeze, a certain odor, a casual question, and her mind would be prodded into creating a surrealist canvas of the bits and pieces of her life. A space would suddenly light, and there it was, all of it—the parts lived, the parts she might have lived—so eagerly had she adopted the feel of the related experience.

So she could later vividly color in for her friends the other elements of that night of December 22, 1880, when she was busy being born. How the stars shone so brilliantly in the darkened New York sky. How no factories or apartment buildings or electric signs spoiled the wintry landscape. How the ring of the horses' iron shoes sounded against the cobblestoned streets, like metal on metal, so deeply was the evening's frost buried. How, inside the carriages that the horses pulled, men and women sat, their collars high, their lap robes pulled tightly around them. Some rode past the brownstone house on West Thirty-fourth Street where Aline's mother lay in labor, while farther uptown, other people rode the Forty-second Street public passenger cars whose bells could be heard tinkling almost all the way to the gates of Central Park and as far south as Madison Square, where many other public and private carriers were heading. Soon a line of vehicles would pull up alongside the Madison Square Theater, a newly renovated building resplendent with a whole series of mechanical wonders. There were folding seats and a modern ventilation system, an elevator stage, and overhead lights installed personally by Thomas Edison.

Inside the theater, backstage, Joseph Frankau, Aline's father, was making up for his role as Met Miggins in the Madison's current, highly acclaimed production of *Hazel Kirke.* He smiled to himself as he fastened his wig to his forehead with spirit gum. *Hazel Kirke,* by Steele MacKaye, was a good play, one he thoroughly enjoyed doing. Unlike many of the extravagant melodramas of the period, it was naturalistic, written with a quiet power. The style was restrained, but it was a restraint that opened up rather than limited Frankau's talents. For Joseph Frankau believed that language should seem to spring instinctively from the hearts and minds of the people living their stories on the stage.

The language of the theater had always particularly fascinated Joseph Frankau. It had not been stage doors he frequented in early life, but bookshops, where he could read the poetry and prose of men who had managed to articulate their passions on paper. One bookshop in particular had become his literary home, for the owner, a Scotsman named McNeill, looked upon his store as a salon, to which he would invite interesting young customers in the evening after business hours. Gathered around the fireplace of the back room, the young men would drink tea and speak fiercely of significant things, and discover, many for the first time, the exhilaration of exchanging ideas, of expressing and defining opinions.

The group included a somewhat older man, Harlan, who was poetry editor for a minor magazine to which Joseph Frankau regularly submitted poems. One gloomy, rainy night, Harlan considerably lightened the atmosphere by telling Joe he would buy his latest effort. But when they walked home together later that evening, Harlan surprised Joe by stating that while talented with words, Joseph Frankau was, in his opinion, putting his talent to the wrong use.

Joe would often draw back the curtains of time to add this scene to his daughter's collection of pictures. He told her how, as he listened to

Harlan, the gas streetlamps cast a long reflection on the wet street, and how "something inside me felt just like the lines of light." He became excited by his mentor's vehement conviction that his talent should be expressed not by writing poetry, but by speaking poetry. Joseph Frankau clearly had "the stuff of an actor," the older man said; he should dedicate himself to becoming a fine and true one.

It was a turning point for Joe, of the kind that many creative people can recall in their own lives: that moment when the picture falls into focus, when all the yearnings and half-formed ideas and dreams take shape, when a commitment is made to the person you only now realize you have decided to become. Aline wrote of this moment in her father's life, and of its implications:

> The years go by, and young men stand in the rain or the sun or under the stars, and they tell this wonderful thing to their friend, and the theater lives forever. That night, standing in the rain, Harlan helped seal Joseph Frankau's future, promising to help him become the kind of actor Harlan knew he could be.
>
> "You must look at life with different eyes, Joe," he told him. "You must look both at the surface and deep down into it, you must search the sources."

In years to come, as he recited these first lessons in acting to his enthralled daughter, Joseph Frankau's voice warmed the child as if passion were a palpable thing, and stirred inside her the beginnings of her own infatuation with the theater. Joseph would continue his story lifting Aline in the air, holding her close while he finished the memory she almost believed she could see unfolding beneath her.

> "Nothing is too small to study, Joe. . . . Don't believe that anything or anybody is too insignificant to study. . . . Watch them, Joe. Watch man, woman and child . . . their manners, their talk, how they use their hands and their feet . . . their eyes and their mouths . . . what they wear and how they wear it. Find out for yourself what makes a joyful face look joyful and what gives the look to a face of agony. Watch and learn."

And as the memory closed, the words of her father's teacher became a part of Aline's own forming self. An intense attention to other people's inner and outer lives would be Aline Bernstein's hallmark, professionally and personally. She would never distort the image men and women projected to fit the familiar comfort of her own design. She averted her eyes from no aspect of the human experience, but embraced it all, celebrated the complexity of lives that fall apart only to reshape them-

11

selves "in the inevitable circle of their character."

Harlan taught Joseph Frankau well; there was little doubt of that. But along with the skills of acting, he instilled in his disciple a craving for love.

"They must fall in love with Joe," he explained, for this was why people would come to see Joe perform. "Cast your spell—then they will listen to you!"

All his adult life Joseph Frankau would want his audience to fall in love with him, and more and more he needed the world to be the audience. There are those who would say the same of Aline, even while they willingly fed her their affection.

Whether or not Aline Bernstein believed this about herself, she clearly saw what price was paid for her father's voracious need for love and admiration.

"Everybody fell in love with him," she'd say later, "and it was the worst thing in the world for him."

She might have added, "and for those who were close to him," for being involved with Joseph Frankau could bring its share of pain. Still, if anyone knew the brighter side of loving and being loved by Joe, it was Aline, the child born that December night in 1880.

As Joe sat at his dressing table, for once he hardly saw his reflection. For he was musing about how this mysterious new role of father would suit him. And even as he was doing so, a small boy was ducking under the doorman's arm at the stage entrance. The doorman had refused to allow him inside because the play was about to begin and the child was breathing heavily and making squeaking noises with his shoes as he jiggled up and down in the cold. But the boy, whose name was Edgar, held off attempts to put him outside the door again, explaining that he had an urgent message for his uncle, Joseph Frankau. Having promised to be quiet, he was finally allowed to tiptoe to Joe's dressing room.

Everything seemed so still as he moved down the hall—the special kind of quiet when the curtain is still down but the overture is playing, that moment just before a particular piece of theatrical magic once again begins.

Joseph Frankau felt the hush, as he felt it every night, and so it was especially startling to see in his mirror the reflection of Edgar coming through the door. Steele MacKaye would have thought the drama too contrived—the way Edgar could only mouth the word "girl" before Joseph must take his place on stage. But that was indeed how Aline's birth was announced. Edgar stayed in the dressing room until the play was finished, and then by way of celebration, Joseph took the child home in a cab instead of the usual trolley car. Holding Edgar's hand, Joseph let himself into the room where his wife lay in bed, and his new daughter slept bundled into a basket. Never one to feel stage fright, suddenly Joe was trembling and his palms were moist. He looked at his daughter for a long while, and gingerly touched her small hands.

Joseph Frankau told his daughter the story of her birth night many times, and when Aline herself recounted the tale, she invariably finished by describing "daddy" 's walk to her mother's bed, where she had lain watching him, to give her a long, "thankful" kiss.

That Aline was unabashed at suggesting her birth was something to be thankful for reflects a quality she would have till the end of her life. Theresa Helburn of the Theatre Guild, who played a major role in Aline's career, summed up this aspect of her personality. "She was so charmingly self-satisfied, so ingenuously boastful. . . . She would tell you about her achievements as if she were reporting a great bit of news, generously shared. She discussed her own and her family's virtues as though she were letting you in on a delightful secret!"

Immodest as it may sometimes have seemed, Aline's pride was usually understandable. Whether it was the accomplishments of her own life, or her parental heritage, her boasting had a solid foundation of fact. Certainly, this was true about the Frankau background, which was, for its day, delightfully bizarre. For her father's own parents were a poor German-Jewish haberdasher and the daughter of one of Connecticut's most prosperous Protestant families.

Aline's paternal grandfather had emigrated to this country with a cultivated mind but very little money. Finding a job in a dry goods store in Hartford, Connecticut, he did more than simply wait on the elegant young ladies who shopped with their mothers. He advised them on which colors best suited their complexions, and tucked flowers into their bonnets free of charge. A Jew, a salesman, nonetheless he was considered charming and was invited to parties by the town's wealthiest families.

Everything about the Connecticut landscape, natural and man-made, the rolling green land and the large white houses that sat elegantly upon it, delighted Aline's grandfather. In one of the loveliest houses of all lived a young woman who seemed to him as graceful and dignified as the world she had grown up in. But when Ellen Griswold told her parents that she was in love with the young Jewish haberdasher, they were horrified. Yes, they had invited him to their home, but that was hardly the same thing as making him part of the family. They forbade their daughter to have anything more to do with Nathan Frankau.

Perhaps some of Aline's dogged determination to accomplish her goals, no matter what the obstacles, had their roots in this particular branch of her ancestry. Aline's sister, Ethel, among others, would later say that Aline "always got her way." She would relentlessly pursue an object or a person who temporarily eluded her until she was victorious. Needing a particular table or fabric for a play, she'd roam the city, poking into antique shops, interrogating craftsmen, until exactly what she wanted, and only exactly what she wanted, was hers. In her relationship with Thomas Wolfe, the same tenacious grip would certainly be evident.

Ellen Griswold stood squarely against her parents' disapproval. No matter what they said, she would marry this Jewish salesman. And so it was that in the middle of the nineteenth century, well before the Civil War, she packed a trunk and left her country home, off to live with a rabbi and his family in Hartford. The rabbi would teach her the religion of her intended husband, and in exchange for this education, she would work along with the rabbi's wife at chores that in her own family had always been done by servant girls.

Before many months had passed, Ellen's parents were asking her to end her exile. They missed her and wanted her to come home and accept their permission to marry the man she loved. She rejoiced in her parents' forgiveness, but had become captivated by the rituals and ideas of Judaism and was determined to immerse herself in them. She stayed in Hartford for a full year, and she married Nathan Frankau in the rabbi's house under the traditional canopy, to become for the rest of her life a pious Jewish wife.

Despite Ellen's religious conversion, the Griswolds were very much part of the lives of their daughter and her family. Although they died when Aline was still quite young, she remembered visiting them, particularly for the annual spring picnics that celebrated the running of the shad in the Farmington River. Aline, with her characteristic relish of eating and cooking, recalled those spring feasts, notable for the fresh-caught fish broiled over hickory logs on open fires until they were charred and then served on hollowed planks along with yellow cream "so thick it had to be put on with a spoon. . . . We ate until we could

14

barely move, then topped it off with chopped lemon pie . . . made of black stoned raisins, lemons chopped fine as sand, flavored with molasses. And it had three crusts, the conventional top and bottom ones, and an extra put in the middle!"

Ellen Griswold Frankau and her husband remained in Hartford after their marriage, and Nathan opened his own shop. It was quickly successful, thanks to Nathan's excellent taste in stock. By the time the Civil War broke out, Nathan had enough money to subsidize a sudden surge of patriotism by equipping a regiment of volunteers from Connecticut. Wearing one of its uniforms himself, he went off to active service. But although he returned unharmed, the war had changed business conditions in Hartford, and after a while the family moved to New York to begin again. He never did as well there as he had hoped to, but he always made a respectable living. More importantly for Aline, the move allowed Joseph Frankau to become a child of the city where he would choose to raise his own family, and where his daughter would be exposed to energies she was fed by all her life.

Aline has said of her mother: "She loved us all too much and that love made her vulnerable." Certainly Rebecca Goldsmith Frankau always lived in the shadow of her husband, making few demands and meeting his most outrageous behavior with quiet, steady devotion. But Rebecca's background had prepared her for acts of male flamboyance. Her father, like her father-in-law, had come from Europe to America to seek his fortune, but he was far better equipped than Nathan Frankau to do so. A lawyer and professor in Holland, he quickly passed the New York Bar examination. Financial success was equally rapid, and when he married the Frenchwoman who would become the mother of his three daughters, they lived as elegantly as any European aristocrats.

Henry Goldsmith savored every detail of living well. Here again, one sees how inherited patterns affect children yet to be born. Like her grandparents Griswold and Goldsmith, Aline would always have a taste for elegance, even while other aspects of her nature were robust and earthy. Indeed, she would spend her life demanding the rewards of both worlds, the bohemian and the conventional, the elegant and the extravagant.

Henry Goldsmith's family lived in a brownstone mansion on Thirty-fourth Street. Aline says of this grandfather that he "had a passion for Thirty-fourth Street." Not being a man to ignore his passions, Goldsmith bought up every available piece of property on the street, presenting each of his daughters at her marriage with a Thirty-fourth Street home. That is how Aline came to be born on a corner where R. H. Macy's now stands, in a room that would later correspond, she always declared in delight, to the store's underwear department.

Mrs. Goldsmith died after the birth of her third daughter, Rachel, always to be called Nana, the aunt whom Aline would worship long and deeply. Some years later, Henry married again, and his thin, quiet new wife was genuinely devoted to her adopted daughters. Henry showed his gratitude by showering her with presents, always faithfully giving duplicates to his big blond mistress, who conveniently lived just around the corner on Thirty-fifth Street.

The lavish spending and real estate speculating that were Goldsmith's style took their toll. At his death, when Aline was less than three years old, it became clear that all his property was going to vanish into a sea of claims. It was time for his three daughters to take stock of their lives. Mamie, the elder sister, who had married a handsome young man from the South, was already discovering that his earning capacity was far less powerful than his charm. Nana, the youngest, was more secure, for her doctor husband was attracting great numbers of patients with his striking looks and almost theatrical bedside manner. As for Rebecca, she worried about the uncertainty of an actor's life. Like her father, her husband loved good living, which to him meant late nights with fellow actors, buying them rounds of drinks or purchasing front-row tickets to their current shows. He had no desire to fill in the time between acting jobs with other kinds of work; and so those intervals, and there were many, were too lean for the comfort of even a loving wife. For this reason, when after their father's death her sister Mamie decided to rent a big house on Forty-fourth Street and run it as a boardinghouse for actors, Rebecca talked Joe into moving there too. Of this home, set in what was to be the heart of New York's theatrical district, Shubert Alley, Aline Bernstein would one day write: "Of all the places I have lived, I loved that place the best." And indeed, inside the boardinghouse at 217 West 44th Street, life surged and sang, bombarding Aline's receptive vision with a million impressions.

A story written by Thomas Wolfe is based on a visit Aline, at fourteen, paid with her father to the legendary actor Richard Mansfield after one of his last performances as Richard III. Aline recalled the visit in great and vivid detail for Wolfe, who later transcribed it almost literally in a story first published in the *Atlantic Monthly* and

16

then as a chapter in his novel *The Web and the Rock*.

A key element in the story is the fictional father's wistful admiration of his daughter's ability to savor even the most mundane incident. Clearly representing the real-life Joseph Frankau talking about his daughter Aline, Wolfe's protagonist tells his more successful actor friend that his child has the wondrous ability to create soaring sensation from the smallest experience. Why, she can go out in a park and remember the shape of every leaf, can tell you what people wore, and invent wonderful stories about their lives.

"I see a million faces, and I can't remember one," he says. "But she sees one and remembers a million!"

As an adult Aline would say in an interview: "There is so much beauty all about us that sometimes I think we should all wear blinkers!" And the beginning of this exultant perception can be seen in Wolfe's recounting of the young Aline's response to her father's comments about her. When Mansfield asks how one gets to the marvelous country she seems to inhabit, she says:

> "It's easy. You just walk out in the street, and look around, and there you are . . . sometimes it's a leaf . . . and sometimes it's a button . . . or an old shoe on the floor. Sometimes it's the markets and the way the chickens smell, or all the new vegetables. . . . Sometimes it's the people in a train that passes the one you're in. You see all the people, you are close to them; but you cannot touch them; you say goodbye to them and it makes you feel sad. Sometimes it's all the kids playing in the street; they don't seem to have anything to do with the grown-ups . . . they seem to live in a world of their own, there is something strange about it. And sometimes it's like that with the horses too; they fill the streets; you forget about all the people; the horses seem to own the earth; they talk to each other and they seem to have a life of their own that people have nothing to do with.

Where did it come from, this ability so to savor life? Certainly, some of its roots lay in the boardinghouse, where her curiosity about people's lives had countless dramas to engage it, and her senses were kept keen by the richness of living the actors and actresses indulged in.

Even the workaday activities were exciting. Aline, as a young child, would run down from the bedroom she shared with her parents—their stately mahogany bed from the old house looming above her foldaway cot—and sit at the kitchen table watching the Irish servant girls pour their strong black tea from the heavy brown pot that was always on the stove.

"They would give me a cup of tea and it made my tongue shrivel ar d my teeth feel as though they were rubbing silk," she remembered. And then she would go marketing with Aunt Mamie, who personally selected every bit of food that went on her table. Aline's lusty appreciation of food surely got a start on these trips down Forty-fifth Street to the butcher and the grocer, holding her Aunt Mamie's hand. Mamie wore lace "mitts," which allowed her many diamond rings to shine brilliantly when she waved her hands in negotiations. And Aline was not simply tagging along. Her aunt made her a very real participant in these excursions.

"I was thinking about ducks for tonight—how does that strike you?" Mamie would ask, and Aline would rub her cheek against her aunt's fingers in happy agreement.

Her memories of these journeys were rich. Lifting the lid of a coffee bin and sliding her hands into and out of the coffee beans, silky and smooth, like satin—how they slid over her hands and through her fingers, the feel and rhythm almost hypnotizing. And the kegs of pickles inside the grocer's store, and the large tin canisters whose lids stood open, inviting you to look at the crackers they contained—saltines and animal crackers, sugar wafers and gingersnaps. Across the floor, inside a big barrel, were plump ivory grapes from Spain, resting on sawdust, and alongside them, heavy coarse sacks bulging with rice or beans. It was all there to touch and see and taste and smell, and the child would bask unashamedly in these sensory gifts.

Once home, she could look forward to dinner, and the noisily gay event it would inevitably be. Aunt Mamie had soon done well with her boardinghouse, so well that she was able to rent the house next door and, in turn, rent its rooms to boarders. She had a connecting passageway cut between the buildings and enlarged a dining room so it could hold everyone. There were one long table and several smaller ones, and Aunt Mamie was in charge of carving and serving from her position at the head of the big table. Gaslight made the scene brighter than day, and the talk was loud and the spirit sparkling. Eagerly the actors and actresses waited for their dish of soup to be ladled out from the big steaming tureen, and just as eagerly took their plates of fish, to be followed by roast. These were not days of cottage cheese and lettuce leaves for an actress's diet. The women as well as the men ate heartily. Aline, who always sat beside Mamie at the table, would fasten her eyes on the big carving knife her aunt waved in the air "like a drum major."

The slices of meat would fall to the serving platter, the diamonds, as much a part of her aunt's persona as her market basket, twinkling in the lamplight.

Uncle Sol, Mamie's husband, would take each plate after she put a hefty slice of meat on it and would add gravy, potatoes and vegetables. One of the Irish girls, now dressed in black, would carry the plates on a tray to the eager boarders. Rarely did dishes remain where they were when emptied, but instead were passed back to Mamie for a second filling. Although Aline ate along with the guests, she held her appetite in check, for she was waiting for the real pleasure. The little bits of meat that fell into the gravy dish as Aunt Mamie sliced would be Aline's to claim after everyone was served. Then, no longer having to worry about etiquette, she would dip in her fork and fish out the pieces, savoring each morsel while the juices dripped deliciously on her fingers. In years to come, Aline would fill many of her hours with cooking, finding immeasurable release and satisfaction in producing a fine meal. She would write love letters to Thomas Wolfe about the dinners she wanted to cook for him, outlining each course in succulent detail. Of her passion for food  first nurtured at her aunt's boardinghouse, and later a vital part of her relationship with Tom—Aline would one day say: "Maybe, if I had not been so fond of food, the whole color of my life would have been different."

Perhaps it might have been. But her musing here is not one of real regret. In fact, Aline always celebrated her lusty appetite, and was grateful to these early childhood experiences which had first shown her the pleasures to be enjoyed when warm friends shared fine food and drink. In the boardinghouse, these pleasures did not end with the evening meal. Still another awaited those who spent their evenings there together. After dinner, Mamie invariably indulged in her only real weakness—cardplaying. One of her greatest satisfactions in boardinghouse life was always having a ready-made game among the guests. Even when she was very small, Aline would try and stay up for the game, primarily because she knew that when it was over, a late-night snack would be served: heaping plates of sandwiches, pitchers of foaming draft beer and juicy garlic-smelling pickles that her Uncle Sol made himself and kept in a wooden barrel in the backyard.

Aline, in recalling those evenings, would wonder whether the generations of children that followed her did not perhaps lead "too regular a life." For after all, she said, "I learned a great deal that I never should have known if I had gone to bed early." When she finally did go to bed, it was not unusual for her father to wake her when he returned from an after-theater "bird and bottle" party. Dawn might be breaking outside the window when Joe, smelling of liquor and perfume, approached his daughter's bed. In a voice filled with love, he would say, "Wake up! Wake up! Listen . . . listen . . . this is better than sleep." And as the child stared up at him, he would recite from *The Tempest.*

> These our actors,
> As I foretold you, were all spirits, and
> Are melted into air, into thin air;
> And, like the baseless fabric of this vision,
> The cloud-capped towers, the gorgeous palaces
> The solemn temples, the great globe itself,
> Yea, all which it inherit, shall dissolve.
> And, like this insubstantial pageant faded,
> Leave not a rack behind. We are such stuff
> As dreams are made on, and our little life
> Is rounded with a sleep.

When he finished, there were tears in his eyes, and Aline even then thought: "He was right. It is much better than sleep."

At heart a poet, Joe was enchanted by a poem's rhythms, and he always shared them with Aline. Later on he would show her how to use their stresses to enliven her walks to school. Moving through the dreary early-morning streets, "Tiger, tiger, burning bright" directed the motions of her feet, choreographing the journey. And often too, when her father was away on tour, she would summon his face to mind by reciting the poems he most especially cared for.

Joseph Frankau went on tour a great deal. He loved the camaraderie of the troupe, the freedom of the road, loved releasing the tension of a week of one-night stands on a Saturday-night spree. Most likely when he went to bed after such parties, there would be a young lady to ease him into sleep. Joe saw no inconsistency in his love for his family and such pleasures of the evening. Sometimes he even invited a young woman of his acquaintance passing through New York to taste one of Mamie's magnificent meals. After all, he'd explain to his wife, the poor girl was not likely to eat like that on her next trip!

To the day of her death Rebecca Frankau worshiped her errant husband, and forgave all his improvidence. That Joe frequently neglected to send money home from his trips was always uncomplainingly accepted. After all, Rebecca would say, it was very likely that "more people were ruined by economy than by extravagance." Nonetheless, worry about money was another cause for the tears she shed on the many nights she slept alone in New York while he worked and played on the road.

Actually, she wasn't completely alone, for when Aline went to bed after the late supper snack, she would crawl into her absent father's space. There, sated with food and warmed by the musky parental scents on the bed linen, she would fall quickly and deeply to sleep. Later, when she woke in the middle of the night, a pattern that would continue all her life, she'd lean over and touch her mother's cheek, and be even more comforted as she gently moved her fingers over skin that was "soft as Lyons velvet." Aline's fingers were instruments of pleasure, as were all the tools of her senses, even when still a small child. She'd look in the mirror sometimes and marvel at that miraculous thing called a nose, which could record so many different odors; how extraordinary the mouth and tongue were to bring you such wonderfully diverse and delicious flavors. Later in life, when her hearing failed, her other senses seemed even more heightened. As her publisher, Alfred Knopf, would comment, it was as if these senses were making up for the one that was diminished; a compensatory development that would produce in her writing an almost astonishing gift for sensory description.

When Aline was six, her sister, Ethel, was born. Joseph managed to be home at the time, and he had supervised the move from the top floor, where the family of three had shared a room, to the third floor of the boardinghouse, where their expanding family could live more comfortably. Aline had a small bedroom all to herself, and while she missed the intimacy of her parents' bedroom, she enjoyed the privacy of the new arrangement. Whatever apprehension she might have felt at being displaced as center of her parents' life was submerged in her zest for a new experience. On the day of Ethel's birth, Aline kept vigil outside her mother's bedroom. Sitting next to her on the stairs was her inseparable companion, Jesse, a boy her own age who lived in the boardinghouse with his actress mother.

The news that she had a sister was vastly exciting. Obviously, Aline had yet to learn how importantly this sister would figure in her life. For now, all she knew was that her family had expanded, a fact she entirely embraced. There was love enough in the Frankau family for new members to be welcomed without making old ones

21

feel abandoned, a concept of loving that would stay with Aline forever.

But while she loved Ethel, she couldn't really play with her yet. And so it was Jesse who remained her real companion. He slept across the hall in a small room just like her own, and when they went to sleep, they kept their doors open, for they found the sound of each other's breathing a happy music to drift off with. Aline would say of New York that she exulted in every stone of it, and it was a response woven into the tapestry of her city child's life. She and Jesse bounced their rubber balls against the boardinghouse stoop and, on the sidewalk in front, played hopscotch or jacks. They would fill containers with water and go up to Jesse's mother's room, and squirt the people who walked under the window, enlivening the game by being selective about who would get squirted—only men with gray derby hats, or ladies with flesh-colored mitts.

Sometimes when she wasn't playing with Jesse, she'd go down the block to a house near Eighth Avenue to visit two "tarts" named Ella and Flora. They were mother and daughter, but looked enough alike in their golden blondness and beautiful clothes to be sisters. A golden aura hung over the house as well, from the delicate figures on the filigreed mantelpiece to the slivers of pineapple kept all over the house in elegant dishes to munch on when they felt hungry. The women were very cordial to Aline, enjoying her unbounded admiration, although they always sent her home by five o'clock, and directed her never to visit after that hour. But Aline did not mind these restrictions. As she skipped along the street, the scent of the ladies' perfume was already being replaced with the anticipated odors of the boardinghouse kitchen, where "the good big dinner was cooking on the stove."

# 2

When Aline talked about Flora and Ella, she would say that spell-binding as they were, "It was never the excitement I knew with Nana"—Nana, the outrageous, excessive, undisciplined woman who added her voluptuous arabesques to the design of her niece's life.

Stories abound about Aline's power to attract men. Never conventionally beautiful or glamorous, she is invariably described as beautiful, or enchanting, or magnificent. Eugene Kennedy, a leading Thomas Wolfe scholar, recalls an interview with Aline when she was well past seventy and he himself was a very young man. He was, to his amazement, persistently conscious that however decorous the meeting, it was a meeting between a man and a woman. And a friend of Aline's remembers her at nearly the same age as a guest at a dinner party, which included several very beautiful young ladies. Suddenly, the friend says (incredulous even now), "I realized there was hardly a man in the living room where we had assembled after dinner. I looked out to the terrace, and there was Aline, plump, gray-haired, wearing a plain silk grandmotherly dress, but laughing that clear bell of a laugh of hers, to the obvious pleasure of the seven or eight men who had gradually come outside to gather around her."

The ability to attract men was as natural to Aline as it was to her Aunt Nana. Indeed, the deeply female side of Aline's personality may have derived from Nana. On the other hand, Nana never restrained her appetites, or tempered her pleasure-seeking with any responsibility. Not so Aline. One of the causes of recurrent arguments with Thomas Wolfe was her insistence on maintaining her involvement with her work. No matter how passionate the meetings with Tom, the hours between were spent in disciplined attention to her craft. It proved hard for Wolfe to understand this capacity to split herself off from their affair. He resented it deeply, and at the height of his own passion, took it as a sign that she did not care enough for him. If she did, he was convinced, surely that feeling would prevail. But Aline had too many memories of such uncontrolled responses to life. Nana had shown her where complete surrender to the senses could take you. She had seen how, in her aunt's life, "each piece of indulgence undermined her morality, until her will was gone, and she crumbled."

However, in the early years of Aline's growing up, Nana was only dazzling. Tall, ample in figure, she moved with "the grace of a full-rigged ship cutting the water." Her clothes were both outrageous and magnificent. Again, while Aline surely learned a love of silk and lace from her aunt's infatuation with beautiful fabrics, her own preference for simple, uncluttered line may well have been conditioned by Nana's invariable excess of dress. Too much would be added to or taken off the most exquisitely designed gown. A delicately made silk skirt would have its line ruined by the extra petticoat Nana would insist on wearing underneath it: she wanted the combined skirts to rustle when she walked, because "the men loved the sound."

And while, according to Aline, in those days "only tarts and short-haired Russian nihilists" smoked cigarettes, Nana smoked. At a dinner party or in a restaurant, when dessert came, she would bring out a package of cigarettes from a pocket hidden in the folds of her skirt, and her request for a light would create an immediate stir, which was, of course, exactly her intention. If, in surprise, a companion did not offer the light quickly enough, she would reach out, her hands heavy with diamonds, for the nearest candlestick and bring its flame toward her lips. How she loved to see the sparkle of her diamonds in that candle-light. She wore as many rings as she could get on her fingers and would

24

never wear gloves, no matter what the occasion. Often in the midst of a quiet interchange with some man, she would suddenly jab him with her sparkling fingers, and inform him that their conversation would be much more interesting if they were lying down rather than sitting. It was so much easier to think of amusing things to say that way, she'd assert giggling, and you wouldn't have all these other people around "to take the edge off things."

On evenings like these, Uncle Ben would glower from across a room or a table, and the angry words they would exchange on their carriage ride home were sometimes the last words he spoke to her for days.

Nana and Ben lived down the street from the boardinghouse. Ben's ability to attract rich patients (he claimed it was just as easy to look at rich people's tongues as poor ones') allowed Nana, unlike her sisters, to live more in the manner of their father. Still, she would dress up every day in one of her bizarrely beautiful outfits and come to the boarding-house for lunch. In between flirting with the actors, she'd fondle Aline, whom, in her own frivolous way, she adored. In fact, when Ben decided to buy a summer house in Newport, Rhode Island, the better to care for his vacationing rich patients, Nana invited Aline to join them. Although she didn't want to be away from New York and her parents, the idea of seeing water and mountains intrigued the little girl and she agreed to go.

Once ensconced, Aline was overjoyed. She loved the place, from the house itself to the landscape it was part of. The house was wooden, with tall turrets, and there was a huge, heavy door, whose thickness was laced with panes of red and blue glass. Sitting on the porch, you looked across to a rocky stretch of land that led down to the sea. The sights and sounds of the beach were especially thrilling to Aline—the coarse, gritty sand, and the wide variety of tiny fish, crabs and clams, whose colors shone in the water.

Unfortunately, the summer's pleasures were cut short quite dramati-cally. Aunt Nana was, even in these early days, regularly ingesting sleeping potions to calm her skittering spirits. One afternoon while Nana was entertaining a gentleman caller in another room, Aline picked up a glass she thought of as her special tumbler and drank its contents. As soon as she drank it, she realized the glass contained some-thing other than water, just as Nana, who was showing her friend out, saw the glass in her niece's hand and knew her carelessness promised, for once, real retribution. She gathered the child in her arms and screamed for her husband. In her panic, she forgot that he was not likely to be home while she played hostess to another man. Tears running down her face and onto Aline's cheeks, she ran from room to room calling Ben. Aline said wryly of that afternoon: "I wish he could have heard Nana's call. It was probably the only time she ever called him straight from the heart, and he missed it."

The stable groom, who was one of Nana's playmates, was sent to find her husband; but by the time Ben arrived, the medicine was already taking effect. Aline vividly remembered the frantic measures her uncle employed to save her—being pummeled and shaken and plunged into alternately hot and cold baths.

In a matter of days, she was home again on Forty-fourth Street, Mama having come up to Newport to take her back. The look on her mother's face was haunted, and when Aline was older, she realized how her mother suffered at the knowledge that the sister she loved so dearly had nearly killed the child she loved even more. Rebecca Frankau's love could and did provide great strength and support for her daughter as Aline grew up; but it was one of the tragedies of Rebecca's life that her love was never able to change her sister's self-destructive course.

But she tried. Often to Aline's very real despair. One day shortly after Ethel was born, Ben came to see his sister-in-law to ask if Rebecca and her family would move into his and Nana's house. There were tears in his eyes. "Beck," he said, "you are the only one who can save her; maybe having the children in the house will be good for her. She needs all the love she can get; you know her heart. I'm trying to do the best I can," he finished, and added, with a resolute sigh, "I don't want to be bitter."

Joe agreed with his wife that they should make the move, and soon Ben and Nana and the Frankaus were living communally in the big house at 201 West 44th Street. It might as well have been across the ocean, so lost did Aline feel at leaving the intimacy with Jesse and the gregarious warmth of the boardinghouse. Despite all the grownups' assurances that life would be the same as before, Aline felt the chill of the "inevitable certainty of change."

Aline's life would always be filled with people. Wherever she lived, men and women would congregate. Her parties were legendary, her welcome a gift generously given. Acquaintance turned quickly into friend (if that was Aline's wish). But although there were many reasons for her vast social network, in part it existed to assuage the ache of loneliness which she suffered far more often than she allowed most people to know. Although she was frequently alone, with her work, with her hobbies, with her own counsel, when she felt the specter of loneliness in the wings of her life, she needed company to dispel it. In the boardinghouse, there was always company. "When you felt that dreadful thing coming over you . . . when you felt that no matter what, you just had to be with somebody, to touch someone, someone was always there."

How terrible, then, to leave it all behind. Particularly so as it quickly was apparent that the sacrifice would reap little reward. Ben and Nana's relationship did not improve, and Ben let some of his anger affect his attitude toward her relatives, the very people he had enlisted to save her. Although he was generous with money, even hiring a nursemaid to help Mama with Ethel, he spent little time with the family. That he turned from Aline intensified her distress. Ben and she had always been so close. Nearly every weekend of her life, he had taken her in his handsome carriage to buy her tea and pastries at Delmonico's. Now he barely spoke to her. Aline did not know then, she would later say ruefully, that she was seeing the combined monsters of jealousy and injustice, and the destruction their unleashing creates.

The tension in the house affected the relationship of Rebecca and Joe. At night, Joe's key would be heard in the door later and later. And while he had always come home to see his family between matinee and evening performances, he stopped doing that too. Consequently, when Rebecca heard he was planning to leave on another six-week tour, she summoned up the courage to insist that she come along with Aline. Dina, the nursemaid, could stay home with Ethel, who was of course too young to withstand the rigors of the road.

Rebecca's belief that she needed to be with her husband to save her marriage meant that Aline would have to delay beginning her formal schooling. But neither parent paid much attention to that fact, and certainly it meant little to Aline. There was far too much going on, far too much to see and think about and absorb, for her to worry about conventional routes of learning, or even to be dispirited by the bleaker aspects of her special education.

Aline's lifelong appreciation of the difficulties of theatrical life was nurtured, along with a love for its glamour, during these first glimpses of the world behind the footlights. She never complained when the company checked into musty boardinghouses or the cheap hotels that invariably stood next door to the railroad station where they disembarked for another round of performances. Often these comings and goings took place at outlandish hours, since train schedules had not been organized around the needs of touring actors. Rarely having a comfortable night's sleep, Aline would take naps on a hard plush sofa backstage during a performance, or most often of all, would curl up on a seat on the train, her head in her mother's lap. She learned how to cope during those days, days she said made her "tough and strong," able to remain undaunted by changing routines and conditions.

There were many times, too, when she had to force herself to stay awake, when they were waiting to leave a town and there was no place to rest, for example. At such times she'd bite the inside of her cheek, or twist her foot at the ankle hard enough to hurt so that she would be too conscious of discomfort to start dozing. Sometimes she actually prodded her eyes open with her fingers. Once on the train, however, she could gratefully doze a little, until, cold and yawning, they would disembark at another station, often as a gray dawn weakly illuminated an equally gray town.

The cast usually ate only one meal a day, after the evening performance. Generally, the menu was steak and beer, the most these small-town restaurants could handle with any competency. Six-year-old Aline would eat her steak along with the grownups and drink a small glass of beer while they downed pitchers, drowsily listening and watching them unwind. Their voices, so beautifully trained and diligently worked on, would ring loudly through the restaurant, and other diners would look up with the kind of smile that seemed to Aline to confirm how different an actor's life was from ordinary people's.

All her life Aline spoke with a soft but compelling tone and diction, and greatly admired those who did the same. The actress Eva Le Gallienne remembers fondly that when Aline's hearing failed, she would pull her hated hearing aid off gratefully when they met, for the actress's precise enunciation was understandable where other people's sloppily slurred speech was not. But long before Aline had reason to be grateful for a fine speaking voice, she had learned to appreciate it from watching her father and his fellow actors work on their voices, and hearing the beautiful results.

The principal play of this company was *Richard III*, and the star of the production was the same Richard Mansfield whom an older Aline would visit years later with her father, and who later still would be set into the framework of the story by Thomas Wolfe. Mansfield enjoyed the young Aline's company even then, and she frequently visited him in his dressing room while he made up, watching fascinated as he made his handsome face slowly turn ugly.

When an actress who played one of the young princes hurt her leg just before a performance, it was Mr. Mansfield who paid attention to Aline's announcement that she knew all the lines for the role. He told the cast that Aline would go on instead, and soon was making up her face with his own powder and paints. Looking at him as he worked, Aline remembered: "I had to close my eyes because I was so dazzled to feel his hands on my face. I was so happy I could feel a smile widening on my mouth until it nearly cut a circle around my head."

*Richard* played only the larger towns, and by the time they played one more, the actress had recovered, but Aline had been on stage long enough to know she wanted to be an actress when she grew up: a great actress who would go through life taking on other skins and creating an infinite variety of Alines.

"I had found out how to do it, how to lose myself, how to attach myself to an image. No matter how life went, I would never be robbed of that." In the theater, she would think, you could tell your story over and over again, and everyone would listen. You could make people understand how you feel when you're sad or lonely or happy. And you could make them in turn laugh or cry or be afraid. Such power overwhelmed Aline, and she told herself proudly that if her life in the theater made her different from other children, she was right to be different. "It was only right," she thought, "that such magicians as ourselves should be marked from other people."

At the same time, however, that Aline was convinced that actors' emotions were grander and larger than ordinary people's, she was also developing the belief that they must assume the responsibility for their gifts—not abuse them by succumbing to weakness and reckless self-indulgence. Unlike her Aunt Nana, these actors and actresses Aline was coming to know so intimately staunchly prevented their frailties from interfering with their professional duties. In later life, Aline would say that the theater was a great moral training ground. "No alibis, no time extensions, no inaccuracies are permissible. You must be there, and you must be alert in every sense." That an actor drank too much or woman-ized, or an actress slept with fleeting friends, did not offend even the child Aline, as long as the night's indulgence didn't delay the morning's responsibility. The ethic that a sharp line must be drawn between one's personal and professional lives took root in her now. It was an ethic about which she would become very serious and speak at great length, but which she could also sum up with succinct and smiling economy: "Till rehearsal call, your life is your own, and you can go all the way to hell, as long as you're back in time for the curtain."

Although she mused about the differences between the troupe and her Aunt Nana—in truth, despite her awareness of Nana's lesser strength—she missed her a great deal. It would be a long while yet before Nana's excitement would fail to override her weaknesses for her admiring niece. Happily, Nana seemed to be making out all right on her own in New York. Her letters to the family were scarce, but matter-of-factly reassuring:

> The baby is all right. . . . Dina is looking sour. . . . Hollander is making me a toque of coq feathers that is going to be beautiful with my green cloth princess. . . . It is getting warmer and lots of Victorias are out in the park. . . . There is some talk of taking up the cobblestones on 44th Street and putting down asphalt, but I guess that will be a long time away; it's too hard on the horses in the winter. Mrs. Hitchcock got drunk last night and locked her daughter out, the whole block was leaning out the window to hear what they called each other. Take care of yourself, Beck, and have a good time, and for God's sake don't worry.

She rarely said anything about Uncle Ben, but at least she didn't say anything bad. And so when the company of actors rode the train back to New York a little while later, Aline could hope that perhaps life would be smoother for them all. Her father, triumphant over his personal success in the tour, was being nicer to Mama, and Aline knew that her own time with him had made them even closer than before. But then, in a few minutes, her good feeling changed, for Mr. Mansfield had come into the car, and was saying that he had an announcement he'd been saving as a surprise. He was going to take *Richard III* to London for an extensive engagement, and any member of the cast who could pay his way over was invited to come.

Aline saw her mother and father exchange glances, and she understood some of the worry on their faces. There was nothing Joseph Frankau would like more than to widen his reputation as a Shakespearean actor, but to go so far away for so long a time would be a serious blow to reestablished family unity.

The dilemma emboldened him to ask his brother-in-law for help. And Ben, who was obviously much warmer to his wife's family when they arrived home, and on much better terms with his wife herself, agreed to foot the bill for a family trip to England. A trip that included everyone. Not just the Frankau family, but Nana and Ben, and even Dina, the nursemaid, to help out with Ethel.

"It was too good to be true," says Aline, "but it was true," and only a little while later she stood on the deck of the *City of Rome,* watching the lights of the city twinkle and grow smaller. Of all the crossings she would make in her lifetime, this one would always be most deeply etched in memory.

Unfortunately, life in England was not all the Frankaus had hoped for. For one thing, while Joe enjoyed great social success in London, the production of *Richard* was a disaster. The Shakespearean traditions of the English were affronted by this American version, and the production was quickly closed and shuttered. Meanwhile, Nana began to act up again, driving Ben to a final bitter attack on everyone connected with his outrageous wife. On her return from a jaunt to Paris with another man, Ben greeted her with violent words of farewell.

"I'm finished!" he shouted. "Done with the lot of you. Whores and rotten actors and their children!"

To hear those words of contempt and rejection was a dreadful blow to Aline. She and Ben had been so close again, and now he was leaving her forever. Although she never saw him after that day, she never forgot him. Life had changed irrevocably when the family left the boardinghouse, and Ben was the first person to walk out on her and abandon her love, the first to teach her the harsh and ugly lesson that people you love may leave you. When, years later, it happened again, she would often remember the pain of this first encounter with emotional loss.

Ben left not one cent behind for his wife, and Joe, unemployed, now had another person to support. He managed to find some work in an English play—a rare experience for an American actor. In addition, he gave some elocution lessons to a man who was a distant relative of the royal family. By the time the British play had run for two months, and "the gutturals were almost removed from the royal throat," they had enough money to take them all back to America. Only Joe and Aline were unhappy at the prospect of leaving London. Father and daughter shared a love for the city's smartness and elegance and its sense of the living past. Much as Aline loved New York, she had discovered in London a new mode of life that was immensely appealing. Staring out the window of the train that carried them to Liverpool, she felt again the deep sadness of change. But when she turned and met her father's eyes, her spirits lightened at knowing that even her sadness united them. That they understood each other's regret at leaving England was another sign that their closeness had continued to deepen during the months of living there together.

Because Ben had quickly and punitively sold the home they'd shared with Nana, it was arranged for Dina and Ethel to stay in the only vacant room in Mamie's house, while the rest of the family went to a hotel on Broadway. Aline would always be able to recall exactly that first March evening of being back together in New York.

She woke in the middle of the night to noisy laughter from her parents' room. Opening the door, she saw her mother and Nana in their robes and a half dozen of her father's friends joining Joe for a boisterous late-night supper. Vast numbers of beer bottles balanced on the washstand, and Joe was holding a huge box of fried oysters. Aline had forgotten about New York's fried oysters. Her father bought them at a place called Mocks on Forty-second Street near Sixth Avenue; he often brought them home for the family to share.

"They were put up eight oysters to the portion, in a pasteboard box with four flaps on the top and a handle. A wilted lettuce leaf was at the bottom and on top was a sour coppery pickle that nearly took the skin off your tongue. . . . The oysters had a crunchy taste and a fried smell that was like home and Broadway. . . . Then you took a drink of ice water afterwards and there was never anything in the world just like it!"

Nobody saw Aline when she first slid her way into the room and into her mother's bed. Everybody had a glass in hand, even Rebecca. Aline fell asleep with the sounds of the party spinning around her. When she woke up, she saw that Nana had fallen asleep in the next bed, with every diamond she owned pinned to her nightgown, every ring she owned on her fingers. Aline's mother was standing looking down at them both. Her skin was ashen from her unfamiliar meeting with drink. And her eyes looked very sad.

By the time Nana and Aline had pulled themselves out of bed, Joe was back in the room, and the family made a rather morose grouping round the makeshift breakfast table. The party the night before had just about cleared out what was left of Frankau's resources after the journey home from England. Indeed, some of Joe's impetus for having the party at all had been the wish to offset the news from his friends that there wasn't a single legitimate show planned for Broadway during late spring and summer. Rebecca sat quietly, listening to her husband and to her sister's pessimistic speculations about squeezing some money from the now distant Ben. Suddenly, to everyone's surprise, Rebecca, in a firmer voice than was ever her style, spoke up. "Now don't all jump on me," she said. "I've got an idea. It's no use trying to save a dollar when no dollars come in to save. I've thought about this all the way over on the steamer, and my mind's made up. I'm going to rent a house and take in enough boarders to pay our living."

Joe and Nana and Aline stared at Rebecca, and then at each other, and suddenly the atmosphere in the gloomy room began to change. Why not? It was certainly worth a try. The room filled up with excited business talk, and Aline was dispatched to Mamie's house to represent them all in kissing the baby good morning. And as she skipped again along Broadway, she grew more and more excited by the idea that still another phase of her life was beginning.

Through the generosity of Ben's brother, who with Ben out of the way was pursuing his brother's wife, the Frankaus rented a house on Forty-fifth Street—just about back to back with Mamie's place. The move was a turning point for the Frankau family. Individually and together they were soon thriving. The boardinghouse did well from the start, and Rebecca was able to hire two young women to assist her. Even with their help, however, Aline played an important role in the house. She and Ethel shared a bedroom, and it became Aline's duty to get her sister up every morning and see to her bedtime at night. These were the very active hours in a boardinghouse, and Rebecca's guests wanted their landlady's attention. But added to Aline's new responsibilities were many of responsibility's rewards. If the world saw her as a little girl, still not even eight years old, to her family she was a valued and productive member, whose opinion mattered as much as their own.

She was very conscious of all the aspects of her increased maturity that first summer back in New York. But she would later say that were she to try to portray that season, she would use one symbol only—a book —for this was the time in Aline's life when she first discovered the New York Public Library and the ecstatic joys of reading.

The writer and producer Bella Spewack, who was to become one of Aline's dearest friends, recalled how the mature, acclaimed Aline would often visit the Spewack home in Pennsylvania when she was worn out from the demands of a current production.

33

"Where are the books?" she'd ask, and Bella and her husband, Sam, would haul out all the new books they had been sent by publishers for comment or to consider for theatrical adaptation. Aline's eyes would light up, and she'd fill a couple of baskets with the books and take them into the guest room with her. Mrs. Spewack says that invariably, after a few hours had passed, and they were getting ready for dinner, she would peek into the guest room and see Aline fast asleep, surrounded by all the books she'd brought in with her, like a child who buries herself in the sand. Their firm covers seemed to support her spirit as the bed supported her body. It was as if the very contact with the possibilities of their contents refreshed her, and when she'd join her friends for dinner, she seemed already renewed.

The reading she did during that childhood summer gave rise to all kinds of romantic fantasies, and indeed, influenced attitudes she could smile at but not completely erase as she grew into womanhood. The novels of the late nineteenth century, such as Grace Aguilar's *A Mother's Recompense,* or the works of Thomas Bailey Aldrich, generally presented women as the instrument of either pleasure or inspiration for some man. Aline would grow up to despise the restrictions on her own potentialities that being born female had placed on her. But at the same time she would say that the ultimate statement of a woman's life was to complete a man through joining him with her womanliness. Those friends who would deplore her loss of autonomy in her relationship with Thomas Wolfe failed to understand how deep this conviction was, a conviction that first took shape in her early exposure to the stories of men and their women in reality and in print. For her reading was certainly supplemented by the ongoing romantic dramas of the boardinghouse, Nana's continual intrigues, and the succulent tidbits of gossip actors and actresses handed each other like chocolates when they made their rounds for jobs on Broadway.

Joe was relieved when summer ended because it promised work at last. But for Aline, fall meant saying goodbye to timeless days and self-directed pleasures. At last this actor's daughter was joining the ranks of other people's children. She was, if two years overdue, being sent to school. Who in that large, ugly building could know what it was to be her? The darling of the boardinghouse was just another school child, and the anonymity of it outraged and even frightened her. More and more she turned inward to her "secret life"—replacing the teacher's sour face with Nana's, the chipped desk with the shiny surface of the dining room table.

Aline's daughter, Edla, remembers her mother's amused tolerance for Edla's own lack of enthusiasm for early formal education. Less secretive about her distaste than Aline, Edla was frequently accused of some infraction that demanded Aline's presence in the principal's office. Aline did her best to mouth the proper words of concern and cooperation, but she'd come home and do imitations of the principal for the family.

Although Aline felt altogether different about serious learning and, indeed, regretted never having had any significant higher education, the mechanical process the public school system of her childhood called teaching appalled her. Still, she went through the motions, accepting it as a "distasteful necessity," one that was considerably lightened by knowing the pleasures that awaited her at home when the school day was over.

But as the new century approached, those pleasures began to dim. Rebecca's health was clearly failing, and it was not long before the family was told by her doctor that she had widespread cancer and that her condition was extremely grave. After a prolonged hospital stay, she did not resume her normal life. The bedroom, not the kitchen or dining room, was her environment now, while the rest of the family struggled to maintain the boardinghouse without her supervising strength. Unfortunately, though they pretended to Rebecca that they had it all under control, conditions were chaotic. Nana, who had tearfully promised to take over many of Rebecca's tasks, would give money intended for the household to her rather sinister new lover. A distracted Joe rarely found this out until supplies ran short or angry creditors appeared at his door.

For Aline, her mother's deterioration promised a loneliness too unspeakable to bear. She clung to the hope that one morning she would wake up and all would be the way it used to be, with Rebecca humming in the kitchen and grabbing her daughter up in her arms for a sweet-smelling kiss. Instead, Aline woke up one October morning in her eleventh year to learn that Rebecca had died in the night.

It *was* too much to bear. Too much, and too little. For this child of the theater was outraged at death's lack of drama. She was enraged that her mother could have died while she herself was calmly asleep. How could the passages of real life be so random and nondescript? An old friend of Joe's who had become a priest tried to help her deal with her confusion. One night, sitting in his sanctuary study, Aline asked again how it was possible, if people had souls that lived on, that Mama's soul hadn't called Aline from sleep to say goodbye. He began to tell her that

35

far wiser minds than hers or his had tried to understand the issues of life and death, when his housekeeper entered the room carrying a tray of cake and wine. The cake was brilliant yellow, Aline remembered, with plump dark raisins embedded in it. The taste of the cake in her mouth brought her a surprising feeling of solidity, a deeply comforting sense of knowing there would always be lovely things to see and taste. Watching her eat and drink, the priest said that there are things in life one simply knows, in much the same way as she knew the excellence of Bridget's cake. The difference was that the cake's meaning could be physically tasted, while other meanings must be absorbed through faith.

Father Flanagan assured her, too, that grief was as natural a part of life as the food one ate, and must be accepted as such and allowed to run its course. And she should understand, he said, that when this finally happened, she would again know peace, for it was obvious to him that she had a great capacity to enjoy life, and would always, no matter what befell her, "have your pack on your back."

Although she was still shocked by how love had been ripped from her life, Aline understood what he was saying. If her mother's dreams were over, Aline's were beginning, and it was her obligation to herself, to her mother and to her life to see that they came true.

After this, Aline and Joe spent more and more time together. It became Aline's custom to walk down to Joe's theater every Saturday and watch some of the matinee and then join him for dinner before the evening performance. Surely some of her gift for stage design was cultivated during these afternoons that she sat in the wings on a rickety chair watching her father in various productions. Although she was enthralled as ever with the stories and the way actors through their magic could tell these stories, she remembered also, "I learned to look at objects," becoming fascinated by the way in which the most ordinary became so much more than ordinary because of its integration into the dramatic whole.

On one of these afternoons, in mid-adolescence, Aline waited as usual in her father's dressing room while he removed his make-up. Suddenly she framed a question that had been increasingly insistent in her mind. Did Joe think, she asked seriously, that her mother would have liked her to become an actress? It was a question of particular significance, because, despite her late start and her distaste for formal education she would soon be graduating from high school and must begin to think of the future.

Aline remembered that her father had been laughing at something she'd said just before her question and that his laughter abruptly ended.

"It's a dreadful life," he said soberly. "Too hard for a girl like you. Your dear Mama never said anything to me about it, but I know what I think, darling. I would hate to see you do it. . . . I wish I could be a stern parent and say I forbid it."

Aline was alarmed at his response, and she expressed the dilemma she felt. She needed, she said, to be able to tell people how she felt about things. How could she do this apart from being an actress?

"There are more ways than acting to do that," Joe said, and added that they would go to see Tom Watson soon and talk it over with him.

Tom Watson was the only lover of Nana's who had captured the hearts of her family and kept their affection long past her breaking off their affair. His house was filled with beautiful works of art, for Watson was a highly respected and dedicated collector. For years Aline had visited Watson often, marveling at his treasures, and he would patiently explain the intricacies of various pieces. It was Tom, too, who had encouraged her own attempts at painting, presenting her with her first set of watercolors. Since then, she frequently brought him examples of her work and he would carefully point out their strengths and weaknesses.

It was to this man that Joe Frankau came with his daughter on a sparkling June afternoon, seeking advice about her future. To match the collector's never-failing elegance, Joe was wearing a black-and-white pin-check suit with a pearl-gray bow tie, and a brand-new straw sailor hat. Aline was dressed in a fawn-colored ankle-length dress with a belt and collar made of Dresden ribbon. Emulating the older women's fashion of the time, she had a big bow tied at the back of her head. Arm in arm with her father, she knew what a snappy picture they made together and the image made her proud.

As always, coming into Tom's house was like entering a beautiful, timeless world. Every pore of her body opened to the accumulated impressions of the rooms, and she let her father tell their story so that she could drink everything in.

"She wants to tell people something," Joe explained, continuing earnestly to confess his worry about her doing this as an actress. "Still," he finished, looking troubled, "she has to be ready to take care of herself someday. What do you think, Tom?"

Aline and her father studied their friend's face, waiting for him to speak. But before he did, Tom's eyes, as Aline's had been doing, began to search the room they sat in, his gaze resting every now and then on

37

a porcelain or painting. And Aline understood the message of his search, even before he spoke. Of course. Why, she knew exactly how these various artists had felt about trees framed against a sky or the seas changing colors. Until now she had looked at her attempts at painting only as aesthetic experiments, but why not think of them as a way to reach out to other people, just as she would have done on a stage? So when Tom told her he would help her get into art school when she graduated, and would even supply her with the equipment she'd need for her classes, she eagerly accepted his offer. And her hands, which had been lying quietly in her lap, suddenly felt a tingling, as if they were coming awake from sleep. Her fingers felt, she remembered, "as the twigs of trees must feel when the first green feathery leaves break through." Holding her hands out to Tom, she said simply, "I'll do what I can with them."

It was almost immediately after this visit, so filled with hope for the future, that new challenges to Aline's and Joe's optimism appeared. The boardinghouse, which had been holding together under the combined efforts of Nana, Joe and Aline, had to be abandoned, its contents sold at auction. Nana had become involved with a gang of jewel thieves, a situation perhaps related to her continuing morphine and alcohol addictions, and she had barely escaped being sent to prison with them. As the story became known, those few tradesmen who had let their self-interest be lulled by Nana's charm circled around the Frankaus like vultures for the money owed them.

Joe was at a loss as to how to care for his daughters, but Aline convinced him they would manage. Most pressing were arrangements for Ethel. Although various relatives offered to help out, the best decision seemed to be to send her to a convent school in the Bronx run by one of Father Flanagan's friends. Here Joe and Aline could visit as often as they liked and would still clearly be the center of Ethel's life. While the house was being broken up, Aline parted with her father also, going to stay with some actor friends of his who had a restaurant on the New Jersey shore. They were getting their place ready for summer visitors, and Aline worked out some of her anxiety by painting furniture and learning to cook the restaurant's specialty—a chowder of long-necked soft-shell clams, flavored with sage and whole black peppercorns. It was so good to be around a bustling kitchen again that Aline was almost willing to accept the invitation to stay all summer. But when her father came to claim her, she was concerned about how he looked. Some of the light had dimmed in his face, and his eyes were unhealthily puffy.

So she packed up her things and took the train back to New York with him. There they would move into the home of one of his sisters, who was married to the city's police commissioner.

Joe knew Aline didn't much care for her Aunt Gert, and he tried to summon the old bravado into his voice when he assured his daughter that they would be there only a little while, "till my ship comes in." Very soon they would pick up Ethel and move into a beautiful flat on Madison Square that he had already picked out, one with a great big studio room for Aline's painting. "And when they send for you to come down to the White House to paint Grover Cleveland's portrait, your old Daddy will put on his galoshes and ear muffs, grasp his crutches, and come along!"

As they bumped along the railroad tracks, Joe gave Aline other news. Nana had married her persistently dreadful lover in a ceremony performed by the Mayor himself, no less, right in City Hall, with Joseph Frankau as best man. Although Aline was hurt that Nana hadn't asked her to be there, her father's description of the event soon had her roaring with laughter, and she read the disjointed letter Nana had sent to her through Joe with no bitterness toward her aunt for her part in their current troubles.

As Aline said of that time: "It was incredible how soon I was happy again." She still didn't like Aunt Gert's miserly spirit, but the rest of her life was rich. Classes at the New York School of Applied Design for Women were absorbing, and always, indeed even more than before, her life with her father cloaked her with love. Although he was barely fifty, Joe was having difficulty getting parts, as both his hearing and his memory were failing, and recently he'd gone up in his lines during a revival of *Hazel Kirke;* even persistent prompting from the wings could not bring the words back to mind. The incident frightened him, and for the first time in his life he tried to find work outside the theater. But he was still wonderfully entertaining, and beloved by great scores of people, all of whom he now shared with his maturing daughter. Unlike her mother, Aline went along to all Joe's parties and enjoyed them every bit as much as he did. There were also other social pleasures. In the summer the St. Nicholas Skating Rink housed a series of concerts, and father and daughter attended as many as possible, feeding the passion for music Aline would always have. Often Father Flanagan and another priest would join them, and after the concert they'd all go to a local restaurant to drink and talk. Aline learned much about music during those evenings, and sitting with the men, sipping champagne, she would feel that the music they'd heard and were discussing was a description of herself. "My mind, body and senses were a resolved chord, and out of the chord I broke into other harmonies, and I had a vision of the self's endless combinations."

It was at the peak of all these budding feelings, soon after her sixteenth birthday, that Joseph Frankau suddenly took ill. In their rooms one night, he began to gasp for breath and collapsed in his daughter's arms. By the time the doctor arrived, Joe had died, the apparent victim of a heart attack. Aline fainted at the physician's verdict, her grief too great to bear consciously.

When Aline woke from a long sedative-induced sleep, her Aunt Nana was at her bedside. Aline had avoided seeing Nana since her marriage, for as much as she still loved her wayward aunt, she despised the man Nana had made her husband. Now she saw that her aunt had changed. The hand she held against her niece's cheek was not as soft as it used to be, and when she lowered it again, it shook in a way that held obvious and unpleasant implications. She asked Aline to come and stay with her in the little house she had taken in the country. She needed her, she said. They could help each other. Aline could come to art school every day on the train. Nana had already checked on that. She started brushing Aline's hair, and Aline let herself enjoy the feeling. And she remembered suddenly the solace Father Flanagan had given her when her mother died. "You'll be all right wherever you go; you have your pack on your back."

And Aline sensed that this would always be the answer to life as long as she did not deny reality, did not deny "truth, nor faith in living, nor love." She had loved her father beyond any measure, and burned with the pain of his loss. It was a pain she would not turn from, would not try to deny, even though she knew she must move beyond it.

She drew herself from the bed and, still shaky, let Nana help her dress. She would go to see Ethel very soon, and be with her as much as possible. Maybe soon they could really be together all the time. Meanwhile, she would do what she could for Nana, and take what comfort she could from her aunt's chaotic kind of love. Together, she and Nana left the bedroom and went down the stairs hand in hand. And Aline felt that if she turned her head, she would see the specter of her girlhood watching her leave, while in the downstairs hall, the shadows seemed to form the shape of her woman's life.

# Part Two

1898-1925

# 3

Nana did not prove to be a very stable surrogate mother for Aline, despite her good intentions. She and her husband fought constantly, and more and more she tried to recapture happier yesterdays by blotting out the present with a hypodermic needle or a bottle. Standing on the edge of her own future, Aline felt pulled down into the chaos of her aunt's life.

So Aline came back to New York. Although she could stay with Mamie, Gert had offered to take both Ethel and Aline into her home, and there they would have more living space than in Mamie's boardinghouse. Aline accepted the offer mainly because Mamie was getting on, and it would have been hard on her to move a young child like Ethel into her life. And Aline did want to keep Ethel with her. Gert and her husband, ever concerned about money, also told Aline they would take charge of the nearly two thousand dollars Joe had left for his daughters —a legacy whose implications Aline understood well. She counted up the drinks and handsome clothes and theater tickets the two thousand dollars might have bought her pleasure-loving father, and wept with appreciation for this evidence of his devotion.

Emotions were restrained in Gert's house, except for the querulous chipping away at joy that seemed to define her aunt's personality. Years later, after Aline married, Gert would sometimes visit her (the older woman lived, despite a lifetime of physical complaints, till the age of ninety-eight—at which time, Aline recalled mildly, she died "quite reluctantly"). At the announcement of Gert's intended visit, all the servants, with stony-faced solidarity, would hand in their notices. Aline would then have to cajole and plead and offer inspirational remarks about the value of rising to a challenge, ending usually with the promise of a bonus if they stood by for the two-week invasion.

Actually, Aline was remarkably forgiving to continue their association into these later years, for Gert disgracefully abused her brother's wishes for his daughters. She criticized them all the time; nothing pleased her —it was useless to try. As for the inheritance, it might have been better spent by Joe, for Aline never was allowed to feel the security two thousand dollars might have brought had someone more generous and caring been in control of it. As it was, she felt penniless and helpless. Without Mamie and other relatives close by, the situation would have been even worse. How many evenings when the Hesses would go out for dinner did Gert, instead of arranging for her nieces' meal, snap, "Go around the corner to your aunt, ask her to give you something . . . she should have something left over for two kids."

When their situation simply got too bad, Aline took Ethel back to the convent and she herself drifted from relative to relative, staying as long as it was practical to. Those that could contributed some money so that Aline could finish her course at the art school. Not able or wanting to be beholden, she sold greeting cards door to door, and designed the pictures on their covers for a minimum fee. She also grew adept at designing and sewing hats and dresses. Most clothing manufacturers parceled out the handwork they required, such as buttonhole or embroidery trim, among women who sewed at home for pitiably small pay. Aline took in such piecework as often as possible. She'd bring any left-over material to Ethel, who at eleven had become the principal supplier of their own clothes, thanks to a talent for needlework that would have been unusual in someone twice her age. A cousin, Mrs. Willard Loeb, recalls her mother saying how much the family admired "the two orphan sisters . . . they were practically destitute, but somehow or other they always managed, and even with a kind of gaiety—only it seemed to everyone, because of their extraordinary creative impulses."

Certainly there was nothing heavy and bitter about them in these tenuous days, an early indication of the adults they would become. Both sisters, in different ways, would accept fate's whims without chagrin or complaint. While Ethel would cloak her responses in stoicism, Aline would always be freer in revealing her feelings, but just as clear was her accepting the fact that these feelings must sometimes be painful, that life would bring agony as well as rapture, and that both must be woven into the tapestry of existence. Aline's friend and associate Eva Le Gallienne sees this attitude as crucial to any artist's life, and understood and admired it in Aline. "It all feeds you, after all," she says. "As an artist, you must take in all experience if you are to give it out again. You can reject nothing. Aline knew that always, and knew that life, all of it, is there to be lived."

The New York City of Aline's young womanhood was filled with contrasting experience. "The gay nineties" was a "whopping misnomer," she later told a friend, adding that for many people they were painted a "dull, brown shade." Rich New Yorkers might live in splendor along Fifth and Madison avenues, or on Riverside Drive, but there were many other sections of the city where men and women lived in terrible poverty.

The worst neighborhood of all, in terms of numbers of people in appalling need, was the Lower East Side. Its streets were jammed with immigrants from Central and Eastern Europe who had been drawn to America in part by the fantasy of making a fortune—a fantasy that too often became a nightmare of abject squalor, disease and early death.

Aline walked among these people often, drawn to the neighborhood by foods and scents that had been a cherished part of her childhood. "My Jewishness runs through me like a strain of gold," she would say many times in her life, and she never felt that heritage more keenly than along the tangled sidewalks of the Lower East Side. At the same time, her empathy for the torments and humiliations of poverty began to forge an artistic and political consciousness that craved expression: she must bring flashes of color into the dull brownness. Hers wasn't a once-removed benevolence. She felt a definite kinship to these weary men and women despite the energy that coursed through her. She had already formed the conviction that a common humanity links people irrevocably to one another, and that one's position on the social ladder is largely an act of providence.

Peggy Murphy, Aline's housekeeper during her last years, remembers how worried she used to be when Aline was confined to a wheelchair and the nurse would take an afternoon off, leaving Aline and Peggy alone in the apartment.

"I used to get so nervous," says Peggy, "about doing the right thing for her, and I'd say, 'My goodness, I hope nothing will ever happen to you while I'm taking care of you!' " At this expression of concern, Aline would smile and tell Peggy she was lucky to have anyone in the apartment with her at all.

"Look, Peggy," she'd say matter-of-factly. "If I were poor, I'd have to rattle around by myself, wouldn't I? So however you take care of me, I'm better off."

And even when she was living on Park Avenue, Aline would ride buses and subways to work. The Park Avenue address embarrassed her.

"Mother always said she 'wasn't the Park Avenue type' and had sworn she'd never live there," says her daughter, Edla. "But then I found us a simply marvelous place and suddenly she had this terrible conflict!" Indeed, there was a Madison Avenue entrance to the building, and Aline tried valiantly to get the post office to allow her to use it as her address; they refused to cooperate in her attempts to soothe her social conscience.

But she always felt proudly separate from her Park Avenue neighbors. Thus, in middle age, in a letter to a friend, she affectionately recalled a very different social climate: "Saturday I had lunch with the quality, at the Metropolitan Museum. . . . We ate rather poor food surrounded by masterpieces . . . it was a wonderful assembly of capitalists and capitalistesses, and any anarchist would have had a happy hunting ground there. He could have shot off billions. (Where is the old-fashioned nihilist of my youth? The ones who used to take pot shots at steel magnates? They are gone with the white Christmases, and snowballing in the city streets, two kinds of dessert and tight gloves!)" And after this bit of nostalgic whimsy, the letter finishes: "Did you ever know Emma Goldman? I knew her and she was the first to open my eyes about a lot of things."

The famous anarchist Emma Goldman had come to the United States from Russia in 1886. In New York she edited a radical magazine called *Mother Earth,* and founded the Ferrar School as an anarchist center. Although her own interest in the arts was negligible, the idea of artistic freedom was important to her. She also wanted to give underprivileged students an opportunity for artistic expression. Consequently, she invited several artists of sympathetic views to teach at her school.

The lines between social and artistic revolution are often not very far apart. Aline's struggle to tell her story and discover what was to be in that story was a struggle felt by many more established painters. A vital new group of artists, including George Bellows, John Sloan and William Glackens, later to be identified as the "ashcan school," were challenging academic and popular ideas of painting. They felt that art must relate to real life, must capture character in all its diversity. Their acknowledged leader was Robert Henri, who was also one of the American artists instrumental in introducing new developments in European painting to his native United States.

Aline did not study under Henri at the Ferrar School, but at the more conventional New York School of Art where he also taught. Since finishing her study at the School of Applied Design, she'd longed to return to serious training in art. And so, by pooling carefully saved money from her assorted jobs and contributions from some of her relatives, she was able to raise the tuition to become Henri's pupil. Thus, toward the turn of the century, her path crossed with Emma Goldman's. It was Henri's habit to invite friends and students to Tuesday-evening get-togethers in his home, where he functioned as if he were a conversational concertmaster, and Emma Goldman was a frequent guest, railing against censorship and imposed value systems, asserting her right to walk naked down Fifth Avenue if she was so inclined, and demanding to know how many in the room could be counted on to join her in this declaration of freedom. Certainly, Aline would have been one of the yea-sayers, although Emma never went beyond the planning stage with that particular idea. But surely her dedication to unbridled liberty thrilled Aline, particularly when it was combined with all the other excitements around her. In this room Aline began her lifetime friendship with men like Moses Soyer and Man Ray and Stuart Davis. She attended the Tuesday-evening sessions regularly, bringing work in progress for Henri and the others to criticize.

Robert Henri was a gifted teacher. Long before it was fashionable, he questioned the teacher's role as instructor, seeing it more as that of an "encourager" who awakens and nurtures a student's uniqueness. He also believed that any subject was the legitimate province of the artist. "Draw your material from the life around you, from all of it. There is beauty in everything if it looks beautiful to your eyes." At the same time

47

he demanded from his students total discipline and commitment. He would turn his dark eyes on the class and tell them to "work both mind and body to the limit of endurance," if they wanted to present truly their vision to the world. As Aline listened to him and worked for him, she felt herself emerging, becoming more and more a person distinguishable from all others, able to show through her art what she found significant about life and beauty and love.

Love—being loved—was increasingly present for her now. She had developed into a magnificent-looking young woman. The skin whose rosiness and smoothness would always enchant all who knew her glowed in these budding days like a petal—as if a rose had been polished with a pink velvet cloth. Her deep brown eyes seemed to hold delicious secrets, and when she turned them to a young man, she made him feel that no one in the world existed or mattered but him. She wore womanliness like a richly enveloping cloak, even when her features still had a girlish outline and her waist was barely eighteen inches around. Above the waistline her bosom swelled, full and curving, and she invariably wore clothes that made the most of it.

One of the men who was drawn to Aline was Theodore Bernstein, who had emigrated from Germany in the mid 1890s along with a great wave of educated, ambitious compatriots. They all, explains Aline, "went straight to Wall Street," and, indeed, the German-Jewish hold on a significant segment of the banking world became quite firm. As New York evolved into an increasingly important financial center, German-Jewish families formed their own society—their fortunes and life styles becoming the stuff of legends that persist into our own time.

Aline's cousin Mrs. Loeb believes it was her mother who introduced Theodore Bernstein to Aline, for it continued to trouble the older woman that her young relatives had so little security. Although Bernstein was still only a clerk, his future on Wall Street looked bright. Seven years older than Aline, he was clearly a mature and steady young man. Besides all this, Theo, as Aline quickly began to call him, was handsome, a quality important to a girl whose image of romance was tightly bound to the dashing figure of Joseph Frankau. In fact, Theo's features were almost as regular as her father's and had the same aristocratic look, while his dark hair and mustache provided dash.

They balanced each other, these two. Though not nearly as reserved as his Wall Street colleagues would assume, still Theo was a far more moderate person than Aline. At the same time, he enjoyed immersing himself in her headier emotional climate. In many ways, she filled in the spaces of his own personality. In some, if opposite, ways, he did the same for her. Here was the bourgeois strand that was part of her heritage— here was the careful approach to life that she admired but too often chose to ignore. This exchange was an element in their relationship which many people failed to understand or, if they did, interpreted as a rational compromise dispassionately decided on. In fact, while Aline certainly knew Theo was good for her, she married him with love and good faith, while he adored her with entire abandon.

There were many guests at their wedding in November 1902, for Aline's circle of friends was already a large one. But of all the guests, there was undoubtedly none happier, although her smiles remained subdued, than Ethel Frankau. Thanks to this marriage, she would be able, once and for all, to come home. In fact, the joint living arrangement they were about to embark on would set the pattern for the rest of their lives, but Aline could only know how grateful she was to be able to give her sister, in her teen-age years, the kind of care their parents would have wanted her to have. Theo had never once objected to the idea that his married life would immediately include a young sister-in-law, and this attitude remained constant, making his relationship with Ethel as solid and full of feeling as the tie between the sisters themselves.

Their first winter as a family was spent in a brand-new apartment on Seventy-eighth Street near West End Avenue. Aline had left Henri's classes, although she knew that one day she would return to them. Indeed, his feelings about color and form greatly affected the delight she took in everyday life. Wrapped in a new winter coat, her face cold and glowing, she would watch the children playing in Central Park, where "the snow was over everything, feathery and perishable, smoothing and blurring the outlines of shrub and rock." The air would be clear as a diamond, and the city sounds would float toward her, providing a musical cadence for her walk home to the welcoming apartment and the warmly sweet space of her kitchen. There she would begin to make supper, filled with a sense of her own power, for in that cozy room it was as if she had "divine permission" to do exactly as she chose. Theo and Ethel would come home to stews the shade of "Rembrandt brown," and chicken casseroles cooked to a "molten gold." Theo might bring with him from lower Manhattan huge paper parcels filled with greens and fruits from the Washington Market, and she would immerse herself in the artistic possibilities of the vegetables, creating salads that ran the whole continuum of green from the yellow-white green of endive to the darkest watercress. Or perhaps she would arrange a combination of tart fruits, "made suave with avocado."

More often than not, guests would join them for dinner. Usually they were friends of Aline's because, for the most part, she found the young lawyers and investment bankers of Theo's business world quite dull, a fact she could not be counted on to hide in their presence. The only compensating factor in her deafness in later life was being able to turn off so many dull conversations. Good friends learned to recognize the benign look on her face at a boring dinner party—a sure sign she had turned the switch on her hearing device. Later she'd giggle about the virtues of the otherwise tedious-to-manage equipment: "It's a dream!" she'd say gleefully. "A flick of my fingers, and they can prattle away for hours!"

Rarely was the company boring at her own parties. "You didn't turn down an invitation from Aline," is the judgment of all who knew her. Wherever she lived, even in this first apartment, there were large sofas and chairs where guests could settle in comfortably for the afternoon or evening—and always, somehow, Aline would be in the center, usually telling a story in rich detail and carrying off each listener into vicarious adventures. She would tell about Nana, about Joseph Frankau, about London skies and road-company tours. Sometimes Theo would smilingly protest: "Now, Aline, it couldn't have happened that way." And she'd turn to him, shaking her head earnestly, and swear it was "the God's truth, Theo. It happened *exactly* that way." And everyone believed her, even Theo. Or if they didn't, it hardly mattered, for her own version of the truth was so captivating.

Ethel was thriving in their life together, making plans to study teaching. Often, on quiet evenings, Aline would sketch her sister's serious face as she sewed on a dress, for even with more money available for clothes, Aline preferred her own and her sister's needlework. Ethel's designs for Aline exactly captured the elegance and bohemianism that would always be her style, a mode of dressing that would become more pronounced as she grew older and took to wearing saris or flowing Oriental robes. In the early years of her marriage her clothes were more conventional, but they always had the flair that announced they had been made for a distinctive woman. She wore suits of unusual materials and linen shirts that draped across her bosom and were often embroidered in intricate, delicate designs.

As much as Aline admired her sister's talent, she marveled, too, at Ethel's steady temperament, as regular as a healthy heartbeat. The convent had perhaps left more of an imprint on Ethel's personality than Aline had first thought. Her inner life was, Aline knew, filled with feeling, but it remained concealed. And although Aline was puzzled by her sister's reluctance to show emotion, she understood that Ethel's controlled temperament would serve as ballast for her own volatile disposition. From the start, Ethel frequently smoothed Theo's feathers if he and Aline got into some heated political discussion, a not at all uncommon occurrence. Theo was extremely tolerant of his wife's liberal views, but he himself was true to his conservatism, and Aline could sometimes push him too far with her passionate declamations on the need for social reform.

"Nonsense!" Theo would yell, and standing up from his chair at the dinner table, he would throw his napkin down and stalk out of the room. Whether remorse or hunger brought him back, he did usually come back, no more than five minutes later, but it would be Ethel who then engaged him in placid conversation, lowering his emotional temperature while she eased him once again into the family scene.

Aline would smile into her dinner plate at her sister's skill and marvel at how mature she was—far too mature to give Aline's maternal impulses much room for expression. So it was welcome news to learn in her second year of marriage that she was pregnant. Welcome is far too pallid a word: she was ecstatic, overjoyed; she embraced this new aspect of herself with unrestrained rapture. All her life Aline would be a lusty human animal, hearty in all her appetites, satisfying them with robust pleasure, and without regret or apology. Similarly, she had none of the inhibitions, aversions or self-consciousness about her body that were common to young women of her time. Pregnancy was to her a cause for public celebration. Her swelling belly delighted her. "I look magnificent," she'd tell her friends, and pull their hands toward her stomach, hiking up her shirt so they could feel the baby's movements. Even the shyest man or most squeamish woman could not help but be warmed by her climate of perpetual summer, while she basked in her own animal heat and in the new life she was growing inside her.

In 1904, Theodore Bernstein, Junior, was greeted joyously. Experiencing the wonder of birth, Aline felt a new kind of connection with her sweet and gentle mother, who would have loved so to see

51

another generation of their family begin. Agreeably, the Bernsteins were able to afford a nursemaid for Teddy. "Anyone who had two sticks to rub together could have some help," Edla explains, and Theo was certainly accumulating more assets than a few sticks. He was moving rapidly along the often bumpy road of business success. If he was not considered creative, neither was he plodding. A future partner would say he never had the "sharp, cutting edge" needed really to make a mark, but it was always apparent that he was a bright, meticulous, dedicated worker. By the time his son was born, he was firmly ensconced in the investment banking world, having moved easily from clerk to cashier, and was clearly on his way now to becoming the broker he would be in later life.

Thus he was able even in these early days to provide his wife with some of the domestic help she needed to free her own time. That she preferred painting or political involvements to a full-time domestic career never prompted an apology. She accepted her need to have more experience than could be found within her family as easily as she accepted her love for her family. And indeed, by the time her daughter was born, two years later, Aline made a still greater commitment to her other interests, even as she exuberantly embraced the daughter she'd yearned to give birth to. In their new, larger apartment on West End Avenue, there was room for a studio for Aline. And now when she and Theo wheeled their children down the wide street—Teddy in an imported wicker carriage, the baby in a high black one—her eye registered with new concentration each dramatic detail of urban life.

But her private musings would end when they stopped for tea at a café, where they could chat happily while watching the sleeping children. For their Sunday outings, Theo usually wore a silk scarf casually tied around his neck, while Aline clasped her linen collar with one of the brooches Theo delighted in bringing her. It often irritated him that she took so little interest in jewels, for as a European and a proud man, he gained pleasure from ornamenting his wife with the symbols of his growing success. But of course he knew Aline's beauty needed little ornamentation. Her seemingly endless number of admirers attested to this, and Theo understood their impulses, even seemed to enjoy them. He bragged to his friends on Wall Street about her beauty and charm, just as he bragged about her talent and its renewed development. For Aline had returned to studying with Robert Henri.

She was thrilled to see that nothing had changed about Henri except for his moving his studio to the Lincoln Arcade Building, on Sixty-sixth Street and Broadway. The spirit of the classes was exactly as Aline remembered it, while the evening receptions were also still in glorious session. Every week the same sort of assemblage gathered in Henri's house, artists, writers, political activists. Perhaps the most notorious guest to visit there for a while was young Leon Trotsky, who was studying art at Emma Goldman's school while living in exile in the United States.

But Aline needed no controversial figures to make the evenings intoxicating, especially now that maturity and greater sophistication made her more a peer of the group. Indeed, Sloan and Davis and Bellows and even Henri himself were becoming her intimate friends. "They were always in and out of our house," Edla remembers—a situation that Theo apparently also enjoyed. He felt no self-consciousness about the disparateness of his own interests, although, in fact, he most often bid everyone good night long before his wife was ready for sleep.

Even then Aline was doing battle with insomnia. Somewhat later, when she and Theo had separate bedrooms, the reason given was her sleeping habits, and it is true that her tossings in bed and middle-of-the-night trips out of it influenced the decision. It's doubtful that she ever slept more than three or four hours a night all her life. She'd stay at a party till near dawn, and wake another guest with a phone call at seven-thirty the next morning, amazed that the other wasn't like her, going about the day's business.

It came as a great piece of news to Aline when she learned that Benjamin Franklin had had trouble sleeping, and immediately she adopted his declared method of dealing with it—making up your mind it didn't matter. As soon as she did that, she said, "I was eased into a wonderful relaxation, and was able to use that quiet pre-dawn time for sketching or writing or painting."

No wonder that her evenings with Henri's crowd were so nourishing. The good talk about art and music and books would stay in her mind and feed her during later, wakeful hours. Joseph Frankau's love of literature, transmitted to his daughter, now flowered as Henri discussed and recited Whitman and Zola and Ibsen. And other names and ideas took on new life in those sessions: Emerson and Rousseau, Dostoyevsky and Tolstoy. The gaps in her education were being rapidly filled in, thanks to the enthusiasm Henri generated for the works of his favorite authors and philosophers. As Stuart Davis reported: "When Henri spoke of writers . . . what he did was inspire [us] to go out . . . look up all this stuff and get completely involved with it!"

Aline would come home from Henri's classes or gatherings and over a brandy and soda would recreate some of its excitement for Theo, who was still awake because he had perhaps played bridge that evening, for surprisingly reckless stakes, or gone to the club he had lately joined. Or he might have stayed quietly at home, lingering in the living room to discuss what he was reading with Ethel—the first of a lifetime of evenings when Ethel Frankau would step into a role and a responsibility more properly filled by her sister. If life was a wonderful drama, Aline was the star and the other members of the company, important as they were to the unfolding story, had accepted their lesser billing.

# 4

While Aline mingled uptown with the artists and intellectuals who couldn't have cared less what a person's religion was, and Theo continued to advance close to the center of German-Jewish nobility on Wall Street, another story was being acted out on the Lower East Side.

Every year something like ninety thousand Jews were landing in New York City, escaping the poverty and pogroms of Russia and Poland. Many of them had taken part in workers' strikes in their native land, and they brought a fierce political sensibility to their new life. It was a sensibility that alarmed the uptown Jews—those aristocratic Germans Theodore Bernstein counted as his peers. As Stephen Birmingham reports in *Our Crowd:*

> To most well-to-do Germans, one of the most terrifying things about the Russians (the blanket name given to Lower East Side Jews, even when they came from Poland or Lithuania) was their interest in forming trade unions. This threatened the German's pocketbook, always the most vulnerable part of the anatomy of any rich man. And so, to the uptown German, the Lower East Side Russian became the enemy. . . . It was

worker versus boss, mass versus class, vulgar versus genteel, foreigner versus American, Russian versus German, Jew versus Jew.

The vulgarity Birmingham speaks of was perhaps the most painful cut of all to those privileged Germans who had made themselves wealthy in America. To those still fighting the anti-Semitism of the old-line social elite, it was a miserable embarrassment to be identified with these socially unwashed coreligionists. As the city's newspapers printed stories of the dreadful poverty and ensuing problems of the immigrants "in the Jewish quarter," wealthy Jews squirmed in their board room and drawing room chairs. How could they progress into real social acceptance as long as they were tainted by these unsavory associations?

Mrs. John Loeb, herself a Lehman, and the wife of one of Theo's eventual partners, recalls how Aline's attitude toward this situation differed from her own family's.

"In the world of my parents, the one thing you never wanted to be was Jewish. You never said someone was Jewish out loud, you always lowered your voice when you discussed 'it,' like you do when you say someone has cancer, or you'd use some euphemism like 'one of ours,' or he's 'you know what.' . . . I remember one night at the dinner table, when my father whispered that someone was Jewish, asking, 'Why do you lower your voice, it's just our family, there's nothing but Jews here.' . . . You'd have thought I had thrown a bomb in the middle of the napery!"

Not so with Aline, says Mrs. Loeb. "She was amused at this kind of denial and was completely relaxed about her heritage. Her artistic and theatrical friends were Jewish and non-Jewish—some had changed their names for professional reasons—but mainly you never thought about whether a person you met through her was Jewish or not, while in my other worlds that was the immediate measure you made."

Actually, John Loeb's parents, the legendary Carl Loeb and Mrs. Loeb, Sr., were among the few people Aline Bernstein ever really liked in the financial world; and part of the attraction was their comparative lack of hysteria about assimilation. The elder Mrs. Loeb, her daughter-in-law reports with a smile, "often made remarks that were considered great social boners, but I think Aline recognized them as more likely being her own kind of absolute directness." When meeting someone at a party, it was not uncommon for Mrs. Loeb, Sr., to tune out a name change that had taken place and sweetly say, "How nice it is to see you,

Mr. Goldstein," to a man who had legally become Mr. Gladstone. If he sputtered an indignant correction, it was waved away impatiently. "Oh, what difference does it make?" she'd say, and Aline, if she was present, would grin with mildly malicious glee.

A good deal of the behavior that was so offensive to Aline stemmed from the Jewish paranoia suggested by Mrs. Loeb—the desire to "fit in." It was a desire fed by reality, for even wealthy Jews experienced club and school and career discrimination. But ironically, prejudice only heightened their own "in-house" anti-Semitism. If they could have, many of these uptown Jews would have thrown a wall around Hester and Division streets on the Lower East Side, where unkempt street vendors in sagging suits hawked shoelaces and handkerchiefs in broken English, where impoverished parents doled out pennies for stale meat and fish, whose odors mingled with the sodden garbage underfoot.

Aline, of course, responded differently. The late designer Russel Wright explained that "her range of sympathy, and understanding for people, ran to the very lowest, coarsest and ignorant." And it is true that Aline Bernstein was, if such a quality can be defined, truly democratic. Her measure, her elitism, had to do with character and talent and capacity for life, and these could be found as abundantly on the Lower East Side as on Park Avenue. Feeling this way, and with increased time free from family duties, it was natural that she should begin to look for a way to make some contribution to the city's impoverished immigrants.

By 1910, Ethel had already begun volunteer work at the Henry Street Settlement House on the Lower East Side. She brought home excited stories about the woman who led it, a woman whom Aline knew slightly but whose reputation she admired profoundly. Lillian Wald, an extraordinary, charismatic person, had created an oasis of care and comfort and, increasingly, culture, right inside the bruised heart of the ghetto. A trained nurse, Miss Wald had decided years before to use her medical knowledge to do social work among the poor. She wanted to help them learn to be clean and healthy and productive, and, she hoped, prideful. She had grown weary of bureaucratic systems whose generalized programs were often callously impersonal and even, sometimes, brutal.

To raise money for her plans Lillian went uptown, visiting those wealthy, mostly Jewish men and women who were not afraid to admit responsibility for the immigrants others in their world preferred to ignore. The settlement house concept was a new one in America, and Miss Wald explained its origins to her patrons in fervent detail: how it was begun by Samuel Augustus Barnett in England and had spread to Chicago, where her good friend Jane Addams had created the already famous Hull House. Like its predecessors, her settlement house would be dedicated to active participation in the lives of the poor. Affluent families, like the Schiffs and the Loebs, were sufficiently stirred by Lillian's magnetism and passion to make really significant donations to help realize her dream.

The children's plight in particular had seemed horrible to Miss Wald. In summer, they often moved outdoors to escape the sweltering heat of the tenements, sleeping in the filthy streets or in empty, smelly pushcarts. Child labor was of course in full and unregulated force, and by the age of eight, boys and girls were sent into dank factories to strip feathers for bedding or paste linings on fabrics or roll cigars. Often they carried work home after a twelve-hour day, and worked into the night for extra money. Even before Henry Street was functioning, Lillian called again on her uptown friends, asking them to come downtown on Sundays and take the children back into their world for a few hours, take them into homes where they could see beautiful objects and art, take them to Central Park, where they could see bright flowers and lush lawns, and could spread their arms and imagination.

Out of all this energy and the energized support of benefactors, in 1893 Henry Street Settlement House was born. Even today, it sits as a bastion of elegance and warmth in a neighborhood that has little time for either. It is a red-brick Georgian building, a relic of a still earlier time in New York when the neighborhood was younger and not crowded with tenements. Lillian's restoration work made fireplaces glow once again, wood shine, and moldings reveal their original hand carving. Gifts of furniture made their way downtown, none of it in any way bearing the "institutional" stamp. This was to be a home, a house where friends would gather.

There was a huge backyard attached to the house, a rarity in these streets, and it was promptly turned over to the neighborhood children. In good weather, kindergarten classes were held outdoors, and there were special hammocks designed for infants who were in an older brother's or sister's care while their parents were working. In the evening, the hammocks were put away and there would be dancing for the young men and women of the neighborhood under the warm glow of Japanese lanterns.

Because Lillian Wald believed in encouraging people to take pride in their environment, the idea of dramatic clubs took hold on Henry Street. They would, for one thing, offer a chance for people to celebrate their heritage, reflecting in pageants and playlets the richness of their cultural origins. For another, they would afford familiarity with the adopted country, through reading and dramatizing America's folkways and literature.

One of the uptown women working as a volunteer at the settlement house was Rita Morgenthau, who wholeheartedly agreed with these ideas of Lillian's. A theater enthusiast, she gladly became leader of the girls' dramatic clubs. Two other people who were deeply and devotedly involved were Irene and Alice Lewisohn, wealthy young copper heiresses from the German Jews' inner circle, whom Aline had grown friendly with uptown. The sisters defied conventional wisdom by actively working to develop Henry Street's theatrical life, and this streak of independence, plus their complete devotion to the theater, endeared them to Aline. Through them, her own interest in the settlement house began to grow. By 1911, she was joining Ethel on her trips downtown and working along with her sister to create costumes for the drama club productions. It was the first time Aline had put her sewing talents to such use. She had made clothes for herself and for Ethel, but never for people playing a role. Although she had learned through her father how important the clothing an actor wore was to his interpretation of a character, she had never thought of her talent in that light. Now her entire life was being illuminated in new ways.

There were also the props and the sets to work on. She found she was really adept at making blueprints, setting up entrances and exits, placing furniture so that the movement of the play could proceed smoothly. Her excitement mounted, both for her expanding abilities and for the place that was stimulating them. It was important to Aline when she worked on a club production to mirror exactly the ethnic culture it was depicting, and in the future, attention to historical and cultural accuracy would always mark her work. "We do not create life, we recreate it," she would say about theatrical design, adding that the truth must be seen and respected before illusion can evolve from it. Nowhere was this conviction more important to her than in this early work in the ghetto. She fed her creative instincts with the scenes from real life pulsating around her. One day she would recreate these scenes for Thomas Wolfe, stimulating his own talents by her description:

> Everything had a melting mellow color, old woolen clothing, old brick walls, old carts . . . lovely old faces with the sorrow of centuries; one old, old man with an ivory-white beard dressed in a dusty ragged caftan had a pushcart full of babies, there must have been eight or ten, maybe he was taking care of them while their mothers did the marketing. His old head bobbed as he pushed the cart, his little white side curls blowing in the breeze from under his old silk skullcap. He must have been a red-haired Jew when he was young, for there was a faint carroty stain at the roots of his beard. His back was like a bow. He had stooped, and his father, and his father's father, to the burden of his race; still, there was the light of love in his watery old eyes, and I could see him muttering to the babies, babbling to the fat little seeds of Abraham riding in a pushcart on a Friday morning. . . . I saw a young woman with a little baby in her arms, looking at heaped-up raisins on a pushcart, I saw her shake her head and try her thin pocketbook; and I saw the fat woman who owned the cart take a handful of raisins and stuff them into the young woman's sweater pocket. . . . I saw mothers nursing and arms waving, Jews wagging, people fast and people slow, shuffling old feet and clicking high-heeled slippers, cats eating things from the gutter . . . and I saw the pulsing loyalty that has held them all together.

In 1913, when Aline's involvement with the settlement house was still quite fresh, the idea grew in Miss Wald's mind that the house's twentieth birthday should be celebrated, that she should use the talents of Miss Morgenthau and the Lewisohn and Frankau sisters to create some spectacular pageant that would not only commemorate the anniversary but also document the social history of the streets it served. When she broached her plans to her friends, they excitedly agreed. No question; the Lower East Side would have in June the biggest, gayest, most elaborate birthday party anyone had ever seen.

All winter and spring, a large group of neighborhood women worked under Aline's direction in a small apartment lent for the purpose, assembling the wardrobe for the pageant—creating costumes from their own histories that would help dramatize how they came to be who and where they were. Aline and Ethel would leave the brownstone at 233 West End Avenue in which where the family was now living—the house with such wonderful big doors and high windows, filled with Early American and English and French antiques coexisting in perfect harmony—and push open the tenement door a little while later, to greet the old grandmothers in their brown sweaters with elbows worn thin, and the pregnant wives with stomachs pressed against dresses whose cheap fabric could barely stand the strain. Together they would sit in a circle and sew. At lunchtime Aline and Ethel would unwrap their sandwiches as the other women opened their own—and the smell of garlic and herring hung in the airless rooms while they all sipped strong tea from chipped thick glasses and Aline giggled at the jokes the women told.

Theo's bridge game improved during these months; he had plenty of free time in the evenings to play cards. It would often be very late indeed when the two women in his family returned home. His comfort did not suffer, however, for their household staff had expanded to meet most of his and the children's needs. Peggy Murphy explains why Aline would never have any trouble keeping domestic help. "She paid you to do your work, and respected the work you did, and left you alone to do it. . . . Nobody would leave her." She sighs. "You had plenty to do, but it was all enjoyable, . . . It was done and you felt everything was right."

As for the children, they seemed to accept the idea that they didn't have the kind of mother who would take them to the park after school and gossip with other women while they played. "I don't know what we did on our nurse's day off," Edla says somewhat defensively. "One of the maids probably took us out." Nor did Aline concern herself much with the children's schooling except, as in Edla's case, when she had to make command appearances in the principal's office; and one might speculate that Edla's misbehavior was a way of forcing her mother's involvement in her life. There does seem to be some discrepancy between Aline's genuine feeling for her children and the way the children, or at least Edla, perceived that feeling.

"Mother was principally involved with her own life," Edla says. "She was only really happy when she was working. . . . It wasn't just something she did to fill out her life . . . it *was* her life."

Certainly, without her work Aline would not have been Aline. But her family was also fundamental to her. Teddy seemed to have less trouble than Edla in grasping this, a difference in perception that would soon widen.

"My schoolgirl complexion was of the pimply variety, and I wore glasses long before it was chic," Edla continues deprecatingly. "Mother had that completely enviable skin that never needs rouge or cream. . . . I was skinny with stringy hair and Mother was curved and lush with soft, fluffy hair she could leave completely alone. . . . It wasn't easy," she finishes with a smile.

As an adult, Edla was in fact quite striking, and Aline's letters to friends tell how "beautiful" her daughter looks, how "handsome," how "stunning." But in childhood what seems to be is often as painfully real as what actually is, and can affect relationships for years to come. In any case, it is hard in other ways to live with a person whom the world seems to adore, to see the feet of clay that are always shod for others in silken slippers.

"Mother had a very low boiling point," Edla explains typically. "Very few people saw it outside, but she made no attempt at all to hide it at home. . . . Without Ethel's keeping everything anchored and steady, I don't know what would have happened."

Although the testimony of various servants would dispute this view of Aline's temperament—"I never heard her raise her voice"; "They were always so loving and polite to each other, all of them"—it seems fair to assume that to some degree Aline let her public face relax at home; the ethic of keeping your personal life apart from your work would have led her to express her feelings more freely inside her private world.

The public Aline was very evident during the days and nights of preparing for Henry Street's pageant. This was not to be some amateur event, clumsy and more conspicuous for good intention than talent. Everyone involved was determined to make the performances as professional as possible and, by this achievement, force New York to pay tribute to its overlooked citizens. And the rest of New York was paying more and more attention. City officials offered to pave Henry Street for the occasion, and then the Edison Company decided to give the street electric lights, so that the celebration could be gloriously illuminated.

On the day of the festival, Aline and Ethel worked tirelessly, stopping for nothing. The streets around the settlement house began to fill. Ten thousand people looked down from rooftops or windows, lined the tenement stoops, were held high on older brothers' shoulders. There was music, there was dancing, there was singing, there were speeches, and then, as the sun sank in the sky, a thousand brand-new electric lights snapped on, and the five hundred "actors" and "actresses" who lived in these streets began their scenes.

One after another, the episodes that told the story of New York fell into place: its purchase from the Indians; the Dutch and British settlers;

colonial times. Finally, there came the greatest episode of all—the procession of immigrants coming to live in this bewildering new place. In costumes that proclaimed a native Russia, or Poland, or Italy, or Ireland (costumes that Aline had kept to a fifty-cents-each budget), men, women and children moved proudly down the street, singing songs of their old countries, dancing the remembered folk dances. Their faces shone. Tonight, at least, each of them felt his own value.

When the procession ended, there was a cheering salute to Lillian Wald, a salute that was now underscored by a peal of bells from the old church on Henry Street, the last one left in New York with a slaves' gallery. The music seemed a tribute to the men and women who had left ancient oppression behind, and tonight were celebrating their hope for a way of life that would be truly free.

The magic of that spring night lingered in Aline's and Ethel's minds in the months that followed, giving them increased enthusiasm for settlement house projects. But by summer of 1914, a new bid was being made on Ethel's attention. The Bernsteins summered in those years in Woodmere, Long Island, where they had become friendly with Edwin Goodman and his family. Mr. Goodman owned the fashionable women's specialty store Bergdorf Goodman, and one night at a dance at the local country club he commented on the particularly flattering dress of purple taffeta that Aline was wearing. Dancing with her around the ballroom floor, he asked where she had bought it, intending to tease her about patronizing a competitor. Instead, Aline remembered, "I told him my kid sister made it." Surprised, having known Ethel only as a kindergarten teacher, Edwin half-jokingly invited Ethel to come into the store when they returned to the city and talk to him about a job.

One could not have guessed that Ethel Frankau would thus begin an association with Bergdorf Goodman that would last for sixty years. All that was clear to Edwin Goodman when they chatted more officially about her coming to work for him was that she had a rather "awesome gentility," a quality that he rightly perceived would be almost as important as her talent when working with the temperamental women who made up Bergdorf's custom clients. Bergdorf's, in those days, was strictly a custom shop, where clothes were made to order (for a great deal of money) for wealthy customers, many of whom were Ethel's social companions through Theo and Aline.

Mr. Goodman went regularly to Paris on buying trips; there he would purchase "originals" from leading designers, which were then copied in his workroom, line for line and in the original fabric, for his American customers. This called for a delicate calculation: if he failed to buy enough material to meet the demand for copies back home, important customers were unhappy; if he bought too much, the store lost money. Furthermore, since his customers tended to move in the same circles, he needed to maneuver so that no one would either feel "left out" or —most horrible of all—find herself wearing the same splendid frock as a friend.

Ethel proved to be adroit in all these matters. Almost immediately after she went to work for him in October 1914, she heard that Mr. Goodman had decided to cancel his upcoming trip because of the war, and she asked a bit timidly, but quite determinedly, if she might go instead. He agreed. Trips to France and Italy and Spain would become as much a part of Ethel's life as the store itself, but in 1915 it was wildly dramatic to travel across the ocean alone.

"But it's dangerous," Aline worried. "But it's such an opportunity," Ethel countered quietly, and of course Aline knew she was right. And she also knew that once Ethel made up her mind to do something, it would be extremely difficult to influence the decision. If anyone could, that person would have been Aline. Still, "this was a highly powerful lady too," Edla says of her aunt, and goes on to say that growing up flanked by Aline Bernstein and Ethel Frankau could make one feel occasionally "quite crushed between them."

In truth, Aline respected her sister's steely resolve, and so she paused only a moment before smiling her approval. Not too long later, she was presiding over a farewell party on shipboard, her own gaiety almost obscuring the quiet young woman who was about to sail.

Of course, Ethel never seemed to mind such eclipsing—as Mr. Goodman commented, "Ethel thought her sister the loveliest thing that walked"—and indeed, her excitement about the journey was tempered only by the idea of being away so long from Aline and the rest of the family.

The crossing involved dodging U-boats, and after a delayed arrival in Paris, a shell from Big Bertha landed on the building next to the hotel Ethel was staying in. But nonetheless Ethel was enchanted by Paris and excited by her work there. Near the end of her life, in 1969, France honored her contributions to its fashion industry by awarding her the Order of National Merit. By that time she had made more than fifty trips to see the Paris collections. But as she sailed for home in 1915, she knew only that she was embarked on a profession that would make increasing demands on her time and talents.

As Aline listened to her sister's enthusiasm when they celebrated her return, she began to think even more about her own life and work. With the success of the pageant, the Lewisohn sisters were inspired to concretize their theatrical experiments by building a real theater to house them. They believed that what they were doing for the neighborhood had cultural implications that extended far beyond it. And so they began, to the chagrin of many of their uptown friends, to raise money to build a permanent theater, which they would call the Neighborhood Playhouse. Aline was caught up in their plans, but she was also feeling confused. For while she vastly enjoyed designing sets and costumes and of course was devoted to the magic of theater, she still thought of her vocation as fine art practiced on canvas, not on a drawing board or cutting table. Yet the closer the Neighborhood Playhouse came to becoming a reality, the more excited Aline was about remaining actively involved with it. As the months passed, and she continued to contribute her ideas and energies to the plans, she felt herself approaching an important decision. But meanwhile she concentrated on helping to make the dream come true. The Lewisohns and Rita Morgenthau had been joined by two other women who would also become Aline's lifelong friends, Helen Arthur, a lawyer in a time of pitifully few female professionals, and her friend Agnes Morgan, who was skilled in the techniques of production. Already the Playhouse was being called, admiringly, "a women's theater," and newspapers reporting their progress announced that: "No man has anything whatsoever to do with it except by invitation."

Aline's excitement about the Playhouse was being fed in other ways. It would be the first theater in New York to design and make all its own scenery, costumes and properties—thus launching the concept that stagecraft could itself be a significant art form, the fusion of design, sculpture, music, lighting and physical movement as unified and important as the words the actors spoke. Aline would say later that the profession of "scene designer" began at the Playhouse, and the critic John Gassner agrees, adding that in other ways, too, the Neighborhood Playhouse gave birth to an entirely new kind of theater, unlike any the city had ever known.

Gassner doubts that "art theater" would "have made a strong dent in Broadway" in later years without the kind of experimentation that was soon taking place at the Playhouse, where the productions were "revealing resources of taste and style still largely absent in the uptown theaters." And when professional actors began to appear at the Playhouse, he says, "a trip to the Lower East Side became obligatory to art-loving New Yorkers."

Indeed, from the moment on February 12, 1915, when the red Georgian building at Grand and Pitt streets opened its apple-green shutters and doors, professional actors did come down to the Lower East Side in increasing numbers, as did playwrights from all over the country and Europe who were committed to new kinds of drama, works that would stand comparison with the very best being produced in other literary forms. People like John Galsworthy and Eugene O'Neill and Elmer Rice and Clifford Odets would present their earliest efforts at the Neighborhood Playhouse. In fact, even before his first play was presented there, John Galsworthy wrote in the theater's guest book that this was "the house where magic has come to stay."

As Aline began to teach design and stagecraft to theater students in addition to her work on actual productions, the thoughts that had been recurring about her art and her work took a more discernible shape. She went to Robert Henri, as once she had gone to Tom Watson, and told him that she felt great similarities in the work she was doing now and the work she had been doing with him. "After all," she said, "I'm dealing still with people, with capturing my idea of their lives and their character." Henri agreed, and encouraged her to utilize her art training in costume and scenic design. As soon as she had professed the decision, to Henri, to the family, she knew it was the right one. It felt so natural to merge her gifts with the passion for theater that had never left her. She would always paint, but she would be a designer.

"Once she found this talent was growing in her," says Alice Beer, who had also come to work at the Playhouse, "she was determined to nurture it, develop it, use it, and carry it on." And indeed, even more than before, she threw herself completely into the Playhouse productions. Audiences broke into spontaneous applause as the curtain went up on her sets, and complimented her effusively after the show, having seen her name on the program. This itself was a "first" in theatrical history, for no such credits had previously been given.

In the absence of a real profession of stage or costume designer, actors and actresses had for the most part been decking themselves out in ill-fitting borrowed suits and gowns or their own usually shabby ward-

66

robe. Reviews often mocked the bunched-up trousers or gaping neck-lines of the players in their rented finery, or made snide remarks about "shiny serge elbows" that might look all right in the actor's living room but didn't on stage.

As for sets, they were usually hastily painted wooden panels or "flats," so crudely executed that the word "design" might never have been invented. It was all changing now. Changing rapidly. Aline brought home costume sketches and blueprints and took them up to her top-floor studio, often working well into the night.

Life was good. Theo accepted her involvement with the theater; he was proud of it rather than disgruntled. Ethel was becoming more and more valuable to the store. The children seemed relatively happy at the Ethical Culture School, where she'd enrolled them. When in the winter of 1916 the playhouse undertook to produce the American premiere of Stravinsky's ballet *Petrouchka,* Aline was thrilled at the opportunity to supervise the production of the costumes. She was determined to make garments true to the folk traditions inherent in the music which would not in any way hamper a dancer's movements. Her love of music and dance (Isadora Duncan was often a fellow guest at Henri's evenings and was only one of Aline's dance-world friends) lent her fingers new agility.

The production was, for most of its audiences, a vast success, although admittedly, some of the local residents were not quite ready for this unfamiliar art form. On opening night, one elderly Jew rather diffidently walked into the box office to buy a ticket. In broken English, he asked what exactly this *Petrouchka* was. Told it was a ballet, he screwed up his face and questioned some more. "Just what does it mean, ballet?"

"Oh, you know," said the ticket seller. "It's dancing."

"Dancing," the old man repeated contemptuously and, with great annoyance, pulled back his fifty cents. "I don't dance," he snapped in Yiddish to the cashier, and walked sternly back into Grand Street's pedestrian traffic—itself, said Aline later, a ballet, had he only realized it.

Every day she was more and more fascinated by discovering how much you could convey about a person by what he wore. The slightest variation of dress could bespeak some variation of mood, and it was hers to see and capture. Gaiety, passion, fear, anger—all this could be translated into a costume. As she explained with a smile, if "Hamlet had been a well-adjusted and happy young prince, he would never have clung so tenaciously to his inky cloak!"

The connection between clothes and character was always there for Aline, even in private life. When, in later years, she wrote to a friend about the "old lady" settling down and reforming for good, she said, as illustration: "my next evening dress will be black lace over lilac satin, just escaping the ground in front with a train in back, a grey marcelled wig and the old Dinkenspiel cameos, a black velvet ribbon clasping the sagging throat, lorgnettes on a chain worn around the neck and a hot water bottle!"

It would in fact be a very long time before Aline could conceive of herself in any diminished way. Now, everywhere she turned, she saw only expanded images of herself, each more accomplished and productive and attractive than the one she'd just relinquished. And all these images seemed to be at their most triumphant when the curtain rose on one of her productions.

# 5

As the Neighborhood Playhouse story spread through the city, performers of all degrees of celebrity came to observe and take part in it. Ethel Barrymore brought a guest production of *The Shadow* to the Playhouse, and Ellen Terry volunteered to do an evening of readings from Shakespeare. The night of Miss Terry's performance, Aline sat in the audience with Theo. He was already becoming the Shakespeare scholar he would be all the rest of his life, and friends remember that he always carried a volume of Shakespeare in his pocket, which he would read if he was lunching alone or waiting to meet someone, or even in the middle of one of Aline's parties that no longer held his interest.

"You didn't find that offensive, because he was so quiet about it," said Melville Cane, a lawyer, poet and old friend. "And it was clear," he continued, "that he wasn't doing it as any kind of affectation. . . . He simply loved the language, relished it and found comfort, I suppose, or at least a release from tensions by immersing himself in a play or sonnet."

Isadora Duncan and her troupe of dancers were frequent visitors to the Playhouse, and dance students would religiously fill the theater no matter when she appeared.

Aline's friendship with Isadora was heightened by their joint relationship with George Bellows, whose ironic wit and air of spontaneity were extremely attractive, especially to women of such intense sensibilities as theirs. He and his wife were part of the "Washington Square crowd," a group of artists who had settled in Greenwich Village, where rents were low, transforming the quiet streets into the center of New York's bohemian life. The Village was more than a neighborhood; it was a state of mind that embraced change and preached freedom and had nothing but disdain for what it regarded as the bourgeois morality of more conventional neighborhoods uptown. At least theoretically, such behavior as marital infidelity was acceptable to the Washington Square bohemians. Nonetheless, when George began having an affair with Isadora Duncan, Emma Bellows was hardly happy about it. Still, she was able to maintain her dignity while the affair ran its course.

The years have established the legend that Aline Bernstein and George Bellows were also lovers, after his affair with Isadora and before hers with Thomas Wolfe. Years later, Wolfe would accuse her retroactively of her relationship with "the painter." He also, as was often his fashion, created a fictional character based on George Bellows. The fictitious artist was christened Henry Mallows, and Wolfe treated him with contempt. Repeating, for example, Mallows's claim that he was a "primitive" and so had no artistic tricks, Wolfe spat: "God, Henry was almost as much a primitive as Oscar Wilde eating a crepe suzette—as for having no tricks, he had nothing *but* tricks!"

It is difficult to document the rumor about Bellows and Aline. That they were attracted to each other is certain; that they spent a great deal of time together, painting, arguing good-naturedly about their own or someone else's work, lunching late into the afternoon, sipping after-dinner brandy long after Emma or Theo was asleep—all this is also certain. But Aline did not seem to need to go to bed with every man she was attracted to. Her delight came just as readily from the invisible engagement of the senses between two people who reveled in the possibilities of their sensual selves. Thomas Wolfe, again fictionalizing real life, would one day speak of this quality in Esther Jack, the woman modeled so exactly and specifically after Aline Bernstein. He wrote of Esther's "richness" of spirit:

It was not merely a physical and sensuous thing, it was a richly imaginative and delicately intuitive thing . . . and she communicated it to everything she touched. . . . People who have this energy of joy and delight draw other people to them as bees are drawn to ripe plums. . . . People wanted to be near her; she gave them a feeling of confidence, joy and vitality which they did not have in themselves.

And when, another time, he tried to relate her complex mix of strength and softness to the equally complex characteristics of the city she loved so, he wrote: "She was a product of the city . . . she was the natural growth of steel, stone and masonry, yet she was as fresh, juicy and rosy as if she had come out of the earth."

Aline's earthiness, as Wolfe implied, attracted women as well as men, from Isadora to Emma Goldman, to lesser known but equally close friends like Emaline Roche, a designer and architect who worked side by side with Aline for years.

"It was a power," Miss Roche says of her friend's fascination, "a force that emanated from her and drew men and women to her magnetically. . . . She had a womanliness of the most profound sort—animalistic in the sense of being simply feeling, earthy in the sense of being dense, soft, moist, rich." Miss Roche pauses, and says thoughtfully: "I've always wondered whether this wasn't the real attraction for her with Wolfe. His size, his thick sensual features, the chunky neck and great broad shoulders and gargantuan appetites all seemed so totally male; it was as if she had finally found her match in gender definition."

Several people have speculated about the parallels between Emma Bellows's attitude toward her husband's affair with Isadora and Theo's toward Aline during the years of her liaison with Wolfe. That Aline discussed the Duncan/Bellows affair with Theo is certain, for she relished nothing more than a good morsel of gossip, and certainly that connection was rich in tidbits. For example, Isadora insisted that George father a child for her, in keeping with her ideas about eugenics, and she simply couldn't understand George's reluctance to do so. As was her habit when she repeated such stories, Aline's face and voice took on an endearing ingenuousness. She'd breathily begin, "I know I shouldn't really be saying this . . ." while pleasure sparkled in her eyes. But despite her somewhat voyeuristic glee, she also made clear as she recounted the story that she entirely accepted the situation and, more significantly, had never ceased to respect and admire Emma Bellows as a separate and valuable person. Her attitude may well have made some impression on Theo. When, years later, she would write the novel that documented in vivid detail her affair with Thomas Wolfe, friends of the family were astounded by Theo's response. Several people recall scurrying to hide the book when Theo came to call, and remember their amazement when, after looking quizzically around their libraries or living rooms, he would ask, "Don't you have a copy of Aline's book? You must read it! It's brilliant!"

There would be an additional reason for Theo's equanimity. From early in his marriage he had recognized Aline's exceptional qualities, and that "a nature as rich as hers" could not be confined to conventional standards of right and wrong. There was no doubt in the mind of anyone who knew Theo and Aline that this was his view of his wife, and often the measure of his response to her behavior. A friend of the family offers this analysis of how Theo, and indeed almost everyone, saw Aline Bernstein: "When the ordinary person leads a life of conformity, seeking approval," this woman says, "any deviation from that pattern results in criticism. But Aline, although she was generally discreet, never conformed to any but her own value system. She never once measured her behavior by a need for approval. Therefore, when she did something that one would ordinarily be highly critical of in another person, all you ever said, if you found out about it, was, 'Well, that's Aline." You never thought to pass judgment on her behavior, for she had held herself above judgment always, except of course by herself, and she could certainly be a hard taskmaster on that score."

So it was that the Bernstein family accepted Aline's ever growing involvement with her career as something she "must" do, and never complained about its demands on her time. She was, in fact, already evidencing her ability to "stretch the hours," so that all the tasks she set for herself every day could get done. And an important additional factor contributed to the ease with which she managed family and career, her personal and public worlds. The more her outside life claimed her time, the more Ethel stepped into her space at home. Her job at Bergdorf's was becoming increasingly complex and demanding, but unlike her sister, whose work was the very center of her life, and as such could never be separated out, Ethel was determined to keep her work confined to the office and showroom, and never to bring it home.

A woman who was Bergdorf's lingerie buyer and moved in the same circles as the Bernsteins and Ethel remembers Ethel's response when she would try, in a burst of enthusiasm, to discuss the day's activities over cocktails or dinner.

"I'd be all bubbling with something," she says, "perhaps a big sale to a mutual client, and I'd say, 'Oh, Mrs. So-and-so was in today and she—' and then I'd see this look on Ethel's face; she'd just look at me totally silently. She didn't say, 'I'm glad' or 'Isn't that good' or anything. Just that silent stare that told me I'd better keep business inside the shop."

Ethel did, of course, make friends in her field. All her life she would count some of the world's leading fashion talents as her intimates. In later years, people like Christian Dior and Givenchy and St. Laurent would never come to New York without going to dinner at Ethel's, while when she went abroad, they would give luncheon parties for her in their homes. But these were people of far-ranging interests, whose conversation would be likely to turn on music and art and politics and theater.

There was also romance in Ethel's life, though she was typically close-mouthed about it. "You just sort of heard about the relationship," Mr. Goodman says about Ethel's involvement with an American-based French businessman, Charles Thurnauer. They had met through Theo, and indeed, Charles was to prove an important friend to the entire family, fitting into their life together as if he and Ethel were already married. That they didn't ever marry was never totally explained. "For over twenty years, they were getting ready to be married," Edla says wryly. The major reason always given was the resistance of Charles's family to his taking an American wife and settling permanently in another country. But it is open to speculation whether Charles might not have overcome that resistance had Ethel really been ready to make a life away from her sister. Undoubtedly the reasons were complex and several, and only Ethel ever really knew—and would never say—what they were.

And so she continued to contribute quietly to the stability of the Bernstein family, an active if less vocal participant in exuberant family scenes. Mr. Goodman remembers going to the house and playing backgammon with Theo. The "whole family would gather around as if it was the Olympic championship or something . . . and if I'd score, Aline and the kids would all kind of boo . . . rooting very hard for Theo, and very hard against me." Ethel would only smile at times like this, but it was clear to Goodman that she shared the family feeling of "tremendous love and possessiveness," of "us against any outsiders."

The senior Mr. Goodman, his son recalls, was always particularly touched by Ethel's total devotion to her niece and nephew. Consequently, he understood her suffering, even though she did her best to mask it, when twelve-year-old Teddy became seriously ill after a severe case of measles. He had developed a strep throat, which in those days before penicillin could be extremely dangerous because it often affected the patient's heart.

After several days of careful watching by the family physician, a heart specialist was called in for consultation. Aline kept vigil outside the sickroom door while the examination took place. Aching memories of watching her mother decline, and of Joseph Frankau collapsing at her feet, flooded through her, spilled over into tears that ran unchecked down her face. But these memories paled before the immeasurable dread that her son might be mortally ill.

Nightmares can come true. The physician's report was grim. Teddy's heart was damaged, he was certain, beyond repair. They should make the boy comfortable as best and as long as they could. As he shrugged into his expensive coat, it was clear he did not believe they would have to make that effort very long.

"I will not give him up!" Aline shouted as the physician left. She would not *allow* this story to be over so soon. The elderly family doctor shared Aline's anger at the younger physician's cool dismissal of a child's life and a mother's terror. He looked sadly at Aline, but he now saw, along with her pain, a kind of exultant power radiating from her eyes. It said she would triumph over this prognosis, for she knew her strength, believed in her capacity for victory.

Straightaway the Bernsteins and Ethel and the family doctor made their plans. The doctor was convinced that fresh air and bed rest were the two most essential ingredients for Teddy's recovery. Somehow Teddy must have the benefit of fresh air, all the time, night and day.

Done.

Theo immediately found a contractor to build an open porch off the fourth floor of the house, and before it was completed, Teddy was carried up to the roof, where a bed was set up in a sheltered spot. Night and day, professional nurses kept vigil, but more often than not they were seconded by Aline, huddled in a coat, chair drawn up to the bedside, spinning stories that made her son smile.

When the porch was built, Teddy was moved downstairs, and there he stayed for more than two years. Winter snow piled up in the streets, and his mother nestled into the collar of her fur coat when she sat by his side. Spring breezes promised, she told him gaily, better times soon to come; autumn leaves fluttered down around him while his mother triumphantly called his attention to the colors: "Look, Teddy, did you ever see such an orange?" And they would play comparison, analogy games to pass the time and help him transport himself through imagination out of his cage of isolation; the summer sun made him perspire as it beat down, but Aline would carry massive bouquets of vivid greens and beautiful flowers to his bedside. And all the while, as the calendar turned, day by day, week by week, month by month, he came to share his mother's conviction that he would recover. She would have it no other way, and he, above all others, shared her faith in her own invincible spirit.

"My mother made certain the household revolved completely around my brother during those years," Edla remembers, adding impassively, "But of course everyone, including Mother, went on working."

That Teddy as an adult never resented his mother's going on with her career while he was ill seems evidence that she was able to convey the certainty that he was uppermost in her mind even when she was away from him. Indeed, Aline would always say that she had been permanently affected by the years of Teddy's illness. All her life these particular scenes of pain would return to her mind. At such times a look would come over her face that Thomas Wolfe describes in this manner: "a somber and passionate look . . . transformed her merry and eager face with an expression of brooding intensity . . . it had in it a strange, animal bewilderment . . . as if her brain was struggling with some grievous thing in life it could not fathom."

But there was still another side to Aline's pain. It was a response that illustrated a unique aspect of her personality, the resolution of apparent dichotomies. Sorrow and joy were not mutually exclusive to Aline Bernstein, but only different in kind. So it was that the aching despair she felt with Teddy's illness could sometimes be almost healing. Her senses, she would explain, once again using a personally significant metaphor, created in these moments a kind of "music"—a symphony composed of the whole range of her feelings. In the very center of her turmoil, she would know a kind of peace, as if she had been strengthened by her very surrender to pain. The music would emerge from the deepest rent in her soul, "and the hurt, the knife in the heart would start the most glorious chords, swelling, resolving and melting, resounding . . . until I became one with the stream of life."

That Aline did sublimate so much of her suffering in work was spelled out by Wolfe: "It was as worker that this woman was supreme. The true religion of her soul, the thing that saved her . . . was the religion of her work. It . . . took her out of herself, united her life to a nobler image which was external to her and superior to the vanities of the self."

Truly, work was "saving" her now. She was excited by the chance to collaborate with the already famous designer Robert Edmond Jones, who had agreed to design the costumes for a Playhouse production of a fourteenth-century miracle play. He was immediately impressed with Aline's ability to achieve exactly the effects he'd had in mind despite the Playhouse's absurd budget restrictions. Miss Lewisohn remembers the costumes well, and says that even the most eagle-eyed critic "would have been startled to discover that the sumptuous robes of the carved angels and the Virgin were made of oilcloth—gilded and formed to give the illusion of sculptured wood!"

Actually, while Aline was often frustrated by her small budgets, she would look back on them with satisfaction. A meager purse, she said, can "stimulate inventiveness." And later, in an article about design, she explained further: "Wonderful effects can be made with what I choose to call the translation of material. When the curtain goes up on a scene, a magic curtain rises with it, and through this magic curtain the specta-tors look with enchanted eyes. They are there to be amused or in-structed or fooled, maybe all three together. The illusion of the richest stuff can be created with muslin, felt, oilcloth, velveteen and a little paint applied judiciously. Sometimes far more beautiful effects are created by the artist in this way than by the use of real and expensive materials, which often go flat under artificial light." And she ended with a statement that perhaps reveals one of the major attractions theatrical life held for her. "Remember," she said, "everything on stage must be heightened, must be made *more* like itself than it really is."

No matter what her budget, Aline's starting point was always her reverence for beauty. "The intention must always be of beauty," she would declare about any new project, while in private life, friends remember her ability to transform the most mundane experience into something beautiful. "Being around Aline Bernstein," says Clara Weiss, a long-time friend and associate, "was discovering the beautiful. I learned enormously from her, not from being directed to think in a particular way, but by being close enough to be allowed to share in her vision of the world."

With no one did Aline more generously share this vision than with Teddy, lying immobile in his bed. His mother threw open the doors to a world of glowing loveliness. After her workday, she would bring him the day's experiences, all its images packed into stories she would unwrap to reveal their vivid colors. Little wonder, then, that he would come to see the world very much through her eyes. Grown, he would be her constant companion, sharer of all her interests. Almost by definition, what pleased or excited Aline pleased or excited Teddy. Whether the delights of the kitchen or the concert hall, their tastes were compatible and usually identical. Yet Teddy was never regarded by anyone as the "mama's boy" of cartoon or rude joke. Mrs. Loeb says: "He was quite simply in love with her, in the nicest sense of the word. She was his life's central figure." Certainly, he would always have a special place in Aline's life as well. The years devoted to saving him from the sentence of early death had forged a bond, and it would hold them close together forever.

Finally, the exile was over. Aline received her son back into the house as if they had both come home from an interminable war. Unfortunately, however, there were still limits placed on Teddy's return to ordinary living. He would not be allowed to attend school, which was sad news for a boy who had waited so long to pick up the pieces of normal life. But he would triumph here, too, and again it would be Aline who helped him. She scoured the city for exactly the right young man to be his tutor. When she found him, she told him she wanted no half-baked system of instruction. They must duplicate a real school day, so that Teddy would feel organized and productive.

By the time summer came, Teddy was thriving. Still, when the family planned their vacation, Teddy's health was a consideration. They would go no farther than the suburb of White Plains; from there it would be easy to commute to medical care as well as to work, and there it would be easy to transport "the whole entourage," remembers Edla. "We all went—Mother, Father, me, Teddy, the nurses, the maids, the chauffeur, the tutor, the cook. . . . We were quite a spectacle pouring into that rented house!"

It was a very happy summer in spite of the crowd, which actually swelled since houseguests arrived regularly. There were very few visitors from the art world, though, for most of them had gone up to Gloucester, Massachusetts. Aline, when she bid them all goodbye, vowed she would join them the following year, when Teddy was stronger. "I long for the salt water smell," she sighed. But of course, she quickly assured herself, there was a lot to paint right here, if you just opened your eyes and saw what was around you.

When Aline opened her eyes to the future, when she sat outdoors at her easel, she sensed that she was entering the final phase of her apprenticeship in the theater. Every production from now on would move her farther along the continuum of serious designing, and she decided to get herself ready for the progressions of her life. She wanted to know more about architecture and construction, and she decided to find out how she could study these subjects in a more organized way. Her mind was swirling with anticipation. Freed now from anxiety about Teddy's health, who knew what she could accomplish?

"By God," she said out loud, her voice echoing in the summer air, "by God, no one knows what I am capable of! No one knows my capacity!"

# 6

In 1917 the costume and scenic workshop of the Playhouse had been moved around the corner to a connecting building on Pitt Street. Brought in to manage the costume workshops were Alice Beer and Polaire Weissman, who years later would use their firsthand practical knowledge of textile and costume in important new careers as museum curators.

Aline would often visit them in their third-floor workshop by climbing up to the Neighborhood Playhouse roof and crossing over to the Pitt Street side. She loved these connecting roofs very much, and indeed, they were no ordinary places, but had a pulsing, active life all their own. The neighborhood children played here noisily or, in a quiet corner, rehearsed their parts for a drama club production. And there were dances here too. Big hotels were being built uptown with rooftop salons for dancing, but Grand Street was not jealous. At night, local music students played for its own rooftop dancing, and Aline and Ethel, both of whom loved to dance, joined in on many of these evenings.

On the Pitt Street side, the workshop staff dried newly dyed fabrics and freshly painted sets on the roof. The vivid montage of colors lightened the spirits of everyone who walked by on even the gloomiest day. But even though Aline relished every tone as she approached the big windows of the costume workshop, when she climbed down into the room itself she felt happiest of all. For the workshop was filled with the sights and smells and sounds that she loved best of any in the world. She would look at the volunteer workers around the long table in the center of the room busily cutting and painting, and be thrilled by the unity of their efforts and her own.

All her working life, Aline would feel herself connected as an equal in a common endeavor with the men and women who executed her designs. Herself a consummate craftswoman, she respected no one more than a seamstress who sewed a fine seam or a carpenter who sawed a clean cut. This genuine respect for their labors, plus the fact that she had done and was capable of doing nearly everything she asked someone else to do, won her the reciprocal respect of tailors and architects and wardrobe mistresses in every theatrical shop in the city. They never resented her participation when she'd double-check their work, whether it was the stitches of a gown or the hinged corners of a set. In return, she admired their special magic of turning lines on paper into realities. She said: "It is in the workshops that our dreams come true. I take my t-square and triangle and I draw a line on the clean paper pinned to my drafting table; and I know that line will soon be a wall, and all the other lines I put to it will be the doors and windows, the fireplaces and the cornices, and the great sky itself. What I have put down on that oblong sheet of paper will, by a miracle of building and painting, become a drawing room or kitchen or the palace of a king."

In the Playhouse years, of course, sets, like costumes, were made right there, and Aline spent increasing amounts of time in the first-floor workshop, literally feasting on its pleasures.

"You step from the busy street into the sceneshop and the noises make the streets seem comparatively quiet. There is the whirr of the bandsaw, and the hammering, the clatter of lumber being handled, the scraping and moving of heavy pieces. There is an indefinable smell of scenery being built; the smell of fresh glue, of lumber, of canvas that has been fireproofed . . . and the sweet sour smell of sawdust . . . that all mingles into the single smell of scenery being built. Everything is clean . . . wholesome . . . the uncut lumber and the clean new yards of canvas and the fine sawdust on the floors." And she added in characteristic analogy: "when I say I like raw scenery, it is much the same as a cook feels about the assembled ingredients of her dishes—a bowl of eggs, a quart of cream, the beauty of an uncooked cabbage or a basket of tomatoes."

That the pristine and separate ingredients of a meal, or a set, or a costume, could be blended together to produce a new excellence was a perennially invigorating idea for Aline. At the same time, she knew that the finished whole must in itself be pure. Her designs would most often suggest rather than spell out their message, would draw an audience with careful subtlety into sharing her concept of mood and place. Much later, she would try to pass on her belief in economy and simplicity to Thomas Wolfe, an effort that, to her sorrow, met only limited success.

"You are a great writer," she wrote him angrily after he published a story in *Scribner's Magazine,* "but you are going wrong. You are covering yourself with a mass of words that are a fungus growth. . . . Do you remember I always told you not to be fancy? Well, you are heading in that direction, away from the golden core of what you have to say. You could have told that story in two-thirds the words and it would have been a finer work."

As the 1920s arrived and evolved, Aline's work at the Playhouse became both more concentrated and more diffused, in that Playhouse productions were sometimes moved uptown for limited runs. This allowed many more people to take a look at her work, and Broadway producers began to discuss with her their theatrical plans. As Aline thought about the possibility of becoming involved with more ambitious productions, the urge to know more about architecture and set construction intensified. All the work she had done so far had convinced her that the marriage between set and costume must be perfectly compatible, for "Costumes and scenery perform the same function for a play. . . . The scenery is still and the costumes move before it in light . . . so the relation of the two should be perfect." It was a perfection best reached, Aline believed, when costume and set were "the work of one mind."

A man who was achieving acclaim for both sets and costumes and from whom Aline believed she could gain specific knowledge of scenic design was Norman Bel Geddes, a sometimes abrasive man, whose restless ambitions would lead him to design automobiles, typewriters, Macy's Thanksgiving Day parade and the Ringling Brothers' circus. In the theater, he tended to be attracted to elaborate, large-scale productions, and during these years he also worked with selected students at his studio, teaching them construction and architectural principles. They in turn worked on constructing the sets and costumes for his current commitments. Aline was accepted into Bel Geddes's Saturday classes, and now, after breakfast with whatever family members were awake on Saturday mornings, she packed her pencils and rulers in a case and headed downtown, crossing from west side to east, where, in the mid Fifties, Bel Geddes had an entire floor in a large office building. Scattered around the huge space were eight or ten drawing tables, just enough for the small group of pupils Bel Geddes had taken on. The sessions were rigorous, for he was a driven and driving taskmaster, urging his students on and tearing apart their efforts with a minimum of sensitivity—even when, as often happened with Aline, they came not only on Saturdays, but daily, to work on one of his projects.

Gerstle Mack, an architect and author who was Bel Geddes's chief assistant, remembered how difficult it was for many students to cope with Bel Geddes's tendency to look upon them primarily as instruments, as impersonal tools to fashion working models of his blueprinted plans. He was not deliberately cruel, but the effects of his self-absorption were nonetheless painful to those who suffered his harsh and public criticism. It is Mr. Mack's memory that Aline was the one person who would not put up with that kind of treatment, and who never hesitated to tell Bel Geddes when she thought he had acted badly toward her or someone else. Perversely, her lack of awe intrigued him, and they became and remained close friends.

In the winter of 1922, Aline was invited uptown by the recently formed producing group who called themselves the Theatre Guild, to work with another celebrated figure, Lee Simonson, the Guild's chief designer and one of its founders. The enterprise was an elaborate production of Shaw's *Back to Methuselah*. If Bel Geddes was difficult, Simonson was impossible—a flamboyant, complicated and volatile man who would be one of Aline's most enduring and most trying friends. His working behavior was exactly the opposite of Aline's: stormy, temperamental, bewilderingly erratic. The excellent taste he showed in his work was contradicted by his way of life, most noticeably in his deliberately outrageous dress—combining, for example, an electric-blue shirt and a necktie of cadmium orange or lemon yellow with perhaps a crimson handkerchief hanging insistently over a pocket. To be with

Simonson was exhausting, but Aline was able to surmount the draw-backs and enjoy it. After this first collaboration they would work to-gether many times, he and his codirectors hiring her regularly to design sets, costumes, or both, for a variety of Theatre Guild productions.

Later in her life Aline would grow weary of Lee's insatiable needs, but she would never desert him. During his final years he was hospital-ized several times for emotional disturbances, and when he would take his first tentative steps out of this protected environment, more often than not it was to Aline's home that he would go. No matter how busy her work schedule or troubled her own mood, she opened her door to this even more troubled old friend.

"Lee Simonson spent those two hot days here last week," she wrote twenty years after their first meeting. "It was like a bad dream. They called up from the sanitarium just as I got back and said they wanted him to get away for a change and this was the only place he would come to." Later, in another letter, she reported that a mutual friend had called to talk about what could be done for Lee. "But I have spent hours and hours with him of late," she sighed, "and I have reached the end of what I can do beyond just staying with him and holding his hand. I seem," she added without any self-pity or self-adulation, "to be laden with these people, first one, and then the other."

A great number of people looked to Aline when their defense systems faltered. Her cousin Mrs. Loeb, for example, remains grateful to Aline for recognizing the younger woman's despair when her mother died prematurely.

"Everyone was telling me to count my blessings," says Mrs. Loeb with a grimace, "the way we tend to do to ostensibly bolster people who have suffered a loss. They kept reminding me of my wonderful handsome husband, and my beautiful new baby . . . and then Aline came in to see me, and held my hand and said, 'Now this is a tragedy,' and from then on I felt such a bond. She took me under her wing and helped me get hold of what had to be done in my life without making me feel guilty about being afraid of the task."

Although most people remember Aline's support with something bordering on reverence, there were others who, like Thomas Wolfe, eventually grew to resent it. One design protégé, for example, cut off all contact when her own career, nurtured and guided by Aline, really took off. "I wonder," Aline mused, "if she ever remembers the years I put in with her, when she was at her most melancholy, when she felt she could live no longer. Well, we seem to have weathered her storms all right, and our human souls are resilient. . . . But I wish I could see her now," she said softly. "I would like to see her in prosperity."

However, in these years, as Aline's career expanded, she was making many more friends than she would ever lose. People like Theresa Helburn of the Theatre Guild, who would become Aline's confidante during the most trying phase of her life. And Melville Cane, who would soon count among his other clients the great Houdini. It greatly tickled Aline to know that her friend had the secret to every one of the great magician's tricks!

One of the closest friends she made in these years was Alice Beer's brother, Tom, a gifted and highly regarded writer. Thomas Beer has been called "one of the most marvelous talkers to have held forth in the English language since the eighteenth century." Beer's conversation, like Aline's, was luminous with detail and finely spun phrases. "Oh, you are so fine to talk to!" Aline would declare ecstatically. "One of the best in the world!"

During the 1920s and '30s, Beer was a prolific author, turning out more than 150 stories, rich in characterization, for popular magazines such as the *Saturday Evening Post.* At the same time he was writing novels and social histories like the still famous *Mauve Decade,* and a definitive biography of his much admired Stephen Crane. Aline was enormously proud of his talent and of his intelligence and erudition. Her own lack of formal education always troubled her, and although her shelves were lined with volumes on history, and she was a diligent researcher, she did not see herself as a studious person and tended to admire people who were. Thomas Wolfe's Harvard background and the Latin and literary allusions he sprinkled through his speech were not the least of the qualities Aline would find compelling when they met. As for Beer, he never ceased to please her with the wealth of historical detail he generously shared when she worked on period productions.

Beer was generous in every way. Like Aline, he adored giving presents to friends, but his presents were far more extravagant than hers ever were. A fine painting was to him a perfectly reasonable way of saying thank you for an evening of good talk and food. "Oh, by the way," he'd say, when collecting his coat after a dinner party, "I left a trifle in the hall"—which to the host's amazement might turn out to be a painting by Thomas Hart Benton.

Aline never questioned Tom's eccentricities or his susceptibility to

self-destructive excess, even when in later years these qualities contributed to a severe emotional decline. Feeling as she did about friends,
that "we have to take them for the things they have that we like, and
try not to be bothered by the others," she was only grateful for the
affection they'd shared for so long. "Do you think I place too much stress
on love and affection?" she would sometimes ask, but before anyone
could answer, she'd shake her head and say, "No, it can't be stressed too
much, not if it's the right kind."

Till the end of his life Beer spent summers at his family's home in
Nantucket, and Aline had many happy visits there. But beginning with
the summer of 1920, she had for several years fulfilled her promise to
herself of spending most of that season in Gloucester, joining those of
her friends who went there to paint. Renting a large house on the
eastern point of the cape, she immersed herself in this new landscape
that so many artists had tried to capture. Bellows and Sloan and Stuart
Davis were all here, painting in the special light that was a fusion of
rocky coast and foaming sea and clear air. The city seemed far away
indeed. When Theo and Ethel arrived on the businessmen's train on
Friday, they were like visitors from another world, a world she would
always need, but which she was happily exchanging for a while with
this one. Theo would tell her of a new restaurant he'd dined in during
the week, and she'd make him promise to take her there as soon as
she returned. But when the weekend was over, and she took her easel
and paints outdoors, the sandwich she unwrapped at noon and ate
under a sheltering tree tasted like the best meal she could ever hope
to have.

There was one tree Aline particularly loved. It was, she said, "a hoary
old willow, very old . . . with five little shoots growing out of the great
trunk, like the hairs sprouting from an old man's ears and nostrils
. . . you could lie down under that tree, and be hidden and you could
look up and see the branches making a divine cathedral. The Gothic
arches stretching up and beyond on each side, and the dim religious
light of the holy place filtering through . . . and only me . . . alone, under
the tree, in the cathedral."

Back home in New York, Aline sat at her easel and tried to recreate
Gloucester's emotion-charged shifts of color for the stage, making what
Henri called "continual essays with color" in order to invoke emotional
effects in her sets and costumes. Who should be dominant on stage?
Where was sympathy to be focused? Her choice of color could help

decide this. And color could mirror a character's psychological state or symbolically deepen a scene's meaning.

"Every scene that I have ever designed has come to me in its basic color from the very beginning of the process of designing," Aline said, and her method of work was indeed to read a script over and over again until a "psychological color" came to mind. "I see that room as brown," she'd say to Alice Beer, "not much light . . . yes"—she'd shake her head definitely—"this is a dark play . . . a brown play."

And actors and actresses many years after the fact remember with obvious pleasure the colors of the costumes designed for them by Aline Bernstein. Helen Hayes, with whom she would often work in years to come, says: "I remember the little blue taffeta with the pink rose at the low neck for Constance in *She Stoops to Conquer*. . . . I remember the stunning, authentic banquet costume for *Cleopatra* . . . hand-dyed blue taffeta appliqués on cloth of gold in the form of little feathers like the wings of ibis. It was a work of art." But the actors and actresses she designed for are more grateful still to Aline for her commitment to the integrity of the characters they played. Aline saw costumes primarily as "an aid to the actor's interpretation of a role," and would study a script endlessly until she felt she understood each character's nature. Russel Wright, who was a private pupil of both Bel Geddes and Aline, said mildly: "I daresay that often this study was deeper than that of the actress or actor performing the role." While Eva Le Gallienne says that Aline had "that mystic thing that creates the character, and the actor *as* the character."

Aline also wanted the actors to be "comfortable and happy" in the clothes she designed for them. She herself never wore corsets even in days when they were obligatory, and she chose her flowing sari-like robes because she loved the way the fabric fell loosely over her body. Helen Gahagan Douglas recalls that Aline's designs were invariably easy to wear, while Helen Hayes, in explaining Aline's special talent, recalls the costumes designed for *Mary of Scotland* by Robert Edmond Jones. "They were magnificent," Miss Hayes says, smiling, "but they weighed a ton. I felt as if I were carrying around a sofa!"

In 1922, the Lewisohn sisters told Aline that they planned to close down the theater for the 1922–23 season. They felt everyone needed a rest and that it was time to evaluate the accomplishments of the Playhouse. The sisters were also ready for one of their frequent trips abroad to investigate new ideas and productions to bring back to the

Playhouse. For Aline, this hiatus meant the opportunity to do more work uptown with other producers, and indeed, it would prove a decisive year in making her name familiar along Joseph Frankau's Broadway. It began with her quickly accepting a job with the Players Club to design both sets and costumes for a limited revival of Sheridan's *The School for Scandal.* The production opened on June 4, 1923, at the Lyceum Theater, with a cast that included among its stars Ethel Barrymore, Walter Hampden, Violet Kemble Cooper and John Drew.

Even before *The School for Scandal* was on the boards, other offers were coming her way. Her enthusiasm was so great she was even able to put aside her mounting anxiety about a distressing physical symptom. Aline was acutely aware that deafness ran in her family, and for some time she had been conscious of an impairment in her hearing. Joseph Frankau's career suffered because of deafness. At the peak of her career, was the same thing going to happen to her? At her family's insistence she consulted a doctor, who told her nothing to lighten her spirits. The damage was not yet too great, he said, but he was certain it would be progressive, although he could not predict what the rate of deterioration would be.

She kept to herself for a few days to think about what she'd been told. And slowly began to regain confidence. After all, she was behind the stage, not on it. Besides, she had already picked up some tricks to compensate for her loss; it was a rare person who was conscious that she could not hear him clearly. Her attention simply became even more concentrated than before, which of course only delighted her companion. And unlike many deaf people, her voice didn't get louder. If anything, it grew softer and more gentle. "It was really quite beautiful," Helen Hayes remembers, "and simply grew more lovely as her deafness grew greater."

So Aline made up her mind to ignore her handicap. As a result, it was never uncomfortable for other people to be with her. Talking with Aline, whether planning a show, getting instructions for a costume, or selling her groceries, became an intimate exchange. She would read the speaker's lips, and it was the rare person, man or woman, who did not feel embraced by the encounter.

Despite her commitments uptown, when the Lewisohns returned for the 1923–24 season, Aline took on more work for them. Alice Lewisohn says, "She looked upon us as her home or family," and as long as the Playhouse functioned, Aline continued working uptown and down, expanding her career while still nurturing the roots of her past. Actually, these two goals often merged, for much of the work she was now doing for the Playhouse was meeting with critical success from very far afield. For example, one of her continuing contributions was to the annual *Grand Street Follies,* a spoof of theatrical activities all over town. It had started as an in-house joke, to wrap up the fall and winter season at the Playhouse, but had caught the attention of wider audiences and had since become a deliciously irreverent dramatic and musical institution. Many actors and actresses began their careers in the *Follies,* their impersonations of more established talents winning them long-term contracts on Broadway. Aline MacMahon, for example, did a dazzling takeoff of Gertrude Lawrence, who was at the time Broadway's darling, and no sooner had the curtain come down than Lee Shubert was backstage with heady plans for Miss MacMahon's future.

Aline Bernstein welcomed the chance to poke fun at her colleagues and profession, and one of the first segments of a *Follies* program to be singled out by delighted critics satirized John Barrymore's production of *Hamlet.* Robert Edmond Jones had designed an elaborate set to allow Barrymore to lope and climb as he liked to, and when Aline created the scenery for the "Follies" presentation of *Hamlet—Who Killed the Ghost?* she carefully designed a series of steps and a downstage ladder so that Hamlet could leap up and down continuously, bounding purposefully in a variety of directions—which led, as the audience could see, nowhere.

One of the dividends of the *Follies* was that it allowed the whole Bernstein ménage to participate. Theo and Teddy often came down to rehearsals and would make droll contributions to the always elastic script. Edla's and Ethel's involvement was much more direct. Both usually had major roles in the productions. Ethel would come downtown after work at Bergdorf's and, to her friends' delight, briskly strip off her eight-hundred-dollar Vionnet original for the ripped black rags of a washerwoman, or the black and white stripes of a prisoner's uniform.

Aline's sense of humor served her in other productions. In the Lewisohns' presentation of an Indian classic called *The Little Clay Cart,* the villain was a comic character, afflicted with a lisp, and Aline was inspired to dress him in bouffant white muslin, with a swishing skirt that fell to the knees and ended just above his leather leggings. The contrast of puffy, frilly white skirt and heavy dark leather was enhanced by the vast quantities of pearl necklaces she draped around his neck, and the dangling earrings with which she mockingly set off his dark, supposedly fierce mustache.

Despite its humor, the play was taken very seriously and would remain one of the Playhouse's greatest hits and one of Aline's favorite examples of her own work. It also contributed solidly to her professional reputation. She based her designs on seventeenth-, eighteenth- and nineteenth-century Rajput painting, and later Alice Lewisohn would write that "The Rajput setting lent itself admirably to the color and grace of the text. Each moment supplied the senses with some fresh, alluring detail of gesture and movement. . . . For the magical way that the scene transformed Rajput paintings into plastic reality, *The Little Clay Cart* would . . . live on as one of the real events of theater."

Aline's enthusiasm for her work on *Little Clay Cart* was fed by the excitement of having just finished assisting Norman Bel Geddes with his costume designs for the enormously ambitious Max Reinhardt production of *The Miracle*. Hundreds of costumes were involved, and in her capacity as supervisor of costume execution, Aline worked on them all.

With the success of *The Miracle* uptown and *The Little Clay Cart* at the Playhouse, Aline Bernstein's name was definitely and permanently established in the American theater. Her productivity might suggest to people that she worked all the time, and yet she didn't, obviously, because they saw her at parties and came to the delightful ones she gave. But she did spend more and more time at her drawing board at home or in the little room off the Playhouse costume shop that served as her office. It was a room completely bare of furniture, except for her drawing table and a chair. After a long or a late rehearsal, she would sit on the floor with friends from the staff or the cast and drink straight gin out of paper cups. To her the talk was as rich and satisfying as when she nestled into a sofa in her living room.

A sheet of paper would be tacked on her drawing table, covered with sketches of the cast and costumes of her current productions. Thomas Wolfe, as excessive in his portrayals as she was economical, would say with considerable awe that though the figures on the drawing board were usually only outlines, "it seemed as if the figures were always there. There would be just the jaunty sketching of a jacket, an elbowed sleeve, or perhaps just the line and pleating of the skirt. Yet the sketches could not have been more eloquent and moving in their portraiture of life if a whole gallery of men and women had been drawn in."

As her career developed, so did her certainty about her talents. "The most important thing in a person's life is to respect yourself," she'd say, "not conceit . . . but . . . respect." And she was even less likely now to pretend modesty than she had been earlier. In fact, she was beginning to realize that the principal audience for her designs had always been and would always be herself.

"We work for our audience," she'd say, "but I work for myself as well. I think what *I* like, what *I* believe is beautiful and right, what *I* design and strive to make perfect, will also please those in front."

While she did not capitulate to other people's concepts of what was beautiful, neither would their praise warm her if she didn't believe she had done a good job. At no point would she allow success to make her sloppy. Russel Wright remembered how she'd prowl through libraries and museums, notebook in hand, looking up every reference and studying the most minute detail of a painting or textile. One of his most vivid memories concerned going to the Metropolitan Museum of Art with Aline. Holding his hand, she pattered lightly down flight after flight of stairs, turning to him with a pleased smile every so often. And once arrived in the basement, she began to partially unwrap a mummy, having convinced the curator she desperately needed to do so in order to understand Egyptian construction and textiles for her production of *Caesar and Cleopatra*.

More and more often also, she was traveling to Europe to study classical architecture or ancient fabric patterns. Of course, she also embarked on these trips for the joy of experiencing herself in new environments. The lure of the road that had gripped Joseph Frankau was taking possession of his daughter in a highly sophisticated way. Once again, Theo took Aline's increasing zest for new experience in stride. The children were grown, and besides, Aline usually traveled when Ethel was home to watch over things.

Another reason for visiting Europe was to go to some spa for a "cure." The battle with pounds was always there for Aline, although she'd be the first to admit she didn't wage it too seriously. She wrote a friend before one of these trips: "I'm awfully fat and must do something about it. I sit on my tail drawing for too many hours at a stretch. And of course I eat too much. Elizabeth [a maid] is going to dressmaking school, but she comes home at four to cook dinner. Ethel plies us over the weekend with Cordon Bleu dishes, so what is a poor old Mama to do? . . . I never learned to say no."

Since Theresa Helburn also was attracted to spasms of dieting, followed by months of eating, she was a frequent companion on these quests for a slimmer self. They would go to Carlsbad or to some spa in Switzerland and would drink only spring water and fruit juice. Invariably, when their fast was broken, they'd shoot off to Lugano or Paris and cut loose the senses that had been subdued for two or three weeks.

"I've never known anyone who was better fun to travel with than Aline," said Miss Helburn. "She had terrific vitality. . . . We would go sightseeing until four o'clock in the afternoon, at which point I would give up in exhaustion [but] Aline would fortify herself with a drink, and then happily go on by herself!" There was, Miss Helburn said, a "very typical picture of Aline, which never fades from my mind. Very late one night we were walking in Paris. There wasn't a sound. On a deserted street corner stood a lonely young gendarme. We walked past. Then, on impulse, Aline turned back and handed him a single rose from a bunch she carried. He looked after her a long while, completely charmed and delighted."

During these years Aline was also beginning what would prove to be the most absorbing journey she had yet undertaken. Although the idea of psychoanalysis was still mysterious and slightly suspect, Aline had become increasingly interested in it. In her world of the theater and the art studio, people were beginning to discuss the work of Freud and his followers. Alice Lewisohn had been analyzed by Carl Jung himself, while another friend had made a pilgrimage to England for analysis with Ernest Jones. It was Jung who interested Aline most, from her talks with Alice, and when she saw a translation of his *Psychology of the Unconscious* on a shelf of Brentano's bookstore, a favorite haunt of hers, she bought the book and took it home to read. Lying on her bed, with the sunlight pouring in, she became more and more excited by what she read. Contributing to her excitement was the fact that the translator was a woman psychiatrist named Beatrice Hinkle, living and practicing in New York City. Aline made an appointment to see her as soon as it was possible.

Dr. Hinkle was tentative about this plumply pretty, rosy-cheeked lady sitting across her desk. How serious was she about analysis? Was she merely looking for some new intellectual diversion, satisfying some caprice?

Aline was aware of the faddish possibilities of analysis. Psychoanalytic jargon was already falling from the lips of some of her Greenwich Village friends as easily as tidbits about painting or sculpture.

"But it is not so with me," she told Dr. Hinkle quietly, explaining that she had been drawn to Jung's idea of bringing harmony to the self's polarities. Through a Jungian analysis, she told the doctor, she felt she could achieve an integration of mind and body, of conscious and instinctual, that would make her feel more whole, not fragmented, and she wanted with ever greater certainty to feel this sense of unity.

"I am not an idle lady looking for amusement," said Aline, hearing the physician's unspoken question. It was so sensitive a response that Dr. Hinkle agreed to meet with her for a few exploratory sessions.

Aline came away from each of these visits more convinced than ever that this was a process vital to her life. She knew there was no way of charming the doctor into agreeing with her, that only her own sincerity and determination to continue would make the difference. When they met for their final preliminary session, and she waited for Dr. Hinkle's decision, she felt as if she were on the brink of a passionately anticipated journey whose abrupt termination would leave her wandering and bereft. Happily, the doctor said that yes, she would take Aline on as a patient. As the two women stood and shook hands, Aline felt that something seemed already to be moving aside her inner barriers to knowing and being.

The family was concerned about her fitting another new experience into her already brimming life, particularly an experience so profound. But as they watched her, they came to understand what she had instinctively known would be true—that she would have more energy, not less. And they, like Aline, hoped she would get some help in dealing with the sudden sadness that still from time to time assailed her.

And indeed, Aline through her analysis did steadily gain a greater acceptance of the dark as well as the bright side of her nature. In years to come, when insight failed to pull her from dark to light, she would whenever possible go back to Dr. Hinkle, by then friend as well as physician. And she would continue to give Beatrice Hinkle credit for focusing and channeling her creative energies.

As the summer of 1925 approached, although Aline was somewhat chagrined to have been such a "late bloomer" in the theater, she felt the ebullience of being in her mid forties and at the height of her powers. The theatrical season had been long and productive. Spring had seen the launching of *Caesar and Cleopatra* and her homework had paid off—the costumes had won unanimous critical approval.

She had done equally well for the Playhouse with another *Grand Street Follies* and Sheridan's *The Critic,* the setting and costumes for which she had based on eighteenth-century English painted china. Furthermore, in the fall she was going to design a modern-dress production of *Hamlet,* the first time a Shakespearean play would be done in contemporary dress in the United States. Aline made silent promises to Joseph Frankau not to betray his favorite play by his favorite playwright, and she tried to convince Theo too, whose conservatism made him suspicious of such an unconventional project. "Theo," she said, "if anyone can make *Hamlet* beautiful in modern dress, it will be me." And he smiled and said she was undoubtedly right. She was also to design for the Playhouse a darkly mystical play called *The Dybbuk,* based on a medieval Jewish myth and dealing with possession and exorcism in a Jewish village. Primarily for *The Dybbuk,* she decided to take a trip to Europe in order to visit some ancient synagogues.

Should she need another excuse for the trip, she planned to bring Alice Lewisohn a script that had been sent to the Playhouse by a young writer. As a director of the Playhouse, Aline read and passed judgment on every script submitted, but like everything else at the Playhouse, final decisions were made by the governing group. This particular play, entitled *Welcome to Our City,* had struck Aline more than any she had read in a long time. She was strangely excited by it, feeling that despite the excessive images and sometimes unfocused story line, a writer of enormous talent and power was at work. The author was Thomas Wolfe, a young university instructor in English, and a recent student of Harvard's George Pierce Baker.

Aline had convinced Irene Lewisohn that with revisions, *Welcome to Our City* would be an ideal production for the Playhouse, but four other members of the board voted against it, no matter what changes were made. It was finally decided that Aline should take the play with her to England, where Alice Lewisohn was living for a while, as Alice's opinion could be decisive.

A letter was sent to the author, telling him of this plan. He, too, was in Europe, having taken the year off from teaching to write and to find new experiences to write from. The letter about a possible production cheered him enormously as he roamed restlessly from place to place, accomplishing little and somehow always needing to move on from wherever he had settled.

To Aline, who packed the script in the bottom of one of her suitcases, it was singularly unimportant. Her own priorities for the summer were quite clear, and as she boarded the steamship and kissed Theo and Ethel and Edla and Teddy goodbye, Thomas Wolfe was very low among them.

# Part Three

1925-1928

# 7

There is a passage in Thomas Wolfe's novel *Of Time and the River* in which his autobiographical hero, Eugene Gant, shouts in bitter fury: "You call me a big hulking lout—and I feel more, know more, see more, have more life and power and understanding in me in a minute than the whole crowd of you will ever have . . . why, I'm so much better than the rest of you, that . . . that . . . that there's no comparison!"

In that speech, in its implication that there stood a man fully conscious of life, hungry to experience how it is lived—everywhere, by everyone—the connection between the fictional and the real-life Wolfe is absolute. To a considerable degree it explains the extraordinary impact of his meeting another person who shared that hunger, could understand it; and even, through her own eager vision, could help feed it—the woman whom, once met, he would never forget.

That Aline was native to the dynamic streets of New York City intrigued Thomas Wolfe always. His own mind and soul had been bred among very different scenes. Asheville, North Carolina, stands on the rim of majestic mountain country, so that young Tom Wolfe gazed out on what he called "The everlasting rim of hills." Here is where the Appalachian Mountains form their highest peaks and seem to touch in endless rippling meetings the local ranges of Black, Bald and Smoky. On and on they seem to go, these sinuous shapes, so that Wolfe scholar Eugene Kennedy talks of a sense of "unending ascent" as the small city is approached by train.

The train itself had significance for the youthful Wolfe. Its smoke rubbed the mountains gray, seeming to symbolize man's desecration of nature. At the same time, the train whistle haunted him with its images of questing—the search for answers to the countless questions battering his mind and heart. In a letter to his mother, after he had achieved at least the partial escape of college and had begun to put some shape to his dream of becoming a writer, he said: "I want to know life and understand it . . . it is not all bad, but it is not all good, it is not all ugly but it is not all beautiful. It is life, life, life, the only thing that matters. It is savage, cruel, noble, passionate, selfish, generous, stupid, ugly, beautiful, painful, joyous—it is all these and more and it's all these I want to know and by God I shall. . . . I will go to the ends of the earth to find it, to understand it . . ." and he added an almost prayerful promise: "and I will put it on paper and make it true and beautiful."

Certainly, Wolfe's need to see what lay on the other side of the mountain came from drives inherent in his personality. But there is no doubt that the physical environment of his youth contributed to his later way of life, as well as to his writing. From the grandeur of his prose to the painful isolation so many of his characters feel, the influence of Asheville's encircling mountains is clear; while the roaming, the compulsive need to free himself from the restrictions of places or people, was perhaps fostered by the borders that enclosed his childhood.

It was not a very happy childhood for very long, although it started well enough when he was born, the youngest of eight children, to William Oliver Wolfe (who would be immortalized in his son's novels as the Herculean character W. O. Gant) and a former schoolteacher named Julia. That spare, garrulous woman with a photographic memory her son would inherit could and would spin tales that went on for hours, but her personality was completely opposite to her husband's. She, too, would endure, as the querulous, pinchpenny Eliza Gant in *Look Homeward, Angel,* but in real life, despite a capacity for harshness and even cruelty, which Aline Bernstein would one day discover, she was not unkind. And she was filled with love for her youngest son. Six years separated Tom from the next youngest child and thirteen years from the eldest, so he was very much babied by the entire family. However, it was chiefly Julia who prolonged his infancy. She nursed him until he was three and a half years old, and they slept together until he was nine. Mrs. Wolfe, in a published interview, recalled placidly: "He being the baby I kept him a baby. I think he has written it up himself that he slept with me until he was a great big boy. . . . I think we just weaned Tom off by the other children laughing at him and talking to him about being just a baby. He still nursed, but it was a habit with him, that was all," she assures us, and then continues in happy memory: "Tom . . . had beautiful curls, beautiful brown hair . . . I kept it curled every day. He wanted his hair cut off. I told him, 'Oh, no, I want to keep it long.' . . . So I kept putting him off."

It was only when he caught lice from a neighboring child, at about the age of nine, that Julia reluctantly allowed her "baby" 's locks to be shorn. This long-delayed rite foreshadowed the struggle Wolfe was to have before he could break free into maturity. Little wonder that the major theme of Wolfe's first novel, *Look Homeward, Angel,* is the effort of a young man to take full possession of his own life.

Tom was happier in many ways with William Oliver than with Julia. W. O. himself was a giant of a man, six feet four inches, and his personality was also outsized. A hard drinker who went on periodic binges, he once pursued Julia to her room and pounded on the door to break it down. (She climbed out the window and took refuge on the roof, as her children watched in horror.) Yet he was also a richly loving man, and Tom worshiped what he later called "the enormous beating color of his life."

William Oliver was a stonecutter, who made his living carving and selling tombstones, but his talents and temperament were those of an artist. Mourners and graveyards depressed him and his melancholy frequently ended in drunken forgetfulness. His son in turn was early obsessed with what he called "the terrible brevity" of our days. But when not mournful or drunk, W.O. could be magnificently exuberant, reciting, as he strode around the house, the rhetorical poetry he loved. His youngest child walked beside him—just as Aline had once walked with her own captivating father—memorizing soliloquies from Poe and Shakespeare, to remember them all his life. Tom may also have acquired from W.O.'s love of language his sensitivity to the rhythm and flow of words, the need to say something as dramatically as it could be said, rather than settle for simple declarative prose. These were all learned while he still stood short against his father's knees.

If Tom's thirst for language was stimulated by his father, so was his appetite for food and drink. And if Julia's prolonged nursing had heightened the desire for oral gratification, W.O.'s gargantuan gluttony reinforced it. Metaphors of food would become as much a part of Tom Wolfe's lovemaking as of Aline's. In time he would write to her that he wanted to "devour" her, to "taste" her "jolly red face," and in more extreme moments he would fantasize about "drinking your blood slowly like wine." He saw himself as a person feasting on the world's experiences, ravenously taking them all as his own. The "world is a large oyster," he was to write, "but I do not think I will choke when I swallow it." And with youthful grandiloquence, he would inform his old teacher Margaret Roberts: "If you ever hear the sad news of my sudden and tragic extinction . . . I want you to remember that I was not a man who starved to death, but a man who died of gluttony, choking to death on an abundance of food which surpassed everything but his hunger."

Until Tom was six years old, warmth and love still prevailed in the Wolfe household despite its violent scenes. But then, like Aline's mother, Julia Wolfe decided to buy a boardinghouse. She was fed up with her husband's erratic behavior and obsessed with the idea of financial security. However, W.O. refused to leave the old family home, and it is doubtful that Julia really wanted him to. As Tom approached his seventh birthday, the family split apart. Mabel, the second oldest sister, stayed to keep house for her father, and the other children who were still in Asheville floated in a kind of limbo between their parents' separate lives. Only Tom, because of his age, was forced to move altogether into the new house, which he loathed instantly and forever. He hated the roomers, their constant presence, their endless rocking on the porch while he tried to read or think. Most of all he hated their coming between him and his mother. Julia would brush him aside to take care of the boarders, and then further confuse and distress him by summoning him home from his father's house, where he had gone for comfort, because she wanted to rock him, fondle him, enjoy him.

Further undermining the boy's security, W.O. became ill and his powerful personality started to crumble. So now neither home was home, neither parent was the parent figure of his dreams. "I was a vagabond," Wolfe recalled bitterly, "with two roofs and no home . . . my overloaded heart was strangling without speech, without articulation, in my own secretions."

Thus, while Aline's boardinghouse years deepened her feeling of family and enriched her capacity for loving and trusting, Tom's experience embittered him. He began to stutter, and he sank ever deeper into the dark loneliness that was to become habitual. He craved order and guidance and a love he could trust not to abandon him, and he would go on compulsively looking for the person who could be "the image of strength and wisdom . . . to which the belief and power of his own life could be united."

The first person he turned to in this quest was Margaret Roberts, the teacher who discovered in the twelve-year-old boy both burning sensitivity and talent, and devoted herself to nurturing them. She gave him books to read and encouraged his writing, and directed it as best she could. Without her and the escape into books, life would have been truly unbearable. Yet despite Mrs. Roberts, the years of adolescence were painful, his loneliness deepened by his alarming physical growth. His body seemed graceless, raw and awkward, setting him apart even more. As he grew to six feet seven, his mirror gave back the image that would forever haunt him, the solitary outsider.

When Tom was still only fifteen, three years earlier than most of his peers, he enrolled at the University of North Carolina at Chapel Hill, the first of his family to go to college. And, as Eugene Kennedy writes, "The hill-rimmed life was over."

Chapel Hill started off badly, Tom's age and his gangling height making him the butt of the other students, all of whom seemed more at ease socially than he. He committed embarrassing faux pas that crimsoned his cheeks and made his heart beat wildly, and while the other students lived with one or two roommates, Tom Wolfe lived alone in a big, bare room. He was convinced as he sat reading every evening that the remainder of his college life would be spent in bleak obscurity.

Eager as he had been to be on his own, he returned to Asheville the following summer with some relief, and indeed, in the hope of convincing his parents that he should be allowed to transfer to Princeton and make a new start. But things were worse at home than they had ever been. The First World War was on; his brother Fred was already in the Navy, while Tom's favorite, Ben, was morose about being rejected because of weakened lungs. Cancer was causing W.O. to fail rapidly; by the end of the summer he had to be taken to Johns Hopkins in Baltimore for radium treatments. Any thought of transferring schools was abandoned, and Tom went back to Chapel Hill feeling more spent and pessimistic than he had ever felt before. Yet his college life took a dramatic turn for the better. Behind him were hysteria and dying, and suddenly the ability to read and think about great ideas, and even engage in light-hearted campus camaraderie, took on new meaning for him. As he would write in *Look Homeward, Angel:*

> *He greeted everyone with enthusiastic gusto. . . . He began to join. He joined everything. He had never 'belonged' to any group before, but now all groups were beckoning him. He had, without much trouble, won a place for himself on the staff of the college paper and the magazine. The small beginning trickle of distinctions widened into a gushet. He was initiated into literary fraternities, dramatic fraternities, and in the spring into a social fraternity. He . . . went about . . . more pleased than a child or a savage, with colored ribbons in his coat lapel and a waistcoat plastered with pins, badges, symbols and Greek letterings.*

So the big awkward freshman became in his sophomore year a big man on campus. Professors whom he respected encouraged his dream of writing. Still, the extreme sensitivity and intensity that marked his childhood and would always be so fundamental to his personality surfaced when even the most admiring teacher criticized any of his work. There were also times when he would burst into tears at criticism or, in an effort to hide his pain, would jump up from his chair and run from the room while the other students and the already remorseful professor stared helplessly after him.

In October of his junior year Ben died, and the loss was even greater than Tom could have imagined. Called home when Julia learned death was imminent, Tom kept vigil with the family at the bedside. Describing the death of his brother, he wrote: "We can believe in the nothingness of life, we can believe in the nothingness of death and of life after death but who can believe in the nothingness of Ben?" Grief overwhelmed him for Ben, for himself, for the inescapable statement of life's assaults etched in the lines of pain on his brother's face; for the desperation with which this family clung together in what he called "the last terrible congress before death."

> Over the ugly clamor of their dissension, over the rasp and snarl of their nerves, they heard the low mutter of Ben's expiring breath. . . . They grew quiet and calm, they plunged below all the splintered wreckage of their lives, they drew together in a superb communion of love and valiance, beyond horror and confusion, beyond death.

With Ben gone, Tom soon felt that "life at home had practically ceased to be possible," that "the great wild pattern of the family had been broken forever." He had to leave, and quickly, despite Julia's pleas that he stay longer. Staring darkly out the train window that carried him away from Asheville, "It is not hard to go," he said silently to the rhythm of the train wheels, "but when can we forget?"

Thomas Wolfe graduated from the University of North Carolina at twenty, determined to be a writer. His immediate ambition was to study at Harvard with George Pierce Baker, who taught a highly respected, very elite class in drama, known as the 47 Workshop. Finally, Julia agreed to support him for at least a year, and he enrolled in Harvard's M.A. program, having convinced Baker to accept him. As he sat with the talented young men who were his classmates, discussing artistic integrity and the treatment of the artist by society, his hunger for fame and freedom from the restrictions placed on ordinary men intensified. He truly believed in the artist's right to a special place in the world, and that the artist and the world had a joint obligation to sublimate other needs to the sanctified drives of the artistic spirit.

Although his Harvard classmates shared many of these beliefs, and his work was respected by them, he was slow to make friends. These students were far more serious and self-absorbed than those he had left behind in Chapel Hill, and he did not know how to pierce their aloofness. In this urbane setting, too, his own country awkwardness seemed exaggerated. He appeared in many ways absurd as he raced around Harvard Yard with his big loping stride, long arms laden with books, wearing clothes that were ill-fitting and visibly dirty, the cardboard that often lined his shoes flapping loud enough for passers-by to hear. Those students who did begin to visit his room brought back stories of the floors piled high with scraps of writing and Wolfe flailing around among the hills of paper to find a particular passage to read aloud to his guests. Everywhere there were books, open, marked with clips, covering every available inch of space between the abandoned dishes caked with several days' food and dirty linen impatiently dropped and ignored.

His slovenliness was yet another aspect of Wolfe's dualism, for this same person who so craved order and control could not seem to avoid spawning chaos in every area of his life.

Eventually, Wolfe did begin to make some friends, and he would stay up till dawn reading them his work, reciting other people's, or telling stories that were still only in his head about his father, his mother, Ben,

Asheville. Fellow students who came down to open the door for him on the many nights when he returned late and without his key (he got, he would say, "Satanic inspirations from the dark") knew that if they didn't get back upstairs quickly, they would be pinned down by a recapitulation of the night's impressions and adventures. Actually, most of them listened willingly, even with sleep in their eyes, for he was a powerful speaker—his mind driving, eager, restless, his words passionate and stirring and painting pictures of life and its possibilities that made even his most sardonic critic realize he was a man unlike most other men.

Wolfe managed to hang on in Harvard for three years, in the meanwhile receiving his M.A. degree. He lived meagerly, but humbling himself to his mother and eating badly were worth it because the workshop was terribly important to him. He wrote three full-length plays, and his second, *Welcome to Our City*, was selected by the workshop for production in May 1923. It was a play written in pain, conceived after a trip to Asheville in 1922 at the time of his father's death —a deeply mournful visit home after a two-year absence. W.O. had finally succumbed to cancer, his huge, life-celebrating body shriveled to a skeleton long before his labored breathing finally ended. In *Of Time and the River* Thomas Wolfe would write of this homecoming:

> His father was dead, and now it seemed to him that he had never found him. His father was dead, and yet he sought him everywhere and could not believe that he was dead, and was sure that he would find him. . . . He thought he heard his great voice ringing in the street again, and that he would see him striding toward him across the Square with his earth-devouring stride.

Instead, what he saw in the streets of Asheville angered him as he strode up and down them, his heart heavy with mourning. A real estate boom was on, and evidences of get-rich-quick schemes were all around him, defiling the peaceful beauty of the town he had known. Back at Harvard, he wrote to Mrs. Roberts that there was more than enough evil material in Asheville to forge a play from, and that he intended to do exactly that. The play that he wrote proved fiercely provocative, dealing as it did with white real estate speculators buying up all the property in the Negro section of town. Although there was a mixed response when it was performed, Baker was very pleased with it, and told Tom he would submit it to the Theatre Guild in New York for possible production.

Wolfe was ecstatic. Images of coveted fame danced before him—trips to Europe on elegant steamers, beautiful women who showered him with praise and humble devotion. To his mother he wrote: "I know this now: I am inevitable. I sincerely believe that the only thing that can stop me now is insanity, disease, or death."

But the play was not accepted by the Guild. It was far too long, for one thing, and Wolfe refused to make cuts—indeed, couldn't make cuts. Once, attempting to do so, he ended up with a new draft that was longer than the first. For months he went back and forth to New York, seeing plays whenever and wherever he could and trying to peddle his own. Julia Wolfe was becoming increasingly and vociferously reluctant to support his faith in his future, and finally, with considerable reluctance, Wolfe recognized that he must find some way to earn a living other than by writing. When he learned there was a job at New York University at Washington Square, he immediately wrote Dr. Homer Watt, chairman of the English department for an interview. Dr. Watt, a gentle, intelligent man, was immediately taken with the blunt honesty and ingenuousness of the young applicant. Wolfe had made it very clear in his letter that he had no experience in teaching, and that his major interest was in writing. In addition, Wolfe had written that he was exceptionally tall and that this fact often produced "an effect on a stranger that is sometimes startling," a statement that touched Dr. Watt. The letter concluded with the assurance that if he was hired, he would give "the most faithful and efficient service of which I am capable." The upshot was that Watt offered him with hardly any delay an instructorship in freshman composition for the term that began in February and would run through the summer.

And so Tom came to New York. It was distressing to have to give up full-time writing, but it would be good to have a steady income and some order in his life. He checked into the Hotel Albert, a small residential hotel in the Village, where he had stayed before. To be living in Greenwich Village was enormously stimulating. Always an enclave for artists, it entered in the years after World War I its golden era. Eugene O'Neill was here, and Theodore Dreiser, and Edmund Wilson, and Edna St. Vincent Millay, while scores of young men and women flocked to the narrow streets to nurture their own budding careers. As Malcolm Cowley writes in *Exile's Return:* "After college and the war, most of us drifted to Manhattan, to the crooked streets south of 14th. . . . We came because living was cheap, because friends of ours had come already, because it seemed that New York was the only city where a young writer could be published."

But thrilled as he was to be in the Village and in New York itself, Tom found that teaching exhausted him. He had not been aware of the work involved in preparing for a class and meeting the students' demands, particularly students who were mostly children of the lower middle class, the sons and daughters of European immigrants. They were unlike any students he had ever seen before: determined to move beyond their parents' limited orbits and encouraged, even exhorted, by their parents to do just that. They were impetuous, often irreverent, and hungry for knowledge. To Wolfe's fictional counterpart, young Eugene Gant, "the class brought . . . only a feeling of sterility and despair, a damnable and unresting exasperation and weariness of spirit, a sense of having yielded up and lost irrevocably into the sponge-like and withdrawing maws of their dark, oily and insatiate hunger, their Oriental and parasitic gluttony, all of the rare and priceless energies of creation."

Like New York itself, these young Jews alternately fascinated and repelled the young instructor. "I teach! I teach! Jews! Jews!" he wrote a friend, saying also that he came to N.Y.U. "without racial sentimentality—indeed with strong prejudice concerning the Jew which I still retain." He found his Jewish students too inquisitive, too critical of his answers, and colleagues remember that he was indeed harder on them than on his other students. Yet he was, overall, rather an inspired teacher, who was determined to have his students understand the soaring beauty of Shelley or Keats. "Do you see . . . do you see!" he would ask passionately after going over a poem. And often he would follow his ardent analysis with a related monologue of his own. His eyes grew bright, his face flushed with feeling. He would toss his head to emphasize his words, and move in jerky strides up and down the room, huge hands waving the volume that had so inspired him. His criticisms of the work submitted were painstaking and frequently longer than the themes themselves, written deep into the night after an evening of prowling around the city.

Perhaps in no city but New York could his craving to connect his life to all experience be satisfied as it was there. The city was bigger than he was, hungrier than he was, with needs and images as various as those inside him. It stood like a giant rock, while life flowed past it. This truth maddened him. How to make this city a home? How to feel comfortable inside its immense frame of stone and steel? Most of all, how to master its challenge and force it to acknowledge his impress. And rise to the

106

challenge he must, for even though he would call New York City a place of "everlasting hunger," he also knew that it was "the place where men feel their lives will gloriously be fulfilled and their hunger fed." The place where, more than any other, even the loneliest country boy, like himself, could feel most "exultant about his future."

But the future would not evolve as he wanted if he could not write, and teaching had kept him away from serious writing far too long. The idea grew in his head to travel, to travel great distances and for many months. When the summer term ended in September, he would go to Europe, to all the great capitals of the world. He would see how he felt about them, and he would see how he felt inside them. And he would write about it all, and this time people would listen.

He decided to resume work immediately on a play called *Mannerhouse*, which he had started and put aside, convinced now that it was important and salable. His confidence to some degree related to the fact that *Welcome to Our City* had been submitted by one of the residents in the Albert Hotel to the Neighborhood Playhouse, and while they had not accepted it, they had not turned it down. They had informed Wolfe that they were still considering it and were waiting for the response of one of their directors, who was in Europe.

Tom wrote all this to his mother, who proved sympathetic to his travel plans and even offered him some money to supplement his meager savings. After a visit to Asheville, and after declining Professor Watt's offer to return to teaching for the spring term, he sailed for Europe. As he stood on the deck of the great ship and watched the city grow smaller, he was certain that when he returned it would be as a conqueror.

He landed in England and from there went to Paris. Almost immediately his suitcase was stolen, with the manuscript of *Mannerhouse* inside it. In a frenzy he wrote the play all over again from memory, with new additions, finishing in less than a month. Exhausted, he retreated to the countryside, went on to Italy and Switzerland and back again to England. There was never any plan to his nearly year-long odyssey. Suddenly it would be time for him to leave one place for another, and wherever he went, he looked and listened, and noted down what he was seeing and thinking on any scrap of paper he could find.

Yet he had done little meaningful writing, although he had accumulated quantities of beginnings, fragments of stories, dialogue for plays. But he could not get control of the words inside him, could not channel them into one steadily evolving piece of work. He was out of money and feeling ill. When a letter from Watt arrived offering a job for the fall term, he accepted with alacrity. To his surprise, he missed America.

The year in Europe had made him in many ways less innocent, and he was saddened by that but also grateful. He had known, in his own words, "Strange countries, new lives, new cities, new events. He had worked, sweated, cursed, whored, brawled, got drunk, traveled, spent all his money . . . desiring everything, attempting much, completing little. . . .

"And forever," he continues, "in this fury of his soul, he lived alone, thought and felt alone . . . in these wanderings, this loneliness, he came to know, to love, to join no other person's life into his own. But now at last, the time for that had come."

It had been a wonderful summer, Aline later remembered thinking contentedly as she sat on the promenade deck watching the horizon while the great ship moved closer to home. Then she turned to study her fellow passengers and the patterns of color they wove as they moved about. It interested her that her visual acuity had increased as her hearing declined; as though, without the distraction of sounds, her eyes could concentrate on seeing more. That she could choose when to hear made her feel uniquely independent. She could lip-read at will, was becoming more adept every day, and she had also discovered that she could hear quite well by curving her hand to her ear. It was a charming gesture, making conversation with her even more intimate.

She lay in the sun and thought back to the recent weeks of architectural research for her work on *The Dybbuk*. She was already picturing sets and costumes in her mind, confident that they would transfer readily to paper and cloth and construction. Then she let her mind wander over the many interludes with loving friends. She savored again the magnificent meals they'd shared, and the wine they'd drunk, their leisurely motoring through ancient villages with colors mellowed and gentled by the seasons. They had heard marvelous music; she'd dressed up in her loveliest clothes and been admired by interesting strangers. She smiled to herself at her delight in such admiration. But it didn't really seem a fault. Even Theo understood that the young men who peopled her days and evenings and who paid her such court were simply making her feel good about herself. Young, old, male, female, it was so precious to touch someone else's life. Admittedly she took special pleasure in being admired by men, but it was only because she treasured her womanliness.

A pang of sadness suddenly flickered through her musing: all these people in her life, entering it and reentering it with mutual affection. Yet the thought would recur, as it did now, that these encounters always remained unfinished. How much was it ever possible really to know anyone else, however much one might love and be loved by child, lover, husband, sister, friend? Perhaps even the idea of total union was naïve.

She turned from this melancholy thought to happier things. To *Hamlet* in the season ahead, and *The Dybbuk*, which would be directed by David Vardi, a former member of the Habima Theater in Moscow. She thought of her family, who would be at the dock, waiting to take her back to her lovely house and her cool, shaded bedroom. Her sadness began to lift, although its place was taken by a happiness more muted than she usually knew. Was she moving to a quieter time of her life? One less filled with emotional peaks? Would she be able to accept life on such a placid plane? There was no doubt but that the music of her own personality sometimes overwhelmed her, but it was the only music she understood.

She sighed and shook her head, and smiled at her traveling companion, Mina Curtiss, who was waking from a nap in the adjoining chair. Mina was a new friend. They had met in London this summer, but both women immediately knew their friendship would be an enduring one. Mina was an English professor at Smith College, although she was still a very young woman, many years younger than Aline. Of course, that wasn't so uncommon lately, Aline thought wryly. Although she knew she had never looked better, she was forty-four years old and many of the people she knew personally and professionally were no older than Edla or Teddy. She was grateful that artificial boundaries like age had never kept her from making friends.

Just as she was thinking this, a handsome young man approached, an architect whom she and Mina had come to know during the voyage. Though traveling tourist class, he had learned how to sneak up to first, and Aline and Mina greeted him warmly. Delighted to have her thoughts intruded on, she happily accepted his invitation to meet in one of the first class lounges after dinner.

"I've been telling my friends about you two ladies," the young architect said, "and they'd like to meet you before we land." He went on to speak of his friends, one a bookseller and the other a young playwright, a particularly interesting fellow. When Aline heard the writer's name, she started. He must be the author of the script she had carried to Alice Lewisohn, whom she was still trying to talk into producing it. She started to say something about the coincidence, but suddenly thought better of it. After all, it would almost certainly mean having to soothe the young author's anxieties and ego. No, she would keep the strange quirk of fate a secret, and concentrate for the meager remainder of her holiday on having an irresponsibly pleasant time.

It was nearly nine when Aline and Mina excused themselves from the dinner table to keep their appointment in the small café from which one got the clearest view of the ocean. Unlike his architect friend, Thomas Wolfe was uncomfortable in these surroundings, engulfed by the familiar feeling of not belonging, quickly followed by contempt for those who did. He tried to calm down before the ladies arrived, but, turning to say something to his companion, he saw two women coming through the door, and while he did not know one of them was Aline, he was as startled as she had been earlier at the sound of his name. For she was the woman he had sighted at Cherbourg, when he stood on deck looking down on the passengers joining the ship. He had watched the chaotic scene and thought about the hidden stories each man and woman might tell, wondering where their travels had taken them and whether they wanted to come home or were coming only because something forced them to. Suddenly he had caught sight of one particular face, rosily flushed, uplifted, concentrating deeply on something known only to her. In a moment the face was gone, lost in the confusion. But during the voyage he had often thought of her, and it was almost shocking to see her standing in front of him.

Aline felt the intensity of the young man's gaze even from his great height. She felt pinned by his eyes as she might pin a piece of fabric to her drawing board. There was something smoldering and violent in their encounter and it exhilarated her and frightened her. She turned quickly to greet the bookseller, shaking his hand with much enthusiasm. But the touch of the writer's hand remained on her own. It was absurdly melodramatic, she said to herself. But it was also true.

As drink followed drink in the handsome wood-paneled lounge, she told him only that she was a theatrical designer. One by one, the other passengers left to join the party they could hear going on in the ball-room, and when the young men said they had promised to join friends in tourist, Aline, sighing, gathered up her things and turned to say good night. But Wolfe beckoned her aside. The others were busy saying farewell and did not hear when he begged her to meet him later in the evening, and did not hear her agree.

"How foolish of me to say I'd come," Aline thought as she danced with one portly first class passenger after another. To ease her inexplicable nervousness, she'd drunk far too much champagne and her head was spinning faster than her feet. Excusing herself, she went out on deck to clear her head. There was nothing attractive about a woman her age getting ill from drinking too much, she thought ruefully. In the young, illness might sometimes be appealing. . . .

"Twenty years ago, if I was just slightly tubercular, someone might have liked it," she said to herself, "liked the idea of a lovely doomed young lady." But this nervous dizzy woman was quite a different matter.

So she stood very still, letting the cool air restore her, and then made her way down the stairs to the second class deck. This was not like her at all. Despite her pleasure in being admired and her eagerness for new experience, she had no patience with casual encounters. If she now looked to Theo for more peace than passion, she did not spend her passions lightly elsewhere. She loved and respected Theo and cared deeply about the family they had created together. Besides, the daughter of Rebecca and Joseph Frankau had incorporated both their natures into her own. Like her father she was a romantic, who gloried in the sensual, but like her mother she took pride in ordering her instincts. Most of all, however, Aline Bernstein prided herself in midlife on her autonomy, on still "having her pack on her back" and being her own "instrument for living." Her morality might be personal rather than conventional, but it was true and strong, and her spirit could only survive in the "highest place," following the "truest line." Without this, she would turn away from a relationship, remaining gratefully, as she was now, "intact, calm," and her "own mistress."

She thought all this as she moved to meet the strange young man who seemed to have willed her to appear. She prayed he would not be there, that she could turn quietly around and go back to her safe, luxurious world. She prayed that he had not changed his mind.

There he was, looking up the stairs at her as she descended, looking so hard and steadily that she felt shy and awkward. She wanted to say something light-hearted, but she could not find the words. Indeed, she could not find any words of any kind. So, in silence, she moved to his side, and as though by agreement, they turned to the railing together in one joined motion and stood looking into the black waters. Ahead of them, the lights of the waiting city flickered, welcoming them home. Their eyes traveled to the lights and then back again to the sea. They did not look at each other.

And still neither of them spoke. The party noises began to recede. Each moment now seemed to come to her separately, pause to be savored and then move on for another to take its place. Her head felt crystal clear again, and a rush of joy suddenly flooded through her.

In the morning they would both reenter that world of lights, pick up their lives, follow their old routines. But for now, while night still covered them, that other world seemed as distant as the Europe they had left behind and less real than a fairy tale told to a child. Reality was only here—in each separate, jewel-like moment.

She needed to look at him, to drink in that magnificence of size and being. She glanced quickly toward him, and marveled again at what she saw. But once again she felt nervous, and so she started to speak, to say anything that would bridge the silence between them. She began to talk about the city. She told him she had been born there, raised there. "I love every stone of it, stone on stone on stone," she said. "When I was a little girl the buildings were little, there were no fairy palaces like that, blazing in the night." And she told him how her sister and she would walk up Broadway and down again, past streets flanked by little houses and filled with people, and how wonderful it was.

How could she know how divided he was about this home city of hers? Not knowing, she was shocked by the anger that moved across his face. Suddenly he lunged toward her and caught her by the arms and shook her back and forth so that her head rolled and her teeth clicked together. She would write later of the unchecked fury that was so much a part of this man's nature. Although it was discernible in his writing, she said, "no one could estimate his violence who did not know him

113

personally." But on this first night of witnessing it, she was strangely unafraid. His hands on her body filled her with such joy that any pain seemed a small price to pay.

He switched to verbal attack, rage deepening his voice and accentuating the stammer she had noticed earlier.

"Where did you get your face, raised in that dung heap of the theater, among evil and rotten people, strutting and showing their bodies! Answer me! Where did you get your eyes of love, your mouth of love, your flower face!"

The words flew around her head, but she said nothing, fascinated by his gaze, his eyes shining with a light that seemed to illuminate her entire life. She felt that until now she had been a proud flame "burning alone," and that now "another flame, a great roaring, leaping flame," had joined itself to hers.

Perhaps he sensed her thoughts, for he stopped shaking her, although his arms still held her tightly encircled. She must speak, she thought, must move beyond this ocean of feeling to a safer place. And so she twisted her head impatiently and told him his diatribe was absurd.

"You like the theater yourself, you want to be part of it; you wrote a play. I've read it; you didn't know I had read it, did you?" She had been speaking quickly so that he would not interrupt her, and now she laughed out loud at the shock on his face. And then she told him about his play being tucked inside her suitcase, and traveling with her all summer. As she warmed to her subject, her tone grew earnest and brisk. The play was far too long, she informed him, but she still believed in it and would continue to try and convince her colleagues to produce it. The animation that was so characteristic of her speech fascinated Wolfe, even as she began to scold him.

"Now listen, do you know this, or did you ever hear of it with your Harvard and everything?" And she asked him if he'd ever heard of Shakespeare and reminded him that Shakespeare was of the theater, and did Mr. Wolfe see him also as "a common actor, a strutter, a vile exhibitor of himself?"

Wolfe burst into laughter, his arms loose around her now. How extraordinary this was. He could scarcely believe it. He had a million questions to ask her. It was too amazing that she should be who she was, and that he should have felt as he did about her without knowing. God, he wished he had some brandy, but all the bars were closed by now.

"Listen," he said. "Do you have any brandy in your stateroom?"

A bottle of fine brandy lay unopened in her cabin, the gift of a man who had fallen in love with her in Paris, a small, sad token of his feeling after she had turned down far more costly gifts, and the greatest one of all, himself. She told Wolfe about the bottle, and he dropped his arms from her body, and she felt like a little girl pushed from her parents' embrace. The air turned cold and the night grew darker. How could she leave him, even to go to her cabin?

"If you promise not to move," she said seriously, "if you promise faithfully you will not leave while I'm away, I'll bring it to you." And she ran from him, ran all the way. Her trunk was open and she dove underneath its neat stacks of clothing for the bottle, which was blessedly where she remembered putting it. Then she ran past the cabins, where people slept through their last night at sea, dreaming of the tomorrow she didn't want to think about. Along the corridors, down the stairs, along the deck. She turned the corner and breathed sharply in relief, for "there he was," just as she had left him, "mighty and grand."

They asked a deckhand, who was busy folding chairs, to find them a corkscrew and glasses, and soon they were sipping brandy together, resting their drinks on the rail when they turned to embrace. Holding her, or standing at her side, he talked. He never stopped talking, telling her about his life, demanding details of her own. He wanted to know everything about her: how she lived, and what she thought when she woke in the morning and went to sleep at night. What she liked to eat and wear and read. The questions fell so steadily and relentlessly that they almost began to hurt her, but he never interrupted the flow of words so that she might answer. From time to time frustration overwhelmed her, and she'd beat against his chest with her fists, but he scarcely seemed to notice as he went on demanding knowledge of her in his passionate, ringing voice. It thrilled her that he wanted to know her this way, but despair dulled the joy, for how could she ever answer him enough, satisfy his need for understanding, satisfy her own need, which was growing with every minute they shared, to bring him everything she had ever known or felt. Those pictures that were inside her head, that told the story of her life—how could she bring him inside, keep him there long enough to see them all in their true dimensions and color?

Suddenly there was a lull in his talk. Perhaps he had paused to take a long breath. His last question repeated itself in her mind: could she make a good salad dressing? Quickly she leaped into the temporary silence and shouted, "I can make the best salad dressing in the world!" And as she said this, laughter bubbled inside her throat. Later, she would write of this miraculous evening, an evening such as she had never known in her whole rich life, that it "was to be her divine moment, and on this lovely last night of stars and freedom, the wheels of the chariot of fate, were they only tumbling her . . . into a salad bowl?"

The ludicrousness enchanted her and she shrieked with laughter, gasping for air, but within minutes she was crying. Crying as though she would never stop, and indeed, she worried that she might never be able to. They seemed tears out of her past, her accumulated joys and sorrows, all her achievements and yearnings. And they were tears for a future whose bounty and burdens she was yet to know. And they were tears of thanks, for standing with this man, she felt already that touched by the soaring grandeur of his personality, she had finally reached the summit of her own.

He stopped her tears with kisses. His hands were gentle but in their power still bruising as they explored her body, running frantically over every inch of her, clutching, tearing at her clothes until she felt that if she could pull herself away she would have to jump into the ocean, for the feelings released tonight would make every other night of her life a diminished thing.

But when somehow she did find the strength to protest his torrential passion, she did not jump into the ocean. Instead, she also found the strength to deny his urgent pleading that she take him to her cabin. Characteristically, the demands of reality took precedence over her own desire. The ship's steward was stationed right outside her cabin; it would be impossible to enter her room without being seen. More importantly, she did not want to bring Wolfe into that room and that bed. Suffused with longing as she was, the inner sovereignty of her nature said no, wait, decide with a quieter mind and heart.

He accepted her decision, but begged her to stay with him, not to leave him yet. And so, spent with emotion, they watched the sky begin to lighten. Finally, however, she was too exhausted to stay and she tried at last to say good night. But the words came out as a question, revealing her reluctance to let him out of her sight. What if she could never touch him, reveal her life to him? What if he forgot this night and saw no reason to go on from there? She wanted to list her qualifications, as actresses looking for a job sum up their credits.

"Look here," she wanted to say, "this is my value . . . I have lived this long, I can cook, sew, laugh . . . I can weep for the tragic . . . lose myself in the poetic . . . I can walk in any adventure you choose—I know where beauty lies."

But she said nothing. With a final gathering of strength, she turned from him and walked quickly along the deck, shadowed now by the filtering gray light. She heard him behind her, and then there he was again, at her side, his pace slowed to meet her stride, hoarsely telling her that she must believe that what he had said tonight was true and real and had nothing to do with her importance in the theater. Even if she helped him, he would not humble himself to the rulers of that avaricious world. He would make it his way, on his own, and all he wanted from her was herself. Her true nature. Her flower face. Her dear person.

They were standing now at the narrow stairway that led from the deck to her room. If she was truly not going to be with him tonight, she must leave now. She must turn and move down the stairs and go into her cabin alone.

Breathing deeply, she pulled her arm from his grasp, so abruptly that the silk of her dress tore. He looked down at the threads and at her and, to her grateful relief, did not try to follow. But she could not help turning at the bottom to look back up at him, his huge body filling the doorway, watching her as if he were branding her image on his mind.

Years later, Thomas Wolfe would write of this meeting and their parting—would write that he was never able from this night on to see her as she undoubtedly looked to countless others: "a matronly figure of middle age, a creature with a warm and jolly little face, a wholesome and indomitable energy for every day, a shrewd, able and immensely talented creature of action, able to hold her own in a man's world." These things he knew or found out about her later, but this picture of her, which was perhaps the one by which the world best knew her, was gone forever. . . .

She became the most beautiful woman that ever lived—and not in any symbolic or idealistic sense, but with all the blazing, literal and mad concreteness of his imagination. She became the creature of incomparable loveliness to whom all the other women in the world must be compared, the creature with whose image he would for years walk the city's swarming streets, looking into the faces of every woman he passed with a feeling of disgust, muttering: "No, no good. Bad . . . coarse

117

... meager ... thin ... sterile. There's not one like her—no one in the whole world who can touch her!"

And elsewhere in that recollection he would say: "After all the blind tormented wanderings of his youth, that woman would become his heart's center and the target of his life."

Inside her cabin, Aline hurled herself on her bed and fell into sleep. Only when the steward knocked on her door and entered with a note from Mina did she discover that she had somehow taken off her clothes. The steward's startled glance told her she was naked, just as his presence told her it was morning and nearly time to leave. She felt nauseated and sick in every pore of her body, and the thought of rising and finishing her packing and dressing and leaving the ship to join her family repelled her.

She lay there spent, and thought again how she had always set herself goals that seemed unreachable and then pushed herself tirelessly to attain them. She did not feel that way now. She did not want to triumph over obstacles. She did not want to rise to the occasion. She wanted to crawl under the covers and stay right there until the ship turned itself around and started another voyage. Declare squatter's rights, and simply lie in bed while the ship traveled wherever it might go, asking neither her permission nor her opinion. She wanted only to abandon all control over her destiny.

"Your friend the other lady is sick, madam," the steward was saying. "She thinks you might come over and help her . . . she has too many things to get back in her trunk."

And then he discreetly suggested a bracer of champagne for both ladies, assuming that Aline, like Mina, was suffering from overindulgence. Aline was touched. He was so British, respectful but not falsely so, and truly solicitous of the passengers who were his charges.

And she knew that if Mina asked for help, she really needed it. So, taking a deep breath, Aline smiled and told the steward to bring his champagne and she would take it to her friend. Willing herself not to think, she dressed, finished her packing and, ice bucket under her arm, went along to help Mina. As she said later, she put on a "pretty good imitation" of herself, good enough to get them both on deck for disembarking.

Aline even sported the jaunty hat she had planned for weeks to wear for her family's first glimpse of her. The August heat beat down, heavy with moisture, while the passengers jostled each other, pushing toward the railing to see if they could recognize relatives and friends on the dock. They were all impatient for the gangplank to go up, or perhaps it only seemed so. Perhaps, like her, they secretly welcomed the delay, because like her they needed time to adjust. Tom and the night's events kept pushing into her thoughts. She told herself that the episode was insane, a romantic illusion unworthy of her age and worldliness. But even as she finished these admonitions, his face would fill her mind again, the huge body, the resonant voice, the spell of his grandeur would ensnare her again, and she would feel helplessly, irrevocably caught with him inside a "net thrown over them by the hand of God."

The phrase was so melodramatic that it angered her. "No, no," she said to herself. "No more. I will simply get off the boat and I'll meet the family and I'll go home and start to keep house and work and continue existence as though nothing had happened."

"What happened? What do you mean?" Mina was asking curiously, and Aline realized she had spoken aloud. Now that she had, she was grateful to be able to voice some of the chaos inside her, and she started to tell Mina of the encounter that had battered the walls of her life last night. But Mina waved the story away, and Aline reminded herself, as she had before, that life goes on no matter what the loss; one grows hungry and thirsty again, and enjoys food and drink and music and people. And the lights dimming in a theater would still thrill her, and so would the sound of applause for a job well done. This inner litany echoed Mina's words of caution: "Please, darling, don't get yourself mixed up with any such foolishness. . . . You have so much already; you always tell me your life is too full, that each year brings more and more wonderful things."

"Yes, Mina, but never this, never this," she wanted to say, but perhaps her friend was right. Undoubtedly she was right. There was no "divine fire" stoked by some "special fitness" that had fused her soul with Thomas Wolfe's.

She smiled at her friend, and laid her cheek against Mina's and turned back to face the dock. The gangplank was up now and the ship's band was playing *The Star-Spangled Banner,* and Aline remembered her voyage to England with her father and their return. Then, too, she had gone abroad to unknown adventures and come back a changed person.

The crowd on the dock surged forward to embrace in one giant enfolding the entire crowd of passengers. With great whoops of glee single units broke away and greeted one another as she now greeted Theo and Teddy and Edla and Ethel.

"Yes, yes, yes," she said to their questions. "It was a wonderful trip, but I'm so happy to be home with you again."

And she was.

Yet, as she walked with them to the waiting car, she searched the crowd for the face and form of Thomas Wolfe. How could she not see him? And for a moment she wondered if she had made the whole thing up. But the bruises on her arms told her it had happened. All of it. What she did not know for certain was what would happen now.

# 9

It was indeed good to be home. She lay in her bed that first night after Theo went back to his room, and thought about the evening—the glorious dinner cooked chiefly by Ethel, and hours of conversation in which they'd caught up on each other's lives. Mainly, of course, it had been she who'd talked. It was family tradition for her to present the stories of her travels as other voyagers brought material gifts (although she remembered to do that too). Theo often said he didn't need to travel because she gave him so much vicarious adventure. Tonight for the first time she had been weary of that role.

She stretched, and turned on her side, and rested her cheek on the silken pillowcase. Even her face was tired, and every muscle and tendon of her body ached with tension and fatigue. How good it would have been to go straight to her room and not have to speak to anyone. But she couldn't. She was, as she had always been and wanted to be, the focus of this family. Tonight, however, instead of feeling proud and grateful, she felt the twinge of resentment she had experienced this morning in her bed on shipboard. My God, could it have been only this morning that she had left Thomas Wolfe and escaped to her cabin? How was it possible for your world to turn upside down in one day, leaving you an unidentified stranger to yourself and estranged from everyone familiar? Yet she certainly did feel, as she'd felt this morning, that she wanted to get rid of the old Aline—the one who always shone center stage, the one everyone looked to for gaiety and love, the one who always coped and achieved and conquered. A personality larger than her own had come into her life at last, and she wanted to surrender to that knowledge, to let go her own powerful image. . . . She must stop thinking this way. It was destructive and pointless. She was nearly forty-five and had constructed a life that worked in all its parts. If her dominating role was sometimes oppressive, she nonetheless clearly preferred it to one more ordinary and passive.

She tried to fill her mind with pleasanter thoughts of her family. Theo was euphoric about the land they'd lately bought in Armonk, New York, to which he'd added even more while she was gone. Soon she would begin planning a house there, a country place of their own where they could go on weekends and in the summers. She would design it down to the last detail and make it a perfect home for them all. She'd gone to visit the property with Theo before she'd left for Europe, and together they'd walked down the sloping lawns to the bordering reservoir, and they had looked out at the farther hills from the land's crest. She would design a house with marvelous views, and once inside it they would feel they were hundreds of miles from the city rather than an hour away. It crossed her mind that Theo might be naïve in believing the countryside would remain unspoiled, but he seemed so certain. Well, she would bow to his judgment. Certainly her financial stake in this acquisition was minimal compared to Theo's. If she expected him not to question her gifts to indigent actors and artists, she ought hardly complain about his investment in something that would bring them both enormous pleasure.

Theo was happy about the prospect of his country life, but he was happier still that Teddy had recently begun his own career in banking. Now son and father shared the Bernstein car to Wall Street and back every working day. Aline was touched by Theo's obvious joy at having his son follow in his footsteps, and more important, Teddy appeared really to enjoy his work. She shuddered, remembering the terrible time a couple of years back when he'd been ordered by his doctors not to go to college away from home. Aline had encouraged the boy to apply to

Princeton, and she had whooped in triumph with him when the letter of acceptance arrived. The doctors' verdict was a terrible blow, but it had been Aline, not Teddy, who cried when it was delivered. Her son accepted the dictum—as he accepted everything—with fatalistic grace. Tonight he had seemed relaxed, telling funny tales of his co-workers, with an obvious sense of self-esteem. He truly seemed happy with the course his life had taken. She so wanted him to love his work, to know the satisfaction of an honest day's efforts and a job well done. Yes, she thought, whatever Teddy and Edla do, they will do their jobs well, if Theo and Ethel and I had any influence at all.

Tonight at dinner Edla had been wearing the monocle which she habitually wore when riding. It looked rather bizarre on her fresh, eighteen-year-old face, but Aline knew there was more to her daughter's current aspirations for a dramatic career than the desire to make people notice her. She was a serious actress, whose work at the Playhouse was respected, and she made an excellent impression on producers at other theaters, whose auditions she tirelessly attended. Yes, Aline thought as she finally drifted off to sleep, it was a family to be proud of.

In the days that followed, Aline threw herself fiercely into her projects, so that there was scarcely time to think of Thomas Wolfe or anything else. She was designing costumes for the modern-dress *Hamlet*, and doing preproduction work on *The Dybbuk* at the Playhouse. The Staronove Synagogue in Prague stayed in her mind as the example of moodily gloomy, Jewish Gothic architecture she wanted to suggest. David Vardi had already arrived at the Playhouse and had told Aline he'd grown up in a village identical with the one in which the play was set. Aline was grateful for his ability to authenticate her view of the sets and costumes. Vardi was a tiny man—"One of the few people who make me feel tall!" Aline told Theo smilingly—and as soon as she said the words, the image of Thomas Wolfe lit up in her mind, and she remembered how small and precious he had made her feel.

*The Dybbuk* describes the possession of a young girl's body by the soul of a rabbinical student whose love she has rejected. Deeply romantic, mystical, sinister and tragic, it ends with an exorcism that finally unites the lovers in death. As she set to work, Aline was inspired to rise to what she saw as her supreme theatrical challenge. More than any other play she'd done, the sets and costumes would have to be integral to the impact, and to achieve this on her limited budget seemed almost impossible, a drastic test of her talents and ingenuity. She spent her nights at the drawing board, getting up from the bed she had been unable to sleep in, to work out the tonal variations of darkness and shadow that would evoke for an audience the sense of impending evil and the terror of the supernatural.

In vivid contrast were her designs for *Hamlet*—business suits and evening clothes and bowler hats. She had some misgivings about the public's response to a classic in modern dress, but it was an act of humility and love to attempt the feat. Perhaps by stripping the stage of all distractions, the audience could enter into more intimate contact with the play itself. The play might also seem more pertinent, less the product of a different age. At least this was producer Horace Liveright's hope, and it was Aline's as well, although her practical sense told her it might prove otherwise. Theo had warned her against risking her growing reputation on such a problematical venture, but she waved the worry aside. One took risks in life, or what was the point of intellect and talent?

"I think the first most sinful thing is to abuse a talent by letting it go unused or unchallenged," she said to him firmly, and he knew better than to argue.

Why, then, with all the work and love and pleasure, did the face of Thomas Wolfe keep returning? Why did she feel a special tension when she came home at night and looked through her mail on the hall table or picked up her mail at the Playhouse? And why did she start when the telephone rang and strain to hear whom the call was for?

She found herself wondering with uncharacteristic self-doubt if he hadn't told himself by now that she was too "old" for a young man like him. What she did not know was that almost immediately on reaching New York, Wolfe had gone to Asheville for a visit with his family. On his return, the fact that there was no envelope with her name in the corner waiting for him at the Albert made him desolate. For several days he tortured himself with the certainty that she had forgotten him completely, that she had played with him lightly while safe at sea, but would have no use for him now that she was safely back with her family and friends. He, too, threw himself into his work, trying to keep her face from his mind. But the memory of their night together in that "haunting other world" between sea and land seemed more real than the life he was living, and he longed desperately to know that reality again. In the end, he capitulated to his need, pulled some sheets from the piles of paper that surrounded his bed and chair, and began to write Aline a letter. As was his custom, he wrote several drafts, trying to find exactly the right tone and language to bridge the gap between them. He would describe the final product in *The Web and the Rock:*

"It was one of those pompous, foolish, vainglorious letters that young men write, that seem so fine when they write them, and that they writhe over when they recall them later." He did not allow himself to say in the letter how much he missed her, but instead attempted on page after page (the letter ran to eleven sheets) to strike a note of casual independence.

"I believe you spoke of seeing me again," he wrote with attempted nonchalance; "if by chance you should remember me, and should ever feel inclined to see me, my address is here at this hotel." Although he was pleased with this statement since it presumably gave him a slight edge of superiority (after all, it could almost seem as if he were granting her a favor), he felt compelled to be defensive about his own needs. He assured her that should she feel uninterested in picking up their friend-ship, he would certainly understand, "After all, ours was a chance ac-quaintance of the voyage—and these things pass." As these words were written, his belligerence increased and he promised her he didn't ex-pect anything from anyone, would beg for no favors—and he concluded with a rather obscure flourish: "Whatever else the world may say of me, I have never truckled to the mob."

The letter sat in his breast pocket for two days, getting soiled and stained with ink and food when he took it out to reread it while eating or working. He felt cowardly about not mailing it and angry at needing to. Finally, in a spasm of despair, he hurled it into a mailbox late one evening, banging the lid of the box so loudly that the sound rang down the deserted New York street. Predictably, as soon as the act was done, he wished he could undo it. The letter was so young, so mannered, and God, so long—so impossibly long. When would he learn how to say what he wanted to, simply, plainly, without endless variations of thought and theme? But it was too late. The damage was done. Well, she would probably have a good laugh over it with her theater friends. . . .

Aline came into the Playhouse before nine in the morning, ready to confer with Vardi. She stopped at the office for her mail, and her heart leaped as the young woman who handed her the envelope said some-thing jokingly about its bulk. She clutched it to her breast and quickly climbed the stairs to her office, thankful no one was waiting for her.

Without taking off her jacket, she tore open the envelope and read the letter inside, breaking into a broad smile while at the same time tears of pleasure moistened her eyes. She read it and read it again, and laid out the pages on her worktable to study the broad scrawl his hand had covered them with. The thought of his hands electrified her. She sat there so obviously lost in private thoughts that Vardi looked in the door and turned away without speaking. She decided she must see Wolfe again, but that she would see him here on her own ground, where she felt her own strength and might not be so swept away by his.

She rose, feeling a bit breathless, moved to the telephone, dialed the number of the Hotel Albert and asked to speak to Thomas Wolfe. The transaction took perhaps one minute, but she felt that she was suspended in centuries of time. Then there was his voice, just as she remembered it, even with the distortions of the telephone, there it was, for the moment hers alone to hear.

She had obviously waked him, and she quickly announced who she was, recognizing with pleasure that her name made him instantly alert. Still, she felt awkward, and heard herself being excessively brisk and formally polite. She was calling to tell him she had received his letter and had been pleased to hear from him, she said. And she was wondering, she continued in the hurried, impatient tone that sounded so hateful inside her own head, whether he would like to come down and see her play tonight.

To Wolfe the invitation was both startling and pleasing. His fantasy had invented a reunion filled with soft murmurings. Instead, he was matter-of-factly being invited to a performance and was being told how to get to the theater. It was all so practical and impersonal, but still, she was calling him and asking to see him, and that was, after all, what truly mattered.

As for Aline, she could not know what he was thinking or feeling, and she did not stop to wonder.

"Well, then," she said, "I'll be expecting you. It will be nice to see you again," and without even waiting for his goodbye, she hung up and stood with the phone in her hand, taking deep gulping breaths to calm herself. How awkward she had been, but after all, the first time was bound to be awkward; it would get better . . . and as she thought this, she understood that she was already making an assumption about their relationship and its continuation. All day long she was extraordinarily happy. She sang a little song as she sketched, and was playful with Vardi and the crew. Two new design ideas came to her that brilliantly solved certain problems, and she knew her day's work had benefited from her contentment.

It was Aline's habit to be early for appointments and she was early that evening, just as he was typically late. Impatiently she paced up and down in front of the Playhouse, twisting her antique ring on her finger. Many of the handsomely dressed men and women filling the theater were friends of hers from uptown, and she greeted them warmly, if a bit distractedly, while her eyes searched the street.

She looked down at her dress and stroked the silk, taking comfort from its cool touch. It was a sari of deep red; little mirrors sewn into the cloth caught the light and reflected it so that she seemed to stand in an aura of crimson and silver. She had gone home earlier to dine with the family, and afterward had paid close attention to what she would wear to the theater. She'd made a good choice, she knew, as she had with the velvet slippers and their shiny silver buckles. Her legs and feet were quite lovely, among her finer points, her legs slim and shapely, her feet highly arched. All this Thomas Wolfe noticed as he climbed awkwardly out of his cab, just as he also saw the gray strands in her soft hair, and the lines around her eyes and neck, which she made no attempt to hide. He did not yet understand that Aline had as personal a perspective on her looks and age as he did. Although she already recognized the problems a twenty-year difference might confront them with, she nonetheless saw herself as "beautiful, in the real flower of my physical self." Now, and in all the years to come, she would most often believe that her desirability was hardly affected by the passage of time. She felt she could be eternally young in the ways that really mattered, and the response she received from men whenever and wherever she went corroborated this perception. As for Thomas Wolfe tonight, the lines on her face, the gray in her hair, once seen by him were ignored. He knew only her loveliness, her womanliness, her air of gentle strength.

Aline watched him approach and thought she must be dreaming. He could not really be here, even though it was impossible to deny that awesome size. She was still nervous, and again grew brusque as she handed him his ticket, telling him to find a seat with an empty one next to it so that she could join him once the play got under way. They walked together into the theater, and she left him to go backstage. As she got things organized, directing backdrops toward a certain position in the wings, running a last test on the footlights—as she did all this, it was as if she were split in two. The serious worker would not be distracted from the practical problems at hand. But she was also the woman who could think only of the man she seemed irresistibly drawn to.

As soon as the curtain went up, she came back to the darkened theater, enjoying the atmosphere of hushed anticipation, and satisfied with her own contribution. The company was doing a *Grand Street Follies* tonight and when Aline had slipped into the seat next to Tom, she whispered to him at the end of every scene some bit of information about the sketch or the actors playing in it. She felt compelled to speak, but shy about what to say, and so she fell back on giving information. When intermission came, she quickly rose and led him into the lobby, where they would be surrounded by other conversations. As far as Tom could see, everybody seemed to know her, and he recognized many of the important faces and names when she introduced him. He shook hands and muttered polite phrases, but he grew silent when the group traded opinions about the other plays around town. They seemed to have seen everything on the boards and to feel they had the right to make judgments on them all, and Wolfe hated their smugness and easy "knowing." These were the very people whose trivial taste producers pandered to, giving them inordinate power over someone like himself. Would such a shallow, trivial bunch ever appreciate writing like his? He was certain they would not and that no producer would waste his time mounting a Thomas Wolfe production.

His thoughts made him chill with anger, but through it he could still marvel at Aline's behavior. These very people were showering her with affection and praise, and she took it all in with such enviable graciousness. Whatever she might feel about them, she delighted in their compliments, as innocently as a child receiving unexpected attention and reveling in it shamelessly. And once again he wondered how such purity could flower in this tangled garden and whether he would ever be able to "solve" the enigma of that flower face.

They took their seats for the second act, and when the show was over he followed her backstage, where he could not help but be excited by the magic of behind the scenes. Again he was awed by Aline—by her comfort in this hidden world, her command of it. He couldn't imagine ever feeling so at ease with his own talents and their use. His ambivalence about what he really wanted to do with his writing was reinforced by Aline's introducing him to the cast. Close up, illusion was gone. All he could see were the bizarre accentuations of make-up, and he could hear only the actors' petulant, egotistical comments now that they were speaking their own and not some author's language. That people like these could create the effects they achieved both repelled and fascinated him, and he began to feel very sad. Aline sensed his mood, and touched his arm lightly.

"I'm finished here," she said. "Come upstairs with me to my office." And running briskly ahead of him, she climbed the stairway to her little workroom. While she packed a briefcase with drawings and tracing papers, Wolfe looked around curiously. He had never seen a designer's workshop. Aline watched him study her drawing table, her designs pinned to it with little brass pins, and was thrilled by his concentration.

"No one ever asks me about what goes on inside me when I design," she'd often complain to her family. "I know the most wonderful things about color and clothes and what magic you can do with the materials I work with, and no one even cares enough to ask." Such lack of curiosity was incomprehensible to this woman who was curious about everything, which makes it easy to understand why Thomas Wolfe's insatiable desire for knowledge and experience was so gratifying.

She fumbled in her purse for the key to lock the door, and then impulsively, with a mischievous smile, she took out Tom's letter and hugged it to her, patting it and murmuring:

"My beautiful letter . . . my beautiful letter where he says he will not truckle. . . . He does not truckle. . . . He is no truckler!" She was laughing now, and he grew crimson.

"Give that back to me!" he shouted, and when she refused, still giggling, he grabbed her hand and wrested the letter from it. Immediately her laughter quieted, and she grew earnest.

"It's a beautiful letter . . . please . . . I'm sorry I laughed. Give it to me . . . let me have it, please." Her voice calmed him, and suddenly he believed she really did think his letter beautiful and really did care very much about receiving it, and the thought made him break into a wide smile. He handed the letter to her and she put it back in her purse, patting the bag happily when she closed it again. As she turned out the lights to leave, she realized he had not stepped back, and when she looked up he met her eyes and put his arms around her. Until this moment, neither of them had in any way acknowledged their burning memory of shipboard, and now Aline wanted nothing more than to bring the memory into the present, to let herself experience to the full the feelings she had been keeping inside her since they parted. But something stopped her. Whatever was to be encouraged or admitted between them, this again was not the place nor the time. She had wanted to meet him on familiar ground, but to meet as lovers here seemed very wrong. A whole other part of her life went on here, a good part of her history had been shaped here, and would stand in the way of whatever new history they would make with each other. And so she pulled away, and he seemed to understand.

The doorman called a cab, and they climbed inside it, sitting close to each other, neither holding hands nor embracing. But Aline felt covered by the warmth of his body radiating toward her, gently enveloping her like a soft quilt. She looked out the window at the passing streets and felt an ache in her chest at knowing they would soon be in Greenwich Village and at his hotel. The driver pulled up in front of the shabby old Albert, and she motioned him to wait while she climbed out to say good night. Tom did not suggest they have a drink, or that she come upstairs with him, and she was grateful that he knew she would have had to say no. She was not surprised that he knew what she felt, for she had sensed within the first hour of their meeting that they would always have a special knowledge of each other—would be, as Thomas Wolfe himself later said, "the met halves of the broken talisman."

But now, on this second night, they parted formally. Shaking hands, they looked at each other for a long moment, until the taxi driver loudly cleared his throat, and she clambered back inside the cab. Wolfe stood watching as she drove away to where her husband and children and sister waited. Only when the taxi was completely out of sight did he turn and enter the hotel, impatient for the night to be over so that it would be morning and he could call her at the Playhouse.

During the next few weeks they spoke to each other more and more often and met briefly on several occasions. He would come down to the theater and join her for a late supper, or she would come up to the Village to lunch. Aline knew he was becoming more and more involved with her, and she basked in the pleasure this knowledge brought. But yet she made no attempt to move the relationship to another plateau. Although she already believed it would be impossible to stop the course of events, she didn't feel ready to accelerate it. It would have helped to have someone intimate to talk to. But apart from Dr. Hinkle, she confided in no one. Certainly, she could not go to Ethel, who tended to dislike any of Aline's protégés even when the attachments were

130

innocent, and would certainly disapprove of one that was not, no matter how overwhelming the feelings that had precipitated it. Ethel disdained being governed by emotion and would not pretend otherwise, even with her sister.

As for some of her friends, casual as extramarital liaisons were in the theater, she could not share this feeling with them, for they would accept it only because they found it unimportant. Such easy treatment would trivialize what Aline felt, demean its place in her life. Perhaps soon she would have to confide in someone like Mina Curtiss or Theresa Helburn, women of more serious passions, but for now she preferred to remain silent, maintaining her privacy as she nurtured the secret of Thomas Wolfe.

But she did bring her fears and hopes to Dr. Hinkle, and welcomed the chance to sort out her conflicting impulses. For Aline understood very well the volcanic potential of her attraction to Tom. This would be no idle affair, and it would be enormously difficult to fit it into her life without harming the family she cherished.

A lesser worry was the difference in age between them. Although she did feel young and beautiful, richly sensitive and sensual, twenty years seemed too wide a gap to bridge completely. Not that their relationship in any way fitted the stereotype of older woman and younger man, she told the doctor. Tom was so brilliant, so gifted, so deeply thoughtful, that her years of extra living seemed meaningless. She, in turn, could bring him gifts from those years, she could share with him experience he could draw on for his writing. But would he view her insights as intrusive, the presumptuous meddling of an older person?

She had just returned from a visit to Dr. Hinkle, when Tom called the Playhouse to ask her to meet him a few days later for a special luncheon. October 3 would be his twenty-fifth birthday, and he wanted to celebrate it with Aline. As she listened to the hope and shyness and excitement in his voice, all the hesitation of her talk with the doctor disappeared.

"I'll come uptown to meet you this time," she said gaily. "After all, it's a memorable event . . . we should do something special."

They agreed to meet in front of the Forty-second Street library, at the foot of the great marble stairway leading from the street to the main entrance.

"If I'm early, I can stand on the steps and watch for you to come towering over everyone else," she said, and he answered, "I'll be there before you . . . I'd go there now if I could," and she beamed with pleasure as she heard the smile in his voice.

October 3 was a warm, fine day, shining with autumnal promise. Aline dressed carefully to match its mood. She chose a softly warm brown sari, with touches of white. And standing on the library steps, she knew exactly how the noonday sun, reflected from the mellow colors of her dress, must be bathing her in a golden burnished glow. She saw the appreciative look on Tom's face as he hurried excitedly through the crowds to claim her. He'd been standing off to one side and hadn't seen her arrive and had known the bitter disappointment of thinking she'd decided not to come.

"How could you think that?" she asked seriously. "I told you I would be here . . . you must have known I would come to you."

A silence fell between them then, but she broke it by saying, "Well, young man . . . how does it feel to be twenty-five years old?" He told her it felt fine, but better since he'd found her here. And then this man of a million poetic words and images took hold of her hand and said earnestly, "You look so swell in brown." And she was delighted, and told him she was happy that he liked her dress, and she did a little pirouette right there on the steps, so he could see it from every angle.

"All right now," Aline said. "Where shall we go? And don't forget, this is my celebration." But Tom protested it must be his, and she sensed he wanted to be in charge and so she agreed quickly. They had already started walking down the crowded steps to the street, their arms linked, her smiling face tilted up toward his.

It was a short taxi ride to the restaurant he had chosen—a modest Italian speakeasy with stucco walls and red-checked cloths and hearty food. She understood it was important to him to have made the right choice, and she told him quickly how charming she thought the room. They ordered martinis and then an enormous meal—antipasto, minestrone, fish, chicken, salad, cheese and coffee, with a large flask of Chianti to wash it down. They wanted to taste everything on the menu that tempted them, in "the spirit of true celebrants."

As soon as they sat down at the table, he asked her when she'd have to leave, and she grinned back at him. "No time . . . I've taken the entire afternoon off to be with you . . . I have nothing to do but celebrate your being twenty-five." He reached out to touch her hand, but the waiter appeared with their cocktails. Aline picked up her glass and clicked it against his. Thomas Wolfe recalls the episode in his "story" of the meeting. " 'Well, here's to you young fellow,' she said, and then grew silent for a moment, looking at him very seriously. . . . 'To your success —the real kind—the kind you want inside of you—the best.' "

"They drank," he remembers, "but her words, her presence here, the feeling of wonderful happiness and pride that the day brought to him, a sense that somehow this was the true beginning of his life gave him exalted purpose. . . . He leaned forward across the table and seized her hand in both of his. . . . 'Oh, I'll do it!' he cried, exalted, 'I'll do it!' "

" 'You will,' she said. 'I know you will!' And putting her other hand on top of his, she squeezed it hard and whispered, 'The best! You are the best!' "

The hours passed. The table had been cleared and still they sat there. This time he talked about himself, instead of hurling questions at her as he had done at sea. He talked and talked and talked, and his words were finer food to Aline than anything that had been set on the table. In the short time they'd known each other, he had brought her more of his writing to read, and she had hardly been able to believe the luminosity of his language. It seemed to her that he was putting into words what generations of men and women had struggled to express. He gave voice to pain and loneliness and secret hope and humanity's deepest secrets and aspirations. His talent transfixed her. Her love of language and her reverence for the ability to transmit emotion and understanding through it made her exult that she could bring such a person into her life and perhaps even share in shaping his gift.

So now she listened to his voice bouncing off the stucco walls and returning to her. He was telling her the minutest details of his life and she listened with every ounce of her attention, for she wanted him to know that she cared about all his experience and judged none of it.

They drank a second bottle of Chianti and they drank brandy. After a time it was clear to Aline that he was becoming seriously, even impressively, drunk. Several times she tried to get him to leave with her, but he waved her away, wanting to talk more, to make her understand something else, to pour himself out as he had poured the wine into their glasses. Aline experienced a cacophony of sensations. She had exulted in the majesty of his language, in his pulling her into his life, but she was spent . . . exhausted. She needed some time to herself, sitting very still. Otherwise her head might burst from this tumult of new impressions.

Again she suggested that they leave, and this time he agreed. When they stepped into the already darkening street, the night air hit their faces like a sudden rainstorm. Aline welcomed it, would have liked to run up and down the street after sitting so many hours in the little room filled with stale cigarette smoke and the smell of garlic. But she was afraid to delay any longer getting him back to his hotel. She hailed a taxi, whose driver was clearly amused by the small woman helping the huge drunken man into the cab. Aline smiled pleasantly at him, but did not acknowledge his conspiratorial wink. She was already feeling defensive about Thomas Wolfe.

Tom was gentle and affectionate as they drove through the quiet, shadowy streets, and Aline opened the windows to let in the coolness of the evening. She stroked his forehead and told him he must go right to bed and sleep off all that drinking. As she spoke, she once again saw anger leap from his eyes.

"You mean you're taking me back to my hotel . . . and you're going to leave me there!" he thundered. Aline forced herself to remain very still, to meet his gaze and repeat that he must have some sleep or he would be ill. Her calm words made him erupt with uncontrollable rage. He yelled at the driver to stop the cab, and shouted at her that she had abandoned and tricked him. Aline tightened up inside. She was terrified that he did really hate her, would wake up feeling the same resentment he was feeling now. But no matter how hurt or fearful she was, she would not move further along the path of their destiny while he was so roaring drunk.

Again he shouted for the cab to stop, and when the driver pulled over to the sidewalk with a screech, jumped out and thrust his face through the open window space before turning away. "You are a bad woman!" he said, and spun clumsily around to walk off. Aline saw him bump into a passing man and the man turn angrily toward him, only to fall silent when he saw the culprit's size.

She watched him go and wearily told the driver to move on. There was nothing she could do now except pray that he would find his way back to his hotel. Once home, she had no time to compose her inner self, although she did her best to appear calm when she sat down to dinner. She found herself telling the family about Tom Wolfe: that she was trying to get his play produced, and how talented he was. She liked to hear herself say his name, but more important, she wanted her household to be aware of his existence so that she would not have to hide their connection in its more public aspects. She would often say in years to come, "I tried my best, and never did anyone in," and as she sat at the dinner table with her family that night, she tried to believe she could hold to that code.

She was eager for morning. She was afraid to call him that night, although she'd moved to the phone after dinner, before thinking better of it and rejoining the family in the living room. After all, what if he didn't answer? She would never know whether he had passed out in a drunken stupor too deep for him to hear the phone, or had never got back to his hotel at all, was lying helpless somewhere in the street.

She decided to phone from the Playhouse, and as soon as she walked through the door, a little past nine, she placed the call. Once again she awakened him, and sighed in relief that she had. She heard shame rather than surprise in his voice this morning, and she wanted to weep for the pain she knew he was feeling. Yet she only asked him matter-of-factly how he was, and dismissed his tentative apologies with a small laugh, telling him gently that they would talk about it when he was feeling better. Then, in her efficient problem-solving voice, she managed the day's priorities for him. He was to get out of bed and take a shower. Then he must go out somewhere for breakfast. "Don't have it at the hotel; a walk in the air will do you good."

He listened meekly, murmuring agreement. Then, taking a deep breath, and knowing full well she was making a choice—he would have blamed himself had he not heard from her, and very likely would have been too ashamed to pursue her anymore—she invited him to come round to the theater again that evening, after the performance. They would go somewhere and talk, she said, and then he could say whatever was on his mind about last night, and she would tell him what was on hers.

The theater was almost completely empty when Tom arrived at about eleven-fifteen, to find her standing in the lobby. They shook hands in constrained greeting, and she quickly released his, feeling uncomfortable and self-conscious. Once again she led him backstage and up to her office, chattering nervously about being hungry since she'd been too busy for dinner, and perhaps they should go to a Childs restaurant farther uptown. Inside her office, she didn't bother to turn on the lights, just took her coat from the hook. He came toward her to help her put it on, and as he touched her shoulder he begged her to listen to his explanation about yesterday. There was such pain in his voice that tears sprang to her eyes and she wanted desperately to be strong enough to take the pain away. She wanted to comfort him and

135

make him proud at all times of who he was, to help him accept his own nature and respect it.

And so she told him quietly, in the shadowy, silent room, standing next to the drawing board where she exercised her own talent, that he was a brilliantly talented man whom she believed in completely. And she said that from the moment she had first seen him on shipboard, she had known who he was, and would know him in this way forever, and so he need never explain anything, for whatever he did or said was an expression of himself and she wanted nothing more than to accept the gift of himself exactly and completely as he was.

Thomas Wolfe writes of this moment:

> A heavy door had slammed below and for a moment there was the lean and lonely sound of footsteps walking away upon an empty pavement. Then there was nothing, just the hushed, still silence in the house. They stood there, holding each other by the hands as they had done the day before, and this time there was nothing more to say, as if that stormy meeting of the day before had somehow erased, wiped out for each of them all confusion, all constraint, the need of any further explanation. They stood there with held hands and looked at each other . . . and knew that there was nothing more to say.

Aline still felt reluctant to consummate this closeness here in the Playhouse, center of a different life, but she led him silently to a backstage sofa. She had given little thought to what it would be like to be Tom's lover; it was the whole man and the level of intimacy he promised that had obsessed her. From the first moment of meeting he had touched all her senses with all his own, and he would continue to do so even if their bodies never joined. But when she lay in his arms, when he had entered her, she wept for joy. It was as though he had taken her with him, so that she, too, could discover herself. After years of searching, years of nameless yearnings, she had through him "found my own release."

# 10

Every day now, she phoned him to say good morning, to say she loved him, and to feel the wonderful flow of pleasure when she heard him say he loved her. She would wake up feeling as if the day were being heralded by organ music. Every act of living, no matter how minor, took on new purpose and beauty. She marveled at the yellow silk of her nightgown as it caught the sun's rays through her window, at the luscious smell of coffee floating upstairs from the kitchen as if in loving invitation, at the splendor of the bolts of cloth stacked around her workroom. If her senses had been responsive to all this before she met Thomas Wolfe, they were doubly so now. She could hardly bear the number of impressions that flooded in on her through a day of living. But oh, the joy of knowing that she could bring them all to him, lay them all out for him when they met for lunch, or when he came to call for her at the theater. As for Wolfe, he wrote that she became "a world for him—a kind of new America and now he lived in it, explored it all the time." As she "talked about herself and her life, and told in her vivid and glowing manner of her daily little discoveries in the streets," his own vision of the city began to change, to become less fearful and hostile.

Indeed, colleagues at N.Y.U. noticed a new lightness in his manner and recall how he strode back and forth in the faculty room, grinning and shouting, "I'm in love! I'm in love!" When pressed for details, however, Tom grew secretive, saying little more than that she was "a very great lady," or "the best friend I've ever had." He was accommodating his own desire to shout his romance from the rooftops to Aline's determination that they should be discreet.

Aline Bernstein's quite remarkable ability to reconcile what others might see as opposing forces is nowhere more apparent than in her attitude in regard to Wolfe. She made him a part of her life without guilt and without berating herself for being selfish, because she believed that every act is both selfish and unselfish. Similarly, she considered herself neither a good woman nor a bad one, believing that a healthy woman accepts the fact that she is both. However, while she attached her soul to Thomas Wolfe, she felt no less loyal than before to her family, not least to Theo. She had loved her husband before Tom, and she loved him now. And she cared about his well-being. Although she was compelled to follow her destiny with Wolfe, she would do her best not to hurt Theo in the process.

As for Theo, his eventual ability to accept his wife's true relationship with Thomas Wolfe would result from many factors, and be very hard won. Most of all it derived from the depth of his feeling for his wife, but also, to some degree, it reflected his awareness that she had never wanted to hurt him and had done a great deal to avoid doing so.

Thus, while Aline would not be entirely clandestine out of respect for Tom, she would be discreet out of respect for her husband. She knew, of course, that she must be ready to face the possible consequences of her affair, and she considered this readiness only a fair price for her freedom. But she also believed that what guided her attempts to protect her family was her sense, however idiosyncratic, of personal integrity.

When she was with Tom in public, whether across a table at Childs over a late-night supper, at the Playhouse when he came to watch a rehearsal, or at parties they attended together, some of them in her own home, it was within the framework of encouraging mentor and youthful protégé. When she told everyone of his great talent, she was not dissembling. The more Aline knew of him, the more of his work she read, even when she was critical of its form or length, the more convinced she was of his genius; and the more committed she became to nurturing it.

Actually, Tom's writing these days was singularly unfocused. When Aline called in the morning, cheerfully outlining her own day and arranging when they would meet, his plans were vague and formless, despite the fact that he had set up a teaching schedule of afternoon classes only, for the precise purpose of having his mornings free to write. What work he did do vacillated between play revisions and experiments with narrative—some of them quite impressive recollections of his childhood or his recent European travels. However, they were all unconnected fragments that more often than not got mislaid in the clutter of his room or mixed up with sections of unrelated material. Still, though he felt lethargic and unproductive, his exultation at being in love kept him from despair about his career, especially since Aline continually reinforced his conviction that he was surely going somewhere, that he was destined for exceptional fame and fortune. He wrote to a friend that in these months when he searched his life and talents, she gave him "companionship, affection, and the inestimable comfort of human belief."

Meanwhile, Aline was working extremely hard on her own projects, even though *The Dybbuk* would not open until mid December. They had allowed themselves an unusual ten-week rehearsal schedule and Vardi needed every moment of it, just as Aline needed the time for her costumes and sets. She had enormous faith in this production, more than she had ever had before. Eyes shining, she'd tell Tom that all of them at the Playhouse felt almost mystical about the venture, in some way haunted by *The Dybbuk* spirit. Only she was relatively immune, she would say softly, for her soul had already been captured. . . .

They snatched their hours. Sometimes he joined her uptown for the *Hamlet* rehearsals, where again pride and envy battled in him when he saw Aline dealing easily with problems and talking easily with stars and producers. One afternoon she introduced him to Eugene O'Neill, who was on the advisory board for the production. Aline saw instantly how her lover struggled to seem cordial despite the resentment he felt toward the other man's already luminous success.

As it turned out, despite sponsors like O'Neill, Theo's misgivings about their *Hamlet* were borne out. It opened to mixed reviews and not enough people came to see it to keep it going. No matter that the *New York Times* gave it high praise, and that Sherwood Anderson was

139

moved to write a letter to the *Times* saying: "I got a tremendous new feeling of Shakespeare out of the play." He went on to say that on opening night, the audience was "composed of sophisticated people who applauded and cheered as I have not heard an audience in many years. Not only did they cheer; they were moved."

Aline, standing in the wings on opening night, knew that the audience was moved, and that was sufficient compensation for her own faithful efforts. She only wished Tom could be with her to see the faces and hear the lavish applause. But she knew it was wiser that he was not. Her whole family was with her this evening, and they'd all been invited to a small dinner party by one of the sponsors. But later that evening, as she drank champagne and chatted with celebrated people, Tom again entered her thoughts. Not that he was ever completely gone from them. But at moments like these, she gave him a particularly tender secret embrace, for she knew how impressed he would be with these glittering men and women who wielded so much of the power he coveted for himself. She took this privileged splendor so much for granted that she knew she was at times insensitive to his feeling of being an outsider, perhaps a permanent one. Yet she didn't mean to aggrandize herself when she told him that at dinner she'd sat next to Mayor Jimmy Walker or that the acerbic critic Alexander Woollcott had told her one opening night that he thought her designs were splendid. No, it was really true, she assured herself: her admiration for Tom was such that these apparent boasts were to show him that "if he loved me, I was something worthy to be loved, that he was not loving a woman too far below his own great self."

Besides, in many ways she knew he was hungry to hear about that world he as yet had no claim on except through her, and he rejoiced that she could bring it all to him, "still warm with her recent contact." He felt boyishly triumphant that one of the great city's most successful and admired personages had taken him for her lover, although he still wrestled with the darker side of his feelings about New York and the price of success. Aline understood, even this early in their being together, that it wasn't just New York Tom was ambivalent about. The complex dualities of the human personality, which increasingly seemed more harmonious in her own nature, were in constant conflict in his. His shifts of mood had as their cause, she was certain, his inability to fuse disparate feelings into a whole he could accept and respect. She hoped desperately that through her love, through her resolute belief in his genius, through her openness to all that he was, she could help him to be more at ease with his own nature. If only she could be with him more when he hurt; if only they were not so constrained by the public atmosphere of their meetings. There was so much she wanted to do for him —to organize his work habits and cook him fine meals—but it was impossible within the context of their life together now. She looked around the handsome room the party was taking place in, and thought of Tom's shabby, dreary hotel room, and how both of them hated to demean their love by bringing it there.

As it was, their circumstances were becoming more and more frustrating. Although what they shared transcended the number of times they were able to make love, they needed to do so more often than they had the chance. And no less acutely, they needed to touch each other without fear of being seen, to kiss and lie contentedly in each other's arms. Aline had never forgotten Nana's serious counsel that nothing was better than lying down next to the person you loved while you confessed your mind and heart; that you would say things in such circumstances that you would never think of saying while sitting at a restaurant table. Aline smiled at her recurring memories of Nana, knowing they came to mind because her aunt would so completely have understood her niece's passion for this majestically passionate man.

Troublesome as the problem of their meeting was, her concentration during November and early December was of necessity focused on *The Dybbuk*. Although she saw Tom three or four times a week, she was nonetheless caught up in the excitement of the approaching premiere. Everyone who saw the rehearsals, Tom, Theo, Ethel, all assured her that her belief in what her group was doing at the Playhouse was justified; that they were creating a remarkable and unique theatrical experience New York would long remember. But down at the theater, they worried among themselves that perhaps they had lost perspective, that the extraordinary quality they found in every scene might be a kind of communal self-hypnosis. On the day of the opening, Alice Lewisohn remembers, everyone assembled at the theater much earlier than they needed to, "admitting the need to return to *The Dybbuk* world, confessing in turn that it was impossible to stay at home."

Aline came early too. It was hours later when she saw her family arrive, bringing in their wake a number of invited guests, Thomas Wolfe included. She went out to the lobby to greet them all, but her attention was divided. Or more accurately, was suspended, as if she had

141

taken a huge breath and would not be able to release it until the final curtain went down and she could see if their work here had cast its hoped-for spell. Standing in the wings, she watched her sets and costumes and lighting effects, and hugged herself with pleasure. They were good. She knew they were good. They were right. They were the best work she had ever done.

As usual, her judgment of her own efforts was accurate. The audience applauded until she felt her ears would ring forever, and even critics who never allowed their enthusiasm to show until their review appeared congratulated her extravagantly.

They went to many parties that night, Theo beaming with pride, and Tom clearly feeling, if less conspicuously, the same proprietary pleasure. Whole troops of well-wishers and loving friends gathered about her in celebration, and she adored every minute of it and felt she had earned it. Sometime during the evening, Tom left the group, holding Aline's hand long in farewell. She watched him leave, and turned back to her family and friends, feeling diminished, but still content. Her work and its rewards had always provided a road back to stability. Tom envied this, even as he admired and loved it. "In your own work you have been so certain," he would write soon. "You have so fine a talent and you have found the thing you like best and for which you are the best fitted. . . . Dear happy, darling Aline . . . I would give my crooked nose and my weak eye for a little of your strength and ability."

The next morning, Theo brought her the newspapers in bed, but then insisted on reading the reviews to her himself, with dramatic gestures and diction. His face was lit with admiration for this celebrated woman who was his wife. How different she was from the wives of his colleagues down on the Street. How envious they all would be when they read their papers this morning. Aline was touched by her husband's pleasure, and pressing his hand to her cheek for a moment, said happily, "Read me Brooks Atkinson again—that's the best one of all." And indeed, Atkinson's words of praise *were* the best for Henri's ex-student, because he compared Aline's sets to "a Rembrandt canvas."

When Aline came down to the theater later that morning, dozens of messages from friends lay on her desk, urgently asking her to use her influence to get them tickets for a performance. If her career had been soaring before, it had now taken its highest leap, and there was no way to stop it short of her own wish to do so.

Perhaps it was all this attention that prompted Tom to plan a trip to

Asheville for Christmas. Back in the family bosom, he might gain a perspective about his life with Aline that he was unable to achieve at close range. But if these were his motives, they quickly crumbled. Soon after he arrived, he wrote her: "My family is showing its customary and magnificent genius for futility and tragedy." Various members of the clan were either ill or hysterical, and Tom could hardly wait to leave them all behind again and return to the woman who had truly become his life. He knew when he thought about her that she was giving his life "a kind of frame, design, and purpose" it had never yet had. That indeed, "She had herself become a kind of goal and purpose . . . a kind of target," so that he could now aim all his "tremendous energies, so long exploded, scattered, misdirected, or diffused into thin air." When Aline read avowals like these in his letters, she could scarcely believe in her good fortune. And she longed again to give it an environment in which they could truly live with, as well as for, each other.

Tom would write later that "she solved the problem in a characteristic way, in a manner typical of the indomitable purpose which he was to find that small figure housed." He was referring to Aline's decision to rent a place to work in. She began talking, to her family and to him, about the dwindling light in her top-floor workroom on Seventy-seventh Street. This was not an invention; real estate operators were buying up the lovely private houses on their block and putting up massive modern towers, changing the landscape the Bernsteins saw from their windows and shutting out the light and air. Aline and Theo were determined to resist the encroachers, but as their neighbors surrendered one by one and sold off their homes, their own capitulation seemed inevitable. They would be smothered by skyscrapers, driven out of the warm, wonderful rooms that held so much shared history.

"I'll go into mourning when we leave," Aline often said, and was already grieving over the slow changes they had no power to halt. One of these changes was indeed the loss of light in her workroom, which suggested the idea of renting a loft in another part of the city. It would not do simply to spend more time at her office in the Playhouse. For one thing, it was used as a catchall for unused costumes; and for another, she simply had no privacy—people were continually parading in to see her. She explained all this to Tom when she first broached the idea of taking a place of her own, and in December, soon after she had introduced the idea, and not long after her forty-fifth birthday, she rented a loft on Eighth Street, in Greenwich Village, to start the new year of 1926.

"I've found a studio," she said ecstatically to Tom when they met at a Childs restaurant for lunch. Wolfe remembered the scene. "It's simply wonderful," she cried. "In all your life you've never thought of such a place. It's up at the top of an old house . . . the kind of house I used to live in when I was a child. Only this one is all rickety and gone to seed. You think the steps are going to give way on you and it's very dirty. . . . But it's been a beautiful house," she cried, "a noble house. And I've taken the whole floor!" And she finished gleefully: "In all your life you've never seen such space!"

In fact, the house at 13 East 8th Street was appallingly run down, although it indeed had signs of an earlier elegance. Now, however, a dreary-looking tailor shop was on the ground floor, and the stairs going up were broken and tilting, giving off outrageously loud creaks under Wolfe's heavy tread. Aline told Tom she thought the rooms had recently been used as sweatshops, and when they peered in, that seemed a fair assessment. Electric wires hung from the ceilings, and piles of litter lay on the floors—empty boxes, string, and stuffing of some kind. But when Tom stepped over the threshold of Aline's top-floor loft, he understood her sense of discovery and marveled anew at her ability to see past surface deficiencies. For although the room was as filthy and shabby as the others, there was a sense of grandeur about it because of the huge skylight in the center of the ceiling. And the space was truly enormous, particularly compared to the cramped little hotel room he spent his days and nights in.

"Walk up and down," she urged him, beaming, and he caught her mood and strode with military dignity up and back on the sagging floor and then up and back again.

"There now," she said proudly. "What did I tell you? Isn't it fine?"

She stood under the skylight and the sun's rays poured over her, and Tom felt himself so moved he could hardly look at her anymore. But when he did, he felt a great peace wash over him, as if this place with its showering sunlight or moonlight could be a vast, silent refuge.

She told him she had already hired someone to come in the next day and scrub the windows and walls and floors. And as soon as that was done, she would send down her drawing table and equipment and some old furniture she didn't really need at home. And before she put the key back in her purse, she gestured with it in a way that confirmed what he had felt since he followed her through the door. She seemed clearly to be saying, "This place is not mine, but ours."

144

Very soon the loft was fixed up to accommodate both Tom's and Aline's needs. Her drawing table was under the skylight, while a sofa and his books were in the back. He had to stoop a bit when he reached the far corner, for the ceiling sloped downward from the skylight toward the front and rear windows. But he reveled in the tranquillity and space of this place they were making together, and Aline felt inordinately wealthy each time she looked up from her work and saw him so naturally, simply, there. And when, soon after she was settled, he broached the subject of his leaving the Albert entirely and moving in permanently, she gave a prayer of thanks. She had hoped fervently this would happen, but would not have suggested it herself. She did not want to take over his life in any way that he wouldn't spontaneously concur in.

Now, however, that he *was* there all the time, that she could think of him as there when she was elsewhere was a joyous and wonderful thing. He had insisted on sharing the thirty-five-dollar-a-month rent and she agreed, knowing it was important for his pride, and also because it validated the image of the arrangement she was presenting to her family. For she made no secret about his being at the loft. After all, it seemed logical enough for her to be sharing such a huge space, particularly when she could thereby help someone she had so much confidence in.

There is good reason to believe that Theo's easy acceptance of the news was in large part due to the difference in age between Aline and Tom. If one is eager to believe that only friendship exists between a man and a woman, the fact that the man is barely older than the woman's son, and that the woman has always accepted growing older with ease and grace, helps sustain that rationalization. Clearly, this was the case now, as Aline went about her life, fully and lovingly, at 333 West 77th Street in her luxurious, many-roomed house, and fully and lovingly in the sprawling loft, still always messy with Tom's debris, at 13 East 8th Street.

After breakfast with the family, she would go down to the Playhouse, where she was doing a number of plays in the winter and spring of 1926. She was also, because of *The Dybbuk,* increasingly in demand uptown, and so, when she left the "Neighborhood" and came to Tom, her briefcase was filled with scripts to read and sketches for work in progress. But her heart would dance with excitement when she hurried up the stairs and the work in the briefcase would be temporarily forgotten. It was only his face she wanted to think about, to see, to touch. As soon as her key turned in the lock, he would be at the door waiting for her. He would gather her up in his arms and hug her tightly and she would cover his face with the eager kisses of a child. Twenty years fell between them like dust in a breeze. Sometimes he would be so full of emotion that he would do a clumsy jig, and Aline, knowing and feeling his mood, would gracefully waltz around his leaping body. They would sink down into the worn sofa and she'd tell him tales of her morning. About the fruit vendor who was dusting his apples with a feather duster, about the wonderful antique shop she'd found, where just exactly the ancient curtains she'd been looking for were hanging—"an awful, faded, greeney plush . . . they looked as if all the germs and dust and microbes in the world had nested there!" or she'd earnestly pull out a tiny folded-up piece of tin foil from her pocket and spread it out for him to share her wonder at its colors. "It's the wrapping off a piece of candy. . . . I saw it this morning as I was passing a stationery shop. The color was so strange and beautiful that I went in and bought the candy, just to get the wrapping. . . . I'm going to see if I can match it somewhere with a piece of cloth. . . . I've never seen this shade before. . . . It would be beautiful!" she'd finish reverently. And he would marvel at the "thousand shifting plays of life" contained in this remarkable woman who had gotten "into the conduits of his blood."

Soon it would be time for lunch. If she had not stopped on her way to do the marketing, they would leave the loft and go out to shop together. She didn't know which she liked better—bearing her parcels of food when she arrived, succulent, pungent evidence of her love, or having him link arms with her and trail along as she talked to butchers and grocers, eating her up with his eyes as she negotiated for the finest chicken or melon or fish. They "bought food," remembered Wolfe, "with the passionate intensity of poets," and "found the lost world not in Samarkand, but on Sixth Avenue."

Aline was in her glory amid the homely, spicy colors and odors of the market. Although shopping for food had remained a consistent pleasure for her since the days when she skipped along with Aunt Mamie, there was nothing to match these expeditions. The life she led as Mrs. Theodore Bernstein made her delegate much of the marketing and most of the cooking to other people, although she supervised all of it carefully. But with Tom's meals, she did it all—planned, shopped, cooked and cleaned up. And every step of the process was rich with meaning.

She felt mother to the earth, quintessentially woman.

And Tom, when he watched her cooking in the small kitchen area of the loft, found his love and hunger almost too much to bear. He'd begin pacing the length of the entire room again, or start to shave to look handsome for the meal; but then, with the lather still covering one side of his face, he'd need to see her, and would come back to where she was working and grin foolishly, for once wordlessly—and she beamed back at his half-white face, her own flushed pink from the heat of the stove. Often while he waited for lunch, he would read poetry to her, and this she loved most of all. As she listened to the cadences of Blake or Browning, her father's remembered voice would blend into her lover's.

They would sit down to eat, inhaling the delicious fragrances, serving themselves with relish. "I make you meals to make you believe in God, sir!" she'd say proudly, and he could only agree.

Yet with all the passionate intimacy of this place, it was not only a temple of sensual love. It was a room that adhered to its original purpose—a workroom, where visitors from N.Y.U. who came to see Tom, or producers who came to see Aline, would find her, spectacles on, wearing one of the loose linen smocks she loved to work in, busy at her drawing table, while Tom, sprawled on the sofa, read students' work or corrected their compositions. Aline was doing her very best to bring order into his life, to organize his energies into a pattern that allowed neither love nor teaching to impinge on his writing. She fed him lavish meals not only because this was for her an integral part of lovemaking, but because it helped punctuate and shape his day. She bought him large legal-size ledgers and suggested that he write in them rather than on the pieces of loose paper that invariably got lost. One of her tenderest images of Tom was the way he would place the ledger on top of the refrigerator and write standing up, his big body pressed against the squat white box.

Increasingly, he was writing straight narrative. In those days and weeks and months they shared together, Aline was growing more certain that the theater was not the medium for her lover's creative gifts. Not only did she feel his stories could best be told in another, less concentrated form; she reminded Tom that theatrical writing involved collaboration; that many other people—directors, producers, actors—made their imprint on your work. A personality like his would have difficulty functioning in such a framework.

Tom had begun to feel this himself, particularly since it was becoming obvious that the theatrical world was not eagerly waiting for Thomas Wolfe. Through Aline, he had submitted his plays to the Provincetown Playhouse and to the Theatre Guild, and had been rejected at both places. As he thought about the situation, he realized that he was putting his talents to the wrong use. Years later, in a speech about writing, he would say that his youthful dream of being a playwright was "not only wrong, it was as fantastically wrong as anything could be. . . . Something in me very strong and powerful was groping toward a more full, expansive and abundant expression than the stage itself could physically encompass."

Aline was gently guiding this perception. The hours and hours she spent listening to his stories convinced her that there was a novel to be written out of the accumulated substance of his personal experience. Gradually, as they talked, the idea of his novel took shape for him. Ardently encouraged by Aline, he began to jot down notes for it. It would tell the story of a young man's odyssey and would be peopled by all the men and women of his childhood; especially, it would be about his family, would give voice to all the yearnings, despairs and wonder at being a mother's and a father's son. It may be that Aline's experience with psychoanalysis prompted Tom's interest in mining his own unconscious. Perhaps, by putting his experience on paper, he could better understand the man who had been shaped by heredity and environment into the person he was.

As Aline cheered these ambitions on, and cared for him and cooked for him—"Why do you take lunch with me nine days a week?" he asked her one day with a grin—he grew more and more dependent on her. Had they been more prophetic and less blinded by love, they might have recognized this as ominous. They might have seen that the very story he would write, the story of his struggle to break free of dependency, was playing itself out in their life together. Her nurturing sustained him, but could it not also alarm him? Had she loved him less well, would he have caused her less eventual pain? For the time being, at any rate, nothing less than every scrap of Aline's concentration was enough to satisfy his hunger, though in retrospect he would write that even in their earliest days together, there was destruction in him, "for what he loved and got his hands upon, he squeezed dry, and it could not be otherwise with him. It was something that came from nature, from memory, from inheritance . . . that drove him forever and that he could not help."

But in real life, the tightness of her embrace at first seemed wonderful to them both. They were inextricably involved with one another, in his case almost to the exclusion of anyone else. He grew more arrogant toward his mother and he wrote to his old teacher Mrs. Roberts about his affair, although he might have known she would disapprove, then responded to her disapproval with great rudeness. Yes, he was hers alone now, Aline knew, but again her own appetite hungered for more. She wanted longer stretches of time with her lover—time that was not limited by other demands on her life. She did not regret her decision to maintain the stability of her family, nor would she let her work be affected, but she still yearned to know, however briefly, what it was like to live full days with Tom, never having to follow the commands of a ticking clock. Accordingly, as spring wore on, she thought more and more about another trip to Europe. With Tom.

She had been asked to supervise a production of *The Dybbuk* in England, which gave her a legitimate reason for going abroad. And she knew that Tom wanted desperately to return to Europe. The lure of travel still gripped him, and he also felt, as many young men of his generation did, that it was in Europe that his writing could best be achieved. So a plan took shape in her mind and one afternoon, lying on the sofa on Eighth Street, nestled against his side, she offered him the gift of time. A subsidized year to write his book, free of teaching, with an extended visit to Europe to begin it. They would travel together this summer, sharing all the wonders. And then, when summer ended, although she would leave him, he could, if he wished, remain several weeks more to start seriously on his book.

Tom wept with joy at the offer. What a magnificent, loving, wondrous woman she was. He buried his face in her neck and vowed he would love her forever, be faithful till the day he died. And Aline gave him promises of her own, and it was an interlude tender with feeling, shimmering like a delicate and precious jewel.

Their plan was for Aline to precede him in early June. She had work to do for *The Dybbuk*, and he had to wait for the semester to end officially. He would sail to meet her on June 23. An earlier separation while he went to Asheville only whetted their appetites for each other. Aline wrote him frequently in the brief time he was away, and in one letter she told him she was depositing money for his passage in the safe at the Playhouse, since she would already have left for Europe when he returned to New York. It was a letter that ended with eager projections

149

about their reunion. To soothe his anxiety lest she not miss him enough, she added, "The way I care for you is like a cube root. It just multiplies in every direction."

Soon she was embracing her family in farewell and watching them descend the gangplank. They all took their positions on the dock, where Aline knew they would stand faithfully until the ship pulled out to sea. As she smiled and threw kisses, it was inevitable for her to think back to that frightened day ten months before when she had come to this deck from the arms of a violent stranger and had felt so profoundly dislocated from all that had been her life till then. Yet it had all worked out. She had opened her life to Tom and had managed to keep Theo and Ethel and the children inside it still. She felt strong and protective and sure. The ship was moving slowly out of the harbor, and the breezes cooled her cheeks. She turned and faced the sun, as she sailed to meet her lover.

**II**

She woke up feeling happy, a rush of gladness had come with the opening of her eyes. . . . The casement of her window was open wide onto the small garden, the breeze blew the muslin curtain right into her room and she could see across the road and down the sloping meadow beyond; she could see the lanes and the whitewashed cottages . . . and people beginning their morning work. Clean peace was over everything. She could smell the scent of the clover from the field, and the pinks and roses from the garden, and the air from the wood beside the house, heavy with the odors of earth and wet leaf mold, of ferns and moss and pine. Then her nose was tickled with the smell of breakfast, a magnificent English breakfast, fat, streaky bacon sizzling in the pan, eggs frying, bread toasting over the coals, the thick slices black on the outside and served up dripping with butter.

So Aline Bernstein described the joys of this first summer of her union with Thomas Wolfe. They were sharing a cottage in the lake country which is one of England's most beautiful areas, with its mixture of mountain grandeur and peaceful green valleys and shadowed silver lakes. It was here Aline and Tom had come after weeks of touring, at the suggestion of one of Aline's British literary colleagues. When he'd learned that Aline's young friend was a writer, anxious to begin his first novel, he'd sung the praises of Lake Windermere and the county of Westmorland. The gentle landscape was perfect for the creative spirit, he'd told them.

Aline and Tom were not disappointed. The countryside delighted them, and the little cottage they rented on a hilltop outside the village of Ambleside was to Aline the most beautiful of all possible dwellings —a sweetly simple setting for the precious intimacy of love shared all day and all night. Her mind was crowded with pictures of this trip together—of the day at Bath when they walked in the rain, cleansed of all problems by the misty, rhythmically falling drops; of the way he had held her hand and led her silently down the nave at Chartres until they stood under the great rose window, and Tom had pulled her close and declared his love to be as majestic as this cathedral. But no remembered scenes were as lovely as those of Ambleside.

Aline stretched in her bed, luxuriating in the glow that suffused her and in the knowledge that this day would be as wonderful and rich as yesterday and the day before that and the day before that. She listened intently for sounds from Tom's room, but there were none. They had separate bedrooms, partly out of respect for the woman who had rented them the cottage and was preparing their meals and had clearly wondered about their relationship, but also because Tom's writing habits were erratic and she, despite her love, still treasured privacy. But the bedrooms were adjacent to each other and so Aline was able to see his shadow on the apple tree that stood in the garden long after they had parted, she to sleep, he to work, for it was his custom to write late into the nights. Watching him work had always been thrilling for Aline, but her earlier pleasure was nothing to what it was now. For he had actually begun work on his book.

There was already a proprietary edge to Aline's involvement with this book. Much later, when Tom would lose heart and want to abandon the novel, she would furiously insist that he had no right to do that to her, that it was, in fact, her book. Wolfe described the scene after he had hurled the hated pages at a closet in their New York apartment. She "darts into the closet and comes out clutching a battered fragment to her breast . . . she hugs the whole confused mass of it to her, weeping, saying, 'You had no right to do it! . . . It's MINE! . . . MINE! . . . MINE!' "

On a day washed by a recent rain, they had sprawled on a woody hillside near their house, she sketching in her drawing pad, and he brooding over the empty pages of the big red ledger she had bought for him in London. Her own absorption and poor hearing made her unconscious of the fact that he had begun to put pencil to paper, but suddenly she heard him call her name. She looked up quickly and their eyes met and held, so intently that a shiver ran through her body despite the warmth of the day. She knew something portentous was happening and she smiled eagerly, knowing even before he spoke what he would say: that he had indeed begun the novel. And he then declared that this was a turning point in her life as well as his, because he knew for certain now that she was right. He was going to be a great and famous writer, and so no matter what else she did, on her own, with her own talents, she would be remembered by the world because of her union with Thomas Wolfe. He would see to it that his mistress and muse was forever "entombed in his work."

That night they stayed even longer than usual at their favorite pub, whose ancient sign showed in faded carving shepherds and dogs resting after a day in the fields. Inside the pub, time might have stopped forever: the same ruddy country faces lined the table, the same faithful dogs lay at their masters' feet. To Aline's imperfect ears, the local speech produced a mellow, softly rumbling sound that made her feel drowsily content. Tom would grow boisterous with the men, and she enjoyed seeing him so flushed and happy, but a small twinge of fear sometimes made itself felt; she worried about his drinking. All his life, like his father, W.O., Thomas Wolfe unsteadily walked the line that separates the heavy drinker from the obsessive one. His drinking in the pub was good-humored and companionable, but she had seen other modes of drinking, and their aftermath. When he drank out of shyness or anxiety, he could turn violently belligerent and would attack both friend and perceived enemy. So far she had been witness rather than victim of such attacks, but she took small comfort from this, knowing full well that the situation could change drastically.

These thoughts clouded her mind as she lay in bed, and she sat up quickly so as not to let her mood be spoiled. After all, so far there was no real problem. Tom was devoted to her, and he was working very seriously despite his hours at the pub. Only last night she had been lulled to sleep by watching his shadow come and go on the tree as he paced his room. It was like being rocked by him, as he drifted back and forth in her vision, and it had sent her to sleep smilingly content. No, she would not allow this day to be spoiled; there were too few of them left.

She decided not to wait for him for breakfast. Lord knew how late he'd been up working; he might very well sleep most of the day away. And there was nothing like a fine breakfast to restore her good spirits. She quickly ran a cold bath. She loved taking showers and baths as cold as she could stand them, so that her whole body tingled and glowed, and the rosy coloring that people always noted when they met her, and remembered when they summoned up her image, was in part due to this bracing ritual.

Within minutes, she was in and out of the tub. She drew on a simple dressing gown, then ran downstairs to the sitting room, where they always breakfasted under a big bay window that captured the morning sun. Her landlady was in a hurry and was distressed about having to serve separate breakfasts, but Aline assured her that she would take care of Tom's breakfast herself. She also offered to help make over a bonnet to be worn that afternoon to a church tea and cake sale. While the landlady at Aline's direction went off looking for something that might do for a trimming—"Surely you'll find a feather or fabric flower somewhere in the house"—Aline proceeded to savor every taste and texture of her breakfast.

She ate with deliberate slowness. If he wasn't awake when she finished breakfast, she'd take her sketch pad outside alone but stay close to the house so that he could see her when he looked out the window. The light was so fine today, any spot must be rich in possibilities. Maybe later in the day, they'd go to the church tea themselves, dressing up like country gentry. She smiled at the image, and looked happily at her plate. She had eaten nearly everything—the eggs and bacon and half a pot of marmalade. Only one piece of toast was left, and it tempted her by its slightly burned edge and soft buttery center. She was putting on weight from all this indolent living, but no matter; there would be time to take it off when she went back to her normal routine.

Again she felt a flicker of sadness. Soon she would indeed be back in old routines . . . soon she would feel the pressures of multiple worlds and lives. She sighed and concentrated on the taste of the toast, took another sip of the hot, aromatic tea and once more willed herself to live now, in this moment only.

When her landlady returned with the rose she'd been able to find, Aline exclaimed in delight.

"I'll be right down with my sewing things," she said, and scampered upstairs, moving quietly past Tom's door. She dressed quickly in skirt and sweater, and the English walking shoes she loved dearly. But as she came back down the steps, a nail punctured the heel. Now she would have to visit the cobbler before taking her sketch pad out. Well, no matter. She enjoyed walking through the village, especially in the mornings when everyone was busy buying food for lunch and dinner, and children were going to school. Before she went into Ambleside, she sewed the rose on the hat, placing it so that the stem nodded gently as its wearer walked. Her landlady was delighted, watching her reflection in the hall mirror as she paced back and forth, growing more elegant by the minute. Aline beamed and hugged her close, and started out for the cobbler's shop, whistling a tune her father used to sing when they went for walks together.

The shop itself was a dark little room behind the grocer's store, and the cobbler a young man without a single tooth in his mouth. Nevertheless, he spoke continuously to all his customers. Aline tried hard to grasp what he was saying, but after a while she grew impatient to be outside in the sunlight and hurried him along.

Outdoors again, she breathed deeply of the sweet-smelling air, grateful to be out of the musty little shop and on her way back to Tom. She hoped he was awake; she felt a sudden urgency to see him, and she jiggled her foot restively while she waited for the automobiles and wagons to pass so that she might cross the little winding street. Suddenly a magnificent and unlikely vehicle appeared—a chauffeur-driven, deep-blue Rolls-Royce. And then she was truly startled: seated in the back of the car were Theresa Helburn and her husband. Aline's hand flew to her heart in surprise and she shouted to her friends at the very moment when they caught sight of her and called to their driver to stop.

How they laughed and hugged each other, standing in the little street while curious villagers passed and stared at the beautiful car and the fine folk in it. The Helburns had arrived in Ambleside the night before, hoping to find her although they didn't have her address. Now, although they were in a hurry to move on (they had business in Ireland and Scotland), they agreed, happily, to stay over for a few hours. Aline was bubbling with details of her life here, her cottage and her garden, and the butcher shop where all the ladies gathered every morning. Theresa listened smiling, and then took her friend's hand. She would

155

love to see it all, she said, but she had really come to see Aline's face. Theresa Helburn had become Aline's confidante—Aline had recently decided to share her thoughts and feelings with someone besides Dr. Hinkle—and now, on the street corner in Ambleside, holding Aline's hand, she asked, "Dear . . . are you really as happy as your face says you are?" And Aline looked at her friend and said only, "Yes." For what words could possibly convey her feelings? Indeed, she felt so much, saw so much, knew so much, to be unable to encompass it all in words was often unbearably frustrating.

The Helburns agreed to stay for lunch if that was what Aline wanted and, said Theresa slowly, "if it is perfectly all right with 'everybody.' " Aline assured her it was, but as she climbed into the grand car with them and directed the driver to her house, she began to worry. Tom's ambivalence toward her friends was a continuing problem; his suspicion that they did not take him seriously too often unleashed his dark demons.

As they turned into her road, she caught sight of him, leaning out the upstairs window, smoking a cigarette, obviously looking to see if she was coming. She would often find him there when she came back from marketing in the morning; he'd told her he loved the way the market basket swung in her hands as she hurried along the path. Undoubtedly this was what he expected to see now, and instead, here she was arriving in a big car with two strangers, although he'd met Theresa briefly in New York. Aline's hands trembled as she reached out to him after he had come downstairs to greet them all. To her relief, he was, after a moment that only she could interpret as troubled, warm and pleasant. He was clearly and boyishly delighted by the sight of the big car and the invitation to go for a ride in it. The Helburns wanted to see the countryside and Aline wanted to show it to them. While Tom dressed, she took them for a walk, pointing out their pub and the fields near the house where the mowing machine rested and the sunlight fell so beautifully on the stacks of hay.

Back at the cottage, she ran upstairs to help Tom find the blue shirt he was calling for, and to kiss him tenderly so that he would know he mattered most of all. By one o'clock, they were ready to be off. She sat in back with her friends and he, at his request, sat up front with the chauffeur while the big car made the land seem like a smooth cloth unfolding beneath them.

Aline would later write that this day was "perfect"—perhaps the single most perfect of all her days with Thomas Wolfe. Its "incidents were so clear, so beautifully placed in the hours, it was like one of those primitive paintings where the progress of the life of a saint is shown with all the poignant details; it was like a tapestry, or a fine piece of storied embroidery." And she wrote also that she had wished it were possible to "sew the story of that day, with high-colored silks, stitching its calm and glowing beauty into strong linen," so that perhaps, centuries later, somebody could find it in a "lumbered attic," and would be moved by its glowing amplification of the embroidered title, "A Day in the Lakes."

They lunched at Windermere in an ancient inn—cold meats and salad and gooseberry tart—and while the food was not inspiring, Aline remembered, "there were Gloire de Dijon roses in a Lowestoft bowl on the table," and they sat on "old wheelback Windsor chairs, and the glorious ale frothed in old pewter mugs," while "Lake Windermere spread like watered silk" before their eyes. After lunch, they drove and drove and drove, warmed by the sun and the beer and their shared good humor. They visited tiny villages and went up and down valleys, and turned suddenly into glimpses of silvery sweet lakes. The Helburns were having a wonderful time and did not want to leave, and so they stopped once more, at Grasmere to see Wordsworth's Dove Cottage, and, in an adjoining tearoom, had another meal together.

If lunch had been gastronomically disappointing, tea was sublime. Indeed, Aline's favorite meal in England, besides breakfast, was tea. As she wrote:

> Tea is a wonderful meal, when it is a meal and not just something to fill in that lonely five o'clock hour, or to use as an excuse for a chat. It is a wonderful meal when it has a clean, white cloth spread on the table, and there are pots of jam, and jugs of cream, and different sorts of buns, and toast and thin bread and butter, and seed cakes and raisin cakes.

But tea was particularly delightful when, she explained:

> You know you don't have to save up any of your appetite and hurry home to a big dinner and the theater, only a bit of supper in the sitting room just when you feel like it. You can sit out of doors in the long twilight evening, hours and hours of it, at ten o'clock there is still light in the sky. . . . You feel a quiet to it that you never felt before at home. It might not be a life for one always, but it is a wonderful life to know; tea, and a long northern evening, a glass of beer at the pub, your supper and your book, and a sweet sleep knowing the strong old roof is over you, and your love is resting near.

They were gluttonous, all of them, and ordered everything on the menu, and ate every crumb. They talked lazily but passionately about poetry and poets, about the beautiful countryside, and about the wonder of perceiving life through the "divine awareness" of the artist. Aline looked at Tom across the table and knew that this awareness, this creative fire, kindled his spirit, and she wondered if these dear friends of hers were able to understand and see it, as she did, in his face. She studied all his features: the wide forehead, the eyes whose deep brown could suddenly turn cold and frightening in their flatness. She looked at his mouth, which she loved most of all, for it "held the look and the promise of all his passions, all his violence, all the voracious appetites that fed his mighty nature, and all his beauty and sweetness as well."

She thought to herself that she had seen this face in all its phases: ugly with rage and bitterness, gentle with love and peace. She had watched his face in sleep, and seen it twitch with nightmare. And she "had seen it suddenly come alive, sparkling as it looked now, made glorious by the intense light of his genius." Looking at him over the quiet tea table, she thought his genius made him like a lamp that burned so brightly it might, indeed, blind her. But this thought excited her, exhilarated her, made her proud rather than fearful, so that when at last, as the shadows grew longer behind Wordsworth's cottage, and the steeple of the village church threw its long silhouette across the lawn, and they made a move to leave, she rejoiced that she was going home with Tom and not off with these dearest of friends.

They were all quiet in the car going back, at peace with the day and with themselves. Tom was warm in farewell, but he hurried into the house while Aline stayed to watch the car disappear down the road. She would be meeting the Helburns again in a few weeks, for they had arranged to take the same steamer back to New York, and she knew she would need Theresa to help build the bridge back into her other life. Again she tried to push that life from her thoughts, and she lingered awhile in the garden before going to Tom, deliberately wanting to weave every flower, every shadow, everything from this special day, into her tapestry. When she finally did turn to enter the house, she knew she was again "empty of everyone but him."

Inside, she stood in the downstairs hall and silently embraced the stone and oak and glass and casements that, for so many hundreds of years and for so many people, personified "home." "Yes," she mused, "that is what all these separate concrete things spell when they are joined together," just as Tom and she together formed and defined in the most special way the word "love." And then she thought that it didn't matter how long this interlude lasted—it existed now, just as the cottage did, completely and purely. If she and Tom were suddenly frozen into stillness, "like the sculptured figures on a Grecian urn; love, as they had lived it, had come to life, was forever part of the reality of the world."

At peace, she climbed the stairs, and seeing his door closed, went into her own room to wash and change to something soft and silken for a night at home. After a while, though, she grew alarmed at the silence of the house. Unreasonable fear gripped her: he had gone, left her alone. She moved quickly to his room—to find him lying face down in bed. Her peace returned, and she quietly drew a chair to his bedside, content to sit there and look at him, and wait till he wanted to speak.

But abruptly he turned and clutched her hands, pulling her to him. He had been crying. He was still crying. It was the first time she had ever seen him cry, and she was overcome with compassion. She begged him to tell her what was wrong.

"You love those people more than you love me. You want to leave me and go back to your work, to your fine, successful friends. Dearest," he pleaded, holding her so tightly she could scarcely breathe, "don't ever leave me, stay with me, love me forever."

Gratefully, passionately, Aline swore she would never leave him. As she assured him of her eternal devotion, she could not know that the tears in their future would be not his but hers. She knew only, and would say without shame forever, that this was the happiest moment of her life. For however much she hated for him to hurt in any way, his tears gave witness to how deeply he loved her.

The remainder of their days in Ambleside were beautiful, and it was wrenchingly painful to leave the gentle town. But Aline had business to do in Glasgow and London before she left for home on August 19. Whenever possible, she urged Tom to go to her appointments with her, but more often than not he preferred to wait for her, writing in their rooms, or to meet her somewhere later on. Resentment and shyness kept him from tolerating being "taken along" to her important friends. When she went to meet the one artist he respected more than any other, James Joyce, in order to bring Joyce his royalties in American dollars from the Playhouse production of *Exiles,* she arranged to have Tom call for her, but the actual presence of the master was too much

159

for the young writer. He could only hang back shyly and silently extend his hand in greeting. Aline found this timidity touching, and she hugged him close when they were alone, tenderly assuring him that he would one day be every bit as known and accomplished as James Joyce.

As the time for her to leave drew closer, Aline's spirit crumpled. All her plans to nurture Tom's talent so that he would indeed achieve the stature of Joyce, to sacrifice her emotional needs for his creative ones, seemed to disappear in the face of the fact that they would soon be separated. With all her capacity for imagination, she had not been able to anticipate how acutely painful that separation would be.

The final days in London were particularly bad; her tears spilled over at the slightest provocation. And she was provoked frequently by Wolfe. He welcomed the freedom to write undisturbed, but he resented her leaving him alone. This ambivalence made him frequently and irrationally abusive. That she was going home "on schedule" enraged him. That she continued to keep their bond "in its place" and— more or less—"a secret" induced his open contempt. At dinner one night, the tension between them was so terrible that her weeping became uncontrollable. While other diners cast uncomfortable and disapproving glances in their direction, Aline gestured helplessly to Tom and rose from the table. As they left the restaurant, he informed her that she was ugly, that her nose was "big and red," and she hid her face against a wall until she was calm enough to take a taxi back to the hotel. Once there, Tom, tranquil now, loving now, begged her forgiveness and comforted her to sleep.

Finally, no matter how she willed the day not to come, it was time to leave. At the last possible moment, Aline tore herself from Tom's arms at the railroad station and boarded the boat train to Southampton. Only the pain showing so fiercely in his face eased her own torment. He did love her. He did want her always. He would be faithful to her. He would come back to her.

Aboard ship, Aline sat for hours at a time in a deck chair pulled into a quiet corner, looking out at the empty, rolling sea. She felt as if she were bleeding and that the wound would never heal. She struggled to regain her spirits, to join the Helburns and the other passengers in shipboard amusements. But pain was eroding her always indomitable nature, and that fact was in some ways more frightening than the suffering itself. She poured out her pain on paper, beginning the barrage of letters that would define this time: "In a way, my entire mental attitude has undergone a change. I have never before felt jealous or doubtful . . . but now when I think of you, possibly in an intimate relation with another woman, it is torture." Or: "Forgive me for being this way. I thought I was the strongest woman in the world."

The only thoughts she could concentrate on, that eased the hurt, had to do with work. She wanted to be busy every minute when she arrived home, and she welcomed the fact that her schedule was already quite full. She wanted to work so hard that she would not mark the passing of the hours, or know when day's end signaled the aching recall of those shared "green and silver" twilights of Ambleside. She would work until, despite her weariness and sadness, she would be able to "summon an idea, a vision of pristine freshness . . . strike a vein of gold." And she was confident that she could, for it had happened time after time, if not as often as she would have wished, "often enough to give her faith in her spirit."

Yes, she must look ahead, to who she was and could still be. Otherwise, she feared, she would spend her time only hurting, "wishing back years that had rounded themselves out and passed into limbo."

In truth, Aline, to her own surprise, was increasingly conscious that the decades separating Tom's life from hers could not be wished away. Although she still felt powerful and beautiful, the twenty-year difference between them seemed a wide, wide chasm that defied even her certainty that she would love him unchangingly all the rest of her life. These concerns about her age were exacerbated by Tom's recent insistence that she leave Theo and marry him. No matter how she protested that it would not work out because of the difference in their ages, he refused to accept that as her true reason. After all, hadn't he told her many times how much he loved every line on her face, that he no longer thought of young girls, that he was born "with an autumnal heart," and that in her he found a timelessness profoundly powerful. "For me," he would say, you are "timeless, the harvest of all desire."

No, he didn't believe it was her age that kept her at home with her husband. It wasn't because she feared what the homely bonds of marriage would do to their lives as she grew into old age and he remained a relatively young man. Tom was, instead, convinced that it was the opulence of her role as Mrs. Theodore Bernstein that kept her playing the part—as well as a deeper commitment to her marriage than she would ever confess to him. He felt dallied with and was tormented by the idea that she would soon tire of him and move on to a new young playmate. Once a New York colleague of Aline's had commented that "she likes young men," and the phrase came back to mock him over and over again, even though Aline had repeatedly and tearfully assured him that it had been the meaningless, malicious jibe of a competitor.

Aline had realized during their recent months together that these anxieties about the depth of her devotion intensified Tom's own maliciousness. For if Aline's Jewishness ran through her "like a vein of gold," Thomas Wolfe's anti-Semitism coursed through him like a dank, festering stream. That Aline was Jewish had always delighted Tom; it was glamorous, exotic, exciting. But she knew that he also had brought to New York from his Southern town and his bigoted mother a view of Jews as repellent, avaricious and even dangerous.

Aline had managed to deal with this ambivalence. When he tenderly called her "my Jew," as he so often did, she tried to hear only the affection and not the hint of insult. But too often, in the last days in London, as his panic about her going home increased, insult was inescapably there. He shouted that she was going home only because of the money that was to be found there. "You are a Jew and like success . . . and success and I are strangers."

Tom Wolfe loved Aline's elegance and lavishness; he even praised the perfection of Theo's haberdashery. Jews knew how to "enjoy money," and to someone bred in Julia Wolfe's atmosphere of arid miserliness, that flair was captivating and enviable. But nonetheless he still feared and was contemptuous of Jews as people. And if it was some kind of victory to have taken an exotic, sensual woman from one of New York's princes, he could not help but wonder, particularly when he was upset and alone, what fearful damage she would do to him "in the name of her race." There is a passage in *The Web and the Rock* that records this perverse vision of love with Aline:

> When she had gone . . . the dark and fatal light of absence . . . menaced with its thousand intangible treacheries, fell upon her, and the . . . light of servitude, possession, and health . . . vanished utterly. Fixed in an arrogant power, her face as he saw it then flamed like a strange and opulent jewel . . . he saw a dark regiment of Jewish women in their lavish beauty, their faces melting into honey, their eyes glowing, their breasts like melons. Swathed in power and wealth, he saw their proud bodies opulently gowned and flashing with the somber fire of ancient jewels. . . . They were the living rack on which the trembling back of all their

Christian lovers had been broken, the living cross on which the flesh and marrow of Christian men had been crucified.

As she sailed farther and farther away from Tom, Aline tried to believe that her absence would not intensify these hideous fears and feelings in her lover. She recalled the night she had lain by his side in England and had suddenly known a hollow and aching sense of impending doom—so real that she dared not reach out and touch his face for fear of his response. But then he awoke and she was able to lose her anxiety in his evident love for her. Now there would be no such moments or reality to bridge her fantasied terrors, and she was deeply frightened of what would happen.

So great was her fear that almost immediately upon arriving home she wired him: "Arrived—pain worse—leave—" But although Tom had already written her a self-pitying letter predicting she would soon forget him— "I shall make fainter and fainter music. . . . I am really sure that my charm is not so conspicuous that it may not be bettered"—his response to her cable was measured and even annoyed. He took issue with its peremptory tone after first picking it apart as he would have done a student theme: "I could not construe 'leave;' I did not know whether you were leaving or . . . asking me to leave. . . . But if you were asking me to come back now, why didn't you say, 'come'?" After this he made it very clear that while he loved her, her demand that he come back was "not quite playing the game."

The criticism struck home, and Aline applied it now to other aspects of her life. To her family, for example. She knew they had sensed that her homecoming was not as joyous for her as it was for them, and once again she felt frightened because her sense of loyalty and fair play was being tampered with, by herself. The erosion of spirit she had been aware of on the boat was continuing and she felt she was embarking on a long personal battle. The strong, resolute, autonomous Aline was being displaced by a raw new Aline, stripped of all attributes except those called into being by Thomas Wolfe.

On Labor Day, she wrote him that "Tomorrow will be three weeks since I left. I feel as though I have passed an ordeal of fire. I feel absolutely burned clean." If such statements affirmed the purity of her love, she knew they also implied that her defenses of forty-five years were being taken from her. As she sat at her desk, she was determined not to let them go entirely. She sat thinking for a long while, listening to her family in the kitchen busily preparing a Labor Day picnic. With a firm shake of her head, she rose, gave her letter to a servant to mail, and joined Theo and the children and Ethel in the kitchen. As she passed, Theo looked up from the basket he was carefully packing and gently touched her cheek as if to ask if she was feeling better, although no one had suggested she was troubled by anything more than the fatigue of a long trip. His concern touched her so that she felt a new flood of tears rise in her throat and only the awareness that she had no right to such an indulgence gave her the strength to turn the tide back, to smile and take Theo's hand again to her face, to her lips.

Soon they were climbing together into the family limousine, and she could smell the tantalizing fragrance from the baskets, filled with superb examples of Ethel's cooking. She herself had done pitifully little for this particular picnic, something which she vowed silently would not happen again.

As they drove out to Westchester, it was impossible not to remember that wonderful day of driving through the lake country. But as she had done then, she willed herself to put the past aside, except for the past shared with this family. Together they were a force no outside person or event had ever been able to shake. And as she began to tell them an anecdote of her trip, touched deeply by their eagerness to have her really with them in spirit, she prayed fervently that this truth of their life together would continue to be inviolate no matter what private pain she must endure.

# 12

abor Day was several days gone and the summer was officially over. Aline had sent the children's old nursemaid, who still did odd jobs for the family, down to the loft to clean it out. It didn't take Aline's fertile imagination to picture the shape Tom had left the place in when he took off for Europe. She knew very well he had simply closed the door behind him without a thought of the decay and odors that would accumulate during the summer months. His capacity for disorder was staggering, and it often amazed her that her normally fastidious nature wasn't offended by his disgusting personal habits. Of course, she knew they weren't willful. He was simply incapable of paying attention to the minutiae of daily living. Many critics of Wolfe would later agree that only when Aline was around to take care of him was he able to live at all wholesomely.

Tom's dependence on her for "wholesomeness" contributed to her sense of herself as a nurturing figure. In many ways it was easier to be a surrogate mother, whether to Tom or to the countless young men and women she gave so much time to in and out of the theater, than it had been to mother her real children. For this chosen role was one she had more control over. But as she walked along Eighth Street in the early September morning, she was not analyzing herself. Instead, she was wondering how it would be to work in the loft alone. Would it help her or would it interfere to have traces of him around her, knowing that they were all she could have right now?

Hurrying up the stairs, she felt the old lift to her spirits, and she was struck by the intricacy of human responses. For she was responding from the past, feeling again what she had felt each time she ran up these stairs to join him, kiss him, hug him. And then, even though her mind knew what she would find, when she opened the door and saw no one, only that huge space, her spirits plummeted so sharply that she gasped for breath. The summer's recent intimacy only accentuated the emptiness of her heart. She had grown so used to his presence, feasted on it so, that it was deeply painful to be robbed of it completely, especially in this place where they had first been truly together.

Only that morning she had written in her daily letter: "You cannot imagine how I want to talk to you . . ." and had gone on to tell him how glorious their shared summer had been for her and how horrible it was to be bereft of that communion.

She went to the closet and saw his blue suit hanging there, and she took the jacket down and wrapped it around her, inhaling the stale tobacco smell that even careful cleaning couldn't get rid of. God! How she missed him! She went into the kitchen, tears streaming down her face, and opened up the cupboards, looking at the china and pots and pans Margaret had carefully washed and stacked for future use. She put some water on for tea, and stood there fondling a favorite cup, remembering how many times she had placed it alongside its matching plate on the table where she and Tom ate. Inside her head, Tom's face lit up more brightly than ever; she saw his hair and eyes, and his mouth smiling that foolish eager grin as he urged her on with the cooking, sniffing loudly and moaning that she was torturing him by making him wait.

For a long while she sat at the table sipping her tea, and then, with a great effort of will, put memory aside. She went to her drawing board and began to work. And soon she was blessedly absorbed in "doing her job," with all the solid satisfaction that it had always brought her.

Three projects were occupying her attention. For the Playhouse, *The Lion Tamer*, by Alfred Savoir. Joseph Wood Krutch, reviewing it in *The*

*Nation,* would point out that its stage design and acting clearly demonstrated how profoundly the Neighborhood Playhouse understood that "a role is something to be created by a mind which uses the body as a sculptor uses clay." Uptown at the Booth Theater in October, her sets and costumes would enhance *White Wings,* a new Philip Barry play, on which Tom had already focused his jealousy, accusing her of being two-faced in her enthusiasm for what was wholly a commercial project. His demeaning words still burned in her mind, even as she went on with her designs—designs, Tom had sneered, that she "dispraised" to him, but that were in reality part of her ongoing, predominant activity, "making obeisances to fame."

Perhaps the major undertaking of the three was the Theatre Guild production of *Ned McCobb's Daughter,* by Sidney Howard. It would open at the Golden Theater November 22, starring Alfred Lunt, and featuring Morris Carnovsky and Margalo Gillmore. The sets for this play still appear in anthologies of stage design, and Aline felt the special tension of a more than ordinary challenge as she worked on them. Perhaps the play's subject matter—the evils of prohibition—engaged her, since she deplored the fact that you couldn't get a decent bottle of whiskey in New York even through a bootlegger, and if you did, it cost you fifteen dollars. She wrote to Tom often on the subject, and worried a lot about his not being able to get liquor easily when he came home. While she certainly would have welcomed an end to his drinking, she knew how much enforced abstinence would enrage him.

Howard's play was set on the Maine coast and called for two principal sets: Carrie's Spa, a run-down eating place next to the ferry terminus, where Carrie, the "icily competent daughter of Maine," worked, and the living room of Carrie's father, Ned McCobb. Alfred Lunt, who played the bootlegger brother-in-law, remembered Aline as having "exquisite taste," but clearly considered it exquisite because it completely met the needs of the story. The very construction of the set for Carrie's Spa seemed temporary, as if it had been carelessly tacked on to the main ferry building, and Aline scoured the city to collect the props that would convey Carrie McCobb's random, amateurish attempts at decorating. In contrast, her specifications for the living room provided an aura of stability through big, solid pieces of furniture and dark woodwork. And although Ned McCobb had long since retired from the sea, she placed several nautical mementos in the room to establish the significance of his old career. No one who saw the sets and costumes, whether in rehearsal or at a performance, failed to recognize that the power of Sidney Howard's play was greatly heightened by Aline Bernstein's designs.

These designs were being worked out at the Neighborhood or at home as fall took hold. It had turned out to be simply too painful to continue working at the loft. She'd found herself jumping at the faintest sounds, foolishly imagining that if she turned her head, she'd find Tom there, smiling at her. The old sofa looked primly back at her, and she would find herself walking over to it and running her hands across its worn, soft fabric. And so she let Alice Beer, who was between apartments, take over the loft until the lease ran out in late fall. By that time, she hoped, Tom would be back, but it was Aline's plan to find him a larger place, with separate rooms for each of them, because he would probably want more privacy to work on his book.

Her letters were as filled with plans for his future as they were with the stuff of her own inner and outer lives. She wrote him faithfully, and sometimes frantically. A soothing note, light-hearted and gay, would be followed, perhaps even the same day, by a deep sigh of longing, and a plea that he follow their original plan of a six-week absence and come back to her. His own swings of mood, of course, continued. Cries of loneliness and his fear of losing her would be followed by abusive spasms of distrust and free-floating rage.

Aline's genuine wish for his success and happiness clashed with her need of him and with the persistent whisper inside her head that if he really loved her, he would want to be with her: he would dismiss the foolish conviction that he wrote better in Europe and do his writing where they could be together. She tried very hard to keep these thoughts from him. They were unfair to his talents, and to her promise and her own integrity. Yet they would creep into her letters in spite of her, and the cycle of her hurt, recrimination and apology would begin again.

In between the extremes of feeling, they continued to report the details of their daily lives, each of them believing that here was the person who could really grasp, as no other could, the nuances of the other's individual experience. This was especially so for Tom as he traveled alone, feeling himself "a phantom in a world of people, or the only person in a world of phantoms" and convinced that Aline was "the only person who seems to me to have flesh and blood substance. . . . I want you to understand that I am living in a mighty dream, where I wander about, extensively examine everything, and find everything unreal."

The need to "wander about" was still strong, and by mid September he had already left his rented flat in London for a two-week sightseeing trip to Belgium. It was on a sightseeing bus, from Brussels to Waterloo, that he saw James Joyce again, traveling with his family for the purpose, as it turned out, of collecting material for *Finnegans Wake*. Tom was still too shy to talk to Joyce, but he scribbled furiously in one of the notebooks he always carried with him now, and later that night transcribed every word into a long letter to Aline. The letter ends rather wistfully with the thought that by the time she received it, he would be twenty-six years old. And when he returned to London in time for his birthday, there was a letter from Aline which had crossed his own, recalling with great tenderness his birthday the year before, when she had stood waiting for him on the steps of the library, and he told her how "swell" she looked in brown. "I can't believe it was only a year ago," she wrote. "You have come into that year and expanded it to four times its size!" Both lovers had clearly invested Wolfe's birthday with extravagant importance, for there was still another flurry of letters around the event. They saw fit to tell each other how they had marked the day. Aline had literally declared it a holiday, not going to her office and not even working at home. As important as her work was to her, she felt the need to acknowledge Tom's preeminence by giving herself over to lonely celebration. So, she reported to Tom, she took a long walk around the city, which had now, in early October, "reached the bronze age." She came home to lunch by herself, and indeed, left most of the meal untouched—one of the few times in her life when her appetite failed her. In general, she seemed to have lost her taste for meat and was mostly eating vegetables and drinking milk. She'd lost nearly eight pounds since returning from Europe, but while she liked the difference it made in her figure, she lamented the reason. After lunch she left the house again and went to the Eygptian room of the Metropolitan Museum, finding in the ancient statues and artifacts a sense of what Tom would call the "always flowing river of time."

As for Tom, he visited, as dusk fell on London, a favorite Spanish restaurant of theirs. Aline, as she read his letter, could instantly see the small table laden with aromatic rice and meat, and the fragile glasses full of golden sherry which began their meal. Tom reported delightedly that he had ordered sherry in her honor on October 3, asking the waiter to bring two glasses. Since he had said there would be only one for dinner, the waiter was properly confused and asked Tom if he was in fact expecting someone. Wolfe looked at him a moment after pouring wine into the second glass and then said quietly that yes, he was expecting "a ghost. He was so frightened," Tom wrote gleefully, "that he didn't come near me the rest of the time!" Aline smiled tenderly at his exuberance but even more tenderly at his description of lifting his glass to its mate across the table and toasting her missing presence. "You *are* a ghost my dear, that will walk down the passages of my heart as long as I live."

But Aline's joy was short-lived. In his next letter he sneered contemptuously: "You speak grandly of having stayed alone on my birthday. . . . My dear Jew, I stay alone from waking to sleeping to waking. . . . Every damned day through." And continuing to attack her self-imposed (and to him self-congratulatory) isolation, he added: "Of the other days when you jig about wantonly with your retinue, you say nothing."

In fact, she had quite deliberately curtailed her social life since her return. Weekends, she often went to Pleasantville, New York, where Ethel shared a little cottage with a friend from Bergdorf's, and where Helen Arthur, of the Playhouse, also had a house. They were weekends of women being together, respecting each other's need to be quiet, but present for each other when company was wanted. As was her habit, Aline rose early and would take a walk in the clear predawn air. She would sit in the garden watching the sun come up, thinking of how it must be on the other side of the world, and wishing she could reach out to Tom as he worked or slept and describe to him how the birds sounded, how the dew glistened, how the sky looked as night turned into another day.

Theo would generally drive up with Teddy to fetch her on Sunday, and often they would stay and have dinner with Helen Arthur and then drive everyone back to New York.

One weekend when she was feeling particularly grateful for her companions' hospitality, Aline asked Theo to bring up one of her grandmother's huge iron pots, and she and Ethel went to a local farmer and bought some freshly killed chickens. All day long she simmered on Helen's stove a golden, buttery soup with big chunks of white chicken in it and softly green strands of celery huddled next to tapered orange carrots. They sat around the dinner table ladling the soup into deep pottery bowls and breaking off wedges of homemade bread that was too hot and fresh to cut with a knife. The next day she described the meal to Tom and wondered as she wrote whether she was not trying to tempt him to come home.

Meanwhile, her own appetite for work, if not for food, increased. Sometimes she sat at her drawing table till one in the morning; and while she certainly was never too busy to think of Tom at all, he did leave her thoughts for significant stretches of time. Occasionally, in reply to her reports of her progress, he would complain that she was "bragging," and would then launch into his familiar diatribe about the meaninglessness of fame. At the same time, in his equally familiar and paradoxical fashion, he would rage against his own obscurity, filling page after page with self-pity about his thwarted hopes. To this Aline would cable or write fervent reaffirmation of her faith in him and his artistic future. Yet such encouragement often angered him more. He felt pressured by her faith and by his own dependency on it, and he would lash out, ordering her never to say again how wonderful he was, that it was cruel to feed his hopes this way. Of course, Aline's reassurances continued, and there is little doubt that Wolfe drew strength from them and that her resolute faith in his talent at this time contributed significantly to its development. He desperately needed the kind of "love and certitude" she unfailingly brought to him.

But by November Aline was weary of professing her feelings by letter. Tom's habit of leaving London to travel in all directions disturbed her, and she complained angrily that every letter from him seemed to carry a different postmark. She worried about his keeping his promise to be faithful as he wandered around Europe, always meeting new people—even though he continued to swear he was essentially alone and not really interested in being anything else. She worried even more about his writing. Although he was obviously applying himself to his book, her own disciplined habits convinced her he would do better with a regular schedule and consistent working conditions. She sharpened her pleas and commands that he come home, but at the same time she continued to send him money and tender solicitude. Did he want the New York newspapers sent, and did he need some warm clothes for the English chill? Any friend who went to Europe was entrusted with some gift for Tom: a muffler, gloves, new pajamas. She tried also, in her letters, to deflect through humor his recurring personal attacks—to convince him and perhaps herself that he did not really mean the abuse.

When he accused her of being unfaithful, or avaricious, she wrote back that she wished there were a Jewish nunnery she could join. Of course, she added wryly, it would have to be one where they wore "velvet habits, with gold and ivory rosaries, and sleep on the best mattresses—but nuns, nevertheless." Or, after attending a Theatre Guild opening, she reported teasingly that every rich Jew in the city had been in attendance. "You could have made a lovely pogrom—you could have cut all their throats and seen the dollars trickle out!"

Notwithstanding her mocking assessment of a Theatre Guild opening night, the opening of *Ned McCobb* added to her laurels, and her satisfaction was great. There was a particular reason for satisfaction this time —professional recognition in the most concrete terms.

In recent years, as the scenic designer had emerged as a significant contributor to the theater, many of her colleagues had begun to feel the need for some kind of union representation. To Aline, long committed to a belief in unions, the need seemed important and immediate. But it had taken a long time to decide whether the designers should have a separate artists' union, as friends such as Norman Bel Geddes would have liked, or whether they should join an existing crafts union that had been organized before the concept of the designer as artist ever took hold. About two years earlier, word had come down that there would be no artists' union; instead, the designers would be allowed to join the Brotherhood of Painters, Decorators and Paperhangers Local Number 829, of the American Federation of Labor.

However irritating the union's refusal to distinguish artist from craftsman, not to belong to 829 was rapidly becoming a professional handicap. Most of the designers swallowed their annoyance and joined. Not only was the union demanding such rights for designers as full program credit, pay for extra work and permanent ownership of their original designs; it was also enforcing restrictions on what a nonunion designer might do in the theater, making work for the outsider increasingly scarce.

Aline, like her friends, capitulated to the decision and applied for membership. But, to her dismay, her application was turned down. The union's concern for the designer did not extend, it seemed, to the female designer. For two years, Aline had been agitating to batter this resistance down. She enlisted a number of influential friends, in particular producer Gilbert Miller, and a correspondence with union officials, almost as active as hers with Tom, had been continually in progress. When Aline didn't write, Miller did, and together or separately they met with union representatives. Finally, just before leaving for Europe, she had been allowed to take the union examination, and just a few days before the opening of *Ned McCobb*, she received the letter telling her she had passed and would at their next meeting be officially inducted into the brotherhood.

She and Theo lunched with Gilbert Miller that day and Theo toasted his resolute wife and her colleagues, delighting in their victory. The only problem at this celebratory luncheon had to do with induction, which fell on the Bernsteins' anniversary and conflicted with a dinner Theo was planning.

"It's all right," Aline said after a moment's thought. "The meeting's not till later in the evening. I can leave the restaurant and then come back or join everyone later at the apartment, where we can finish up the party!"

The juxtaposition of the elegant Mrs. Bernstein and the painters' and carpenters' union tickled Theo, and so on the night of November 19, 1926, Aline appeared at the union hall with Theo at her side. He had insisted on accompanying her because she was in evening clothes and in the shabby neighborhood where the meeting was held she was certain to be conspicuous. Aline, rosy and golden in her pink and gilt sari, smiled at the doorkeeper and insisted that she was not there by mistake.

"Here," she said sweetly. "I'll show you my credentials," and opening her beaded purse, presented her union card and letter of acceptance. The doorkeeper looked the card over carefully and then, after a long, long moment, swallowed hard, threw open the door and shouted hoarsely to the boisterous, shirtsleeved men inside: "Let's give a welcome to a new member—Brother Bernstein!" Smiling prettily, Aline, with Theo behind her, made her way into the hall and took her seat.

Amusing as the story was when she returned to her party, this was no idle exercise for Aline. Her work on the Lower East Side and her own role in developing the theater as a vocation had convinced her that the welfare of professionals needed the protection of organized labor. That she was the union's first woman member was no small part of her triumph, for she knew she was opening the doors for other women who wanted to be judged by their accomplishments and not by their sex. She was soon to express her hope that the only criteria for membership in this union would be "hard work and talent," and that every man and woman would help one another "earn and maintain a dignified living in this American theater."

For the rest of her life Aline would be a committed union member, serving on committees, staunchly supporting its causes. One of Peggy Murphy's last memories of her employer was hearing Aline, confined to her bed, shout happily to a painter on a scaffold outside her window: "Hey, there . . . you and I are brothers—did you know that? We belong to the same union! How's everything going for you? Do you get to many meetings?" And soon the man had clambered in through the bedroom window and sat down near her bed, and they had become engaged in a conversation more animated than Aline had taken part in for weeks.

Such men were of course old friends to Aline, for in the early days of her union membership, they, not the artists, were still the predominant group in the local. Particularly at the beginning, they were often red-faced with discomfort when she'd slide past them to take her seat in the hall. It was clear they were agonizing over what to do and say. "They treat me with kid gloves," Aline reported to the family, "and they offer me cigarettes and Life Savers and chewing gum at intervals of fifteen seconds just to have something to say!" And then she'd open up her purse and pour out their tokens of friendship, abrim with warm and affectionate laughter. They were tough and often truculent, she'd tell her sophisticated friends, but they respected her courage in joining and they "played fair."

Meanwhile, the postmarks on Tom's letters continued to change. His letters were sporadic—sometimes nothing for days at a time, when her heart filled with fear, and then pages and pages almost bursting their envelopes. One letter took two and a half hours to decipher, so scrawled and overblown was its prose—the result, Aline knew, of too much beer or brandy. When such letters arrived, she would answer cautiously: "My great fear for you always is about drink. But I really do have faith in you there, too. The book is stronger than that and will pull you back."

But God, she would cry to herself, when could *she* pull him back? No matter how many letters piled up from him, even the loving ones were not compensation for his absence. Still, she carried the most ardent in her purse, putting the others in a large wooden box she had bought to hold them, a box with a lock and key. To her chagrin, when she told Tom about the box, even though she made it clear that she always kept the key with her, he flew into a rage. These things "have a way of being found," he told her, and angrily demanded that she burn his letters after reading them. That he was just as likely to grow furious at her insistence on keeping their love affair secret did not seem a contradiction worth bothering with.

174

She was able to accept his outbursts thanks to the same reasoning he would often, if somewhat shamefacedly, offer when they were over. He wanted her to know all of him, all his sides and moods, even the ugly ones. And she, in the name of total union, believed she wanted this too. So she tried to restrain her response, not only to his attacks but to her own growing susceptibility to intemperate emotion. She wanted, as the days of his absence mounted, to howl and scream and demand his return, but she forced herself to hold back, to catch herself before she was swept away by need. Once, after not hearing from him for a while, she went into a Western Union office to send an imploring cable, but the message as she wrote it seemed a long moan of self-pity, "like the wailing woman character in *The Dybbuk*." She was already handing it across the desk to the operator, when reason surfaced and she pulled her hand back.

"I'm sorry," she said quietly. "I've changed my mind." And she turned and walked out into the late-autumn air, and along streets all broken up by excavation for a new subway. Her beloved New York streets were once more being altered by "progress." Although she welcomed growth and change, her heart was saddened when she realized how little remained of the city she had grown up in, and she made an inevitable analogy, as she skirted the rubble, between the city and herself. Tom, she felt, whom she had looked on as a new way of experiencing herself, an ultimate development in her ever developing life, was causing her too much of the time to lose sight of old and important parts of herself. She had never intended to abandon the old Aline, only to expand her. Yet here she was, so often going against her most passionately held beliefs. She, who believed so in love's integrity and generosity, threw herself at him, hung around his neck, made love into a burden. She, who had vowed he "would never feel the weight of my hand upon him," reached out across the ocean in her efforts to control his behavior.

The only saving factor was that she knew that overall her hand steadied him, and clearly, despite his surges of anger, he still frequently acknowledged his need for her. His letters were erratic, but they contained everything he did or thought or felt. He would send her long bulletins about his writing and details of how prolific he was being, down to estimated word counts and projections of when the novel would be finished. The projections varied widely, however, in large part because of his continuing inability to apply the brakes to his prose.

Aline was troubled by this, not because she worried about supporting him for too long, but because she was so anxious to have him reveal his talents to the world, to receive the recognition she knew he deserved. His verbosity would, she felt, not only delay this but might even prevent it. Publishers were not inclined to deal with manuscripts as huge as this one promised to be. She continued, therefore, to encourage him to leaner language, and Tom for the most part took her advice to heart, if not to practice. He was becoming more and more impressed with her own ability to be so "plain" and "straight" and "pungent" on paper. He marveled at her letters in contrast with his own. "Your letters have a beginning, a middle, and an ending," he wrote wonderingly, and went on to further analysis of her writing form. "They do not sprawl, they work up swiftly to a note of passion and decline accurately to one of despair. . . . While I grope darkly about in [my] letters . . . you obtain a sense of form, proportion, perfection of your woe into two-and-a-half pages, and all according to the most approved laws of dramatic and fictional technique." And he added, rather petulantly: "Isn't it queer?" Yet he was not always without humor about his own style. If he were a reporter writing about a crime, he said, the murderer would be in Canada before he'd even mentioned where the body was found!

At last, in November, he wrote the letter she had been waiting for, announcing his intention of coming home. Obviously, staying in Europe was not the answer to finishing his book. On the contrary, he knew he needed her help to do so. "Somehow or other," she must help him finish this task that was dominating his life. He seemed worried that she would withdraw her support, financial and emotional, and Aline quickly cabled him a message of eternal devotion and enough money to pay for his ticket home and another round of touring before he left. She insisted he must not think of going back to teaching, even though he'd been offered a job at N.Y.U. for the spring semester. He might hate her career, but it paid well. Well enough for her to continue supporting him for the year she had promised.

Now all the pent-up feeling of the last few months was released. She discovered new energy and forgotten peaks of joy. She dashed around New York, Gramercy Park, uptown, the Village, trying to find a place they could share, big enough for both to work in and Tom to live in. But she finally had to admit it was a fruitless search. Everything was over-priced or dark or cramped. And so, admitting defeat, she called the Eighth Street landlord and arranged to take the old loft back. She would have preferred more space, but she would make this do, she assured Tom. She promised never to get in his way when he was writing.

The family rejoiced in her new high spirits, without questioning their source, and together they began planning a huge Thanksgiving celebration with several dear friends. She and Ethel left their offices the day before the holiday to go down to the Washington Market, where they bought the biggest turkey they could find. It weighed twenty-three pounds, and they carried it across their laps in the taxi going home and giggled like children at the driver's annoyance with his extra passenger. The Bernstein cook was no less nonplused when she saw them struggle through the kitchen door with the bird.

It looked like an eagle, she told them testily, and she'd never be able to make enough stuffing for such a creature. Aline beamed at her "Cooky" and said of course she would, and what's more, Aline would help. After all, it was more than just a Thanksgiving dinner, although that was always one of the family's happiest feast days. It was also a going-away party for Edla, who would soon be off on a six-week trip with Ethel. The tour was to be a birthday present, and they had all chipped in to arrange it, Aline somehow finding time in her schedule of work, apartment hunting and family life to organize her daughter's wardrobe. Edla, of course, could have anything she wanted from Bergdorf's, but most of the clothes there were too mature, and Aline knew the kind of clothes her daughter looked best in. "I'm going to make some of your dresses myself," she'd told her, and was indeed doing that —mother and daughter getting together at odd hours for fittings, and Aline happily inventing effects that were "just right" for her tall, personable girl. In Europe, Ethel's designer friends would supply endless numbers of escorts, and Edla would be assured nights of dancing and festivity. It made Aline happy just to think of it.

The turkey was a huge success, the chestnut and sage dressing well worth every minute it had taken. The dining room gleamed. A delicate lace cloth covered the table, the brown wood turning the lace warm and creamy beneath the English silver and Dresden plates and pewter bowls. The florist had delivered flowers to Aline's exact specifications, and she'd arranged them in a cut-crystal bowl set in the center of the table, a floral harvest to accompany the harvest of good food and good will.

The dinner was a triumph, from the clear soup that began it to the lemon pie made from the recipe of Aline's childhood. But as soon as

177

dessert was cleared away, she excused herself and went to bed. She had been developing a terrible cold, and her head was beginning to pound with feverish discomfort. If there was any truth to the idea that a sudden chill can cause colds, she knew unhappily where this cold had come from. For on Sunday night she'd gone to bed early and quickly fallen asleep, only to be awakened by a telephone call from Alice Beer, who had gone down to the Playhouse to go over some work and found a cable from Thomas Wolfe for Aline. She thought perhaps Aline might want to know about it before morning. Irritated at her own compulsive behavior, Aline nonetheless dressed and went out into the bitter cold to take a taxi down to Pitt Street. If there was word from him, even the few hours till morning were too long to wait. The cable announced his arrival on December 29, and apologized for a recent ugly letter—a letter Aline had answered with unusual anger, telling him that he too often sounded "wild and nervous," and that sometimes, "weird and terrible things come tumbling from your hand."

She had let herself back into the cozy warmth of her house that night, and found Theo reading in the living room. She was embarrassed to find him there, suddenly feeling shy. He must wonder why she had left so late and come back so quickly—a real production emergency would take much longer to solve. But he said nothing, only asked about the temperature outside and invited her to have a glass of brandy with him. She refused, only because she was suddenly exhausted, but kissed him tenderly on the forehead before saying good night. In her room, she added the cable to the collection in the already crammed wooden box.

She sat on the edge of her bed, looking at all the sheets of paper, thinking what a story they told. Those gargantuan outbursts of temperament were awesome; they thrilled and impressed her even when they appalled her. And it meant so much to her to believe that she could help Tom channel that energy into fruitful rather than destructive activity. How many times had he told her that she "saved him from madness," or that without her, he "hovered on the brink" of destruction. She sighed contentedly; how much better she would be able to help him once he was home again with her.

The next morning she wrote Tom that she would be waiting for him on the dock when he arrived, and would be with him as much as possible during the New Year's holiday, except—and here her letter seems almost to pause for a sharp intake of breath, gain courage and go on—except that on New Year's Eve she would have to be, as always, with her family.

But she assured him quickly that she would try to have him set up in the loft by New Year's Day, and if that happened, she would cook him the most wonderful meal he had ever tasted, and bring the finest champagne she could find, and they would celebrate together the first day in this new year of their reunited lives.

While she went about her work during the next few days, she worried about his response to her New Year's Eve commitment, and when his next letter arrived she tore it open nervously. As she read, she marveled, although unhappily, at the complicated circuits of his mind and prose. He both rejoiced in and reviled her plans for their New Year's feast: "I should like some succulent Jews' food, with melted butter, spices and fragrant sauces." And then, giving way to the anger so often triggered when he felt displaced by her family or vocation, he added that he wouldn't too much count on their dinner together because "you will probably be in the midst of a show, which you will regret, of course, but which you must do, and I will feed as usual upon the crumbs of weary time that fall from the groaning board of art." Aline sighed, and put the letter in her box, and went to work frustrated and discomfited. Left alone, she could manage all the sectors of her life without feeling fragmented, but Tom's persistent competitiveness pulled her apart. At such times, she worried about what would be when he was home. She desperately wanted him with her, but how hard would he make it for her?

Despite her concern, when she awoke on the morning of December 22 and knew it was the day Tom was sailing from England, she jumped out of bed and threw out her arms in joyful welcome. She closed her eyes and visualized his shabby old suitcases, bulging with the manuscript she would now be able to read and talk about with him. And he would tell her all the other things in his life. Perhaps he would let her see some of the daily entries in the notebooks she had introduced him to, which he said were now so essential to all his writing.

Mercifully, she could not see what he was writing in his notebook on shipboard.

"How shall the years pass, Jew," he wrote as he sailed home to Aline. "What rut of life with the Jew now? Is this the beginning or a final ending?"

On December 29, Aline Bernstein left her house at 7 A.M. The street was empty, gray with snow muddied by city dirt. But in her heart it was all virginal, as white as a princess's ermine cloak, and as she rode downtown in a taxi, her New York had never looked so beautiful. Through the windows she passed she could glimpse Christmas trees, their dark green casting shadows against curtains and glass. She could see people moving about, getting breakfast, beginning another day, and she wanted to shout to them that no one in this entire city was going to have a day more magically wonderful than her own.

Reaching the pier, she paid the driver and went out onto the dock. In the distance she could see Tom's liner, the *Majestic*. It had been locked in fog, but was now lumbering its way to shore. Other people were arriving to welcome loved ones of their own. (But did anyone here know love as she did?)

As the ship churned slowly forward, pushed by its tugs, Tom stood on deck, watching the skyline of the city he feared, adored, and felt more a part of each time he left it and experienced the pull to return. And then, as he lowered his eyes and scanned the dock and the crowd—people with sleep still on their faces—he saw, as he had done that first time, Aline's upturned, brightly shining flower face. She was wrapped in fur, and her cheeks were even pinker than usual from the cold morning air as she studied the passengers lining the ship's deck.

She saw him! My God! There he is!

Shrieking his name, she began jumping up and down for joy, then danced back and forth along the dock, skittering to the end and back again to the middle. He roared with laughter, and she could see his grinning face, and her heart all but burst. "Tom, Tom, Tom!" she kept calling, and he waved back and drank her in, and for now at least, ambivalence fled. She was there, his "grey-haired, wide-hipped, timeless mother," the woman he loved beyond anything he could now or ever imagine. And when at last he ran down the gangplank, his large body shouldering past the other passengers, and he scooped her into his arms, they knew again that they had both come home. All that day, until she had to leave him to return to the family, she convinced him through the totality of her passion that the promises of his life would richly and inevitably come true, now that he was back where she could care for him.

# 13

Aline was able to meet Tom after all on New Year's Eve. The family had been invited to so many parties that they decided to split up and go to some separately after their traditional dinner together. Dressed in their most gala clothes, they toasted each other around the dinner table with the finest champagne Theo had been able to buy (for an extravagant price) from Wall Street's principal supplier.

When the equally extravagant meal was completely consumed, they left the softly lit room, gathered in the hallway, put on their coats and scarves and, chattering happily, moved together out the front door.

"Good night, good night, good night . . ." Their voices echoed in the air as they found taxis and kissed each other in temporary farewell, and went their separate ways for a few hours, a tightly knit, loving family of individuals with independent lives. Aline's cabdriver was a good-humored young man who didn't take offense at her urging him to drive faster, even though the streets were filled with revelers. She wanted so much to get to Eighth Street before midnight. Now that she *was* going to be with Tom, she wanted the ceremony of welcoming the New Year together. If some time with him was good, more time, particularly in shared ritual, was even better.

The driver came through with minutes to spare. Aline tipped him lavishly, and her smile was radiant when she clambered out of the back seat and ran into the building. She hurried up the many flights of stairs with the energy of a girl, but before she even reached the top landing, the door was flung open by Tom, resplendent in evening clothes.

"Oh, how handsome you are!" Aline said when she stepped back and looked him up and down. "Come, see how grand we look together," and she pulled him toward the mirror. They stood smiling at each other's reflections for a few minutes. Then Aline shouted, "Quickly! Open the window!" She wanted to hear the bells herald the new year, and she needed the night air to carry the peal to her imperfect ears. The lovers stood there listening to the New Year's music, and Aline told Tom that the bells were for him, for the talent he would surely fulfill this year of 1927. And she said that this city, hers by birth and his by adoption, would one day boast that he had made it his home.

When the chimes stopped, they put on their coats. For some reason, Aline wanted to appear with him in public tonight, and celebrate among handsome and happy friends, and he had agreed to accompany her to a couple of parties. He bowed ceremoniously to her as he opened the door, and she curtsied back, and then skipped down the stairs in front of him, her feet already dancing.

Within minutes they had arrived at the Fine Arts Ball, which was being held in a huge rented hall on Eleventh Street. No sooner had they checked their coats than Aline spread her arms and invited Tom to dance with her. They were, despite her gracefulness, a rather awkward couple, the difference in their heights a problem, and Tom's innate clumsiness ill suited to the waltz. However, he was feeling festive, and he could lose his self-consciousness at such times. For a while, it was evident that he had. They wove in and out among the other couples, many boisterous and obviously drunk, oblivious to the people they were bumping into. Oh my, life was good tonight, Aline thought.

When the orchestra broke off for a rest, Aline led Tom upstairs to a box the Neighborhood Playhouse had taken for its own small party. Many groups had done the same, necessarily bringing in their own liquor, and loud sounds of drunken gaiety rose from every box.

Aline's friends greeted her effusively, cheeks flushed, voices high. Their glasses were filled and Tom could barely keep up with their hospitality, which, for the moment at least, he seemed able to accept and enjoy. People came and went, and Tom was introduced to them all, and when Aline glanced over at him he looked comfortable and as though he was having a good time. She wanted to sing out her own joy, so filled was she with it.

It was somewhat later that a young man, a sometime beau of Edla's, came into the box, cheerfully drunk and expansively affectionate. He started sloppily embracing one after another of the party, egged on by some of them, particularly by the one person Aline had been worried about, Albert Carroll, an actor from the Playhouse who was flamboyantly homosexual and famous for his female impersonations. He was a good friend of Aline's and Ethel's, but Tom hated him. Carroll was to him the epitome of the decadent sophistication of the theatrical "dung heap." Now Aline could see Tom smoldering as he watched the two men playing with each other, and although Tom had smiled with real amusement when Edla's ex-beau had embraced him on meeting, his eyes had grown cold and fierce. The young fellow had turned his attentions to Aline and was babbling about Edla's charms and her own. As she tried nervously to extricate herself, over her shoulder she could see Tom, and she grew cold with anticipatory dread.

The young man's chatter about Edla and his easy intimacy with Aline made Tom's blood boil. He shouted to Aline that she should not allow anyone to speak of her daughter so casually, and should not treat her own body so lightly. When Aline urged him not to get so excited, said no one meant any harm, it was all in fun, his fury mounted. If this was what it meant to be sophisticated, he wanted no part of it. It was corrupt and degrading and vile. He shouted all this as he grabbed the young man by the arm and hurled him into a chair. Around them the conversation stopped. The music still playing below emphasized the silence inside the box. Then, abruptly, the young man pulled himself from the chair and came at Tom.

"Tom, Tom, come with me. . . . Please come with me now," Aline begged. "Let's dance. . . . I want to dance some more." She looked toward her friends for help, and they quickly formed a circle around Tom, trying to keep the two men apart. At that point, he began to bellow obscenities about Aline and her family and friends. God, why won't he stop? Aline cried inside herself, while she continued to plead with him to be quiet, to come with her. Finally, he heard her. Like a puzzled child after a tantrum—why was everyone making such a fuss

183

just because he got a little upset?—he turned to her quizzically, and without another word or backward glance, pushed through the circle and moved after her as she ran downstairs to the dance floor. She didn't look back either—her shame was too great. They had barely reached the bottom of the stairway when he took her arm to dance, but Aline shrugged off his touch.

"I don't want to dance, you fool," she said. "We have to leave." Her voice was more tense than he had ever heard it, and he said nothing more, not wanting to make her angrier. Once outside, the freezing air whipped their faces, and Aline welcomed the chill; her cheeks were burning with embarrassment. She set off down the street, taking quick, almost jumping, steps. There was a terrible pain in the middle of her stomach and her heart was filled with anguish.

Inside the apartment, she began to weep quietly, as if she was immensely weary, even of her own sadness. Tom knelt down beside her, and took her hands in his, and said he was "cut to the heart" by her anger. But his remorse suddenly infuriated her. It was easy to apologize after he had done his filthy damage.

"There was no reason for you to do that," she said. "It was completely unnecessary. He's a lovely young man who adores my daughter and respects me. Your jealousy is insane and destructive."

She wanted no more of his "heroics," she said coldly, and if this was what he was going to be like, they could never go among people again. Tom, though still remorseful, was unimpressed by her scolding. "They can't put their hands on you," he said simply, and then he told Aline that he might indeed have acted badly, but he had acted the only way he could, and she would have to accept his behavior because it was part of him, and she professed to love all of him, didn't she?

It was very difficult for Aline to pretend a holiday spirit when she rejoined her family later that evening. They were drinking a final bottle of champagne in the living room, exchanging reports of their respective parties. Aline said very little. There was not much she could tell them after all, and she only hoped they would never learn the details of this dreadful night. The possibility that Theo or the others might hear some gossip didn't seriously upset her, for the people they knew rarely engaged in such malice. Tom had been accepted until now and could easily continue to be if he acted reasonably—like a gifted younger person she was helping, as she had so many others. If some people were beginning to suspect that the relationship went beyond this, they kept their suspicions to themselves. As Eva Le Gallienne explains: "In those days one was more reticent than one is now—we respected privacy and didn't expound on our own or other people's personal lives," and she adds: "Aline and I were part of that period where such reticence still existed."

There's little doubt that this circumspect climate made it easier for Aline to live clandestinely without facing many of the emotional hazards of clandestine behavior. On the other hand, it also isolated her, for even with friends like Terry Helburn and, later, Bella Spewack, there were limits to what she felt she should confide. And so she turned to Dr. Hinkle again for guidance through love's bleaker and more chaotic moments. Dr. Hinkle's help went beyond emotional support, for Beatrice Hinkle was also an authority on the creative personality. Her feeling for creativity had helped to release Aline's own talents, and they now explored together those aspects of the artist's temperament that affected Aline's relationship with Tom. Many of Dr. Hinkle's theories seconded Tom's own beliefs about the artist and what he required of life. Whether society approved or not, the doctor said, to a true artist his creation "is often what he offers to the world as his contribution in place of himself as an ordinary, adapted being." So when Tom said to Aline, as he had on New Year's Eve, "You must accept any behavior of mine, because that's who I am," he was stating the principle many artists lived by. Dr. Hinkle explained to Aline that such absorption of the self in creative activity can, in terms of conventional maturity, produce a man who remains in many ways a child forever.

Aline read Dr. Hinkle's book on personality over and over again. Among the many passages she marked one seemed chillingly prophetic, and she was destined to recall it on far too many appropriate occasions. When the artist falls in love, Dr. Hinkle wrote, he loves the woman primarily "for her stimulation or value to him as a creator. However, another person also brings in the problem of reality, and reality has claims of its own and cannot be completely submissive to the will of another. Therefore . . . the artist . . . cannot maintain for long the reality relation he has assumed, for what he actually wants and needs . . . is a mother who will sacrifice all willingly for him, give much, and demand little in return. He desires to be the spoilt and favorite child, for his own interest is occupied primarily, and often exclusively, with his creative activity."

185

Tom read Dr. Hinkle's book too, and was fascinated by, if not always in accord with, her reasoning. Psychoanalysis continued to intrigue him, and he urged Aline to speculate about the reasons for some of the incidents of his past that he was currently writing about. Recognition of the existence and importance of the inner life seemed to validate his decision to write an autobiographical novel. Aline believed passionately that through understanding one man's experience, one might understand a good deal of life itself, and she encouraged Tom to pursue this path.

Louis Rubin, in the introduction to his critical study of Thomas Wolfe, speaks of the sense of discovery countless young men and women have felt when they first read *Look Homeward, Angel.* "There are writers," he says, "who in the way they interpret our experience for us . . . exist in a special and personal relationship to us. Particularly when we are young, we may, if we are lucky, come upon a writer who can speak to us so eloquently and so pointedly that he sets our imagination on fire . . . our experience has been so intense and so personal that when we talk about that writer and his work, in part at least, we are talking about ourselves." Mr. Rubin also recalls that Thoreau said once of Whitman, whom Wolfe has often been compared to, that no writer "can communicate a new experience to us; but what he can do is to make us recognize the importance of our own experience so that we become aware, for the first time, of what it is that we feel and think and what it can mean for us."

As her conviction of the universal significance of Tom's writing deepened, Aline's determination that his book be completed and published intensified. "I was the muse," she would always remember proudly, and she took her responsibilities very seriously. He needed her nurturing more than ever before, for he was completely absorbed in his writing. He was also, of course, wholly dependent on her financially. He wrote by day, and he wrote by night, a blanket wrapped around him after the heat went off at midnight. He had no time for anyone or anything but Aline.

She saw him as often as possible, though her time was increasingly difficult to apportion, in part because she was involved in the preparations to close down the Neighborhood Playhouse. Although it still was a respected and successful theatrical source, mounting costs and increased competition from uptown theaters meant making significant changes in size and format if it was to survive commercially. After careful and painful review, the Lewisohn sisters had decided to close it down at the end of the season.

As Wolfe toiled alone, feeling driven and isolated, he resented these additional claims on Aline's time; the impossible pace he had set for himself was deepening his paranoid self-pity. At the same time, his chronic resentment at having to compete for her attention with so many other loyalties and interests began to erupt in bitterness. That she divided her life into neat little compartments—"your life, your many activities, your feelings for me"—often caused him to shower her with abuse even when she was most loving. No matter how much devotion she demonstrated when she came to him—cooking and cleaning and discussing his work—the idea that she had come from somewhere and would be off again somewhere else, while he sat alone in his room, could fill him with seething rage.

Many people believe that the mounting difficulties of this period stemmed from Tom's extreme dependency. But others suggest that his resentment of the woman to whom he had given himself over was fueled by his reliving the past in his writing, that many old hurts were being exposed and many old wounds probed—particularly those connected with his mother. In other words, perhaps for the first time, Aline's age and maternal tenderness began to work against her, allowing Tom to identify her with his mother and to experience again, in Aline's leaving him for her family or her work, the deep sense of injury he had felt when Julia dismissed him in order to attend to her boarders.

Some such confusion and conflict may have led Tom to start pushing at the boundaries of his relationship with Aline, calling her at home in the middle of the night to hear her assurance that she loved him. One night, when she had gone with Theresa Helburn to an opening, she came home late to find a message from Theo, marked "Important," on the table in the darkened hall. The note informed her that "Mr. Wolfe" had called her several times after midnight and wanted to speak to her as soon as she came in.

Aline's heart clenched like a fist as she looked at the neat Germanic-looking script. The maids were instructed to answer the phone when she was out and only Mr. Bernstein was there, and though they were not fooled, they respected both Aline and Theo enough to agree blandly with their mistress that Mr. Bernstein shouldn't be disturbed. They would also, on Aline's instructions, leave messages for her in her bedroom rather than relay them through someone in the family. Why then, must Tom call when he knew the maids would be asleep? Why must his intemperateness ruin her careful design? Why must he ignore every need but his own?

She sat on the edge of her bed, her face in shadow from the lamp the maid had lit when she turned down the silken quilt. As she listened to the phone ringing in the loft, she pictured that other, so different setting, the rumpled bed and the stained blankets that held Tom's body. There was no answer, but she wasn't alarmed. She knew his propensity for crawling the city while it slept, letting his imagination people the streets and darkened buildings. Or he might have drunk himself into a stupor and be lying there passed out in some nightmare land. She hung up the receiver, and undressed, and slid between the sheets. Only an occasional haunting whistle from the river broke the silence, but she could not relax enough to sleep, out of fear that Tom might call again; she was determined to answer before the ringing woke anyone else.

In the morning, despite her fatigue, she was out of the house early —she wanted to get to Tom, and there were things she had to attend to at the Playhouse first. Neither Theo nor she mentioned the message on the hall table, although, to her deep dismay, when Theo looked down from his newspaper at breakfast, she saw a new sadness in his expression. For a moment their eyes met and held. Theo looked away first and Aline knew with troubled certainty that he was restraining himself from bringing out into the open thoughts that might better be left unsaid.

Thomas Wolfe captured Theo's attitude that morning when he described the scene in his later novel *You Can't Go Home Again*. Frederick Jack, Theo's stand-in, has been going over in his mind the intrusion of the young man's telephone call the night before. Wolfe wrote of Mr. Jack: "He was not a man to rip the sheets in darkness or beat his knuckles raw against a wall," but Jack's anger at the emotional and physical intrusion is deep and real. It was, he thought, "intolerable" that he "should be pulled out of his bed in the middle of the night by a crazy young fool—it was intolerable, and by God, he had half a mind to tell her so!"

But he didn't tell her so, not in the novel and not on the actual morning, about which Tom learned from Aline when she complained that he was troubling her family unfairly. Jack kept silent, Wolfe wrote, because he had learned that "the secret of wise living was founded in graceful compromise, a tolerant acceptance," and that while it was wise to keep your eyes and ears open as you tried to make life go your way, if a man "wanted to live in this world without getting hit over the head, and without all the useless pain, grief, terror and bitterness that mortify human flesh, he had also better learn how *not* to use his eyes and ears."

By the time Aline got to Eighth Street, Tom was gone again. Liquor bottles lay empty near the unmade bed, and sighing, Aline put them in the garbage and mopped up the liquid that had spilled. Then, after studying the bed, she stripped it and made it up again with fresh linen. Only when she had done all this did she write him a note that angrily expressed her feelings about his bothering the family. Later that day, she phoned him and accepted his apologies, but she begged him, in the name of their love and regard for each other, to honor her wishes in this respect.

Partly to compensate for the restrictions she placed on them, Aline, in spite of the New Year's Eve debacle, continued to invite Tom to parties she thought he might enjoy, and where he might meet people who could be of future help. But he nearly always refused. And indeed, too often, in this overwrought period, when he did go along, the evening turned out disastrously. In early March, for example, she took him to a party given by Philip Moeller of the Theatre Guild. Nervous about the party and irritable from the day's tension, Tom drank heavily before he left for Moeller's duplex apartment on Bank Street, a part of the Village very different from the area around the loft. Carl Van Vechten, a good friend of Aline's, who had taken and would take many superb photographs of her, and the poet and novelist Elinor Wylie were among the special guests. Wolfe took an instant dislike to them and to Elinor Wylie's husband, William Rose Benét. Undoubtedly it was their very celebrity that antagonized him; they seemed to him so arrogantly sure of their accomplishments.

"I hated them so that I managed to insult them all," Wolfe would say later, and jotted down in his notebook a few days later that thinking of the party filled him with nausea. He might well have felt ill, for within a very short time after his arrival at the party, he had consumed so much liquor that he could barely stand. He leaned against the dramatically stark white wall, his giant body casting a grotesque shadow across the room, listening to the easy discourse around him. It was, he said, exactly the kind of conversation he most despised: facile literary judgments about what was to him unimportant writing, which turned writing itself into some cheap, superficial diversion. That this was a distortion of the

189

actual conversation did not matter. He heard the words through his own perceptions, and grew hot with rage. Flinging out his arm, stumbling to keep from falling, he shouted his contempt. They were all revoltingly pretentious, the "literature" they wrote or discussed so seriously was pap beside the majestic language that came from his pen. Then his attack shifted to a free-floating barrage of incoherent curses. Apologizing—but what apology could deal with this?—Aline asked for help in getting him downstairs and into a cab, took him to the building on Eighth Street and left him there rather than go through the commotion of trying to get him up the stairs. Let him sleep in the street if he wanted to. His cries of outrage and his demands that she come back rang in her muted ears as the taxi carried her home, the driver tactful enough and wise enough in New York ways not to comment on the scene.

Considering the decline in their stability, it was probably a good thing, she felt, that as spring drew near, Tom began to go out of town occasionally to visit friends. Although she missed him and worried about him, she needed the respite. Her work schedule was increasing as the end of the season approached and plans were being made for the fall and winter. These included a challenging new enterprise in the shape of an offshoot of the Neighborhood Playhouse. With three colleagues from the Playhouse—Helen Arthur, Agnes Morgan and Alice Beer—Aline was starting a new production company called the Actor-Managers. Reluctant to let the spirit of the Playhouse die, the four women determined to carry on independently with the kind of theater they had worked on there, producing plays of their choice in New York during the winters and in out-of-town stock in the summers.

Aline loved the process of helping to put together a company. Theo gave her advice on finances and budgets, and she took to it as though it were a recipe for a new dish. She was, after all, in many ways what Abe Feder, the master of theatrical lighting later called her: "a merchant at heart." She enjoyed business and hard-headed planning, and she especially loved it with the Actor-Managers because she was proving again, as she had with the union, that women can be effective and comfortable in traditionally masculine roles. The Actor-Managers would be the first all-woman production company in the city, perhaps in the country, the press was soon reporting with some surprise, for male directors had been invited to participate even at the Playhouse. And the most skeptical drama reporter had to take this effort seriously, for these women had all proved their worth long since.

The decision had been made at the Playhouse itself to "go out laughing," and so the final production was to be another *Grand Street Follies*. It would run for two weeks only, ending on May 29, although such a clamor had arisen at the announcement of the closing that arrangements were made to move the "Follies" uptown for a summer run. On the final night, the theater throbbed with the stored resonance of its history. Everyone connected with the current productions came on stage for a bow, from scrubwomen to directors. Edla and Ethel, who were both in the cast, joined Aline on the packed stage, while Theo and Teddy raised their voices in bravos and joined the rest of the audience in a standing ovation. It seemed the applause would never stop, and then a voice sang out from the stage (was it, as some insisted, Aline's?): "Goodbye, goodbye . . ." and soon the cheers turned to cries of farewell. "Thus ending," wrote Brooks Atkinson in a lead article in the drama section of the *Times*, "the noble career of the most inspiring acting organization in this city, which began its magnificent history among the pushcarts and gents' furnishing shops of the east side."

Alexander Woollcott also bade farewell to the Playhouse in his column in the *Herald Tribune*, singling out Aline for special tribute. After first dipping his pen in irony—"There was," he wrote, "a tinge of commencement, so that you looked around for a few fond parents and old grads and were vaguely disturbed by the omission of the class prophecy"—he went on to say that there *should* have been a prophecy, for "I, for one, would like to know what theater will use henceforth the fine imagination and rare wisdom of Aline Bernstein in her sorceries of light and color?"

Of course, there were many producers who wanted Aline in their theaters, and the response of critics like Atkinson and Woollcott only whetted their interest. But Aline already knew she would like to continue the kind of theatrical experience she'd known at the Playhouse. She wanted to work within a structure that functioned as a unit, to help create theatrical experiences which synthesized all the forms of dramatic art. The Actor-Managers could do this to some degree, but not as if they had their own theater and a full company of actors. Also, while she enjoyed many of the challenges and certainly the money of Broadway, she was committed to the principle of bringing theater to the people. In truth, she shared much of Tom's feeling about Broadway audiences. She knew that many of them went to a play only to be in the swim at their next dinner party. But she had first come to Henry Street because drama and good writing could enrich people's lives. The push-cart peddlers and butchers and factory workers who first heard English spoken beautifully on the Henry Street stage were audiences she loved and felt responsible to. The bleaker a person's life during the day, the more important it was to watch a curtain go up on magic at night.

She thought about all this in the days following the Playhouse closing. All this and more: her head literally buzzed. Indeed, the Playhouse closing seemed to signal how vastly her world had been transformed since she had first been a child looking with wonder into the next century. Airplanes and telephones and subways. And the tensions that seemed so much greater as the world became more complex.

At this time Aline, like many artists and writers, was deeply involved with the case of Sacco and Vanzetti. Outraged at what she considered a vile injustice, she went to protest marches and meetings and raised money and solicited names for petitions, often, it should be said, in such bizarre places as among Theo's banking associates. Their conservatism horrified her, even though she'd always known it was there. But she felt so passionately about the case that she could not help trying to convert even these bankers. Theo and she had a number of heated arguments on the subject. He found her insistence on speaking out in inappropriate places willful and pointless. But he did not stop her. Instead, in a typically pragmatic solution, they stopped attending too many parties where a clash might take place.

Tom did share her feelings on the subject and listened to her outbursts sympathetically. But for the most part, his passions, like his frustrations, persistently focused on his own cause. Although his demonic pace of working continued, the book seemed as if it would never end. He would not, could not, abandon it before he said all that he felt must be said. Aline knew for certain that the size of the manuscript would be a problem, but she also knew she could not sway him from his compulsion to capture every nuance of his experience. The few times she raised the question of length, he grew so furious that even she, accustomed to his rages, was alarmed. Their quarrels were frequent enough now. She did not want to precipitate any more.

The fact that the heat this June was unbearable contributed to his being so overwrought. Tom could barely think in the sweltering loft, and when Aline came to see him, he lashed out at her for being so insulated in her thick-walled, well-ventilated fancy house—despite the fact that she came laden with fresh greens for cool salads, and bags of fruit to make him refreshing drinks. The hotter it was, the more he roamed the streets at night seeking relief. These nocturnal wanderings, too often accompanied by too many drinks, darkly stirred his discontent. He was lonely for companionship, for Aline's companionship, and she was not there to give it to him. He would come home from these aimless, desperate walks convinced that Aline was being unfaithful to him, that it was not just her family and her work he had to compete with, but also a new young lover, probably many young lovers. He even dreamed of her being unfaithful, and would wake up feeling as violently angry as if the dream had been real.

At these times, waking from a dream, or stumbling in from the street, he would call Seventy-seventh Street at two, three or four o'clock in the morning to make sure she was home. His jealousy was pathological and beyond the reach of reason, and no matter how Aline begged him to stop the calls and to believe in her fidelity, the pattern continued.

So once again, when Tom was invited to wait out the heat in the upstate home of Owen Downs, an old friend from Harvard, Aline was not altogether unhappy about the separation. Besides her wish to be free of his jealousy for a while, she also believed he would work better if he was more comfortable. Owen's family was immensely wealthy, and Tom was to have the gatekeeper's cottage all to himself. He could work there undisturbed as long as he cared to.

When the weather lightened a little, Aline went down to the loft to get it ready for Tom's probably imminent return. She would have gone earlier, even in the hot spell, but she was busy with fall productions. Two plays besides her work with the Actor-Managers were on her agenda: *The Taming of the Shrew* for the Garrick Players and a Theatre Guild presentation of Shaw's *The Doctor's Dilemma*. The star of *Dilemma* would be Lynn Fontanne, and Aline had decided to have Ethel and Bergdorf's execute her designs. The production had a big budget and Miss Fontanne was extremely knowledgeable about design. Aline wanted the best work possible, and her sister was without fail the best, she told her happily. "Besides, Ethel," she said grinning, "it feels so good to be able to afford you!"

On this day in mid June, then, Aline and Ethel lunched together at a midtown restaurant, looking at sketches, discussing technical problems. (Even with her sister, Ethel liked to keep business confined to business hours.) By the time they were through, it was late afternoon, and Aline decided to go down to the apartment rather than do any more work.

It was unbelievably awful.

Remnants of food, rotted by the heat, spilled over from tables and littered the floor. Flies and other insects circled her head as if she were in a jungle. The filth was so appalling that she felt it could never be cleaned, and yet she was too embarrassed to bring anyone to help her, to let anyone know she was in any way associated with such a place. Her face grim, she rolled up her sleeves and began to clean, barely making a dent by the time she had to go home for dinner. The next morning she came back wearing her oldest clothes. She worked for hours, her arms and legs stiff from the strain of kneeling and scrubbing. As she moved aside a pile of garbage, she was suddenly startled, for a piece of paper with her own handwriting had appeared. Sifting through the debris, she fished out two notes she had recently written to Tom, filled with her love for him. Tom had barely written her at all since going to Owen's; his treatment of her letters to him made her wonder what or when he would ever write to her again.

She sat down on the couch and read the two letters, remembered sitting at her desk, pouring out her heart in them, and she felt as if her heart had been trampled on by his big, careless feet. Savagely she ripped the letters to shreds and scattered them around the room, turning them into the garbage he had obviously likened them to. And she laid her head down on her dusty arm and, hating her sadness, wept, needing the cooling tears.

That night she wrote to Tom, asking how he could hurt her so, could treat her love so lightly. She also enclosed a check from his uncle that she had discovered lying like her letters among the filth. Even this had distressed her. While she expected no gratitude for her financial support, neither did she want him to take the support so much for granted that he didn't even have to bother with a check from another source.

But she didn't say that now. Like Theo, she knew some things were better left unsaid. Instead, she ended the letter quickly and signed her name, but before putting the letter in its envelope she sat at her desk thinking. An idea that she had not been fully ready to deal with had been flirting in her mind for weeks. The idea of spending another summer in Europe with Tom. Theresa had already asked Aline to sail with her, and there were several business reasons for going. She'd been unable to come to a decision, however, and so had said nothing to Tom even about the possibility of another season abroad. Reviewing her silence, Aline knew she was ambivalent for several reasons. Did she want to leave her family? Did she want to shower Tom with so much more, perhaps excessive, indulgence? Did she want to live so intensely with him when his emotions were so unstable?

Now, faced with the pain of what she saw as rejection, and the fear of what that implied for her future, she could only answer yes to everything. Reason gave way to need. She closed her eyes and saw the silver lakes of Ambleside and felt the joy in her heart when she looked out on them each morning. And she knew she must try and recapture that happiness. And so, lifting her pen again, in another remarkable demonstration of the psyche's influence on action, as she recognized when she reread the letter, she added a postscript in a hand suddenly so light it was almost illegible. It was as if she was resisting her own impulses, fighting her need to say to him, as she did now, "Would you like to go to Europe with me?" And then, knowing Tom's taste, in a hand that was lighter still, she offered a self-consciously tentative, but quite manipulative, temptation: "Vienna? Prague? Budapest?"

# 14

Of course, Tom accepted Aline's offer with gleeful alacrity. He came home quickly from Owen's, refreshed and loving, and filled with hope for a wonderful summer of new experiences—new smells to provoke his appetites, new faces, new languages. Oh, Aline, my love, my "good and beautiful spirit," yes, yes, let us travel together again.

And so they did. By early July they were already reunited in Europe after separate crossings. The problems of the last months lifted like a layer of dead skin. He was filled with remorse for the pain he had caused her. Love had "driven me mad," he told her. Love tortured him especially when he was so filled with self-doubt. But now, together, when she was almost exclusively his, for her work abroad did not take her away as it did at home, he felt more secure. And his writing was going well, and finally, finally, he could see a real end in sight. Every word he entered in his ledgers or in his notebook brought him closer to a foreseeable conclusion, and they both felt the relief of his reaching the end of a thrilling but debilitating journey.

They went to Paris because Aline wanted to buy some clothes, and because she wanted to see a production of a play called *Maya,* which the Actor-Managers had scheduled for the new season. Their trip would also take them to Munich, which Aline loved, and to Vienna and Prague and Nuremberg. Along the way, they fed each other's curiosity, as if they were handing each other rich morsels of meat. "Tom, look, see the pain in that old woman's face when she looks at the younger woman. . . ." "Aline, that fat man is fondling the waitress's thigh! See, she's pretending not to feel it. . . ."

Week after week, it had been sweet and peaceful and filled with memorable moments. When he announced that he had completed the prose poem he wanted to begin the book with, so as to introduce the reader to the theme, he read to her as he had done at Ambleside, his voice excited. Aline felt a stab of sad recognition along with her pride. For beyond the poetry, which she considered really magnificent in its lyrical intensity and cadences, she heard a cry of loneliness and yearning.

"Aline, you read it to me now," he said shyly, and she reached over for the notebook.

" '. . . a stone, a leaf, an unfound door; of a stone, a leaf, a door. And of all the forgotten faces.

" 'Naked and alone we came into exile. In her dark womb we did not know our mother's face; from the prison of her flesh have we come into the unspeakable and incommunicable prison of this earth.

" 'Which of us has known his brother? Which of us has looked into his father's heart? Which of us has not remained forever prison-pent? Which of us is not forever a stranger and alone?' "

Her voice broke and she could not continue. For once, both of them were speechless, but they reached out their hands to clasp the other's in gratitude.

Yet, as the summer wore on, old strains surfaced. Aline would say: "You can change your skies, but not your soul." They would have a happy, busy day of sightseeing: the National Museum in Nuremberg, perhaps, followed by a marvelous dinner—they both liked German food, and especially enjoyed the light Riesling wine. And then something would happen to change Tom's mood. He would decide the bill was too high, or Aline would seem too interested in what some other man was saying at the bar, and she would be exposed to the old misery of his abuse, felt even more deeply now because she wasn't prepared for it.

Just before they were due to leave Vienna, they had a terrible quarrel for no really important reason, and she burst into tears and walked aimlessly through the city she thought so beautiful, unable to go back to the hotel and face him. She'd left him standing in the street, and he'd made no attempt to follow her. For a moment she felt trapped. She did not want to see him when she was so upset, and yet she had nowhere to escape to. And though she felt relieved that he hadn't come after her to prolong the scene, she hated the idea of having, in effect, to crawl back to him like a helpless, tired child.

Her tears were not always shed because of a quarrel. One day at a train station, Tom embraced her and, happily, she raised her face for his kiss. Some soldiers standing nearby began to laugh, and she pulled back, mortified, her face crimson. She knew too well what they saw— how the older woman and the young man looked to them—and the degrading distortion filled her with shame.

By the time they got to Munich they were both far more irritable than they had been all summer. Tom was suddenly critical of the Germans' appearance, "young gentlemen," he sneered, "with dueling scars on their faces, and older ones with shaven bullet heads, small porky eyes, and three ridges of neck over their back collars." They stayed in a Bavarian hotel that was immaculate, but to Tom, annoyingly sterile. As he recorded in his notebook with unusual understatement: "I was touchy, on edge by this time."

So again it was not without some relief that Aline left for home ahead of Tom, who was to join her in a week or so. Clearly, the simple golden joys of the Ambleside summer had not been granted them this season. Still, there had been many, many moments she remembered with joy and encompassing warmth, and it was these she vowed to concentrate on and be grateful for.

Similarly, when she thought ahead to fall, she told herself not to worry because Tom had accepted a teaching job again. With the cooperation of Dr. Watt, he had arranged to teach mostly evening classes and would thus have large blocks of time for writing during the day. And she also thought, as she sat alone on deck, that it might be better if Tom were less dependent on her financially. She knew his mother was highly critical of their financial arrangements, as she was of the relationship itself, and she let Tom know so in her letters. Moreover, Aline felt that his compulsion to hurt her derived often from his feeling of powerlessness because of her total support. It really could be better for them this fall in a number of ways, and yes, she had good reason to feel optimistic about their future. Fortunately, she did not know that even as she comforted herself with these thoughts, Tom was visiting a brothel in Paris. A notation in his journal clinically marks the event: "Cafe at corner of Faubourg Montmartre. I have just come from a whore house . . . in over two years, first time I've betrayed her."

Thanks to ignorance and hope, Aline thoroughly enjoyed her return home and going through the mail on her desk. There was a whole stack of letters from Harry Woodsend, the architect she had hired some months before to oversee the building of their house at Armonk. Theo had written to her during the summer that building had actually started, and she was impatient to go out to the site and see how the plans were translating themselves into reality.

"It's going to be beautiful, Aline, you've surpassed yourself," Theo said proudly, and he awakened her early the next morning so that they could all ride out to inspect the work. When the car stopped at the site, Ethel and Theo climbed out quickly, wanting to lead Aline ceremoniously to the crest of the hill in the distance. From there she could see the beginnings of the stone Cotswold cottage that would be their new home. As she climbed briskly up the hill behind her husband and sister, and saw the framework clearly marking off a set of spacious rooms, Aline felt a thrill. Till now, she'd been so preoccupied with other matters, her life already so full, that even though she had worked carefully with the architect, she'd thought of the house as meeting Theo's and Ethel's and the children's needs far more than her own. But all that changed now.

She realized that when they were finally forced to sell the house on Seventy-seventh Street, a prospect that still depressed her terribly, she would not have to be spiritually homeless. Clearly this new home could contain them all in a circle of comfort. She took Theo's arm and they walked together into what would be their living room, and looked across the rolling wooded hills, already planted with peach and pear trees, and down to the Croton Reservoir, which bordered the property and provided the expanse of water that always soothed her spirits. She foresaw their watching the sunset together and winter's pristine snowfalls, and suddenly she had a million ideas for how the rooms should be decorated and furnished. She set off around the construction, darting in and out, drawing little sketches in the notebook she fished from her purse.

"I think," she asked, "mainly white walls and plain curly-maple floors, don't you, Ethel?" or: "Theo, look here, let's not have any doors off the living room at all, just archways, like this . . . see?" and she'd flash the paper with the sketch under his twinkling eyes. Theodore Bernstein was indeed very happy at his wife's enthusiasm, wanting to believe— and believing—that she was glad to be back with them and eager for this new stage of their common life.

"I want to show you what *I'm* going to build, my dear," he said with a smile, and he took Aline's arm and led her to where a small mound of land had been cleared on a hill. "I'm going to have a gazebo built there," Theo told her, "so I can sit and read Shakespeare outdoors in every season and also hide when the theater talk gets too thick."

"It's a wonderful idea, Popsie," Aline said, with an affectionate hug. "I promise I will never intrude on it."

Indeed, the whole house had been planned to respect everyone's privacy. The downstairs rooms would all be open to each other, but the personal space was to be private, with each member of the family having what virtually amounted to a separate wing. Ethel's apartment even had its own staircase, while Aline's would have a private entrance from the outside, a little stairway leading up from a small flagstone terrace to the Dutch doors that opened onto her bedroom. There would be those who would soon refer to this as Tom Wolfe's stairway, but in fact it existed so that Aline could go outdoors in the early morning while the rest of the family still slept, or simply merge the indoor with the outdoor environment when a particular light lay on the lawn or an especially lovely scent drifted through her window.

Aline was, however, making other living arrangements this fall that did specifically include Tom. Clearly, they needed a new place to live and work. The loft on Eighth Street was too dilapidated, the dirt too resistant, for Aline to bring clients there. And now that the Neighborhood Playhouse was closed, and her assignments were so diverse, she needed an office where she could meet with people as well as work on her designs. Besides, the tensions of the presummer months had made them both disenchanted with the loft. When, soon after Tom's return, they went back to visit it, they saw what anyone else would have seen —a run-down, filthy garret, hot in summer, cold in winter, and depressing for the people it inadequately housed.

That very day, over lunch at Marta's, on Washington Place, they talked about getting a larger, more expensive apartment. After all, with

200

Tom working, they could afford a considerably higher rent. The idea was exciting to them both, and as soon as he went off to N.Y.U., his bulging black briefcase slapping against his thigh, Aline went house hunting. The very idea filled her with hope. Nothing had ended. They were simply beginning again.

She had hoped to find something before his next birthday, and happily, she was able to. With great ceremony, she took him to the lovely old building on Eleventh Street that, with his approval, would be their new home and studio. The building was owned by a well-known artist who had cared for it with full appreciation of the beauty of fine wood and brick. They were to have an entire floor, consisting of two huge rooms, a large kitchen and a bath. The back room looked down on a private, flower-filled garden. It was old New York at its finest and Aline adored it, and as she had anticipated, so did Tom. They would split the rent of $135, and if they traveled in the summer, they were free to sublet it, which would further reduce their expenses.

Here, then, Tom would start his twenty-seventh year, and as usual, he regarded the event with solemnity. Aline and he talked for hours about his life past and present and future, and it seemed certain that his love for her was as pure as it had ever been. When he was not driven by old ghosts or anticipatory specters, he said, his view of Aline was clear: she was "the best and truest friend" that he had ever had, and his love for her "was the most enduring thing in my life, and will hover above our bones when the great towers of America are forgotten."

Within a week they had moved in, Aline ensconced in the front room with her drawing materials, Tom and his writing and personal effects in the back. When someone came to talk to her about business, Aline could close a door on the amazing mess he produced. Despite her heroic efforts to keep him and his bedroom tidy, the "cyclonic chaos" of his living habits continued. Clothing, most of it stained, lay in a heap on the floor; correspondence, students' themes, were thrown all around; books of every sort were piled up in tottering stacks in a kind of circle around his ash-strewn bed. Dishes and cups held the remains of food and drink, adding their odors to the dense, tobacco-stale air. And sprinkled through it all like a crazy snowfall were his scraps of notes to be transcribed into his notebooks or ledger. Russell Kraus, a colleague from N.Y.U., recalls with wonder visiting Wolfe at what he calls his "stinking lair." After describing the terrible disorder, he says: "I refused coffee from the pot in which superimposed grounds accumulated until there was no more room for the liquid brew. I viewed . . . the heap of putrid white shirts from which, from time to time, he would re-select for current wear the one to him least dirty and wrinkled, but to the neutral observer, hardly selectable."

Wolfe himself would speak of the extraordinary contrast between his and Aline's sections of the apartment, recognizing it as a metaphor for the differences in their personalities, as well as a clear indication of her devotion. He described her work area with something close to awe. There, under the window, was her table, "trim, spare, certain, alert and orderly and ready instantly for work . . . right and left, the instruments and materials she loved so well and could use with such sure magic were arranged and ready for her instant touch . . . the tubes and boxes of paint, the fine brushes, the sliding rule, the gleaming compass, and the long, neatly-sharpened pencils . . . behind the table, hanging from nails driven in the walls . . . the square, the yard measure, and the triangle." Aline had once told him that one of the most beautiful sights in the world for her was the window of a hardware store with its countless implements and instruments, each having its own clear purpose. He understood her pleasure in these tools, but his own life continued to be lived in grubby confusion. Cigar boxes filled with pencil butts were the sources of his own writing, and a motley collection of papers, from tissue to butchers' wrappings, were what he poured his talents onto, shoving them under his bed when he was done with them, where they collected little balls of dust that sometimes threatened to obscure his smudged scrawl.

Henry Volkening, another N.Y.U. colleague from this period, who subsequently became a distinguished literary agent, says that only Wolfe could have worked in such disorder, and he was able to only because Aline was there, providing loving encouragement and, in herself, a model of certainty and productivity and control. That model was particularly important now, as Tom came closer and closer to the point where the book must be considered finished. Aline's decisiveness stood in firm opposition to his tendency to procrastinate and evade and to dissipate his energies. With her help, he created a new design for his day that included teaching and its attendant responsibilities, completing the final portion of the novel, and perhaps most exciting of all, beginning to have transcribed those portions that were already written. Abe Jones, a devoted student from N.Y.U., was recruited to type the manuscript, and often when Aline arrived laden with groceries, she would hear Tom's voice dictating in the back room. The sound filled her with happiness, and sometimes, when she stood at her table, the combined pleasures of her own work and his all but overwhelmed her.

Her own work was going well. Play after play lay ahead of her: more modern-dress Shakespeare for newly courageous producers . . . the Fontanne play (Miss Fontanne in an interview had told the press: "I adore Aline Bernstein, she is simply a superb designer") . . . a Robert Sherwood play . . . the Actor-Managers' productions . . . and more after that. She was making more money and winning greater acclaim than she could ever have hoped for, yet the project that was most inspiring would pay her comparatively little.

Eva Le Gallienne had got in touch with Aline and asked to meet with her at Miss Le Gallienne's own repertory company. When Aline walked up to the theater on Fourteenth Street, after preparing some trout for Tom's lunch, she felt suspended in time. For she had watched her father perform on countless occasions in this very theater, heard his glorious voice raised in Shakespeare, watched his handsome face beaming from the stage. A nostalgic smile still on her lips, Aline entered the cavernous building and found Miss Le Gallienne's office. The young, beautiful actress, much closer to Tom's age than to Aline's, greeted her guest warmly, and as they began to talk, the two women felt a kinship that was to last all Aline's life. Like Aline, Miss Le Gallienne was committed to the idea of a "people's theater" that combined fine plays with popular prices. Tickets at the Civic Repertory could be bought for thirty-five cents, with the top price only $1.50, and Miss Le Gallienne was determined to keep productions scaled to that price range. But she did not intend any compromise with quality, which was why she was so anxious to have Aline work with her. Aline's experience with the Neighborhood Playhouse must certainly have made her knowledgeable about stretching every dollar, and this, combined with her great talent, would enrich the Civic Repertory Company. The actress knew, of course, that Aline could have her pick of uptown assignments, but she hoped Aline would agree that the repertory concept could serve audiences as Broadway was still unable to.

Without a moment's hesitation, Aline said she would love to be a part of this noble project. She would find the budgetary restrictions a challenge rather than an obstacle, just as she had done at the Playhouse; the artistic triumph was far greater when ingenuity rather than dollars was your creative capital.

The two women sat over tea, and Aline felt the phases of her life flowing together again. Superimposed on the actress's beautiful face were images of Lillian Wald and the Lewisohn sisters, women, like Miss Le Gallienne and like Aline herself, who were strong, and bravely creative, and sure of their talents. As for Miss Le Gallienne, she knew immediately that they had a "common bond. Aline was a person who served the theater," she says. "We both felt that this was what we wanted to do . . . this was the immediate and continuing sympathy between us." And she continues thoughtfully: "Too many artists are so busy exploiting their own ego that they often swamp an entire production, they're so anxious to put their own stamp on a show. . . . But Aline was never like that. She was only concerned with the validity of the play, and serving the author—always she cared about the writing, and doing her part to insure its most accurate translation."

Aline was altogether enthusiastic about her new collaboration and felt more comfortable about discussing it with Tom than she did her work for Broadway. As he came closer to submitting his own talents to the marketplace, his ambivalence about his desire for recognition grew. Those people who had first denied him recognition, theater people, were "base and vile" and cared for nothing but their own pretensions. But he could hardly accuse the Civic Repertory of this, and indeed, he seemed to approve Aline's feelings about working within the repertory structure. "The theater becomes rather like your family," she explained to him. "The crew gets to know your likes and your dislikes. . . . Why, I can just say to our electrician, 'Give me a pool of light over there on stage left, the way we had it in *The Green Cockatoo,*' and he knows just what I mean!" And then, in an inevitable analogy, she said: "Well, it's just like this, isn't it? Working in a repertory theater is like dining at home, instead of out in a restaurant."

Yet despite Tom's relatively benevolent attitude toward this aspect of her career and Aline's euphoria about his novel, the tensions between them were growing more electric. For one thing, Tom was bitterly disappointed that the book wasn't moving along on the schedule he had planned. He'd convinced himself that it would be done by Christmas, and that date came and went, with chapters still to be written. In a letter to his mother, he wrote sadly: "I know you will understand my reason for not coming for Christmas. I am trying to do something with my life; it is right that I make every effort to do something with it now. And I must finish what I have started."

His despair caused Aline misery of her own. Her work on the Armonk house, all her theatrical projects, the family plans for the holiday, conflicted with Tom's insatiable need for reassurance. Before and after the holiday, as winter deepened, his evening wanderings grew more desperate, ending in those dreadful late-night telephone calls.

"God only knows what I suffer from your jealousy," Aline told him tearfully one morning, for at breakfast Theo had again let her see the flash of pain in his eyes, and her children had tried to mask their embarrassment when she entered the dining room. She wished Ethel were there to smooth things over, but Ethel was away on a buying trip, with young Andrew Goodman under her wing, teaching him her part of the business. Perhaps, though, Aline thought ruefully, it was just as well that Ethel wasn't there, for her sister was obviously aware, at least in part, of what was going on, and while she would have tried to make life less difficult for the family, her disapproval would have hurt Aline acutely.

Later Tom would apologize for the pain he caused her during these months, but his apology was offered in the expectation that Aline would understand and forgive the inevitability of his behavior. After all, he said, "I was obsessed with the work I was doing, driven on desperately to finish it. . . . I think you must have seen and understood some of the agony of those months—my job to do, the horrible pain lengthening out day by day, and no escape—until I roamed the streets of New York by night, cursing like a madman, bolstering myself . . . with doses of raw gin, and so far losing myself as to call your house at unexpected times, day and night, in an effort to keep track of you."

But when she heard those drunken shouts in her ear, accusing her of having come in from one of her "bawdy missions," Aline would shudder, and sometimes wonder forlornly how much easier her life might be if she *could* distract herself with random little adventures. Over and over again some handsome young actor would indicate that he found her desirable, and whether he was simply hoping for some extra professional attention from her or actually meant it, "how amused she could be if she allowed herself to be amused," she thought. She could float into the "delightful casual pleasures, hardly more than sensations, which often make up the brief intimacies of an actor's life," like Joe Frankau in his fleeting encounters with young actresses.

She would sit back in her bed after hanging up on Tom's call, her tension so great she knew sleep was over for the night, and she would let her imagination wander. Tonight after rehearsal she could go to that handsome young actor's dressing room, regale him with the stories of her life, which she knew she told so well, "go out for supper, get a little drunk, let him slip his hand down the neck of her dress, make a little love, have a jolly time, only skin-deep; and a few weeks afterwards, another one, another chap to call you darling and put his arms around you when he felt blue, so long as you kept your figure and your fragrance, looked pretty and played up to the fun. Not a heartache in the dozen," she told herself bitterly, "nor an ounce of anything to hold dear."

But of course that was exactly why it was all fantasy. If it wasn't important enough to risk the heartache or to hold dear, why risk anything at all? Why waste herself in such a meaningless, cynical, soul-denying way?

It was only Tom she would give her peace over to, despite the danger that he would disrupt it forever.

Even more tormenting than his telephone calls, and his hysterical accusations of her unfaithfulness to him, was the continuing and inescapable evidence that Tom was being unfaithful to her. Out shopping for food with Aline, he would leer at some young wife, obviously hungry for more than the meat and fruit Aline was buying for their lunch.

"I saw you looking at her," Aline would fume, and he would try to tease her out of her anger, not realizing that she felt far more than anger, that she was experiencing a terrible new fear, a sense of hollow inadequacy because of the other woman's taut young skin and gleaming hair untouched by gray.

Or, cleaning the apartment, Aline would find a sprinkling of face powder, or some hairpins under Tom's pillow when she went to change the case for the freshly laundered one she had brought with her. Other times, she'd look for her apron or the slippers she often worked in, and they would be missing from their customary place in the closet. They would be tucked away on a top shelf, out of sight. At these times she'd accuse him again, her velvet voice suddenly scratchy, like coarse cotton.

"You don't want anyone to know about me . . . you don't want those cheap silly little tarts to know that there is a woman in your life who takes care of you night and day . . . in ways they would never even think of."

"Don't you ever hide my things again," she'd command him, her cheeks burning with anger, and when he denied that he had and tried to make her believe she had imagined it, she didn't know whether she had more contempt for him or for her own need for self-delusion. As she would later say in rueful apology for her desperate attempt to deny the truth: "I wanted to think that all he needed in the world was for me to love him, and for him to love me. I knew he needed other voices than mine, but I couldn't bear that, so I would not admit it."

Yet in fact, she was far too realistic to believe Tom's feeble excuses. Their quarrels grew fierce and more frequent. His destructive behavior intensified, and her defenses crumbled. He began to invite young instructors from the college to come by for dinner, without asking her first. While her dinner overcooked, she drank the cheap gin they brought or watched them drink her own expensive liquor which Tom generously offered, glancing slyly at Aline as he did so. Until now, he had never brought people home when she was there, respecting the fact that she might find it awkward. Obviously, her reaction had ceased to matter to him, and this particularly disturbed Aline. More often than not, she left them still drinking, her dinner abandoned, and Tom barely acknowledging her going. It took all the strength she could muster to say a pleasant, dry-eyed good night.

There were worse times, when she demeaned herself.

"The dignified, balanced, intelligent woman I fancied myself to be disappeared; there was no trace of her, in her place was a tearful, petty bore . . . I saw my immortal soul sitting inside of me like Buddha, calm, immobile, allowing this vulgar fishwife to have her say."

One evening when her heart felt like "a piece of burning lead, twice its natural size," she came down to the apartment when he did not expect her. As she approached Eleventh Street in the twilight—"an unseeing, liquid light" with "no shadows, and no forms"—she felt resurgent hope. She seemed to herself to be coming together again. After all, she thought, despite their quarrels, they still shared many glorious moments, and in his calmer moods, he told her over and over again how important she was to him, and how much he adored her. She still had "the two great elements to make a life—work and love." As she walked, she smoothed herself out as she would smooth out a fine piece of fabric that had been crumpled.

But then, in this shadowless light, she saw a shadow in his window, the form of a young woman. Reason left her, and adrenaline poured into every cell as she flew up the stairs and threw open the door, screaming at him in the voice of that "vulgar wife," that other, new, unwelcome Aline.

"I've caught you. . . . I've caught you and your little hussy," she shouted, too blind with fury to see the startled faces of two young men and one rather plain young woman, seated on the floor beside Tom. They were eating steak from Aline's china, drinking cheap jug wine they'd poured into the crystal glasses Tom had long ago chipped.

Tom, in the middle of a story, leaped to his feet and came to her. He was terribly embarrassed, but his eyes were kind.

"Aline," he said, stammering, "Aline, calm down; it's not what you think."

But of course she already knew that. As she knew her own mortification. What did it matter what there really was to see in that room? She could only see her own distorted reflection. She would recall, sadly: "My image of myself was shattered, as though I was looking in a glass, and I had thrown a stone at my mirrored face and broken the glass and the image into cruel jagged edges." Mumbling an apology, she left the apartment, and stood outside on the street, shaking. She had, she felt, "deserted myself when I needed my strength and all the command of life I possessed." And then, trying to hide her weeping face, she thought in abject horror that perhaps this tearful woman who watched shadows from a street corner was in fact "the real one, and the beautiful one was all made up, a fantasy. It may be that this noble talented woman never existed."

No, God, no. She could not let herself believe it. She must take herself in hand, be the woman she had believed herself to be all these years. For a while, as she rode home in a taxicab, she hated Tom. Hated him for reducing her to this rawness of undisciplined feeling. Once home, she looked into the study, where Theo and Teddy were working on reports, and she wondered how she had strayed so far from the serenity of this house. And later that night, alone again, she lay in bed thinking for a long time. She wanted to call Tom, but would not allow herself to do so. She tried to analyze his hostility—and its corrupting effects on her, his increasing need to destroy what she had built for him, what they had built together. Her head and her stomach ached and she could not deal with it all. Prayerfully, she told herself it would be better when his book was accepted for publication. Surer of his own strengths, he would not have to hurt her in order to prove them.

She vowed to herself then, as she had once vowed about Teddy's health, "he will recover" . . . "this book will get published." She would do everything, anything, in her power to find the publisher who would wade through the more than eleven hundred pages she had read every word of and see the genius she had believed in and nurtured for so long. A great deal of her life was invested in this novel. She had taken inordinate risks to see it to its conclusion. In a matter of days it would be ready to be seen by others. She had promised Tom that she would take charge of getting it published, and as soon as the final word was written, she would. No matter that she had so many new shows to do, or that the Armonk house was demanding more and more of her attention. She, who prided herself on never asking anyone for help, would ask favors —recall favors she had done so that she would not be refused. She would violate the boundaries she herself had set, to prove she had been right in investing so much in loving this wild, tormented, gifted man.

Aline and Theo, with their children,
Teddy *(left)* and Edla *(right)*, 1906.

Aline *(center)* in early production of *The Grand Street Follies*.

Set for *Ned McCobb's Daughter* by Sidney Howard. Produced by the Theatre Guild, 1926.
© The New York Public Library at Lincoln Center, Astor, Lenox and Tilden Foundations.

Helen Hayes as Cleopatra in Shaw's *Caesar and Cleopatra*. Produced by the Theatre Guild, 1925.
© The New York Public Library at Lincoln Center, Astor, Lenox and Tilden Foundations.

Tallulah Bankhead in *The Little Foxes* by Lillian Hellman. Produced and directed by Herman Shumlin, 1939.

© The New York Public Library at Lincoln Center, Astor, Lenox and Tilden Foundations.

Thomas Wolfe, c. 1930.
From copy in North Carolina Collection, UNC Library, Chapel Hill.

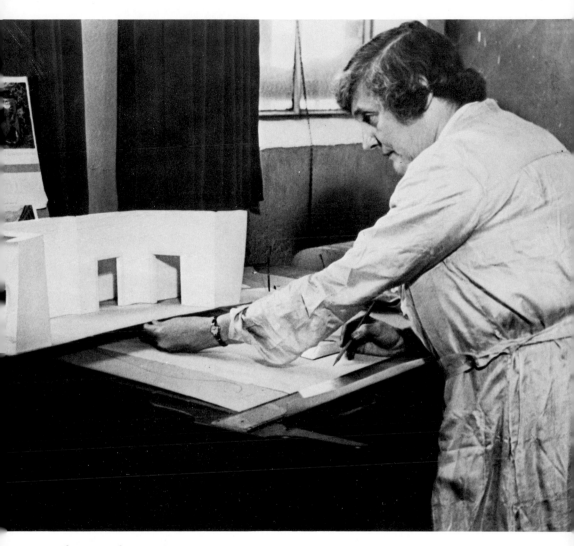
Aline at work, c. 1938.
© Pix Karger Studios.

Aline in her publisher's office on
publication of *An Actor's Daughter,*
1944.
Photos by Alfred A. Knopf.

Theo at Stratford, England, 1951.

Aline, 1953.

# Part Four

1928-1934

# 15

The novel was finished at the end of March. Aline and Tom packed the manuscript into two small suitcases, and she placed a call from their apartment to a friend who was an editor with the publishing firm of Boni and Liveright. Yes, of course he would read it if Aline felt he should.

"It's rather . . . long," Aline said.

"How long?" her friend asked.

"Oh, dear." She giggled into the phone. "I'm afraid, very long, but he's willing to do some cutting."

Indeed, Tom had conceded that he might have to trim the book, relaxing the stubborn resistance to revision of his playwriting days. Whether from a sharpened taste for success, or a mellowing, he was willing, at least to some degree, to consider portions of it less sacred than others.

He even enclosed an open letter to the publisher with the manuscript, explaining that several pages had been written primarily as catharsis—to release his ideas and energies so that he could then write more directly to his subject. He said he would willingly eliminate such pages. While Aline was pleased at these signs of cooperation, she knew very well that extensive cutting of the manuscript would not be accomplished without bloodshed. And even if one could overcome Tom's avid clinging to his prose, she also knew it would be hard to find an editor willing to undertake what must surely be almost a halving of the novel to make it commercially viable.

Nonetheless, despite her misgivings, she and Tom took the suitcases down to her friend's office and then went back to the apartment to toast the occasion—and to begin what would perhaps be emotionally the longest period of Thomas Wolfe's life. For the first few days he was euphoric. In a typical swing of mood, he was convinced that his having made the decision to publish the book assured its enthusiastic welcome by the publishing world. He was particularly confident, too, because Aline had undertaken to act as his agent. Writing to his sister, he implied that because she had, his past difficulty in placing his work was over. "My greatest deficiency is total lack of salesmanship," he explained to Mabel Wolfe. "I never sent my plays to more than two or three managers, and if I got no answer within a month, I wrote insulting letters demanding their return. I have never known where to go, where to turn, what to do."

On the strength of his newly optimistic feeling, he wrote to Professor Watt a few days after the novel was complete, resigning from N.Y.U. for the following year because he felt that dealing with students' compositions was dissipating his creative energy. "I want to get the energy of my life directed towards the thing it desires most," he wrote. "In short I am going to try and support myself by writing—if necessary, by hack writing of any sort, stories, advertising, articles." He added that if his book should be accepted, he would of course begin work on another, and was in fact planning to do so anyway, perhaps because at this point he believed so strongly that it *would* be accepted.

Meanwhile, Aline was helping him plan more immediate ways of getting money through writing. She spoke to her friend Mrs. Helen Resor, who ran the J. Walter Thompson advertising agency (Aline had designed some of their offices), about giving Tom a job writing copy. Although she had laughed with Tom often about the entire concept of advertising, it was clearly a growing and profitable business in America in the twenties, as the country became more and more prosperous. Once, while Tom had been away, Aline had written him wonderingly about dining with Theo at Mrs. Resor's house in Greenwich, Connecticut. She described how splendid the house was, its paintings, furniture, appointments each "worth its weight in gold—gold mined by Lux Toilet Soap, Pond's Cold Cream, Fleischmann's Yeast, and General Motors wheels going round and round."

Despite Aline's "I think the world is a screamingly funny place, I was vastly entertained by my visit," she now felt, and Tom was inclined to agree, that turning out advertising copy would be a realistic and undemanding way to earn enough money to support his serious writing. Aline showed Mrs. Resor sections of the manuscript, and that astute person was impressed enough with Tom's talent to offer him a job at considerably more money than he would be able to earn at N.Y.U. However, she stipulated a three-year contract, and Tom immediately felt his interest wane.

"I don't want to commit myself to anything that long," he told Aline, and she felt a slight but familiar chill in her heart.

In fact, although Tom spoke of seeking work, there was no room in his mind for any thought beyond the fate of the novel. His good mood was rapidly disappearing, and too often when Aline came to the apartment, she found him in a state of increasing gloom and frenetic impatience.

She tried to find words to soothe him, but he would mimic her and lash out at her as viciously as if she were deliberately keeping him in the dark. At the same time, his resentment of her full life increased. He was obsessed with the book, could find no distraction from it, and she was giving it only a small part of her attention. Her days and nights were filled with all manner of things that made the success or failure of his novel insignificant. He would not believe anything she said about how deeply she cared, and more and more often, she became the target of his impotent rage. Somehow she was to blame for his being in this position of tremulous uncertainty.

For Aline, all this was simply torture, a dreadfully bleak obbligato to those other aspects of her life that he felt so competitive with. She had also been having some rough going professionally. *Maya*, the play she and Tom had seen in Paris, opened with her designs in New York in late February and created an immediate scandal. The central character was a prostitute who wanted to raise and educate her own child. She was far more "eternal female" than social deviant, and the city's moral watchdogs were outraged. After fifteen performances it was

215

closed by the district attorney for "tending to corrupt the morals of youth."

"I hope I'm not causing you too much embarrassment downtown, Popsie," Aline said to Theo after reading her morning paper one cold February day.

"Don't worry about it, my dear. It's good for their blood pressure to get stirred up a bit." Aline watched him leave for work, a small smile on her lips. It occurred to her, not for the first time, that if Tom was in some ways the embodiment of what she would be were she less disciplined, she filled the same role for her husband. At work, he was the antithesis of anything that smacked of unconventionality. But through his wife he would experience vicariously a wider range. She could picture him this morning if someone raised the subject of her connection with the *Maya* controversy. He would shrug his shoulders as if to say: "What can I do about a bohemian wife?" The fact that many of his colleagues envied him her success would, she was sure, enhance his secret pleasure in having escaped through her a tediously impeccable life.

Nonetheless, the reverberations from the *Maya* opening interfered with the rest of her schedule. She was preparing another uptown production of *Grand Street Follies,* and two more productions for the Civic Repertory, one of which, *Hedda Gabler,* would be the major event of the company's season.

So it was not easy for her to come to the apartment to comfort Tom as regularly as she did, or to concentrate on her own work once there, what with his thrashing around and starting increasingly ugly fights that usually culminated in half-hearted but shrill scenes of renunciation.

"What is it you want?" she would scream. "Do you want me to walk out on you entirely? Is that it?"

"Yes, that's exactly what I want . . . because that's what you want to do, isn't it? Go to your fancy friends and your grand family?" And he would spew out hideous insults about everyone in her life he had ever met, until she either held her ears or found new levels of rage in herself to attack him from. Sometimes he would demand that she leave, grabbing her by the arm and pushing her to the door. Sometimes she was so afraid the end was really imminent that she offered the one seduction that still seemed to interest him consistently—her ability to cook a superb meal.

Wolfe later described just such a scene, setting the stage by introducing a man and woman in the midst of a clearly familiar confrontation. The woman, as she is about to leave, gestures toward a large market bag she has deposited on the table. "Do what you like with it," she says angrily. "Throw it in the garbage can, give it to the janitor. . . ."

> He: (looking up and staring at the bag curiously) "What's in that bag?"
> She: (lightly) "Oh, nothing much. . . . I just asked the butcher if he had anything extra special in the way of a sirloin steak. . . . And . . . some little spring potatoes . . . you know how much you used to like the way I fix them . . . and a few oranges and apples, a couple of pears and a grapefruit . . . you know how much you like a fruit salad the way I make it. . . . Well, it's too bad to see it go to waste but I suppose it can't be helped. . . ."
> She turns as if to go but lingers on.
> He: (rising and putting a restraining hand upon her arm, licking his lips reflectively) "Did you remember to get some butter?"

They waited five weeks, while the tension between them mounted until the rooms they shared could scarcely contain it. And just when Tom was feeling a new surge of hope and had allowed himself to admit again his continuing love for Aline, a letter of rejection arrived from the publisher. A copy had been sent to Aline at home, and as she climbed the stairs to the apartment that day, her chest was tight with apprehension. Quickly she moved through her office to his room, to discover him sprawled on his bed, one leg stretched out, the other dragging the floor, the letter lying across his chest. He was utterly desolate: no one would ever be interested in publishing his novel. What's more, he moaned to Aline, he felt like a fool for having written it at all. The publishers had done more than reject the novel. Their letter of rejection seemed to dismiss the story entirely, as some all too familiar, predictable, naïve exercise. After first pointing out that the book was far too long to hold a reader's interest, it went on to say that although it did have some quality and originality, "on the whole, it is a pattern—the autobiography of a young man, and so much of it has been done, and so often, that we hesitate to take another chance."

For days afterward, Aline tried gently to argue Tom out of his deep depression. "They don't know what they're talking about . . . they're fools. . . . It's my fault for showing it to them in the first place," she repeated over and over again. It was then that she scrambled after the pages of manuscript as he hurled them around the apartment, protesting that he had no right to destroy "her" book.

In desperation, she went next to her friend Melville Cane, who was legal adviser to the publishing house of Harcourt, Brace and who some-times informally brought new authors to them.

"Please see him, Melville. It's very important to me, and I wouldn't ask you if I didn't think it is a brilliant book, destined for extraordinary success in the right hands."

Because of his affection for the Bernsteins, Mr. Cane agreed and made an appointment for Tom to come to his office. He recalls the event rather ruefully.

"Promptly at the appointed hour, Wolfe was announced. My secre-tary held the door open to admit him, a six-and-a-half-foot, lumbering giant [Mr. Cane is a small man] struggling with two weekend suitcases, which he deposited on the floor beside him." As Mr. Cane sat back, Tom rambled on about his background, stammering that "Aline was sure you could be of help." Then he picked up one of the suitcases and set it down with a loud thump on Mr. Cane's neatly organized desk. He snapped open the lid, revealing a huge pile of manuscript. "This is the first half," he said. "The rest is in the other one."

Tom read the shock on Mr. Cane's face and with some embarrass-ment said he didn't expect him to read everything, just sample enough to get some overall idea of the quality of the writing and the develop-ment of the theme.

In spite of this assurance, the lawyer found highly unpalatable the project he had committed himself to out of friendship for Aline. Later he recalled that as he tried to go about his legal business after Tom left, he became depressed every time his eye fell on "those two pieces of luggage." For his own peace of mind, he decided to tackle the chore immediately, and that night he left the office "carrying suitcase number one, for after-dinner investigation."

At first, as he soon reported to Aline, he shared her enthusiasm, recognizing "the driving, passionate force behind the writing, as unre-strained as a force of nature, the words gushing forth, like a spring torrent, bursting all barriers and overflowing river banks."

But as he continued reading, while his admiration for that force continued, the undisciplined quality of the writing grew more trouble-some. He doubted that any editor would want to assume the herculean task of whittling the book's many excesses, and he urged Aline to tell Tom, as he would himself, that he would do well to compress the manuscript before submitting it elsewhere.

"He'll never agree to that," Aline said simply, and of course she was correct. She thought now of another route to try. Through Thomas Beer, Aline got the novel, still in its two suitcases, to Ernest Boyd, a literary agent and respected critic. Unfortunately, Boyd did not care for novels very much, and generally passed them along to his wife, Madeleine. At the time Tom's novel was delivered, however, the Boyds were in the midst of a serious marital battle, and Mrs. Boyd didn't look at the manuscript for several weeks. Since Aline had emphasized to Tom the significance of having the Boyds involved in his work, to encounter only silence again fueled his self-pitying fury.

So Aline gave a small prayer of thanks when she hung up the phone one morning after a conversation with Madeleine Boyd. Mrs. Boyd was tremendously impressed with the book. She had sat down one day at noon, and at 3:00 A.M. was still absorbed in the story. Only when she'd come to a description of one of the extraordinary meals consumed by W. O. Gant did she realize she herself hadn't eaten for more than twelve hours. The fact that she had been so engrossed made her jump to her feet, and in light-headed excitement, she rushed into the hallway of her apartment building, shouting to her sleeping neighbors: "A genius! . . . I have discovered a genius!"

A few days later, Aline arranged a meeting between the author and his potential agent, after exuberantly telling Tom that Mrs. Boyd was setting up her own company and wanted Tom to be her first client.

"She knows everyone," Aline told him encouragingly. "I really think it would be much better for her to take the book around than have me continue to do it. . . . And she's got just as much energy as I have, I promise you!"

In fact, the meeting was strained, each party finding unappealing characteristics in the other. "He talks so damn much," Madeleine said in an irritable aside to Aline, "and he's so suspicious of everything." And back in the apartment, Tom sulked about Mrs. Boyd's having taken offense at his asking about fees. "Her voice is so strident . . . it hurts my ears to listen to her." Still, she had agreed to act as his agent and they had shaken hands on the arrangement. After all, she was the first person in the publishing world to express any interest in his writing and he knew too well that he was hardly in a position to reject any kind of literary support.

Mrs. Boyd used to hire taxi drivers to carry the suitcases down from her apartment and up into publishers' offices, an impassioned speech for the defense always on her lips. But despite her persistence, the manuscript was quickly rejected by two houses. A junior editorial employee of the second house remembers that "My fellow reader and I jockeyed about for a good while before I managed to stick him with reading it. . . . He read 50,000 words . . . some of them aloud to me. What I heard of it was terrible. Finally, we sent the manuscript back, presumably in a truck."

It was all too much for Tom to bear. Here and there, of course, he got some encouragement. Publishers would "like to see his next, perhaps shorter novel." "There was much about this one that was original and well done." Still, the rebuffs scarred his heart and mind. Although he had indeed begun a new novel, which would later become *Of Time and the River,* he wanted desperately to publish this one. Even though Aline assured him that sometimes writers have a reverse success—their first novel being published after a later one wins approval—he could not abandon his yearning to achieve acceptance for his initial effort. He wanted recognition now. It was time. He felt old and used up, and his comparative youth was no compensation for the weariness of his spirit.

Predictably, as his despair grew, their battles exploded into a warfare neither could control, until too many ugly things had been said ever to be forgotten. In *The Web and the Rock,* Wolfe himself described count-less such scenes drawn from their life. He would tell Aline she'd "grown fat and prosperous on my life and energy. You've sapped and gutted me; you've renewed your youth at my expense!" And she would scream her own contempt. His mind was "poisoned," filled with "filth and evil." And: "You leave my family alone! Don't you open your dirty mouth about them. . . . I'll smash you in your face if you say a word about my family! We're too good for you, that's the trouble . . . you think everyone is as vile as your low corner-drugstore mind makes them out to be!"

There were other, no less dreadful times, when she wept and pleaded to stay, and went out into the hall and sat on the stairs waiting for him to come after her, and when he didn't, calling him or writing him or coming back to Eleventh Street with some lame excuse of needing a pen or brush.

At night, in her house on Seventy-seventh Street, or working with Eva in the theater, surrounded by gifted, committed people who respected her talents, she wondered how she and Tom had come to this terrible juncture. She had believed so passionately in him and what they might be and do together.

There was hardly a shared moment now that was not filled with pain.

More often than not, he was drunk when she came to see him. He was even drunk going to class, something he had never done before, no matter how great his distress. Aline was appalled; her beliefs about work and responsibility made her unable to accept such self-indulgence. That they were heading for a final quarrel was clear, and Aline felt the terrible weight of anticipatory dread. Furthermore, Tom's aggressive womanizing left him little time and apparently little desire for sex with Aline, and she would rage at him for rejecting her.

"You've gone with dirty, rotten women all your life," she'd tell him furiously, "and that's the only kind of woman you know about. That's the only kind you understand!" Tears of wounded pride glistened in her eyes, and she fought them back fiercely so as not to suffer further humiliation. But, in truth, his behavior was so outrageous, his promiscuity so compulsive, that its very excess provided some consolation. For surely it was nothing so simple as no longer finding her attractive that prompted such obsessive, depersonalized sex.

Finally, there was Aline's Jewishness. Tom hurled at her uglier and uglier epithets about "her race," and the very qualities that had attracted him to her—her warmth, her capacious personality, her loyalties and earthiness—now became negative attributes. His paranoia about his treatment in New York was projected onto Aline and the way she lived. He saw the theater, success, money and elegance as Jewish things, false and corrupting and arrogantly denied to people like himself.

In short, all the pain and defeat of these last months were identified with Aline, and only by freeing himself from her could he recover some peace of mind. Yes, he told himself one night, lying in his dingy bed, wondering where she was, or how easily she rested between her snowy sheets, yes, he must again "draw his breath alone," or in this melodrama he had created surely he would die. And as usual when his inner turmoil come to a boil, his thoughts turned to escape. He had money coming to him from N.Y.U. and some other money saved, since outside of paying his share of the rent, his personal expenses had been minimal this year. So he would go to Europe yet another time, travel, look for himself. He would tell Aline his plans in the morning, and he would listen to no arguments.

Wolfe himself described the scene in which he announced to Aline his plans for his "Grand Tour of Renunciation," calling it an act of "single and brutal violence. He told her he was through with her forever, their life was finished, he wanted to forget her utterly, to tear and strip her very memory from his blood, his brain, his heart, and go away from this accursed city . . . put a wide ocean between them, and let its raging waters wash away the last remaining vestiges of their life together."

Aline said little as he spoke. She looked at him from behind her drawing table, where she had gone as if to take refuge in a world she could better comprehend. What she felt most of all was fatigue. These months had left her too weary even to feel her pain. But what she would not allow him to do was demean what they had been in order to justify his destroying what they were now.

"You want to hate me and what we've known together, but you are lying to yourself. I know who I am and what I feel and what I've tried to be, and you will not change that, no matter what you say." And as she turned to leave the apartment, she said, "I have comported myself with honor."

In the days that followed, Aline clung to her dignity, despite her torment. They avoided each other's intimate presence, and Aline restrained herself from taking part in any conversation that might push her out of control. At times, both when she was with him and when she was alone, she felt so angry she believed she could commit murder—stab him with a knife so that he bled as he was making her bleed. She'd stuck to him through all kinds of abuse and allowed him to treat her as no one else would ever dream of doing, because she had seen in him the same streak of gold that ran through her—only his shone even brighter. He was crazy and destructive, but he was "the best"—there were "more beauty and more glory" in his "mad, tormented spirit" than in anyone she'd ever known, and it was an act against *her* to deny all this in drunkenness and cheap women and pointless roamings around the world.

But she needed time to think about it all, to understand and to plan. And so, when Terry Helburn called to propose that Aline join her in a weight-reducing "cure" in Carlsbad and then travel awhile, perhaps to Italy, Aline accepted immediately.

"We're not going to see each other," Tom said coldly when she told him her plans.

"I'm quite aware of that," she answered quietly, and put some papers into her briefcase to take home. It was too painful to work in the apartment now, even when he wasn't there.

As she left, he shouted, "I'm not even going to give you my itinerary," and she only nodded and closed the door behind her.

They did meet several days later, on the morning when Aline was sailing. She had called to invite him to the ship to say goodbye, along with some other friends and her family. He refused. Instead, he said he would meet her on the corner of Seventh Avenue and Fortieth Street. Aline stood at the intersection, scanning the streets, until she saw him lumbering toward her. The years fell away, and she remembered the library steps just a few blocks away, and how joyous he had looked when he first caught sight of her there. Now he was scowling and his face was flushed with drink and strain. As soon as he joined her, he repeated his vow of not wanting ever to see or hear from her again. There was little point in standing there, Aline thought, feeling suddenly rootless as people pushed past her on their way to their jobs in stores and offices.

She took a deep breath. "Goodbye, Tom," she said softly, and as she crossed the street to begin her walk to the pier where her ship waited, she did not allow herself to look back.

What followed this parting was a sequence of wild emotional swings, extreme even for Thomas Wolfe. Almost immediately after she sailed, he wrote her, saying seriously: "Since you have gone, I have thought more clearly about you. I think of you with pain and with love and I think I always shall. And it is very bitter for me to know that I have acted meanly and badly towards you." And after further apology, he added: "I am still stupid and numb over what has happened to me. But I have lost my ugliness and bitterness and I cannot deny, Aline, that I love you more than anyone in the world. This is as honest a record as I can make at the present time."

He no longer wanted not to hear from her, but instead gave her his full itinerary, and announced various shifts in it once he himself arrived in Europe. As for Aline, while she was at first overjoyed at his apparent change of heart, she wondered whether his original decision against any communication might not in the long run have been kinder. For although she clung to the hope that they would be together again, particularly in view of his continuing protestations of love, she felt something chillingly different in their correspondence. There was an element of reverent nostalgia in his letters that was both haunting and enraging, particularly when she thought back to his sexual rejection of her in the last weeks of their life together. Now, time and again, his passionate declarations of love would be followed by his expressed hopes for future meetings in "loving friendship." Sometimes Aline would respond in kind, but at other times she would write back angrily: "I feel that I will never be satisfied with this loving friendship you talk about so much. The phrase stings me with helpless anger."

This exchange was going on while Aline and Terry were embarked on a drastic three-week fast. The lack of food was making her light-headed, so that images of Tom seemed to float in and out of her mind even more easily than before, and fantasies of his response to her new, gorgeous self returned persistently. She wrote to him about her shining hair and her flat stomach, but he seemed either uninterested or concerned that she would somehow impair her "womanly loveliness." As for meeting, their letters vacillated between their joint desire to see one another and concern that they might find a brief reunion more of a strain than none at all. Also, both were aware of how easily they fell into patterns of manipulation when they were emotionally keyed up. These patterns appeared in their letters too, but could be dealt with more dispassionately on paper than in person.

Thus, when Tom wrote to her about people taking advantage of him because he was too trusting—a clear bid for her sympathy—she answered tersely: "I do not know who told you you were too trusting. They certainly have not heard you speak to me!"

And when, in a fit of despair, she sent him a drawing of a heart pierced by seven swords, saying that was how her own heart looked, and if he stabbed her once more she would bleed to death, Tom wrote back: "I think this is the first time in a letter that you have used your great cleverness of head and hand in a bad way. . . . You know very well that you are in no danger of 'bleeding to death' and that you have had a very good time this summer."

Aline *was* having a good time. Certainly, she endured days of bleak despair, but there were also days of excitement and fun. Terry, a tower of strength, was "tactful," knowing just when to make her presence felt and when to leave Aline alone. She also, like Tom, understood her friend's capacity for drama and often punctured Aline's darkest moods with ironic but loving jibes.

They took to the life of the spa like mischievous schoolgirls, poking fun at their fellow guests—the portly Germans with their sullen-looking wives, the Frenchwoman with her bleached hair and wrinkled skin and dainty little-girl dresses. At night, in the room they shared, they'd plan down to the last dessert sauce the enormous meals they'd eat when the fast was over. Every day they thought they could not last through another one without eating, but the improvements in their measurements spurred them on. More often than not, Aline felt dreamily languid, and took great pleasure in her own stoicism, as if it signaled that underneath the frantic despair she could still sink into at the thought of Tom, her strong self, however bruised, remained intact.

When the two ascetics left Carlsbad, they were joined for a few days by a cousin of Theo's and then by Terry's husband, Oliver, and together they visited Pisa and Rapallo. Aline went for long walks, following the rugged coastline, or rowed out in a small boat to watch the people on the beach and invent stories about them. Terry encouraged her to do some modest mountain climbing, and in her handsome English shoes and with a thick walking stick, she followed her friend along the mountain paths, enjoying the sensation of healthy fatigue.

She wrote Tom about everything she saw and said, but too often her letters were also laced with protestations of love, couched in language so intensely emotional as to seem threatening. There is reason to believe, however, that at this point her rhetoric was more intense than her anxiety. Her faith in her own powers was still too strong for her really to believe she had lost him forever, and she was using what weapons she had against the one opponent she had ever had real difficulty in conquering. Wolfe would say with a note of awe: "Behind this flowerlike and rose-lipped face, were stored the energies of an indomitable will . . . this exquisite and lovely little creature who could weep bitterly . . . was beyond comparison, the most determined and formidable antagonist."

So although she wrote him bitterly about his deciding not to meet her in Berlin after all—she herself had at one point expressed similar doubts —she was hardly in a state of despair when she arrived there. She had talked Terry into taking an airplane from Prague to Berlin, and although she felt a bit guilty during the bumpy, noisy flight whenever she looked across at her friend and saw her green complexion and acute discomfort, she herself was almost drunk with excitement. She could not believe how the earth looked from the sky—what a magic glimpse of the planet that housed her life. How far she had traveled from buggy rides with Aunt Nana around Broadway!

Her letter to Tom reporting the flight, however, stressed her lack of fear. After all, without him, what did it matter whether she lived or died? When she wrote the letter, she probably felt that way, but since, in other moments, she still believed they would ultimately find their way back together, she could continue enjoying a good deal of her life on her own, whether she admitted it to him or not.

And indeed, by the time she sailed for home in August, she was more irritated with him than longing for him. Not only was he treating her badly; he was wasting his time with his foolish wanderings. All summer she had been urging him to work seriously—to try and revise the first novel—"You can't just spill your heart on paper"—or to work seriously on the new one. In a shipboard letter, she repeated her admonitions and finished with an impatient scolding: "I wonder if you know what you do. Take care of yourself, and be faithful to your own goodness, and don't, for God's sake, waste everything as you have me."

# 16

I t was not easy to come home to New York this time. She felt as though she were in a state of suspension, her footing uncertain on the path of her life. One particularly jarring note was the news that Theo had finally capitulated and sold their house. He had written to tell her this while she was away, but she hadn't had the time or concentration to confront what the fact would mean to her. But she knew now, as she walked around the dearly beloved rooms, and fingered the familiar walls and handsome mahogany doors.

"Oh, Theo, where will we ever find something so wonderful again?" she asked sadly, although she quickly assured him she understood he had no choice but to decide as he had.

"It almost makes me share your contempt for capitalism," Theo answered, with a pained smile, and he explained again, as if to convince himself of the rightness of his choice, that a large company had bought up every inch of ground except for the plot their own house stood on. If they didn't move, they would be completely surrounded by construction, and eventually by huge apartment buildings that would smother their beloved little home.

Edla said she would concentrate on finding a new place for them to live in, and tried to hide her own sadness to ease her mother's very real pain. Teddy said he had spoken to the builders, and they probably had till May before things got really oppressive. This meant they wouldn't have to think of moving immediately, but to Aline even such tender words of cheer were not very helpful. She was totally bereft and her grief underscored the loss of Tom's presence. Did it make her feel better or worse that he seemed to miss her as much as she missed him? She hardly knew. And she did know all too well how erratic his feelings were. While she was heartened by his words of love, her fear as to its duration remained. Still, it helped to hear how much he missed her, how frightened he had felt when he realized she had actually left Europe and that his seesawing about seeing or not seeing her was now irrelevant.

Moreover, however certain he was about his love, he was still unsure of the place he wanted it to have in his life.

"For me," he wrote in the first of a typical sequence of letters, "this is the most poignant and bitterest moment of all. . . . I have never felt so keenly the certainty of our parting as I do now, writing to you on the ship that will take you thousands of miles away from me."

Yet his next letter only celebrated their past and gave no hint of irrevocable doom: "It has been three years since we met. I have crossed the ocean five or six times during that time, a thousand scenes have passed before me. It seems very long. How long it must seem to you, who have carried it along with fifty other things, I do not know. Everything I have said or seen during the past three years has been radiated by you, or has streamed in towards you. . . . My glorious and beautiful Aline, who are one immutable youth to me, I love you, I love you."

And still another, that spans both moods: "My dear, my darling, we were the only lights in the enormous dark. All the pain, all the weariness, all the agony, all that has happened and that has passed between us could not outweigh the miracle and power of love which in a wild and winter place has kept me warm. And now you are going back into your way, and I am going on somewhere into mine."

Her own replies crossed the sea in an uninterrupted flow. Apparently she could not mark a day as having been lived if it did not include a letter to Tom. They carried stern reminders that his first duty must be to his work: "You are now in the most precious time of your life, and it seems to me you are doing the same thing you did years ago, aimlessly wandering."

But they were also filled with love and lament:

"We are in a curious place now, my dear, and I must wait. I do earnestly want you to have time to recover your self . . . maybe to get a clearer view of what there is for us in life."

"If I feel no happier soon, what shall I do? Just go on. Well, my darling, an ache only aches the person who has it. I've found that out by now. Time is a dream. I love you."

In the midst of such uncertainty, she thanked God for her work. She was about to unveil at the Civic Repertory Theater an architectural construction she had designed to solve the continual problem of scenery storage which plagues all repertory companies. With rapidly changing programs, hanging and hiding scenery was a costly and far too time-consuming process. Aline had therefore designed a basic scenery hull, with evenly spaced openings and an innocuous background color, which could be varied in many ways merely by dressing it with appropriate arrangements of doors, fireplace, windows and curtains.

The first production of the Civic's 1928-29 season would be Molière's *The Would-Be Gentleman,* quickly followed by Chekhov's *The Cherry Orchard*. Mounting two complex productions within days of each other would normally have involved a major expenditure of time and money, but it was easily achieved now. As *Theatre Arts Monthly* pointed out, Aline could and did create "with the simplest means, interiors of quite different feeling."

Moreover, the economies made possible by the hull permitted Miss Le Gallienne to adhere to the concept of repertory, which Aline shared with so much fervor. With expenses reduced, the company could take chances on scripts uptown producers would have been reluctant to gamble on. While more obviously commercial plays were being done on Broadway, *The Cherry Orchard* could be seen on Fourteenth Street by people who might otherwise never experience it.

Aline was particularly proud of her subtly understated sets and costumes for *The Cherry Orchard,* which focused the audience's attention on the poignant dilemmas and failings of the characters. She wrote to Tom, admitting her pride in her designs, and his responses were often enthusiastic. Perversely, it troubled her that he seemed to be encouraging her in the career he had always regarded as a rival—as if he was trying to ease her absorption in him over to another area. When he wrote how sure he was that her work was beautiful and how fortunate she was to have such a rewarding vocation, she felt newly anxious.

If the family wondered about what the future would be, they did not indicate it. They seemed only grateful for Tom's absence. It was evident that Aline had spent her summer entirely with Terry, and they knew Wolfe was still abroad: it was hard to escape that knowledge with the constant flow of correspondence, discreet as Aline tried to be. But letters were easier to rationalize than four-in-the-morning phone calls, and so Theo's and Ethel's spirits lightened. Despite the impending disruption of their family life, its emotional integrity seemed reclaimed. As a result, old habits reasserted themselves, just as when someone has been ill and certain topics have been avoided, but once the person has recovered, conversation can again be spontaneous. So Theo took to teasing Aline as he used to about her penchant for taking over the lives of aspiring young writers or artists, feeding them, guiding their tastes in music and art, helping them financially. And, Aline had indeed found a new protégé, thus encouraging the family in their desire to read her association with Wolfe as that of nurturing mentor and gifted aspirant.

Although many of the young artists and writers whom Aline helped or guided did not achieve success, others did, particularly those who were students of design. Russel Wright always remained grateful for Aline's tutelage, and later a young Indian woman named Sointu Syrjala would refine her talents under Aline's direction. And now Irene Sharaff, who would go on to a major career in the film industry, had been hired by Aline as her design assistant. As a friend recalls, Aline tutored her directly and indirectly—"not only in design but in living." "Irene really enjoys music like Brahms now, and knows so much about fine painting," Aline would report, as if a plant had grown so strong under her care that it needed no further help from her.

But although the family had taken heart and she herself was certainly absorbed in the many aspects of her life, she sometimes sensed a spiral of decline. Her energies seemed slightly sapped. She would speak of being "tired," a word hitherto almost unheard in her vocabulary. Her concentration was too often dissipated by nostalgic reverie, and she would find herself, at dinner or at her drawing board, losing touch with the immediate present. It was really for this reason that she had hired Irene, for she was concerned that her work might suffer, and she was not only proud of but grateful for Irene's eager energies and obvious ability.

230

As late summer turned into autumn and Wolfe's twenty-eighth birthday approached, his letters carried postmarks that testified to his undiminished restlessness. To Aline these wanderings denied all the growth of the last few years. At the same time, never knowing where he was made her dreadfully anxious. Days, sometimes weeks would pass without a word from him, and she would have welcomed any postmark, just to know where to send her own letters, and to know that he still wanted to hear from her.

Each time a letter did arrive, it was painfully clear that he was shifting back and forth emotionally as well as geographically. They were often drunken scrawls, smudged and rambling. One was so bulky that she had to go down to customs to claim it. But when she read it, it made her cry in frustration. Sullen, meaningless digressions interrupted the lyrical professions of his love. Nor did she ever know what mood her own letters would find him in. She was anguished but not surprised when a letter arrived in response to one staunchly declaring that she still believed in his talent.

"You could not have found a little word that would sting better," he raged. "Do you know what my mind supplied in parenthesis? *Still* (in spite of) *Still* (no matter what other people say) *Still* (although you are thus far a failure) *Still* (because it makes me feel so noble and grand to keep on saying I believe in you when no one else does)."

Or he would analyze her page count in comparison with his. There may be more letters on her side, but his were longer. Hers were written "in haste," and besides, he knew how easily a turn of phrase came to her. She hadn't read one of his carefully enough. It must have bored her, or she was too tired to waste her precious time on it. As Aline told Dr. Hinkle with a troubled sigh: "He actually expects I will respond to every line, point by point, even"—she had to giggle at the thought—"when the points are so pointless."

Dr. Hinkle continued to supply the psychological insight and friendly encouragement Aline so needed now, and at home Ethel went on with her own brand of steadfast assistance, stepping in wherever Aline needed help, whether it was work on the house in Armonk, cooking for the dinner parties Aline continued to give, or providing Theo and Edla and Teddy with companionship and devoted concern.

They were all preoccupied at this time with the change in their living arrangements. They had decided not to buy another city brownstone, but instead to rent an apartment, and the Armonk house would in effect become their family home. Ethel's talents and her willingness to use them were consequently important to Aline: she wanted the house to be perfect, but she did not always have the patience or time to make sure on her own that it would be. She wanted the Queen Anne dining room chairs she had been collecting lately to be covered in needlepoint, but much as she loved to do needlework, the project would overwhelm her now. So it was Ethel who picked up her needle.

On weekends Aline or Ethel or, when possible, both went up to the country to check on the progress of the work, bringing samples of woods or paints for particular rooms. Neither the architect nor the building crew ever seemed to resent either of the sisters. They were won over by Ethel's calm and Aline's good-natured enthusiasm and their evident personal competence.

Thanks to Aline's research into eighteenth-century manor houses, many of the rooms evoked the architecture of that period, although on a larger and lighter scale. The fireplace wall in the living room, for example, was copied from a house built in 1740, except for a moderation in scale, and the pine paneling had been gathered from barns she had scoured the countryside for.

Each time she arrived on the site, with her drawings and samples, the architect and the workmen were astounded. Standing behind her, they watched as she layered plaster so that it was completely smooth, and sitting on the hillside over a picnic lunch she had contributed many courses to, they watched her demonstrate how to achieve colors unavailable commercially. Through her experience in stage design, she knew that an adaptable, almost translucent wall color could be achieved by underpainting with a darker tone and adding two light coats. While the color will appear to change, depending on the degree of sun or shade in a room, it never becomes dark or drab, even under electric light. Now, as the workmen finished their lunch, she said, paintbrush and plank in hand, "See, boys, what I want is a special blue—one that has a kind of soft glow." This was for the dining room, because it was part of her aesthetic philosophy that meals should be eaten in an atmosphere of quiet welcome. "So," she continued, "I discovered if you first paint the wall scarlet"—and she showed them the plank brought from home and painted that color—"and then you cover it with this lighter shade of blue, what you get is exactly the pale, glowing color I have in mind!" When they applauded affectionately, she dimpled and said, "And you'll be among the first people to have dinner in that room.

... I promise you that. ... And I'm a terrific cook. Probably better than any of your wives!"

These visits to Armonk were increasingly helpful to Aline as she prepared to uproot herself from Seventy-Seventh Street, and actually did uproot herself from the apartment on Eleventh Street. The lease would soon be up there, and with Tom's plans still so uncertain, it seemed romantic foolishness to hang onto it, particularly when working there had become oppressively lonely. Nonetheless, it was hard once again to pack up traces of their life together and make the rooms ready for strangers. She thought it endearing that Tom had told her to keep any of his things she wanted, as if there was anything in that rubble she could have any use for. But of course, she would save his books and the manuscript copy of the novel he had given her, held now in several binders. He was in fact very agitated about this copy, terribly concerned that the wrong person might see it.

It was during this period that Wolfe had the first glimmering of what certain reactions to the book might be. Although Aline had raised the issue several times, he would never pursue the question of what Asheville would feel about the easily identifiable and generally hostile characterizations. But now he wrote Aline from Europe that on impulse he had offered Mr. and Mrs. Roberts the use of the apartment on their intended visit to New York, and he was terribly worried about their having access to his papers. Aline, although annoyed that he had issued the invitation without consulting her—"After all, it's still half my place" —assured him that he didn't have to worry; she would take the manuscript out of the apartment.

In September, Tom took up temporary quarters in Munich, where he vowed he would begin to work seriously on his new novel. But in truth, he could not settle down to writing. As he had done in college, he lost himself instead in other people's books, visiting every store and stall to buy their work, devouring their stories and ideas until they in some way became his own. He needed to know what everyone had ever thought or said, and despaired of how much was left to read and understand. He spent his meager savings on these books, not only for himself but for Aline, writing her exultantly about the perfect book of poetry or history he had found for her. She answered each time gratefully, but always with the hope that he would leave these other writers for his own important work. No one else's writing would help him with his own, she told him.

She wrote one such letter to arrive on his birthday, but Tom spent that day in a hospital bed in Munich, victim of a drunken brawl at the city's *Oktoberfest,* the annual festival that celebrates the dark, extra-strong October beer. The festival lasts for days and the fair site is filled with merry-go-rounds, amusement stalls, gambling games and, above all, beer halls. Tom visited all the beer halls and became, even for him, spectacularly drunk. When the fair closed for the night and he started to leave, a man on his way out with a group of friends said something to him, lightly touching his arm in what was probably a comradely gesture. But for some reason (Tom sheepishly told Aline he didn't know why), Wolfe swung and knocked the man down with a heavy punch. Then he ran from the place and his pursuers as fast as he could, but because of his condition this wasn't very fast. A steady rain further confused his drunken vision, and he ran down an alley that proved to be a dead end. As the avengers attacked him, Tom kept slipping in the mud, and his wild blows fell like raindrops on his antagonists. He heard the awful scrunch as the cartilage in his nose broke, and he began to choke from swallowing his own blood. Finally, somebody in the gathering crowd called for help, and he was rescued by the police. He spent the next six days in the hospital, recovering from a broken nose and severe head wounds. There wasn't an inch of his face that wasn't swollen or bruised, all of which he described in minutest detail in a letter to Aline, a letter he continued writing for two weeks. When it was done, he sent it in two separate envelopes, wary now of the post office.

Aline was of course appalled at the news, despite the genuine remorse and love that accompanied it. The accident had sobered him and made him realize how lost he could be without her presence. He wrote that he would soon be coming back to her and that he would do everything in his power to make their life together work. Her answer told him how much such a promise meant to her: "I am yours forever. . . . I don't know what you want, but I am here for you." But she felt called upon to add

> You write that you are coming back to make something of your life, you said you were going away to make something of your life. The thing to do is to do it, and no one can do it but yourself. There are plenty of places in the world to get your head cracked and your nose broken, if that is what you are after, but why? Isn't once enough or did you like the way it tasted? . . . As soon as you come back, we will sum up what you want, and what you can do, and for once in your life make a plan

and see where you stand. You are too good to waste. We will hold together.

By the time Aline sent this message of encouragement, she knew there was something to be truly encouraged about. Earlier that week, Madeleine Boyd had called her in great excitement to say that Maxwell Perkins of Scribner's had expressed real interest in the novel, and wanted to talk to Tom about possible publication. Madeleine had tried to cable Tom, and Aline did so immediately, but both cables were returned undelivered. Now, of course, Aline knew why, and by now another cable from Madeleine had reached Tom, so that he also had heard what to Aline was such wonderfully cheering news. But he was maddeningly unexcited even when he received a letter of praise and a tentative commitment from Mr. Perkins himself. Maxwell Perkins was already legendary as an editor, and when Tom referred to him as "Mr. Peters," and wrote that "In my present state, Scribner's does not make even a dull echo in me," she could have wrung his naïve neck. He would continue traveling, he informed her, until he felt surer of himself, and meanwhile, he hoped that Aline would help him "get back a little vanity, a little self-belief."

And so her nightly bulletins bearing witness to his promise continued even in this whirlwind period of her life. As the weather grew colder, apartment hunting, which they were all involved in now, seemed particularly bleak. "Everything is too damned ugly or expensive or usually both," she reported wearily to Theo at night, echoing the experience of the rest of the family. She was also feeling upset by the impending presidential election. As usual, Bernstein politics were in conflict, with Theo unwaveringly behind Herbert Hoover and Aline vociferously supporting Al Smith. It enraged her to hear and read the anti-Catholic smears, to see how people's prejudices were once again keeping them from seeing a man's true value. Ethel did her best to moderate the dinner table debates, but more often than not Aline, in her own words, "stormed and fussed and yelled at Theo until he cried stop, and now he will not discuss politics while I am present, which suits me just fine." She even told Ethel that if she were "a young woman, I'd go into politics myself," to which Ethel rather acerbically muttered, "Thank God, then, you're not."

They had all been invited to the Goodmans' for election night, and Theo rather curtly requested that Aline try to moderate her passions, since many of the people in the room would not share her views. He needn't have worried; after drinking several glasses of champagne, Aline curled up on the sofa and went to sleep. "I'm sorry, Ethel," she apologized later, after they'd left for home, "but I knew Smith was going to lose, and I would just have gotten too excited. It's better for them to think I'm some old souse than to realize I think they're a bunch of short-sighted bastards." Actually, Mr. Goodman had been amused and had set the tone for the other guests by ignoring the fact that one of them was taking a long, peaceful nap in full view of everyone. "Aline did what she pleased," Andrew Goodman says with a smile. "We all always knew that."

Aline was now designing an uptown production, *Caprice*, for the Lunts and an unorthodox version of *Peter Pan* for Eva. *Caprice* had an out-of-town tryout in Boston, and as she walked the cobblestoned streets, she thought of Tom walking similar streets abroad and wondered again how she could induce him to come home and get to work. She had cabled him several hundred dollars before leaving New York, with the idea that he might have run short of cash and would not have immediate money for a ticket home. She was right, for when she got back from Boston, to her utter joy she found a letter from him saying he accepted her check and its intent gratefully and was booking passage back to America.

"I am coming home. I am an American and I must try to take hold somewhere. . . . I am tired of struggle and should like to fall in step if only I knew how."

Oh, she would show him how—who better than she could show him how?

And so, once again, Aline Bernstein stood on a dock, her breath making little puffs of steam in the early January air, waiting for Thomas Wolfe to come home to her. The sight of his giant figure on the deck of the Italian liner made her swell with so much feeling that she felt as large as he or it. As in the past, she jumped up and down with impatience until he had run down the gangplank and gathered her up in an embrace that would mark the beginning of what he would later call "the Indian Summer of their love."

The next two weeks were perhaps the most wonderful of Tom's life. After settling in temporarily at the Harvard Club (Aline had already started to look for a new apartment), he made an appointment to see Perkins. Aline had informed him of Perkins's reputation. The man who had introduced F. Scott Fitzgerald and Ring Lardner and Ernest Hemingway to the reading public was reported to be a kind and sensitive person, as concerned about his authors' egos as he was committed to their work. When Tom stepped into Perkins's office, he felt at once that here was a man he could trust, and when Perkins pulled from his drawer page after page of meticulous notes on the novel, Tom was in a frenzy of renewed optimism. Here was someone whose criticism he could follow and believe in, who could truly help him in concrete, specific ways. When he told Aline, she felt no sense of competition with the editor. Someone would later refer to Aline and Perkins as the "twin engines" that got Thomas Wolfe off the ground, and she was quite willing to share that role with someone who could bring to it skills she did not herself possess.

In the days that followed, she encouraged Tom to set down a plan for revisions that would indicate to Mr. Perkins that Tom had taken his suggestions to heart and understood their intent. Perkins read the outline in Tom's presence a few days later, and when he looked up from the pages he was smiling. Wolfe's first question was whether publication was certain enough so that he could mention it to a "very dear friend," and Perkins gently said he believed it was. Hearing this, Tom rushed out of Scribner's to meet Aline. And two days later, when an official letter of acceptance arrived, he brought that to her too. He then recorded the event in a ceremony that linked her to it. After writing the date, "Jan. 9, 1929," in his notebook, he continued: "On this day I got a letter from Scribner's confirming their acceptance of my book." Then he handed Aline a pen, and they both signed their names to the notation: "Aline Bernstein—Thomas Wolfe."

In a letter to Mrs. Roberts, Tom was equally open and grateful about Aline's connection with this life-changing event, and expressed his appreciation of her deep and genuine generosity. "Because I was penniless and took one ship instead of another," he wrote his old teacher, "I met the great and beautiful friend who has stood by me through all the torture, struggle, and madness of my nature for over three years, and who has been here to share my happiness these past ten days. That another person to whom success and greater success is constant and habitual, should get such happiness and joy from my own modest beginning is only another of the miracles of life."

Aline was willing to go on supporting Tom, and indeed continued to give him money, but he took a part-time job at N.Y.U., which again

237

allowed them to take an apartment of more comfortable size. It was similar in layout to the one on Eleventh Street, but a few blocks farther uptown, at 27 West 15th Street, very close to the Civic Repertory Theater. Aline could thus run over from a rehearsal to make lunch, or spend a snatched hour there, even though she might not be able to stay for any length of time. Her own life was still in flux (the Bernsteins had had to move into a hotel, because they had not yet found an apartment, and it was difficult to handle all Aline's professional assignments even with Irene Sharaff to help her), but she and Tom were enjoying a genuinely peaceful interval. And Theo and the rest of the family seemed to accept Wolfe's reentry into her life.

Aline was even able to accommodate his more actively independent social life, for it seemed that the commitment to her he had vowed in his letters had really taken hold. Thus she was not too upset when she arrived at the apartment one morning to help him get ready for an appointment with Perkins, and found him sprawled across the bed in all his clothes, including his shoes, his face and neck covered with sweat. When she got him awake, he explained that after he had been working till five in the morning, two Asheville friends had suddenly appeared with a bottle of corn liquor, and after a while he had decided to try on for them the new blue suit he had meant to wear to today's appointment. When his friends had finally left, he had fallen asleep without remembering to undress, but he felt quite unconcerned about it as he pulled Aline down beside him. "You smell like goose grease," he said to her with perverse tenderness. "All Jews smell like goose grease, but you smell like a flower too, a fresh dewy flower just out of the bathtub."

He was impossible, Aline thought to herself, but she loved him, and was proud of him, and it was as simple and as complicated as that. "I've bought you a tie," she said with a smile, "a blue polka-dot one to make the suit hum . . . and all the lunch you don't spill on the suit, you can sop up with it. Just you tell your friend on Fifth Avenue that he had better bring an extra fifty cents along to feed the clothes."

Laughing, Aline pulled herself from his arms and hurried him into the bathroom to shave, while she brewed some coffee, and did her best to remove the stains he had already got on the suit jacket. And as she watched him shave, she saw him peering out at her, a look of intense concentration on his face, and she knew that despite this period of calm, his mind was still "a battlefield," that he still wanted a million different things to happen at the same time. But while this hungry excess continued to frighten her, she was less fearful now, because of her renewed importance in his extravagant life.

Wolfe's meeting with Perkins was, as they all were, reassuring, although it was clear the editor was getting concerned about Tom's meeting the schedule for his revisions. They had in fact begun to have long working sessions together after Perkins's business hours, because Tom, left to his own devices, tended to put in more than he took out. When Tom complained to Aline that his work was being ruined, she assured him he was in the hands of a sensitive expert whom he must trust. Similarly, she encouraged him to cooperate when Scribner's asked him to change the title, *Oh Lost,* and they went over their favorite poems from Donne and Milton together, until one day Tom seized on a phrase from Milton's *Lycidas*—"Look homeward, angel"—and Aline knew, as he did, that it was the perfect choice.

His revisions were finally finished by April, but Perkins wanted even more cuts made. Tom would go into paroxysms of rage each time he came home from a meeting at Scribner's. "Those sons of bitches are taking the balls off me!" Only Perkins's suggestion that he might use some of the expunged passages in other work, and Aline's constant affirmation of Perkins's value, kept him calm enough to do eventually what Perkins asked. And he was pleased when the editor arranged for an excerpt from the book to be published during the summer in *Scribner's Magazine,* so that the novel, due to be published in October, would have some advance publicity. The prospect of seeing his name in print in a national magazine that he himself had read enviously for years lifted Wolfe's spirits immeasurably and, again, his happiness reached out and touched Aline.

Tom rented a cottage in Maine for most of July, and when Aline managed to take a few days to go up to New England with a friend, she visited him. He was supposed to be going over the galley proofs of his novel to make sure nothing had been misprinted or left out, but the task was awesome, nearly paralyzing. The knowledge that this was his final chance to determine what a reader would see overwhelmed him, and he looked to Aline to help him stop worrying over every phrase. She began to despair that he would ever send the proofs back to Scribner's, and it took infinite patience and encouragement to make that happen finally. By the time she parted from him, he was nervous but he was also feeling the triumph of completion.

Meanwhile, the Bernsteins were all ecstatic about their Armonk home, reaping the fruits of the perfectionism Aline had insisted on. They went up there as often as they could, and to her surprise, Aline did so most of all. She had a new love now, her garden. Much as she'd adored the house on Seventy-seventh Street, it had not given her a garden, and she took to this new esthetic expression instantly.

"I only want trees with a clubfoot!" she'd tell the nurserymen, meaning that she wanted those that would grow into interesting shapes. And she planted her flowers as if Robert Henri were overseeing her work; each bed was a still life. "If you knew Aline at all, you would know immediately that these were her gardens," her friends said. And they had ample opportunity to view them, for from the moment the Bernsteins moved into the house, it was open to visitors.

When Tom's story appeared in *Scribner's* that August, and the Bernstein family read it, they agreed that it was the work of an exceptionally talented young man who had vindicated Aline's investment in him. They seemed more than willing to put their suspicions and fears to rest without ever voicing them, and they were no doubt grateful to Aline for the lavish love and concern and devotion which encouraged them to.

Tom took a brief trip to Canada after leaving Maine and planned a visit to Asheville in early September. Aline did not mind. Her life was crowded with good things and she had all the delicious anticipation of *Look Homeward, Angel*'s appearing in the fall. She was proud of her own unshaken faith in the book, as if she had been midwife at a tortuous birth that someone less resolute would have given up hope for. Her pride was rewarded when Tom brought her the first copy to come from the bindery. She fingered the blue-bound, colorfully jacketed book, too moved even to open the cover. But when she did, at Tom's insistence, she read under the printed dedication, "For A.B.," words in Thomas Wolfe's hand meant only for her:

To
Aline Bernstein

On my 29th birthday, I present her with this, the first copy of my first book. This book was written because of her and is dedicated to her. At a time when my life seemed desolate and when I had little faith in myself I met her. She brought me friendship, material and spiritual relief and love such as I never had before. I hope therefore that readers of my book will find at least part of it worthy of such a woman.

# 17

After the happy summer in Armonk, the Bernsteins and Ethel moved into a large and lovely apartment at 270 Park Avenue. (The only negative factor was Aline's reluctance to be a Park Avenue lady.) It had five bedrooms and an equal number of servants' rooms and occupied almost an entire floor. Long corridors separated the wings, and the living room, with a vast marble fireplace at one end, was regal in its proportions. The dining room opened off the end opposite the fireplace, and Aline draped its large glass doors with filmy white fabric. When the table was set for one of her buffet suppers, guests sipping cocktails in front of the fire could look through the doors with anticipatory pleasure. The size and arrangement of the apartment made Aline feel it was "almost like a house . . . if you could just block out the view of the elevator, you would never know you were living together with strangers."

And then she'd add: "I mean when you think of all those rich people's apartments you see, there's something so wonderfully warm and real here." She continued to ignore the fact that she herself was one of the rich she disdained.

"Oh, no," she'd protest, if someone pointed this out to her, "we're not rich like *they* are." And, Thomas Wolfe reported with affectionate mockery, she would prove her point by looking "for confirmation not at the hundred and thirty million people there impossibly below her . . . but at the fabulous ten thousand who were above her on the monied heights . . . who by the comparison were 'really rich.' "

Wolfe explained that her justification lay in her being "a worker." No matter how much money Theo was earning as a partner in the investment banking firm of Hirsch, Lilienthal & Co., or what investments he himself might hold, she was never simply a rich man's wife. She earned a great deal of money on her own, and she had built that success herself with only her talents and courage to rely on. As Wolfe said admiringly: "She had needed the benefit of no man's purse, the succor of no man's shielding strength. . . . She had made her own way. She had supported herself. She had created beautiful and enduring things. She had never known the meaning of laziness. . . . It is no wonder that she never thought of herself as being 'rich. ' "

Actually, although she loved the apartment, its grandeur had troubled her somewhat. But Theo was determined to make the move. He always enjoyed opulence if it was in good taste, and he could count on Aline to provide that. If he could afford it, why not have it?

And who could have foreseen that he would soon not be able to afford it? They were hardly settled into the apartment when the Wall Street crash occurred. Actually, Theo had been aware of impending trouble, and had taken some precautions with his own holdings, but he never anticipated a disaster of such dimensions. Despite his foresight, he suffered heavy losses and came home every night to the grand new apartment taut with strain and physically exhausted. Aline was conscious of the irony of the situation—Tom so exultant about new beginnings, Theo so worried about a possible ending. Many of their friends were literally broken by the crash, and Aline read the fear on people's faces when she went around the city during her day's work. She was reminded of some of the people down on Henry Street years ago, struggling to escape the tyranny of poverty or its threat. It made her own life seem almost sinfully good, and she vowed to hold herself together and give Theo the support he needed and deserved. And although she would enjoy the apartment as long as they were able to stay there, she would make it clear to him that no loss of face would be involved in leaving it. Though who at that time could afford to take over a lease of $15,000 a year?

Her concern made her more receptive to uptown assignments even though her work at the Civic was particularly rewarding that season. In their shared devotion to Chekhov, she and Eva had mounted a new production of *The Sea Gull*, which received excellent reviews, Aline's contribution having again been singled out for comment. But Broadway paid her a great deal more and money was important now. Although she had always supported herself, she wanted to contribute more to the household expenses. As long, then, as there were still people who could afford to go to the theater and were willing to pay good prices when they did, she might as well reap some of the benefits. And it was really a pleasure, too, to be free of a restricted budget. Challenging and rewarding as the Civic's jobs were, it was nice once in a while to indulge in an orgy of affluence, to order the most expensive fabrics and hire enough production people to help her.

Perhaps the person least conscious of the market crash and its potential effects was Tom, who was completely absorbed in the publication of his novel on October 18. Some reviewers qualified their praises, but overall his debut was an impressive one. He was acclaimed as a major new writer and that recognition filled him with exhilaration. "Listen to this one . . . Aline, listen to this one," he would shout, waving the reviews in his hands. He collected every one. None was too obscure for him to dig out and savor if it was favorable, rage over if it was not. He began to get fan mail from other writers. Sinclair Lewis wrote: "I wish I might have some fresh phrase with which to express my profound delight in *Look Homeward, Angel*. There is, you needn't be told, authentic greatness in it. . . . God, your book is good!"

And he got letters from ordinary readers—mothers who found in his story new understanding of their own sons, young men who, after reading it, found courage in themselves to break out of confining lives.

"Oh, Tom, I knew it . . . I knew it . . . I knew it all along," Aline would say proudly when he read her these letters, and she would embrace him tenderly. But too often these days he pulled back from her embrace impatiently. It was becoming chillingly clear to Aline that the demon of renunciation was again invading Tom's consciousness. Their interlude of love and peace was fading, for all the old reasons, and for new ones as well. Perhaps after all, she thought as she watched him frowning at her, perhaps he had come back to her only out of fear. Now that he felt strong again, he could break away from her love—finding it, as he

243

had before, too binding, too claustrophobic, no matter how hard she tried to repress her jealousy and refrain from making the slightest demand. And she was trying very hard indeed, under immensely difficult conditions.

Among Tom's fan letters were many from young women, who were greatly excited by the restless, undisciplined passion they found in the novel. They unabashedly wrote or called him, and he was seeing some of them. For some time now, Aline's sexual life with Tom had been waning again, and it did not take much imagination to understand that he was satisfying his sexual needs elsewhere. Yet this time she said little, hoping he was only carried away by the first heady excitement of his success, and that he would tire of these superficial involvements fairly soon.

If he did not want her sexually, she would try even harder to be important to him in other ways. But even here, perhaps especially here, there was difficulty. Although she had never resented Maxwell Perkins's role in Tom's life, now she could not help but worry about the effect of his displacing her as Tom's literary mentor. It was obvious that his need to attach himself to a sympathetic guide had begun to transfer itself to Maxwell Perkins, and that as far as Tom was concerned, Perkins was responsible for the "miracle" of his publication. Editorially this was certainly true. But it was jarring for Aline to hear Tom rave on and on about Perkins's genius, Tom's undying gratitude to him, and worst of all, his dependence on him. She could not help but feel that Perkins was in some way contributing to Tom's restlessness in regard to her, and this feeling was confirmed when Tom began to drop heavy hints that Perkins did not entirely approve of their relationship and had even advised Tom to end it. Perkins would later deny this, maintaining that he had not at this point even met Aline and knew her only as the "very dear friend" Tom had alluded to. Yet Tom did try to confide in the editor about his private dilemma, and although Perkins did his best to short-circuit such discussions, Tom persisted in asking for advice. And so, said Perkins, "I said that in the circumstances I did not see how the relationship could continue, and that since she was so very much older, it would certainly have to end. That is as far as I went."

Perhaps it was the need to enhance her value to Tom that made Aline even more comprehensive in recalling her past life for him. He was worried about what to write next, and he looked to her experience as a possible source. She began to write down the details of her life for him,

and when they were together, he gave her reminiscences his complete attention. Wolfe himself recalled such scenes:

> She would say: "My father used to go to Mocks. . . ."
> "Where was it? Never heard of it."
> "It was a kind of restaurant; he used to go there almost every night."
> And then he would ask her to describe what it was like, and she would recreate it down to the last remembered detail. . . .
> "And the name of it was Mocks?"
> "The name of it was Mocks."

Her father's visits to Mocks appeared years later in a story by Thomas Wolfe, which Aline read under the drier on one of her rare visits to a hairdresser. To encounter the borrowed data of her own experience was startling when so much time had elapsed since she'd explored it with Tom. It gave her, she wrote Thomas Beer, "an awful wallop to see it all in print under his name." But when she was struggling to hold on to Tom's love, she was quite willing to hand over her experience for whatever literary use he chose to put it to. For one thing, he was discovering how much trouble he could get into by writing about his own.

Asheville, North Carolina, had not responded well to reading about itself. Not just Tom but his mother and his whole family were being vilified by enraged citizens, and only the fact that the Wolfe family itself had received unflattering treatment saved them from being totally ostracized. Tom got letters warning of a lynching should he ever show his face in Asheville, and his phone rang with tearful complaints that he had broken the hearts of people who had always treated him kindly. Several lawsuits were threatened, and the Southern press generally denounced the novel, seeing it as an attack on the entire South. Jonathan Daniels, a friend from Chapel Hill, and at this time a young reporter for a Raleigh paper, wrote in bitter distress that Tom had cursed and spat at the State of North Carolina.

To Aline's amazement, Tom was astounded at these reactions. "But I didn't think anyone there would even read it!" he'd yell, or he'd protest that he hadn't really intended any harm. Why was everyone so excited about a story? It is of course possible, as Eugene Kennedy suggests, that Wolfe's anger at Asheville was primarily unconscious.

What was especially grievous for Tom in all the furor was Mrs. Roberts's response. His family had rallied around him, despite their distress, but Mrs. Roberts was deeply hurt and angered by his portrait of her husband as a "bully and a pedant." She wrote him that in *Look Homeward, Angel* he had "crucified your family, and devastated mine."

Aline understood that Tom felt orphaned as a result of all this, cut off more than ever from the sense of family. It would be a long time before he would be comfortable walking down the streets of Asheville (in fact, he went into self-imposed exile for seven years), and Mrs. Roberts made it clear it would be a very long time before she wished to see him again, anywhere at all.

This did not, however, turn him toward Aline. The presence of Maxwell Perkins and the autonomy of success impelled him to break free of any relationship that demanded an emotional price. Contributing to his mood of wanting to move on was the fact that the writing he'd been doing in the months before *Look Homeward, Angel* was published no longer interested him, and he was growing increasingly agitated about his next novel.

"People are always asking me what I'm going to write next!" he'd wail to Aline, and she knew he didn't have an answer. His worry did result in some softer moments between them. He would still look to her for approval and comfort when he felt especially vulnerable. Burying his face in her neck, he would whisper, as though confessing a humiliating secret, that perhaps he could not do a second book at all. Perhaps he had written himself out. Aline, of course, would jeer at such a preposterous thought, and croon her love and respect and conviction. But even when, with Aline's help, his ego was considerably restored, the nagging question of being a "one-book writer" blistered his spirits. He had become intensely nervous, and his apprehensions triggered new quarrels, worse and more frequent than ever.

The more he worried about what shape the new book would take, and when, the more he fretted over his commitment to N.Y.U. He had signed on for an entire year of teaching, but now he begrudged the time it would take. Perkins himself was concerned about his newest protégé's schedule, and as the sales from *Look Homeward, Angel* continued to rise, he talked to Tom as Aline once had about finding some way to live without teaching. Sizable royalties were coming in and Perkins felt he could talk Scribner's into advancing some money for Tom's next novel.

Tom was more than eager to agree to this plan, and when Perkins suggested he apply for a Guggenheim fellowship to subsidize his work for the coming year, he was euphoric. As he sat in Perkins's office grinning happily at this genie with the key to his future, he realized that winning the fellowship would solve not only his economic problems but his problems with Aline. He would have both a reason and the money to leave again, this time forever.

Immediately, he resigned from N.Y.U. as of the end of that semester, and without telling Aline, also set the Guggenheim application in motion. That she was ignorant of this part of the plan enabled her to express her real approval of its other aspects. No one wanted him to return in earnest to his writing more than she. In part, she felt it would keep him from his disquieting diversions, but far more important was her wish that he continue growing as a writer—that he build on his new fame to produce another book that would confirm his talent. Henri had once told her, and she passed the statement on to Tom, that "if an artist has but one other soul to believe in him, he can go on to conquer the struggle."

Aline, of course, continued to see herself as doing this for Tom. She would gladly have gone on supporting him financially while he went back to full-time writing, but at the moment it wasn't possible. Nor did Tom want that bond to continue. Aline chose not to look for any reason other than pride to explain his stand. Christmas was approaching and she wanted to enjoy the holidays. Thank heaven, Theo seemed less worried, and Teddy's job with the investment company owned by Maurice Wertheimer had remained relatively firm in spite of the crash. And enough ladies continued to shop at Bergdorf's to guarantee Ethel's job. What with Aline's own relatively secure career, the Bernstein family had good reason to be optimistic about the new year. And indeed, on her birthday, celebrated quietly with the family, Aline looked around the dinner table, and a rush of tenderness flooded her.

"I think we should have a party," she announced, "the housewarming we never had." As the family murmured approval, Aline grinned and said she had to celebrate her remarkable good fortune." "After all," she said, "look at me! I have everything I need in the world: two homes, a sealskin coat, two canned hams in the icebox, a dozen pairs of stockings, lots of shoes, a husband, a sister, a daughter, a son, and a sunny nature!" Her tone turned a bit more serious. "My God, my life is so brimming with work and love . . . oh, yes, we must enter this new decade with a celebration."

It would be a long time before Aline was to feel so celebratory again. On the night of her party, however, January 3, 1930, she was still able to look with eager anticipation to the decade that awaited her. As she finished dressing, scene after scene from the past ten years lit up in her mind. Eva Le Gallienne's ringing voice speaking as Irene Lewisohn walked on stage . . . Airplanes flying over horse-drawn wagons and lumbering motorcars . . . Thomas Wolfe's face floating past, and joining the images of Theo and her children . . . The miracle of time overwhelmed her, made her sad and happy together. These feelings stayed with her on her tour of inspection through the front rooms of the apartment. It was all truly perfect. The new cream-colored carpet she'd installed in the living room only last week captured the glow from the fire in the hearth, the soft shadows making secret, ever changing patterns. Everything glistened that was glass, everything shone with burnished warmth that was wood, every book of the hundreds that lined the walls lent color to the room. She hugged herself with pleasure and with pride. It would be a marvelous, wonderful, glorious party.

There was special reason for her delight, for she was giving her guests what she considered to be a rare treat. Alexander Calder, at the start of his path to world-wide fame, had recently created an entire circus troupe of wire dolls and animals, which he put through their paces on wire trapezes and flying swings. Aline did not know Calder well, but she was certain he was a sculptor of exceptional inventiveness. In early December she had visited a show of his work at the 56th Street Gallery, where, along with wooden toys, jewelry and other sculptures, some of the circus figures were displayed. When Aline admired them, Calder said that he would love her to see a performance of his circus, but that he knew of no place large enough to stage it in.

"Have it at my house," she said quickly. "It's often a circus there anyway. . . . I'll invite all my friends . . . it will be a great treat for them, and for me."

Aline's party was recorded by Thomas Wolfe in *You Can't Go Home Again,* in a way that Calder took irritable exception to. (He referred to Wolfe as having made "some nasty remarks on my performance . . . in a long winded book.") In fact, this was one time when Tom's unpleasantness was not without some justification.

Aline sensed there might be trouble when Calder, a large, lumbering man, arrived a half hour before any of the other guests, carrying five suitcases and a small gramophone. Seeing a bust by Noguchi on the hall table, he casually mentioned that he'd invited Noguchi to work the gramophone during the show and added that he'd also invited a few other people, but had told them to come only in time for the show. Since they wouldn't be expecting dinner, he hadn't thought it necessary to mention his invitations to Aline beforehand.

With that, he pushed and carried his suitcases into a back bedroom to get ready. The bumping and scraping brought Theo from his room, dressed for the evening. He looked at Calder's retreating back quizzically, and hurried down the hall to help with the suitcases. When he returned, he noticed Aline's rather pensive expression and understood its source.

"Don't worry, my dear. He does seems a little strange, but I'm sure it's just before-performance temperament. You should be used to that by now!"

"Oh, of course you're right, Theo," she answered, smiling. "It will be fine, I'm sure. Here, let me look at you. . . . Oh, you look so grand. . . . There's absolutely no one who gets that wonderful glow about them as you do in evening clothes!" And he returned the compliment, his eyes feasting on her smooth shoulders and graceful arms, framed by her dark-red gown. She was wearing a piece from her cherished collection of antique jewelry, a heavy chain from India with smoky exotic gems laced through it. Her face shone above it with innocent loveliness—the look that Thomas Wolfe always found so puzzling and that Theo quite simply worshiped, as he worshiped the woman it belonged to.

Tonight they pleased each other uncommonly and, arms linked, they walked back into the living room and surveyed what they had created together. They had invited few friends from the banking world, but many from the literary and theatrical worlds whom Theo particularly enjoyed: the Lunts, and Thomas Beer, and Alexander Woollcott. A number of the women were married to wealthy men, whose portfolios Theo was intimately acquainted with.

The party was a success from the moment it began, as Aline's parties always were. Although Ethel had also invited a number of friends, attention as usual focused on Aline, and, as usual, she basked in it. But while she was obviously enjoying herself, a corner of her attention remained on the front door. Would Tom come tonight or not? She'd invited him for several reasons. It would be good for him to meet some of the people here, either for the first time or under new circumstances. Now they knew he possessed the talent she had always claimed for him, and she wanted this recognition for him. Also, to some degree at least, she wanted it for herself. Let them understand, once and for all, that this was not some ordinary young man; let them understand, if they had not yet done so, that there were compelling reasons for her association with him. Furthermore, she wanted the pleasure of sharing all her life with him, and indeed, of having all the people she loved around her at one time. This was an outrageous wish; she knew that. But as long as she remained in charge, could orchestrate the arrangements, she felt she could allow herself such gifts. Yes, she "wanted it all," and still believed she could have it.

Finally, he arrived. He'd obviously been drinking, but not seriously, her practiced eye told her. As he moved into the party after greeting her rather shyly, he seemed to be making an effort to behave well, although he was keeping pretty much to himself, and Aline found it difficult to bring him together with all the people she felt he should talk to. Still, her optimism tonight encompassed everything, including Tom's moods, and she turned back to the friends she was talking with, a bright smile beaming her pleasure in their company, making them feel, although they all knew better, that there was no one in this room whom she would rather be with.

One of the group commented on Fuchs's radiant portrait of her painted when she was in her twenties, that hung over the mantel. Aline turned to look at it, and an image of herself as that young woman appeared in her mind.

"How beautiful I was," she said softly, and it was a statement that seemed completely without vanity. But when her guests murmured that she was even lovelier now, they, too, were speaking the truth, rather than being polite. With her dark-red gown and rosy skin and dancing, innocent eyes, she was a completely beautiful woman who had remarkably weathered the loss of physical youth. Thomas Wolfe stood in the dining room and watched the scene. His eyes followed Aline as she moved from guest to guest, and he thought to himself that all the other people were "ghosts." It was only Aline who had devoured time, who "alone remained immortal . . . stood here, upon the burnt-out-candle end of time with her jolly face of noon."

Suddenly there was a flurry of activity in the living room. Calder had appeared, Noguchi in his wake (he had somehow slipped into the apartment without Aline's realizing it). Calder was wearing a strange uniform of dark turtleneck sweater and football pants with knee pads; he explained that he needed them because he spent so much time kneeling during the performance. To Aline's horror, he began to rearrange

250

her furniture roughly. Books were thrown down from their shelves, and chairs and sofas were pushed into corners to simulate bleacher seats. Posters and signs were attached to her silk curtains and covered the spaces left empty on the shelves. When at last he had finished, he began to set up the circus. It was meticulous work and took over half an hour, and even those guests who were most eager to see the show lost interest in watching these preliminaries and drifted away to get another drink or something to eat. In the middle of his efforts one of Aline's maids appeared, a horrified look on her face. Great numbers of people had suddenly arrived and were pushing past the maid and into the living room. These were Calder's guests—all of Calder's guests. Some of them were familiar to Aline, others looked as if he'd thrown a bunch of invitations down in a trolley car for anyone to grab.

If Aline was disconcerted, Calder was delighted. He commissioned one of the new group to open a particular suitcase and hand out bags of peanuts for all the guests. They would, he told the party happily, recreate every bit of a circus atmosphere, and he opened up a canvas sack and began to sprinkle sawdust over Aline's new rug.

Theo and Aline were on opposite sides of the living room, and their eyes met and remained riveted in helpless astonishment. But it was funny too, and Aline at least could not help but enjoy the ludicrousness of the situation. Finally, Noguchi turned on the gramophone and the show began. And went on and on and on. The delicate sculptures kept coming apart, and Calder would have to stop to fix them. Only Calder's guests were maintaining a high level of interest in the goings on. They passed flasks around, and welcomed drinks from Aline's maid, and good-naturedly cheered every trick and spectacle.

Although the sculptures themselves were fascinating, the difficulty Calder had with them and the raucousness of his guests created considerable confusion. Many of Aline's friends began to drift quietly into the hall or dining room. When Aline, seeing the exodus, went to join them, they offered embarrassed compliments about the performance. Aline heard them out, her face dimpling, and then she exploded into laughter.

"My God!" she shrieked. "Do you believe it?" and in a stage whisper: "Isn't it the most God-awful mess you've ever seen!" Since this was exactly what everyone was feeling, they, too, burst into laughter, until Calder, like a stern schoolmaster, looked over at them with a dark frown. Aline, still giggling, herded her friends down the corridor to her bedroom, where they prepared to wait out the performance.

"It was utter bedlam," recalls Aline's friend Clara Weiss. "There were his pals screaming, and that awful circus music and people tramping up and down the corridors, looking for more peanuts, I suppose. . . . We felt as if we were barricaded in some kind of hideout."

Theo kept leaving the bedroom to bring progress reports. "It looks like all the animal tricks are over," he'd say seriously, adding, at one point, that of all their own crowd, "Only your friend Wolfe is watching. . . . The rest of our guests who aren't gone or in here are in the dining room. . . . Well, if this isn't material for one of Wolfe's books, I don't know what is!"

Shortly after he said this, there was a knock on the door, and they opened it to see Lee Simonson, carrying Calder's sawdust bag back from the living room. Lee had painstakingly crawled around the floor and filled the sack with empty peanut shells, being unable to bear their being crunched into Aline's new carpet. It was a sight that made everyone burst into laughter again, Aline rolling around on her bed with every exuberant whoop.

At last, the show ended. All the guests except for a few very close friends, like the Beers and Tom, had left. Calder, however, was still present, busy now dismantling and repacking. He seemed to have no idea of the havoc he'd produced, despite the fact that Aline's living room resembled the scene of some enormous natural disaster. Theo looked around the appalling mess, a glass of brandy in his hand, a completely bewildered look on his face.

The maids coming in to clean the room stepped on peanut shells, for Lee had by no means gathered them all, and looking at the heaps of books and furniture, one of them burst into tears at the enormity of the task that lay ahead of her.

"Don't worry about it, dear," Aline said, taking her hand. "As soon as Mr. Calder leaves, we'll all pitch in and clean up. Of course you girls can't do this on your own." Her voice was calm, and not only to be soothing. For indeed, if no one else did, she believed the evening had been well worth the price of a torn-apart living room. The performance certainly had not gone well, but the artist was remarkable, and Aline was confident that she would look back with pride on this night when Calder, Noguchi and Thomas Wolfe had been her guests.

But before they could rally their cleaning power, the clanging of a fire engine shockingly pierced the room, and there was a decided smell of smoke drifting in the air. Although Thomas Wolfe wrote about the fire, he did not give himself credit for an admirable act. The building had to be evacuated immediately, but the cook became hysterical and locked herself in her bedroom. As Edla explains: "These buildings then were very solidly built, and no one could have broken one of its doors down except someone as large as Tom." And that was precisely what he did, for Aline would not leave without the poor woman in tow, and they had no time to cajole her to open the door. So Tom threw his weight against the door, again, and then again, and after a few more tries, managed to break it open. Then he scooped up the cook and half-carried her out to the hall, and the family and the others gratefully made their way down the darkened service stairs, since both the elevators and the lights were out. Theo led the way, as they descended through the billowing smoke, and they all carried candles that Aline had found in the kitchen. At every landing, more people joined them, wearing every kind of clothing and revealing every kind of origin. Frightened servant girls from Ireland and Germany and France and Norway prayed in their native tongues, while men and women in evening clothes, probably just returned from a party, reassured one another in quiet voices. There were people in pajamas or coats thrown over their nakedness, naked fear on their faces. And behind Tom in their own little group came Calder, "puffing and blowing and letting the bags bump with loud thuds on each step as he descended." Helmeted firemen led them to safety when they reached the lobby, and they stood outside in the freezing air, watching the firemen trying to contain the blaze in one part of the building. To Aline, there was something horrible and beautiful about it all, something awesome in such ruthless evidence of how little control people have over their own destinies.

A few days later, Tom told Aline about his plans for the Guggenheim. She had been cooking lunch for him at the apartment, and he was unusually loving and gentle. But she sensed something was wrong, and she pressed him to tell her what it was. Finally, he stammered out the news, pleasure and guilt contributing to his excitement. As he spoke, the plate she held in her hands fell to the floor, its pieces scattering. Neither of them even looked down.

"How much?" Aline asked tightly.

"Twenty-five hundred for the year, away from America, no more teaching."

"So you'd let me down, sell me out for twenty-five hundred, would you?" She felt that suddenly, "black wings beat freezing air" all around her. And she shouted at him that when he returned from Europe last year he had promised never to leave her again. He had promised to be with her as long as they both lived. "What on God's earth can you find to balance my pain?" she demanded tearfully.

"I promise I'll come back," he said, not meaning it—loving her, but not meaning it, and she knew he did not mean it, and wept bitterly and lashed out through her tears. "Don't use the word 'promise,' never again. You have no conception of its meaning. It is a golden word, but to you it's only an expedient, it fills in the gap where you're lacking. You think you can fool me once more with that word. You think you can make me quiet with it before you go!" Aline, recalling this scene in a subsequent book, completes it for her readers:

> He tries to comfort her, but there was no comforting in this situation. Either he must stay or go, and his resolve was to go. She was holding so tight to him that he could scarcely move. He hated it. . . . He wanted a world where he could wander at his own sweet will. . . . He wished that he could tell her of his deep love, and still make her see the necessity of his going. He wished he could do all this without having to do it. He wished that he was far away in space and time, far enough so that he could write the book about her. There was so much in his mind, he tried to reach his notebook. He moved and looked at her face. The beauty was obliterated, sobs and tears and grief had made it red and swollen. It was like a battlefield plowed with the harrow of her pain. He wanted none of her grief, no pain but his own. He pulled his arm free, and wrenched the notebook from his pocket. . . . He wrote in the book, "Can there be no revolution without bloodshed?"
>
> She looked at what he had written. "No, no," she answered and her helpless hands beat blows upon his head and chest. She cried and beat until she had no more strength. . . .

And then Aline finishes, weary to the center of her soul: "they sank into the old embrace."

She was desperate, and she began to do desperate things. One morning, lost to any sense of shame, she went to her cousin Mrs. Willard Loeb, who was related to the Guggenheim family.

"Please," Aline whispered, her face flushed with embarrassment. "Please ask your aunt not to grant the fellowship to Tom. He doesn't need it. He can write just as well here. Better. Because I'll be here to help him . . ." Her voice, so faint already, trailed off, and she simply stared sorrowfully at her cousin. Mrs. Loeb, Aline knew, had always admired her, and must be shocked at this new, unlovely image.

As gently as she could, Mrs. Loeb told her that even if she was able to influence her aunt, it would be pointless, since Mrs. Guggenheim did not administer the awards herself. And then, feeling the need to be honest, she told Aline that Mrs. Guggenheim was a very puritanical person, and would not understand or approve of Aline's relationship with Thomas Wolfe.

Aline would say in a pensive moment years later, that loving Tom was similar to a "Japanese maiden's self-immolating leap into a volcano: she knew it would be fatal, but she couldn't resist." Certainly, corrosive flames covered her now, licking painfully at mind and body. There was a wildness to her entreaties, her pleas, her relentless demands that Tom not leave her again. Hers was the frenzy of a woman deeply in love, who had invested complex needs and feelings in another human being, and who could not imagine what would happen to those feelings if they were left suspended in space. Further, her image of herself as mentor, the pride she had always taken in her ability to help others, was being shattered. At the same time, it enraged her to be robbed of her just reward: she had a right to be part of his future when it was she who had shaped so much of it.

Finally, the girl with the pack on her back, the woman who always got what she wanted, felt that the very center of her identity was being eroded. She would fight that truth bitterly and implacably, fight against admitting that his resistance was stronger than her will.

So she continued working at the apartment, cooking elaborate meals for him or inviting him out to restaurants she had discovered and "knew he would adore." He countered her solicitousness with sometimes desperate rejections of it—taking up with other women and flaunting the fact. Friends began to witness the quiet weeping she was unable to prevent, even while she was working. Josephine Hutchinson, then an ingénue in the Civic Repertory, recalls: "She'd be standing there telling the seamstress what I should wear. 'Well," she'd say, 'I think you'd better have a straw hat with a spring band—poppies, daisies, blue bachelor buttons . . .' she'd be thinking very deeply about what kind of flowers would be exactly right, but while she was doing that and talking, the tears would just be rolling down her face . . . and all of us, the seamstress, Miss Le Gallienne, myself, just pretended not to see it . . . we'd go on talking and she would talk to us, and all the time, there were those tears."

Aline, of course, kept hoping that the grant wouldn't come through, and when she believed it might not, she could be less frantic and consequently less provoking to Tom. She could also then recover her personal code and recognize its responsibilities. So when Theo asked her one night to give a dinner party for his new partners, she broke a date with Tom to do so, without a word of complaint. And although the evening was intensely boring, she was able to concentrate on her role as Theo's charming wife. However, after they had left and she had gone to her room, she dropped Tom a note wickedly describing the event. She told him that one of the partners had brought along his married daughter, who had many more teeth "than her allotted number." The teeth made marvelous noises when she spoke, Aline reported, sounds that seemed to "rebound down her throat," but most intriguing of all, the young woman went on and on and on making these noises, while talking nonsense. "I was utterly fascinated," Aline finished, "by her empty endurance."

But her moments of levity were few as the time approached for learning if his application had been successful. One day Mina Curtiss called Tom to say that Aline was suffering terribly, that her friends were very worried about her, and suggested that it might be better for her if they made a real break. Desperate as he was for this to happen, he twisted the conversation around until he convinced himself that Aline, in collusion with her friends, was manipulating him to sever the relationship. Aline was "very clever about people," he sneered in his notebook and to her face, provoking yet another bitter scene.

The day the grant was awarded, in early March, when Tom showed her the congratulatory letter from the foundation, she wished him well in a small voice and, quickly, as if she were fleeing for safety, went home. But there was no safety anywhere, not even there. There was no longer any use pretending that the family did not know the extent and the source of her suffering, and the realization of how she was hurting them doubled her sorrow. "It was a shattering experience for them all," Clara Weiss remembers. "But they were utterly superb in maintaining that determined unity to the world. Not one of them ever discussed with anyone, even their closest friends, what they were feeling about Aline and what Tom's leaving was doing to her."

According to all evidence, they did not discuss it with Aline either. The immediate problem was that the person at the center of their family was in bitter emotional trouble, and this fact took precedence over the sadness and wounded pride she had caused them. This was true even, in fact especially, of Theo.

Tom was planning to leave in early May, and the race with time increasingly obsessed her. Too often her behavior toward him escaped the boundaries of reason, and then she was shamed and repentant. After one such scene, Tom declared he could not see her anymore. They should part now, end it now—not wait until May because they both would be destroyed by then. That night, she wrote him a mournful letter asking him to forgive her and change his decision. "Try to bear with me till you go, Tom . . . just walking out of this does nothing good. . . . I know I have been trying . . . but it's only since this has happened. Knowing you these years has been a miracle. I can't put you out from the innermost part of me. I will do the best I can to be good before you go, and put no more enmity in my mouth."

And she did try. She went to Dr. Hinkle's sanitarium in Connecticut, and when she returned a week or so later, she seemed more in control. But the scenes would erupt again out of their joint confusion and despair. As Tom wrote: "there was no medicine" for their misery, "no check against the marching grief of time."

Finally, too quickly, it was May, and in nine more days he would be gone. There would be an end to "the inner ache, the wild, sterile regret." These last days speeded up their rhythm; the race against time was now quite literally that, with Aline devouring every moment she could have with him, as if she were starving and must scramble for any crumb of food she could find. She would awaken him with a special delivery letter telling him she was "in torture," and only a little while later a telegram would arrive begging him to meet her for lunch at a Turkish restaurant they liked. She dogged his footsteps, going along on his last-minute errands even though every detail of his preparations stabbed her soul.

She woke from a drugged sleep on May 9 and left for Fifteenth Street, stopping at Hearn's department store to buy him some underwear and socks and neckties. When she let herself into the apartment he was gone, but there was a note saying he would be back shortly. Her mind paralyzed, except for its concentration on the details of packing, she folded his fresh laundry (attended to by her) into his valises. When he came home they went out for lunch, hoping to ease the strain. But if anything, it intensified. As they sat across from each other at a small table, with Mario, the restaurant owner, making a ceremony of Tom's leaving, to the point of giving him a bottle of cold champagne to take to the ship, reality seemed almost unbearable. Nervous and wretched, Tom in some ultimate irony began to accuse Aline of looking flirtatiously at some other patron, and she didn't know whether she wanted to laugh or cry, and so she did both.

Back at the apartment, they finished packing hurriedly and carried the bags down to the street, where Aline guarded them while Tom went to look for a taxi. She must concentrate only on the prosaic details of departure, she told herself, moment to moment to moment, and she must not allow herself to confront what the sum of those moments would soon be.

The taxi took them to the ferry, which in turn took them to Hoboken, where Tom's ship was docked. Together they stood at the ferry railing looking out at the city on the horizon. Aline smelled the sea, and immediately a thousand pictures presented themselves to her mind. If only this were the other ship. If only she were going to stand beside him there for days on end, could go with him wherever his restless soul would take him . . . It was dusk when they reached the *Volendam* in Hoboken, and Aline went with him to his little stateroom, a room she would have traded all the rooms in both her houses to be able to share.

"I'll unpack for you," she said in a small, lusterless voice, and carefully she hung up his meager wardrobe, and put his brand-new shirts and underwear in the little bureau. Finally, there was nothing more to do for him. Tom opened the bottle of champagne, and he and Aline sat together on his bed and drank it, all of it. Aline wished there were seven bottles—enough to blur the sharp edges of reality.

She put her glass down for a moment and opened her purse, and out of it she drew a medal that the painter Marsden Hartley had given her many years before, in the days when she studied with Robert Henri and was painted by George Bellows and believed in her own invincibility.

"Wear it, Tom," she said. "I wore it when I was your age," and he took it, and pinned it on his shirt, and kissed her hand. The night grew darker, the voices of other passengers and their friends sounded from the corridor. There were many parties, and much gaiety. How many were weeping at being left behind? Was it only she? Surely it was only she who had reached this dimension of pain, she thought with a touching arrogance. Even in misery, she experienced more of life than other people. . . .

They spoke softly of unimportant things, until inevitably, the gong clanged loudly, announcing to the visitors that they must go ashore and leave the travelers to their business. Tom took Aline by the hand and led her down the hall and out to the deck. A mass of people were shouting farewell and embracing, all foolish babble when measured against the words Aline needed to say and could not. How to articulate what the five years had been? How picture the specters that hovered over this next year without him?

"Tom . . ." she only said, and her face gave tortured testimony of her pain. He reached down, heart full of his own sorrow—for indeed, he did feel sorrow, and fear, and his own kind of love—and amid the babble and the high pitched hilarity, they kissed tenderly. She buried herself in his arms, and ignored the horns and the shouting. In the oasis of their embrace, she was oblivious to what anyone might think of the gray-haired little woman and the tall, dark young man kissing each other on the eyes, the cheeks, the mouth.

"I'm sorry, ma'am, it's time to leave." A ship's officer was pulling at her sleeve. She moved back from Tom dutifully while he began to shout at the officer for intruding. "He's only doing his job, Tom," she said. And with a final, barely audible, goodbye, she went down the gangplank, the tears pouring from her eyes. On the pier, she stood with the others who lingered while the *Volendam* blew her departure whistle and the little tugboats eased her out into the river.

Tom was at the rail, staring at her in the luminous moonlight, and she looked up at him, fixing her gaze on each detail of that beloved face. Neither of them waved or blew farewell kisses, as the men and women around them were doing. They only stared, one gaze upward, one downward, locked into each other's vision. How many times, she thought again, they had found each other's faces in a crowd like this— with eagerness, with relief, with joy, with anger too—but now in bitter and profound despair. Whatever countries Tom might visit, it would never be, she felt, as foreign as the country of herself seemed to her now. She was an immigrant in that country. Weak, confused, helpless. Wearily, she moved along with the crowds out to the street, where they boarded the ferry back to New York. The sky was streaked in milky white, and the water was black with mystery, and her heart was bleeding.

# 18

In a letter urging a friend to return to work who had been too despondent to do so, Aline some years later wrote:

> I have lived through such anguish myself, both in my own life and my creative life, and I have lived it and conquered it to a certain extent. It is never fully controlled, the anguish and disatisfaction. And I am still gripped by a profound melancholy more often than you think; but it inevitably passes, and is translated into something that flowers. So it will be with you if you resolve to work on your play.

Even before Tom left, during those last terrible weeks, Aline had scored one of her major professional successes with her work on the Civic's production of *Romeo and Juliet*. Aline believed, as did Eva Le Gallienne, that one of the most common faults in staging Shakespeare was overelaborateness, interrupting the flow of the play with extensive scene changes. Determined that Shakespeare be given the purest arena for his genius, Aline mounted a production where this would not happen. Her sets were designed so that effects were suggested rather than constructed, allowing the action to continue uninterrupted. Another innovation was to adhere in every detail to the text, which many companies did not always do. Nearly every production placed the scene of the lovers' deaths inside the Capulet vault, so as to focus attention on Juliet. But since this Juliet, Eva Le Gallienne, was far less concerned about her prominence than about the authenticity of the production, they placed the tomb (designed by Aline to approximate as closely as possible the gracefully columned "original" in Verona) stage left, so that the rest of the stage was all haunting open space, suggesting the churchyard the tomb was presumably part of. They were thus able to restore many lines usually cut from the script because they make no sense when the actors are already inside the tomb: when the dying Paris says, "If thou be merciful,/Open the tomb, lay me with Juliet," or when Friar Laurence pleads with Balthasar, "Go with me to the vault." They seemed small matters to some people, but to Aline they demanded respect. She expressed her reverence for Shakespeare in her own way. "Everything he asked for, I tried to give him," she said proudly.

But of course, once the work was over, and Tom was gone, the pain crushingly returned, leaving her breathless. The summer stretched ahead of her like an endless road leading to a life she could not imagine. She loved the house in Armonk, loved every aspect of living there, but it was not enough to answer the question of what life would be without Tom. And it seemed as if fate was being particularly mocking, testing her resilience and her capacity for survival. Almost at the same moment that Tom left, Theo announced that he would like to rent the still new apartment to someone he had managed to interest in it. They had all talked often about subleasing the apartment, but no one had really taken the idea seriously. However, Theo was being extremely serious now.

"I think we must accept the offer," he said at dinner. "We could hang on and see if things get better, but I don't think they will, and I don't know when we'll find someone else who can afford this place."

Teddy, whom Theo had already talked to, explained what they of course already knew, that carrying two homes the size of theirs was absurd in this depression economy. Even before he finished speaking, the rest of the family were murmuring approval, and Aline rose from her chair and stood behind Theo and put her arm on his shoulder. "Of course we must do it, Theo. . . . We've lived here long enough to enjoy it, and besides, I'm an actor's daughter. . . . I'm used to packing my trunk and moving on!"

And so, once again, they mobilized themselves and emptied the apartment, bringing some of the furniture up to Armonk, storing the rest until they could decide where they would live next. But the upheaval made Aline feel more than ever in a state of limbo. Commuting from Armonk also took some getting used to, although she did very little of it. Her work was pretty well over for the summer, and when the family left in the morning for New York, she most often kissed them goodbye like the little housewife she had never been, and was free in their absence to think compulsively and continually of Tom. She had received one letter from the ship and one from Paris when he arrived, but since then she had heard nothing.

In his letter from Paris Tom wrote that her presence invaded the city, her image was reflected wherever he went. There was no café he could sit in without her ghostly presence at an adjoining table, no path in the Tuileries that did not show him her flower face beaming at the beauty of the other blossoms. Such loving messages had filled her with hope, but every empty day that went by chipped away at her desperate optimism. The phase of his life during which he wrote his novel was over, and to stay with her was to stay rooted in the past. He needed to move on unencumbered, to new books, new experience and—she could hardly bear the thought—new people. She knew all this, but she could not accept it.

For a while she soothed her terror by reminding herself that he must be planning to keep in touch with her; otherwise, he would not have asked her to keep recording her past for him. But argument could not prevail against the mailbox, which she watched from her window like a sentry, until the uniformed sleeve could be seen opening the little door and inserting its pile of envelopes of assorted colors and sizes. As soon as the mailman disappeared down the road, she flew out of the house and raced to the box, her heart pounding. With trembling hands, she gathered up the letters and sank down on the grass, not even waiting to take them indoors or to an outside table. If she spotted a foreign stamp her breath stopped, before she realized that the letter was from Irene Lewisohn or was addressed to Ethel.

Reading Aline's letters to Tom during this period is to watch her struggle to remain in control, the tough Aline spirit fighting its way through the flabby helplessness of the woman who has been set aside. But if writing to him involved her in a painful battle with herself, writing about herself *for* him was sometimes equally hard. For the rush of feelings that poured in from the past was all but intolerable when combined with her present torments. The innocence of that world, of that child, who never knew what her woman's life would become, touched her profoundly. Still, the kaleidoscope of life as she had lived it fascinated her, and in her stronger moments gave her that sense of continuity which had always sustained her. She found herself thinking how rewarding it might be to write the story herself, to make this tale of an actor's daughter, of a growing city, of a wild and loving family, into a book of her own. But she quickly put the thought aside, if not completely out of her consciousness. To write a book, challenging as the notion was, still was far less important than pleasing Tom, and so she would go on handing him her past for his future use.

Although all her equipment had been moved up to the long studio on the top floor of the house, she did very little work. She would find herself at her drawing table, staring out the windows at the spectacle of sloping lawns and brilliant flower beds, and she would put her pencil or pen down and go outside. She spent an enormous amount of time in her garden. "The lilacs are literally blazing away, and the tulips are out, and the dogwood make my fingers itch to paint them," she wrote to a friend, adding that she was doing little painting, just as she was doing little designing for her fall projects, for "All art seems a terrible pain now." For the most part, she tried to busy herself with labor that would leave her no time for thinking, the kind of work she really loved— sewing curtains or polishing floors until every grain of the wood shone, or edging the grass along the places where the gardener's mower didn't reach. She would rise around five and step outside to the garden to wait for the sunrise, and after breakfasting with the family at seven-thirty, she would kiss them all goodbye and go inside again to confer with the "Swiss queen of the kitchen." And then, armed with shopping lists, she would be driven into the town of Pleasantville to do her marketing among the local housewives and uniformed cooks. Her interest in homemaking renewed Ethel's, and on weekends when the cook was off, and even sometimes when she was on, they cooked "the best meals in the U.S.A." After one spectacular lunch on a spring Saturday, Theo looked at the two sisters and said, "I'll give you girls ten dollars a month extra to stay on for the rest of the season."

But that lightness of mood did not always enliven their mealtimes. Despite her efforts, Aline's spirit was visibly shaky, and although she seemed better now than she had earlier, the family bore bitter memo-

263

ries of the days immediately following Tom's departure. They remained alert to any sign that she might relapse into the destructive despair whose raw pain had set her on Tom's own route of emotional escape.

"He taught her how to drink." Bella Spewack says bitterly about Wolfe. "I never saw her not know when to stop drinking until she got involved with him. That was his gift to her."

Indeed, on many of the family's last evenings in the apartment, Aline had left the dinner table, her plate untouched, her speech slurred by the drinking begun alone in her room and persisted in as the meal progressed. Once, after a day of arranging for things to be moved and stored, she had declined to have dinner at all, pleading fatigue, and had sat instead at her window, drink in hand, bottle nearby, looking out at the city, at the young couples walking past, at the lights coming on in the buildings. So much taking place out there, such a void in her own heart. The panorama lured her to join it, and, legs shaky, she poured the remaining gin into a silver traveling flask and left the apartment without letting anyone know. She walked among the people, studying their faces, as though looking for someone or some answer. A few returned her stare, and she heard their laughter when she walked by and thought of those pathetic old women who inhabit the city, mumbling to themselves in their loneliness. When she reached Central Park, she walked down a path and sat on a bench. The silver flask felt cool to her hands, and reflected the lights of the city in the descending dusk. Steel and brick and glass blurred in her gin-coated vision into a brilliant mosaic; an hour, and then another, and then another passed. The parade of passers-by never stopped, although their outlines changed as it grew later. Instead of businessmen striding home from work, or children hurrying to the dinner table, there were young couples, love and sensuality defining their bodies as they held hands or brushed against one another while they walked. She sat there, leaning now somewhat lopsidedly against the bench, and cried softly. Suddenly she saw a tall, dark-haired young man walking toward her, dressed in a blue suit like Tom's, and her heart raced with joy. He was not with another woman, not with any young, firm-fleshed girl. He was alone, and he was coming to her.

She sat up, her eyes level with the blue trousers, and raised her eyes to his face, a broad, grateful smile on her own. But it wasn't Tom. It was a policeman.

"Are you waiting for someone, ma'am?" he asked politely. "Yes, I am," she answered, marveling at his sensitivity. How did he know she was waiting for Tom, would wait for him forever? She tried to explain why Tom was so valuable that she would be willing to sit so long waiting alone on a bench, but she knew even as she mumbled her story that she was making no sense; that she had no way of explaining what was in her heart.

Still polite, the officer told her he believed she'd had too much to drink, and she'd better let him take her home, and just where was home, anyway? When she gave him her address, he didn't believe her and, with her permission, opened her purse to find some identification. Closing it with a sigh, he helped her up and took her by the arm. The firmness of his grasp immediately brought back Tom's fierce grip that first extraordinary night, five extraordinary years before. The memory saddened her so that tears began to fall again, and she tried to pull her arm away to wipe her eyes. But the policeman's grip only tightened as he led her to the street, and she realized he was not simply helping her, but making sure she stayed out of trouble. It was a sobering thought, and in the taxicab, the silent officer at her side, her humiliation was profound. She was afraid that the family would still be awake when she came home, was brought home, and she prayed they wouldn't be. She was still quite drunk, despite the shock of this confrontation. She'd been drinking for hours, and she hadn't eaten all day, but she was aware enough to know she had sunk into the kind of irresponsible self-destruction she had always abhorred.

The family was asleep, but her absence had been noted. Theo had gone into her room earlier to see how she felt and had seen the empty gin bottle lying on the floor. Wearily he picked up the bottle and took it to the kitchen and threw it out so that the maids would not gossip when they cleaned Aline's room.

Since coming to Armonk she'd done comparatively little drinking, although there were days and nights when she needed whiskey to pull her through. But she'd managed to stay within the limits she had fixed for herself. The night in the park had frightened her. It demonstrated how she, as well as Tom, could disappear, and she dreaded to lose herself like that again.

Even though the family was encouraged by her recovered sobriety, they were keenly aware that the grief that had led to her drinking was still with her too much of the time. When, in June, Eva Le Gallienne asked her to come for a few days to Smith College, where Eva was to be given an honorary degree, they urged Aline to go. And indeed, the excursion proved a good idea. Eva's devoted friend Josephine Hutchinson came too, and the company of these bright, warm, gifted women restored some of Aline's image of herself. Furthermore, she had never seen a college commencement before, and she was fascinated by the different colors of the academic robes and all the sensory detail, from the parents "moist with tears and sweat," to a pair of visiting "antique professors from London University dressed like beefeaters!"

When Eva received her Doctor of Humane Letters degree, Aline glowed with pride. Her friend looked so regal and she received such thunderous applause. "And you'll never believe what happened then," Aline reported gaily to the family on her return. "She took a curtain call! She stood there in her cap and gown, bowing as if she had just done Juliet."

It was good to hear her laugh, but when more days went by with no word from Tom, the tension returned. As the summer continued, hot and arid, and the grass began to look, Aline said, like "shredded wheat," her spirit seemed to be drying up also. Sometimes she wanted to scream with rage and frustration. What was he doing with himself? How dare he take his ideas for a new novel, many of them *her* ideas, off to Europe, together with his love, leaving her utterly abandoned?

In her letters she begged him to do something that would make all this suffering worthwhile. "If you'll only work and not drink all over Europe, there will be at least some justification for your desertion of me. Will you write and tell me about it, tell me you have started? Not just little scraps when you come home late at night, but real hours of steady work. Please make a schedule and stick to it."

She literally battered him with her demands and her accusations, and predictably, these assaults intensified Wolfe's yearning to escape. Despite Aline's passionate commands that he go on writing, her onslaughts destroyed the quiet concentration he needed in order to work. He tried writing back, but he didn't know what to say. He was too confused about what he wanted and didn't want from her. So her letters kept coming, and his sense of being hounded increased to the point of paranoia. He became convinced that everyone he met in Europe who knew her even slightly was a spy, reporting back every detail of his life.

In town one day to deal with some household problem, Aline called Melville Cane for lunch, in the hope that it would cheer her up to gossip with him about the theater and books. Instead, she found herself spilling over with talk of Tom, his lack of contact, her fear, her need, and her sadness.

"Melville," she said finally, when the torrent at last subsided, "Melville, is it right that people should have to suffer so?" And her old friend took her hand and said that, right or wrong, they both knew life was like that. The only comfort he could give her was to assure her of Tom's talent. Perhaps she could find some solace in that fact.

When they left the restaurant, she did feel a little better, but riding home on the train, she was shaken by the extent to which she had unburdened herself. Melville Cane and his wife, Florence, were good friends of Theo's and she had, with her confession, put a great burden on that friendship. Melville was of course a sophisticated man and, as a lawyer, understood the frailties and complexities of human nature. But she was miserable at the thought that she might have demeaned Theo's image in his friend's eyes.

On August 11, she sent a cable to Geneva. It said: "Help me, Tom." And it produced a response. He cabled that he loved her, but that she must be fair and they must help *each other*. He also gave her his next address and promised a letter would follow. His cable arrived in Armonk at midnight. Aline clutched the phone as though it were an extension of Tom's body, and made the operator repeat the message several times. Then she lay in bed, her head and heart pounding, not knowing what to think. The message had been so short—what was he really saying to her?

Any hope she could summon during the next few days was dashed by the letter he did indeed write. In it he said he would never love anyone as he loved her, that he would never forget her, but that he must give himself over only to his work, and that she must do the same. Unlike him, he added, she had a loving family, and "if you feel the agony about me that you say you feel in your letters and cables, I can only say that you should give yourself completely to those things you have." He added that his words might seem "brutal, but you know what I feel and that I gave everything in me to my love for you."

She read the letter perhaps a hundred times, and although its tone remained what it had been, she felt the spiral of tension relaxing. At least she *had* heard from him, inadequate and unsatisfying as his response had been. And he had said he loved her, even though he was still trying to escape.

So she did her best and for the first time all summer was able to pull herself together. She wrote to Tom more calmly, reporting on her work and implying that she would pick up the pieces of her life and stop mourning for the past. Unfortunately, as she confided to a friend, this decision would only "work for a while, but then that other business starts up and takes me by the throat." But for a while at least, she took pride in going through a day without any stumbling. A day without her writing to Tom was a triumph, and there were many such days, even weeks. And when she did write, her letters were amiable rather than ardent, filled with amusing details about the amazing adventures of everyday life. One letter delightfully described a visit from a "neighbor lady" named Miss Smith, who came to the fence one day while Aline was weeding. She was a nondescript, gray-haired "little old maid," and Aline was careful to keep their chatty gossip innocent and polite. When Aline, on Miss Smith's inquiring, told her she was in the theater, she expected her neighbor to be shocked, but instead she simply smiled benignly at finding someone else in a profession as exciting as her own. For it turned out that Miss Smith had recently retired from a lifelong career as an agent in the United States Secret Service. That nothing in the woman's appearance in any way suggested such a story enchanted Aline. "I'm going to see her again very soon," she wrote Tom. "I want to understand her life."

She was even able to look ahead to the fall and to her work. They would also have to make some living arrangements in the city. Now the idea was to find a hotel apartment, because Theo believed they could thus cut down significantly the household overhead, even if they took really elaborate quarters . . . "which I trust we will," he said with a smile.

Such a plan seemed particularly appropriate because Aline, along with her work for the Civic, had contracted to do a job for Herman Shumlin, a rising producer and director. She was to help him stage a production of *Grand Hotel,* a play by Vicki Baum that dealt with the drama behind the doors of a large hotel. The play was written as a series of episodes that required rapid changes of scene as the action shifted from room to room.

To handle this, Aline designed two jackknifing stages, which made it possible to switch sets in seconds, and the reviews all pointed out that the accelerated action simulated the movement of a motion picture. *Theatre Arts* said: "It has been Mr. Shumlin's triumph that, working from Aline Bernstein's always pointed and practical designs, he has given the play the speed and range which were the virtues of the once silent cinema."

As *Grand Hotel* settled into a long run, she began another uptown assignment, on Philip Barry's *Tomorrow and Tomorrow*, produced by her old friend Gilbert Miller. It was great fun to be working for Gilbert, who was lavish in his production budgets. "I don't have to go to the upholsterer's with my worn out sofa in hand. . . . I just march out to my favorite antique store, and buy exactly what I want. . . . But don't worry," she'd add quickly, "the Civic keeps me my old simple self."

Her latest project at the Civic that season of 1930–31 was *Camille*, which "Eva is simply glorious in," she reported to the family, now comfortably settled in their new quarters in the Gotham Hotel at Fifth Avenue and Fifty-fifth Street. As Theo had predicted, although they were certainly living grandly, with several bedrooms and more than one living room, their expenses were still considerably less than in their other apartment. They kept only their cook, who traveled back and forth to Armonk with them; the other domestic services were provided by the hotel.

On Tom's birthday Aline had sent him a letter signed with a drop of her blood, a melodramatic gesture she'd not repeated, but as her own fiftieth birthday approached, depression began to overtake her. For some reason, the difference between thirty and fifty seemed much greater than between twenty-five and forty-five, and when she looked in her mirror now, her reflection was cruel.

The family, having weathered her earlier, more severe stress, was able to manage these shifting moods, even the darkest. So united were they that people who met Aline in the family circle, even when her misery was most acute, could never imagine her having or even wanting any outside involvement. Thus, while many of the guests at her fiftieth birthday party knew about Tom—Terry and Eva and the Melville Canes—a good many of them did not. They saw a remarkably loving family, enormously proud of their most prominent member. Warmed by their love, Aline wished on that cold December evening that she had Tom's pen to convey to them her gratitude for their resolute support.

Perhaps while Aline had been working on *Grand Hotel* and *Tomorrow and Tomorrow* and *Camille*, her despair had fueled her creativity. These productions launched, however, she felt drained and emotionally spent, and the loss of Tom might have seemed newly agonizing. Whatever the reason, in December her unhappiness returned full force. She sent him a sad and bitter anecdote—care of American Express—about an old jar she had bought on Henry Street years before for sixty-five cents, because she admired its shape even though it was a piece of corroded junk. She took it home to see what she could do to clean it up. "I scraped and polished it and found it was made of copper with circles worked all around. . . . I had it made into a lamp and every night when I put on the light its surface gives me back fire. It gives me this because I knew and recognized its beauty under the grime of its wanderings."

At the end of the month Tom was in London, working steadily on his writing. There he received a cable that hinted darkly at suicide. It frightened him so that he took to his bed for two days, unable to eat without throwing up. He convinced himself she was already dead—that the "spies" scattered around London had decided not to tell him out of fear that he would embarrass the family. When he at last tried to get back to his normal routine, he dreaded picking up his mail and reading the American newspapers. One morning, a call came from Ethel Fran-kau, and his immediate thought was that his nightmares were true. Aline was dead, and Ethel was calling to accuse him. But no; Ethel said Aline was fine, and she herself was passing through London on business and thought she would come by and say hello. Wolfe knew Ethel well enough to take it for granted she would not leave London without seeing him, and he invited her to his flat for tea.

"It's too bad you can't see Aline this season," Ethel said after a pause in their chatting. "She's truly at her peak. She's never looked or felt happier, or been more successful." She returned to this theme several times before she rose gracefully from her chair and extended her hand to bid Tom farewell. But he would not let her leave. He could not restrain himself from asking the question that had been eating away at him while she talked. Why? Why? Why? Why those terrible bleeding messages, those terrifying threats of suicide? Why the accusation that her family had been torn asunder because of him?

"You know my sister, Tom," Ethel said calmly. "You should realize as we do that her emotionalism isn't always to be taken seriously." She smiled thinly and her eyes were steel. "Aline might mean such things when she says them, of course—she is an honest woman—but *we* all know she comes back to herself after really a very little while." And then she added, and her reason for doing so remains obscure:

"Of course, when Aline really wants something, she always gets it in the end."

"You can 'get your way' with people," Wolfe fumed in a letter to Maxwell Perkins after Ethel's visit, "but you cannot 'get your way' with life. She must grow old and die. . . . Also, she has failed this time with me!"

Tom wrote Aline too, a brief and very angry note about Ethel's visit, and Aline seized on her sister the moment Ethel arrived home.

"How could you do this to me?" she shouted, while her sister went on unpacking her trunk before the family gathered for dinner. But then, through her agitation, she saw the tightened muscles of Ethel's fine-boned face, and the muscles of her own heart tightened too, for she knew exactly what combination of pride, love and fury had led Ethel Frankau to visit her sister's lover. She wanted Thomas Wolfe to know that the Bernstein family was still intact, and that Aline Bernstein's spirit and values could not be destroyed by his villainy.

Aline said no more then, but after dinner that night, she returned to Ethel's room, as if by silent invitation. The sisters moved toward each other in a rare embrace, and seated on chairs they had designed and embroidered, had a "long, sad talk" deep into the night.

The next morning, Aline awoke feeling stronger than she'd felt in some time. But the headache that had been plaguing her for weeks was still relentlessly pounding away. Twice lately it had been so severe that she'd lost consciousness, once during a rehearsal on stage, and once shopping in Pleasantville. The family had made her see a doctor, and he hadn't been able to find anything wrong with her except for sinus trouble, but the medicine he'd given her hadn't as yet cleared up the headaches. She was terrified of being ill. If she weren't able to work, if she had to lie in bed, her grief about Tom would, she was sure, overwhelm her.

As indeed it did, on the March morning in 1931 when she opened her newspaper and learned that Thomas Wolfe was back in America, had been for more than two weeks. The cup dropped from her hand, her hand flew to her throat, and her body slumped over in her seat. The family, who had rushed to her side, had difficulty rousing her.

"I'll telephone the doctor," Theo said, his voice flat, and Ethel helped her sister to bed. By the end of the day, Aline was in Doctors Hospital for tests and observation, and it was from there, a few days later, that she wrote to Thomas Wolfe, care of the Harvard Club, accusing him of precipitating her collapse. Wolfe, who was planning to rent an apartment in Brooklyn, largely to escape Aline, was deeply disturbed. He sat down to write her immediately and produced yet one more letter filled with his usual ambivalent passages about loving and being loved and

271

with paranoid self-pity. Aline leaned back against her hospital pillows, searching the pages for sweetness, for words of love. There were, in fact, many. He loved her now, always, forever. "If your present trouble and illness is in any way due to me, I want to tell you that I would rather shed my own blood than cause you any pain."

But the rest of the letter rehearsed his rage at Ethel's visit. "I mean if you were well and happy, and sent me, a young man living alone in a foreign country among strangers, and trying to get on with my work without much money or friends, messages like these which wrecked all peace and calmness in me, it was a bad thing for you, a rich, talented, beautiful and successful woman to do."

Yet he assured her that he needed her as his loving friend. He needed her to go on being "beautiful and lovely and good as you alone on this whole earth can be. . . . I need your help and I need your friendship, and I need your belief."

These words sang in Aline's heart. Never mind that he followed them with the declaration that "the time of madness, darkness, passion is over," for he also said: "Tell your friends and tell your family and tell the earth without fear or evasion that you love me, and that I love you, but that we are not physical lovers."

There was more. And better. "No other accomplishment would mean as much," he continued, as memorializing her in his future writing, so that the world would understand "the glory and magnificence I have known through you," so that "men all over the world will be moved by it." And he concluded:

> I shall love you all the days of my life, and when I die, if they cut me open, they will find one name written on my brain and in my heart. It will be yours. I have spoken the living truth here, and I sign my name for anyone to see.
>
> Tom Wolfe

"Your letter," she wrote back instantly, "has restored me to life." And indeed, a few days later, as Eugene Kennedy reports, she was "back in action." She wrote to Tom saying that soon they must find one another and meet and talk and listen to each other.

First, however, she was leaving for Wilmington for a tryout of her latest play.

But the very minute she returned, she would call him.

# 19

Tom did rent an apartment in Brooklyn, the first of several. It was at 40 Verandah Place in Brooklyn Heights, a small basement apartment, opening on a little garden. It was here that Aline came to see him every Thursday, the only concession he would make to her desire for continued contact. He was still determined to be free. His occasional words of loving friendship were again interspersed with ugly taunts: she only persisted in wanting more from him because of her "glands being out of whack"; she should go home and take up her knitting like a proper woman her age. Yet she would come to Brooklyn by subway or cab, with shopping bags of groceries and a mind filled with memories.

Aline has described a sultry day when she came to the apartment to find him asleep and sat watching him for hours, his presence compensating for the stiffness of her body in the flimsy wooden chair. She was afraid to move in case she might disturb him, and so she sat, her groceries untouched, his face and form the only sustenance she needed. She needed to see him, as a plant needs sun and air. Memories of sunshine do not cause a plant to grow, and memories of Tom were not enough.

"Unheard music" is *not* sweeter, she thought bitterly. "I would look at his face in his most cruel ugliness rather than only remember the angel who once took me to his heart." She mocked herself for what she had become, a woman who would swelter in a stifling apartment, abandoning her own "green hill in the country," to watch a sleeping lover who no longer wanted her. "That this should be my bliss . . . to watch him sleep . . ." His eyelids fluttered and so did her heart. What would his eyes say to her when he awoke: "Friendship this time, or hate, or just that horrible weariness?"

Dr. Hinkle, her work, the family, all of them, none of them, was able to cure her of her need to cling to Tom. And so she clung. And came every Thursday to sit like a waif, waiting for a kind word, a gesture of love, the old vision of herself in his eyes.

"If my love is all turned back upon me, I will drown in it," she thought as he slept, and as if he had heard her, he smiled. His eyes were open but with the blank stare of the sleeper, and he moved to make room for her, patting the portion of the bed that was now vacant. She lay down beside him, treasuring the warmth of his body, despite the heat of the room.

But when, much later, he woke, after she'd lain unmoving beside him, watching the leaves outside "grow richer, darker, in the greying light," he was no more loving than he'd been and she was no more able to repress her sentimental litany of better times.

"For God's sake, don't you know that's dead. . . . Why do you want to wake up dead bodies . . . that's all over . . . look at your old face and your grey hair," he shouted, pulling himself from the bed so violently that she had to hold on to keep from falling. With mingled pride and mortification, she answered that it wasn't dead. Her love was as alive as ever—as alive as if she were "pregnant with it . . . my love beats against my ribs . . . it makes my head ache . . . it pulls me from my sleep in terror. You never called me old until it suited you. When you loved me, I was ageless, beautiful, the most beautiful face you ever saw. . . . Do you think you are King Canute to tell my love to stop? You let me down!" she shouted. "You weren't great enough to hold your love. . . . While I live and breathe, I love you," she declared, like a prisoner defying his jailers. "You can't make me like you are. You talk and talk, but it doesn't change me. It only makes you excited and drags you down."

And finally, quieter now: "You have no idea of my character."

Did he hear her? Did he even listen? His eyes were flat, and he waved her away impatiently. But then he realized he was hungry, and in their bizarre bond, she rose to cook him supper, and quietly watched him eat it until he was ready to satisfy his hunger for more details of her early life.

"Come on now . . . hurry up . . . tell me how it was," he prodded, and once again she handed him the years of her life.

Rarely in any literary relationship does one find such a total gift of one person's experience to another as Aline Bernstein gave Thomas Wolfe, particularly during this period of their lives. As the critic Paschal Reeves explains:

> In the years following *Look Homeward, Angel,* Wolfe made several false starts which he either abandoned or later reshaped. . . . Groping for fictive material that would enable him to produce a novel without resorting to his own experience, he turned to the account Mrs. Bernstein had so vividly given him of her girlhood. . . . He could write about her life with greater confidence than any other outside his own family, and his success in using some of her material helped to expand his scope . . . at the very time that he needed to do so.

And so, from these meetings during the summer of 1931, Tom was compiling much of the material for the book he was calling *The Good Child's River.* To study Thomas Wolfe's notebooks of this period is to see the outline of Aline's formative years. Names alone have been altered, in tentative chapter headings that read: "The Three Sisters," "Bella," "How Esther Drank Morphine," "The Trip Abroad," "Aunt Mary's Boarding House," and so on. Aline even brought Tom a picture of her father, whom he was fascinated by, and he pinned it to the wall above his writing table.

But as Tom depleted her stored experience, he was even more eager to be rid of her than before. And with a resurgence of energy, she became more amenable. It was too degrading to thrust her way into his life, even though she believed she belonged there. So she cut down on her visits, wrote and called less often and, usually, with more control.

Her retreat was based in part on the conviction that he would eventually change his mind. Around her were countless other young men and women whom she had nurtured and guided. They were all thoroughly devoted to her. Why should Tom, to whom she had given so much more, be any different?

Her hope was fed by his continuing dependence on her for the minutiae of everyday living. He borrowed money from her and complained of his high dental bills and asked her to talk to the dentist for him. And when he restlessly moved to another apartment in Brooklyn Heights, he grumbled to her about his noisy neighbors, how their voices traveled up through his ceiling. Aline said she would buy him a carpet as soon as she received her next paycheck, and this man who wanted his freedom accepted eagerly.

Thus, while Aline desperately missed their old companionship and found herself sinking too often into despair, hope allowed her, for the most part, to keep going in the familiar routines of family love, friendships and work. There were many bids on her attention now within those areas. Although the Depression was spreading, John Loeb, who worked with Teddy, was forming a new investment company with his father, Carl, and he asked Teddy to join then. Teddy talked to John about his own father, who, he felt, was ready to leave the firm he was with. The Loebs considered the idea and soon made both Bernsteins an offer of partnership. Says John Loeb now: "We knew we were fortunate to get such an experienced older man as Theo." And he adds: "They were both wonderful, dedicated, hard-working partners, absolutely first-class men who worked beautifully with each other and with us."

But another, deeply distressing situation had developed. Ethel's long-time lover, Charles, had been called back to France by his father some time berfore—to make a proper marriage and go into the family business. Although he was a mature man, Charles had a European concept of family and felt he must obey his father's wishes. Aline knew that despite Ethel's stoicism, the loss was terrible for her, and Aline, of all people, was fully able to understand her suffering. She would try to help her sister as best she could by drawing even closer to her.

And there was, of course, her work. She was preparing, this July and August, preliminary designs for Robert Sherwood's *Reunion in Vienna,* to open in late fall, starring her old friends the Lunts. After that she was scheduled to begin work on another Philip Barry play, *The Animal Kingdom,* a new production of Gilbert Miller's. All this helped her to turn aside thoughts of Tom as 1931 moved to a close.

Early in the new year she called on Tom's mother and sister in Washington, where Mabel Wolfe was living. Aline had gone there for the opening of a new play, and the meeting had been polite—even cordial. Thus, when later in January Aline paid one of her carefully rationed visits to Brooklyn (to hand Tom a five-hundred-dollar loan), she was not embarrassed to find Julia sitting at his dining table. But it was immediately obvious that Tom was in a dreadful mood.

Despite her self-consciousness at being luxuriously dressed in these impoverished times, Aline was wearing her mink coat and matching Russian-style cap because Tom had always favored them. He took no notice of them now. Instead, as she shrugged the coat off her shoulders, he announced the reason for his bad temper. Madeleine Boyd had sold the rights to *Look Homeward, Angel* to a German publisher without getting Tom's permission or giving him any of the money advanced. When Aline tried to assure him that there must be some reasonable explanation for this, he turned savage with anger, working himself up to a frenzy over Madeleine's presumed duplicity. Suddenly he transferred his attack to Aline. It was all her fault that this was happening, because it was Aline who had given the manuscript of *Look Homeward, Angel* to Mrs. Boyd in the first place.

"You're the cause of my getting mixed up with a woman like that," he shouted. "You're two of a kind."

Both Julia and Aline tried to quiet him, Julia with murmured pleas that he not get "nervous and excited," Aline with assurances that she would speak to Madeleine for him. Whatever had to be done, she would do, because "You know how much I love you, Tom."

As if the phrase had triggered a bomb inside Julia, she turned on Aline, challenging her right to profess her love for a person hardly older than her own children. Unless she felt a "mother's love" for Tom, she should be ashamed of herself. She should be ashamed to admit she was such a "licentious" woman. Now the room became a jungle of raw feeling. Aline crouched against the wall like a hunted animal. They were telling her to go, to leave Tom alone, laughing at her tears. But she would not go. She would not let this woman overcome her. No, she said, "I will not leave yet. Not like this."

But unbelievably, Julia came toward her and, with her long, bony hand, began to push Aline to the door. Her fingers pressed into Aline's flesh as her son's once had in love.

Get out, they shouted. Go away. She was outside in the hall, shoved there by Julia's final thrust, her coat and hat thrown after her, lying in a soft brown mound on the floor. The key turned in the lock, and she heard Julia laugh, and she sank down onto her mink coat and remembered how Tom had loved it the first time he'd seen it at an opening in Boston. Blind with tears, she rose, put on the coat and left the

277

building. She walked up and down the streets, for once not seeing anyone else's misery. Unemployed men leaned against buildings that had eviction notices nailed to their doors, and she brushed past them, unseeing. Surrounded by pain, she was oblivious to all but her own, and she wondered how this pain had become her whole life. In a little while she was back, ringing his bell over and over again, her face a cry of agony. Julia came to the window, looked down and waved impatiently for her to go away, as one might wave to an annoying salesman.

She left once more and walked to the Brooklyn Bridge, and stood there watching the beautiful span soaring above the harbor. She walked beside it a little way, then stopped and took one of the five hundred-dollar bills from her purse and threw it into the water.

After a few more minutes, she walked back down to the street, called a cab and even chatted with the driver, conscious again of her fur coat, and not wanting him to think she was a snob. She sipped brandy all night, falling asleep briefly, to waken with a pounding, perspiring start. At dawn she rose from the stupor she'd called sleep and went to her desk to write Tom, bitterly accusing his mother of the uncalled-for abuse that had caused her to lose her own self-control. She told him how she had thrown the money from the bridge . . . and that the love *he* was throwing away was far more enduring than any sum of money could ever be.

Tom read parts of this letter to his mother, and Julia Wolfe reported her own response in an interview many years later.

"I said to Tom . . . 'Call her up . . . tell her that she's a Jew and I've never known one yet that if you drop a nickel but what they'd jump over and scramble for it. And tell her to leave the one-hundred dollar bill on the bridge. . . . I said to leave the one-hundred dollar bill on the bridge and jump for the nickel,' " she repeated, chortling at her humor. She remembered that Tom thought it was funny too, and he kept laughing when Julia said, "Why, she's the silliest woman I believe I've ever heard talk or seen."

It was several days before Aline could compose the letter to Tom she had really wanted to write. "I maintain that neither you nor your mother have any understanding of myself, of the freedom I demand for my mind and my life. I will not be bound in thought or behavior by anything I do not choose myself." She went on to say that she had lived a "fine life . . . have held to the performance of my duties at home . . . have retained purity in the practice of my work. I have been an uncompromising artist in a world that is full of compromise and ugliness. When we met and loved each other, I gave you the whole strength and beauty of my free soul and free mind."

It was in this letter that Aline made the statement about choosing not to live sexually with her husband which has caused Wolfe's biographers to assume that she and Theo had not lived together as man and wife for many years. While such an assumption conveniently explains Aline's affair with Tom, the dynamics of the Bernstein family strongly suggest that the truth of her marriage relationship was quite different from her presentation of it. In fact, while Aline's and Theo's sexual union may not have been ultimately satisfying for her, Theo was enormously attracted to his wife and she was deeply attracted to him, loving the way he looked even as an older man. But it is not unlikely that their sexual passion had diminished after twenty-five years of marriage, and this may indeed have made her vulnerable to a man as passionate as Wolfe.

As for Theo, he never wavered in his devotion and his profound conviction that Aline was a uniquely precious person—with a nature so rare and so much larger than other people's that she required extraordinary sustenance. "He gave her everything she wanted," a friend says. "It was as simple as that," while Mrs. Loeb says: "I don't in any way feel he was thick-skinned. He just had a different kind of skin. . . . He realized the worth of Aline, and I suppose was willing to wait, even when he was forced to face the true dimensions of the relationship, until she got the thing out of her system. . . . Particularly since she was clearly so devoted to him as well. . . . I was at the house all the time in 1930, '31, '32 and '33," Mrs. Loeb continues, "and I remember being absolutely awed by how everyone in the family loved each other so much. . . . I never heard an unkind comment between Theo and Aline—and he followed her with his eyes with the adoration of a young lover."

At any rate, Aline would treasure all her life the way her family stood by her when Thomas Wolfe "almost wrecked my bright soul and heart." And in particular, she would cherish Theo's extraordinary compassion. One spring evening when they were sitting on the porch watching the sunset, Theo took her hands in his and said quietly, "Aline, we must grasp each other's hands and we can pull out of this thing together."

How to express her gratitude for such love? She had no words at all. But, to her own consternation, she still had many for Tom. She wrote to him when she was sad, and sometimes she wrote when she was feeling strong. In a sense, she was waging a battle on two fronts. In her work and family life she was declaring that Thomas Wolfe could not destroy her. But in her letters to Tom, she was challenging his peace, demanding his guilt, making him suffer for his villainy against her. She would give him no easy divorce.

In June of 1932 he retaliated. In an outburst of temper, he took one of those pleading and accusing letters and wrote on the back of it a statement which he read to Aline over the telephone. " 'To Theodore Bernstein, Junior,' " he read. " 'I have to say this to you: If you are a man with a shred of pride or decency left in you, you will see to it that your mother no longer disgraces herself and her family by willfully running after and doing her utmost in her power to wreck the life of someone twenty years younger than she is. I here and now demand, having exhausted every other means long ago, that you see to it your mother no longer tries to see me or communicate with me in any way.' "

"Don't send it, Tom. Please don't mail it. I will not bother you anymore," she said in a small voice, barely more than a whisper. She hung up the phone and looked out at her garden, turned from the window and looked into her mirror, and remembered who she had been and surely still was. And weary and disbelieving, she vowed to try again, harder, longer, stronger.

The shock of Tom's threat did help her regain some strength, and she threw herself into family life that summer. Her compassion for those less fortunate than the Bernsteins heightened, and she invited to the parties she gave every weekend people she knew in the theater and in the arts who had fallen on hard times—people to whom one of her lavish meals would be an uncommon feast. As for those who, like her own family, had made only minor adjustments in their lives, the dishes she carried proudly from her kitchen were nonetheless eagerly received.

"If I invite eight people, eight more come along," she boasted with a pleased smile. "And if we're to eat at two-thirty, everyone shows up at eleven. I don't blame them. . . . They're afraid to miss something!" And she would present her masterpieces to her guests, rolling her eyes at her own triumph. "Taste this," she'd urge, spooning mushrooms and rice and cream from a big tureen. "Tell me, isn't it equal to a Shakespearean sonnet?"

After the meal Theo might walk down the path to his gazebo, Shakespearean sonnets in his pocket, and he would sit there and read until Aline came to fetch him for cocktails. He was content that for another day no cold winds of loss had turned her dear face into a frozen mask of pain.

This was another summer of work, of deliberately keeping busy. In her studio upstairs, Aline was working on a play by new friends, Sam and Bella Spewack, to be produced by an older friend, Herman Shumlin. Bella Spewack is a tough, brilliant New York woman, giving and demanding, and Aline identified with her from the first day they met, despite the considerable difference in their ages. Mrs. Spewack remembers with enormous pleasure how she and Aline would take time off from their work when Aline was back in New York that fall to indulge in what Aline called "Third Avenue crawls." They would prowl up and down the streets under the Third Avenue elevated trains, peering into antique store windows and then going into one or two stores, where Aline would lecture her younger friend about the value of a particular piece. Other days, they would make "gallery calls," visiting the private art galleries along Fifty-seventh Street. "We'd have the owner take out the most expensive paintings he owned," Bella says, smiling, "and we'd feast ourselves on looking at them. Of course, we never had any intention at all of buying anything!"

Aline was also caught up in the political atmosphere. To her joy, Franklin Roosevelt had been nominated as the Democratic candidate for President, and for the first time in a long while she was able to think optimistically about the country's future. Roosevelt's passionate acceptance speech, in which he promised to "pledge myself to a new deal for the American people," was a promise she believed and was grateful for. His handsome face and confident manner were like a stimulant, and along with millions of others, Aline felt a welcome surge of strength. His command of language, the ringing phrases that captured the fears and dreams of a frightened nation, increased her admiration, and she joined her voice to those campaigning for his election. Of course, Theo did not share her enthusiasm, forecasting dangerous patterns of government interference if Roosevelt was elected. But so grateful was Aline to Theo for his steadfast devotion that for once she did not let his conservatism incite her temper.

Yet even after Roosevelt's triumphant election, even as she wept in relief that the country had found a leader to guide it out of its bitter crisis, she wept still for Thomas Wolfe. He remained firmly fixed in her consciousness. Her promises forgotten in the dark of a sleepless night, she would turn on the copper lamp she had described to him, and would write: "Everything else is a shadow and a dream to be slept through. . . . This whole relation of ours to each other, which was like the sun itself, do you ever think of it any more?"

Indeed, he thought of her a great deal, although he was determined not to see her. He had never sent the letter to Teddy, and was deeply remorseful at so ugly an attack, but he did not commit his apology to paper. In every way the blank white page was an enemy now. Although he was writing faithfully and beautifully, he was having great trouble bringing his second novel to an orderly conclusion. Maxwell Perkins was heroically trying to help him, working with him night and day, but even so, Tom was terrified that he would never be able to complete the book. He had sold two novellas to *Scribner's Magazine* to make some money, and they had been very well received, but still, the unfinished novel tormented him, brought back all his old fears and inadequacies. Those feelings drove him into the streets at night as they used to. He would walk all the way to the Bronx, or along the Brooklyn waterfront. Prohibition was over, and his walks were punctuated by visits to bars. If he did enough drinking, thoughts of Aline would invade his night, and sometimes, even if not often, he would find a telephone and dial her number and demand to speak to her. He had to tell her what he was feeling, what he was seeing and thinking about, and she would believe again that he knew, as she did, that she was the only one in his life, now and forever, who could truly understand him.

The renewal of these early-morning calls ripped through the Bernstein apartment like a hurricane, leaving calamity in its wake. One night the shrill ring roused Aline from sleep at 3:00 A.M., and as she picked up the telephone, she was certain she heard other extensions in the apartment lifted. Was there a Mrs. Bernstein living there? The voice on the other end was not Tom's but a stranger's, who identified himself as the attendant in the men's room of the Plaza Hotel, just a few blocks uptown from the Gotham.

"I'm sorry to bother you, ma'am, but there's a very big fellow here, stretched out on the floor, and, well, ma'am, he's terrible drunk. . . . I'm doing my best to get him to go without calling an officer, but he says he won't leave until he sees Mrs. Bernstein, until she comes to get him."

Aline closed her eyes, and said nothing for a moment. "Ma'am . . . did you hear me?" In the background she could hear Tom shouting her name. She told the attendant to say she was coming right over, would be there in a few minutes. Hurriedly, without letting herself think, she got out of bed and slipped on the first clothes she pulled from her closet. As she left her bedroom, she saw light shining under every other bedroom door, and her stomach clenched in grief as she put on her coat and hat and gloves and went out into the cold predawn air. Within minutes she had walked the few blocks along Fifth Avenue to the Plaza Hotel. The city was asleep and a mounted policeman looked curiously at her as she approached the hotel. The men's room was empty except for Tom and she was able to go inside with the attendant and get him to his feet. He was babbling incoherently. She urged him to the sink and helped sponge his face. The whole scene was mortifying, but her first task was to get him safely home. Tipping the attendant substantially and summoning a cab, she bundled Tom in, checking first to see that his keys were in his pocket. She paid the driver and watched the taxi go down the street, Tom's face staring at her through the window, mouthing something in farewell. When he disappeared from her vision, she started home again, wondering as she walked the silent streets, her collar pulled tight around her neck, whether he would call her tomorrow.

He didn't. And she forced herself not to call him. But in the days ahead, when she passed Scribner's or a restaurant they had dined in, she would find herself wondering whether he was inside. Once, at an important business luncheon, an attractive young woman at the next table began to talk about Tom. Aline could hear some of the conversation and was able to understand it all by reading the woman's lips. Talks of contracts and costumes receded from her attention, as she absorbed the news that Tom was having trouble writing and heard the giggling gossip about his latest spate of affairs. She felt herself grow faint. How terrible to hear strangers talking of him so intimately, strangers linking him with still other strangers.

She rose from the table so quickly that she upset her wineglass, and she left the restaurant while her companions looked after her incredulously. Later that day she called her host to apologize, her voice shy and sad, and only the solidity of her reputation allowed him to dismiss the incident as a puzzling but trivial event.

In fact, although producers would continue to hold Aline's work in high regard—her combined talents of economy and artistry and her extraordinary ability to work with production crews making her an asset to any production—students of the theater acknowledge that her work suffered a loss of power at this time.

283

In 1932, because of financial difficulties, her beloved Civic Repertory had to close its doors. The Depression had cut deeply into the generosity of its benefactors, and production costs continued to mount. Although Aline transferred her professional energies to an increased involvement with commercial theater and designed five major shows for five different managements between January 1933 and January 1934, her efforts were comparatively desultory. The only work that really absorbed her was for Elmer Rice's production of *We the People,* a play drawn from life, showing the plight of workers caught in the horrors of the Depression.

Elmer Rice was a difficult man for some people to work with, but he and Aline respected each other greatly. He owned his own theater at that time, and while his wasn't a true repertory company, he did try to offer alternatives to the strictly commercial theater by hiring unknown actors and producing his own work. The combination of a theater that was trying to serve the people and a play that attacked Depression politics roused Aline from her torpor, and she produced some of her finest designs. Years later, Elmer Rice would reminisce about his extended relationship with Aline and speak specifically of her work for *We the People.* "She not only did a splendid job designing fifteen different settings," he says, "she also heartened everyone with her vitality and enthusiasm. . . . She was a truly remarkable woman, warm-hearted, generous, gifted, and endowed with an exuberance and zest for living such as I have rarely encountered."

Because her spirits were so high during her work with Rice, it was even more of a letdown than usual when it was over. Fortunately, she had hired another design assistant, Emaline Roche, because when the Civic closed, Irene Sharaff had gone off on her own, with Aline's loving blessing. Emaline was particularly adept at set design and so Aline could count on her to take over when her own energies seemed sapped.

Except for the night in the Plaza men's room, Aline had not seen Tom for well over a year, but her hunger for him showed no sign of abating permanently. To help her, Dr. Hinkle had suggested that she try to put some of her feelings on paper. Perhaps her need to write to Tom, which she still struggled against (often unsuccessfully), might be eased by writing *about* him.

To her delight, Aline found that this was so. She tried to write something every day, and soon she decided to expand the story into a larger work. She started putting together a book of three long vignettes, each

284

about a man who owned a blue suit. She sent copies of the stories to Tom as they were written, asking him for criticism, but he never replied. In fact, he barely read them, thinking they were only a gambit to get his attention, and not a serious effort. His silence hurt Aline, but she continued writing, challenged by the attempt and enjoying the renewal of her artistic vigor. She decided that when the stories were done she would pay to have them published by a company that produced such books in small editions, rather than try to get them accepted by a traditional publisher.

It was particularly fortunate that she had this newly absorbing project to engage her, for another blow was about to descend. Theo suffered a minor heart attack. The doctor assured them all that there would be no serious damage as long as Theo changed some of his habits, such as smoking the big, heavy Havana cigars he loved, and tried to keep his temper steady.

But it was impossible for Aline not to believe she bore at least some responsibility for this unhappy event. The connection between Theo's illness and her affair with Tom was a question she would have to live with, suffering its pain in the privacy of her own heart. She rarely gave herself the solace of confession, and it was no different now. The only indication of what she was feeling is recalled by an old friend, who visited Theo one evening while he was recuperating. After kissing Theo good night, Aline had poured their friend and herself some brandy in the softly lit living room. As she did, some of the liquid spilled on the rug, and as if mesmerized, Aline stood watching the golden circle darken and widen. And then, looking up at her companion, tears making her eyes shine, she said almost inaudibly, "A stain spreads . . . it cannot help but spread."

Fortunately, Theo recovered quickly and thoroughly, and showed no more concern for his future health than Teddy ever had, Teddy who, Mr. Loeb remembers, "always really lived, with that health history, with the sword of Damocles hanging over his head." Theo did cut down on his drinking and cut out his smoking entirely, and turned even more to his reading, having almost completely given up cards also. But it was all done without complaint, and without a trace of invalidism, and never once did he imply that he held Aline in any way responsible.

Soon it would again be time for Tom's birthday, and predictably, Aline sent him a commemorative letter. It was not particularly high-keyed; she was too weary for that; but it elicited a hysterical response.

He reached back into their past to find some reason for his grave unhappiness, and the result was a letter that made Aline's hands tremble when she read it. "It is two years since I have written you . . . and I may never see you or write to you again, and it seems to me it is better now to try to say what is in my heart than to try and conceal it. . . . You say you don't know how many years it is since we met. Well, I can tell you it is eight." He was only a boy then, he declared, strong and healthy and hopeful. Now he is a "man alone, first youth is gone, the boy's face and figure is gone. I am a gross, heavy figure of a man and I am getting bald." And if he was lonely then, he is lonely now, only now he is also despairing. Aline was the only person who loved him, much more than his family did, who never really had true faith in him. Through her, he "discovered a new world. . . . I want to tell you . . . that no matter what else you did, or what anguish, madness and despair I knew, that that woman who came to my room day after day for years was beyond every standard of comparison, the greatest, loveliest and most beautiful woman I have ever known. And I also want to tell you that I now know I loved that woman with my life, that she is mixed into my blood, and that I shall love her forever."

But then the wind changed. He hoped "vanity and pride is not so strong in you that you can now see nothing but right in everything you did." He told her that the lovely woman turned into an ugly stranger who tried to destroy him with her hysteria and her threats and her deriding of his ability to succeed without her. Yes, this stranger who looked like her "used every rotten and despicable means she knew to destroy me," and he was left with a head so filled with memories that he could not think. He went on to mock her marching for Sacco and Vanzetti. She "entertains fat communists or fat socialists in luxury, and weeps for the poor," while she and her family live in elegance and she can have thirty-four pairs of shoes and shop at Bergdorf-Goodman's. And finally: "Aline the time for your helping me is past. There is nothing that you have now that I want."

Small wonder that after such a letter Aline felt a measure of triumph at hearing from him next in a letter congratulating her on the publication of her book, *Three Blue Suits,* in December. However, after telling her: "You have done an extraordinary thing and shown a clearness and certainty of purpose for which many of us would give our right eye," he turned to criticism of the content. In particular he was troubled by the episodes depicting him in the story of a young writer who ruthlessly abandons the woman who loves and cares for him in order to accept a Guggenheim fellowship he really does not need. The writer is too help-less to care for himself, and lives in complete emotional and physical disorder. Tom protested that he was not such a dreamer. She above all should know how hard he worked at his craft. And, "you say nothing of the bitter and complicated struggle which had been going on be-tween two people for two years," he complained, "nor that the woman is so much older than the man, nor that she is content in her marriage and has refused to leave her family." He went on then to take issue with the character of "Mr. Froelich" in the second story, a wealthy German banker who Tom assumed was supposed to represent Theo. He accused Aline of being heartlessly cynical in her description of her husband, but after all, "in all your stories you show the remarkably sharp, accurate and cynical observation of your race."

Aline replied immediately and in anger. Mr. Froelich had nothing to do with Theo; he was a compilation of several men she had met in the banking world, none of whom bore the slightest resemblance to her husband, "who is an entirely different character, a sweet, fine, good man." As for her representation of Tom, she owed him no apology. And she reminded him that he was hardly the person to object to using personal material.

*Three Blue Suits* was reviewed widely and favorably. The critics recognized the same qualities Tom had always admired and envied: her clarity of thought, her exactness of nuance, the poetry of seemingly simple words.

"Any one of these studies could very easily have been overdone," one reviewer said, but "none is." Another pointed out: "There is a certain kind of bitterness here . . . but there is also great understanding."

She felt, Aline thought grimly, far more bitter than understanding as she closed the pages of another year, and moved into the new one.

# 20

In spite of her sense of accomplishment with *Three Blue Suits,* Aline "seemed to be stuck in something . . . a solid mass from which I struggle to break loose." Although she did a couple of smaller shows in January 1934, after *We the People* opened early in the month, she turned down any further work. "I've decided to take a little rest," she'd tell producers with a self-conscious laugh. "But do call me for your fall and winter plans." Sometimes she'd offer the excuse of wanting to devote more of her energies to writing, and people understood. But the truth was that her creative energies were sapped to an unprecedented extent—partly symptom of her despair, partly contributing to it. The religion of work had failed her for the first time in her life.

"I feel as though I am living in a hole under the mountain," she would say, and increasingly she found it difficult to bring her spirits out into the sunlight. However, she did her very best to keep her misery to herself, particularly since she was being called on to function in a very new capacity: as a person benignly observing rather than participating in the romantic life. Edla was going to be married, had accepted one of her many young suitors, a very handsome, eligible New Yorker named Jack Benjamin. Aline was enormously happy for her daughter, immensely proud of her. "She has such beauty and delicacy, is such a fine instrument for life's expression," she declared to her friends. And yet as she watched the tall young bride exchange vows with her new husband, sadness mixed itself into the day's joy. Aline looked up at her own husband, standing at her side in the reception line, happy in his role as proud father, and next to him Teddy and on the other side of Aline, Ethel—her family, united in sharing another ceremony together. She closed her eyes and saw a montage of other significant moments, but the sight frightened rather than warmed her. She who had always embraced the flow of life now wanted only to retreat from it.

Thomas Wolfe frequently accused Aline of clinging to him because of glandular changes, because of her refusal to accept the disengagement inevitable as people move through life's phases. These were maddening accusations to her, trivializing the extent of her devotion. And yet his charges contained at least some measure of truth. For in her desperate attempts to keep him in her life, surely there was at least some element of the fear a woman can feel as she realizes that far more of her life has been lived than remains to be lived.

One early winter evening when she was walking along Forty-eighth Street after visiting some old friends at a rehearsal, she saw Tom ahead of her, talking to a man she did not know. She darted through the throngs of people going home from work. Her breath caught in her chest from the effort, but quickly she was behind him, and she reached out her hand to touch his sleeve. But her touch was timid, and therefore imperceptible, and instead of turning to look at her, he moved to the door of the Chatham Hotel, where he and his companion entered the bar. She wanted to go in after him, but she was afraid. She could not bear it if he attacked her. The woman who had been able to stand up to his temper, to defend her integrity, was lost somewhere in the city. Tom had accused her in his last letter of turning into an evil stranger. But the real stranger was this invalid. This weak, drifting woman who lived in such anguish. That night she wrote to tell him of the meeting that had not taken place. "To think that you did not know I was there. It scarcely seems possible to me."

He did not answer her. And the ache in her heart threatened to pound her whole body into the ground. Hungry to see him again, even without speaking, she would leave the Gotham in the late afternoon, wondering if she would sight him among the crowds of people once more. The declining sun would cast its long, low rays and her "shadow would be stretched across the streets." She would marvel at how happy everyone seemed: "if they had any sorrow, it did not show." She was certain her own sorrow must be etched into every plane of her face. She walked past the Chatham to other bars Tom frequented, envying the men and women who entered them in little groups.

Her own drinking, and there was a great deal more of it these days, was done at home, her public face still important to her. But as she stood in front of the Plaza Hotel one day, pretending to wait for someone, she thought, in a moment's lapse from her obsession, how wonderful that she *could* have gone inside now by herself and buy a drink. How wonderful that the world had become a place where "a woman could go into bars alone and order a drink and pay for it too, without having to wait until a man invited you." And how ironic, she thought immediately afterward, obsession returning, that just when the world *was* such a place, when the style of living she had always demanded for herself was becoming possible for all women, she stood here desperately searching the streets for a man's face, needing his presence to define her experience.

She looked admiringly at the young women skittering down the avenue on their graceful high-heeled shoes. But their "good lean young bodies so clean and spare" made her feel flabby and old, and the hated bile of jealousy rose in her throat. She turned and began to walk again, heading for the park. Cars and taxis and buses swished past her; in every vehicle more people going somewhere, coming from somewhere. Only she stood apart, as though this were all a stage set of someone else's design, and she "was somewhere else in space, raised or lowered or at an angle to the scene."

She walked that day until dark. For miles, through the park and into the streets and back again, through paths of her childhood and areas that had never existed in those narrow innocent days. Back and forth, east and west, increasingly alone. At last she went home, and to her room, and to a bottle of brandy, although Theo and Ethel had begun to lock the liquor bottles away. They did not know that she knew their hiding places, that she had her own bottles ferreted away like some pitiful drunk or like, she thought with shame, Aunt Nana. Is that what lay ahead of her? Would she allow this to become her fate? It was on a night like this, with these questions still unanswered, that Bella Spewack remembers being called by Theo, who had been unable to rouse Aline from a predinner nap. He didn't know if she'd been drinking, for no bottles were in evidence, but her deep unconsciousness was obviously something more than normal sleep. Ethel was away, and he did not want to involve Teddy or Edla, and so he called Bella, whom he trusted, and whom he knew Aline had confided her story to.

"I went over there and got her up," Mrs. Spewack remembers, "and I made some coffee and poured it into her, and made her show me where she hid the bottles, and I told her she had no right to do this to the people who loved her—the *good* people who loved her . . . and she promised me she wouldn't drink to this point again." Mrs. Spewack pauses, and says with a sigh, "Well, in fact she rarely did, but of course she did a lot worse. . . ."

And indeed she did. But first, only the tears grew worse. As spring approached but her heart remained in deepest, coldest winter, she made frequent trips to Dr. Hinkle's sanitarium, Smokey Hollow Lodge, in Washington, Connecticut. To the physician's distress, however, she did not go with any real hope of feeling better, but simply to escape. For she did not want her family to suffer her agony. As she explained to Tom in a letter written from the sanitarium early in June of 1934, here she did not have to "keep up a face" for the sake of their peace of mind. Here she could at least "curl up and cry or howl when the pain takes me." She no longer bothered to look for responses to such letters. She had long ceased expecting an answer to her pleas, or believing herself powerful enough to force a reply.

The family encouraged her to come home from Smokey Hollow, to let *them* help her, but invariably she would feel the need to return there again. There was only one visit home when she managed to escape the cavern of despair she had fallen into so deeply. One Sunday afternoon, Theo urged her to accompany him to a neighbor's home for tea. The man was a prominent publisher, and this weekend was playing host to Thomas Mann. Aline could feel her spirits lighten as Mann's intellect almost literally illuminated the suburban living room. She had forgotten the joy of observing a fine mind and a wit that sparkled across a vast range of subjects. Mann found her equally fascinating, and Theo, watching her, felt a stirring of hope that the woman he had loved and lived with all these years was not gone, but only resting, storing up strength to climb out of her dark despondency. Later, walking home through the flower-bordered paths, Aline's voice held its old bright

291

timbre when she told Theo that Mann had promised to visit them when he came back to America. He had professed the desire to glimpse America as it was lived away from its cities, and she would take him to see New England.

But the lightness too quickly dimmed, and she fell again into the cavern. Indeed, fell even deeper, for each quiver of hope seemed to make its relinquishing ever more desperate, the disappointment when despair returned more profound.

On such a day, home in Armonk, a day when too much seemed over, when a new summer stretched out too endlessly, dry and hot and joyless, Aline excused herself after breakfast and went upstairs to rest. When she didn't come down at lunchtime, Edla, who was visiting, went upstairs to waken her and found that she couldn't. And this time, Aline was unreachable. As if she were lying drowned "on the sandy bottom of a river." Near her bed were several opened vials of sleeping pills, their emptiness shouting its meaning to the terrified young woman. Needing help, Edla called young Mrs. Loeb, who lived nearby and had been raised in the area. On her way to the house, Mrs. Loeb called her own physician, who, hearing the urgency in her voice, arrived at Whippoorwill Lane almost as soon as she did. The doctor began to massage Aline's legs and arms and chest, periodically checking her vital signs. Finally, although she was still deeply unconscious, he felt she could be, *must* be moved to the hospital. Mrs. Loeb remembers being astonished at the idea that this idealized, idolized woman, whose gaiety and vitality she had so admired, would actually have attempted to take her own life. And indeed, when she reflects on it today, she still believes, as she did then, and as many Bernstein friends do, that while Aline's depression was certainly real, her attempt at suicide was a dramatic impulse and not a carefully premeditated plan born of the conviction that life would never again be worth living.

Whatever the cause, the attempt was very nearly successful. With something almost resembling pride, Aline would declare in later years that in effect she really *did* die. "I was completely gone for three days, but they worked me over and brought me back." Melville Cane was to remember that three-day period very well. He had left New York City early in the morning for a New England vacation, and since his route took him through Armonk, and he knew the Bernsteins were early risers, he decided to stop off at their house for breakfast.

"I rang the bell," he remembers, "and Theo answered the door, looking dead himself. I was shocked by what he looked like and immediately asked what was wrong. 'Aline's taken an overdose of sleeping pills. . . . Aline's in the hospital. . . . Aline's tried to kill herself. . . .' " He spoke, Mr. Cane remembered, in the toneless voice of a person drained of life. Aline, in her book *The Journey Down*, graphically described the experience of coming back to life, of coming up through the layers of unconsciousness to lightness and from silence to the sounds of voices, just as she had done when she was a child and had accidentally taken Nana's "medicine." Her chest felt as if she had swallowed glass shards which drove into her heart each time she breathed. She wanted to cry for help, but her tongue was monstrously thick and large and could not move inside her mouth.

"Little bits of life, memory, floated into her mind," she wrote, telling her own story, "scarcely memory, some the merest sensation, wind blowing leaves, a dress her aunt Mamie made her when she was a little girl, a pink and white silk candy stripe; a birthday . . . a street brawl because of a trolley car strike, the taste of a little jar of strawberry jelly . . . a London square." And now someone was putting a tube between her lips, although she could only manage three swallows. The nurse was a handsome young woman and Aline wanted to tell her so, but she couldn't speak. Instead, she sank again into sleep, swimming through memory and pain and reality. "Water-lilies in her hair, she was diving down to rid herself of melancholy, diving down to renew her soul in the life-giving waters." But suddenly she was feeling not peaceful but frightened, drifting now to a thickly matted place, tangled with plants and weeds and ugly eels coiling themselves around the vines, and she struggled up to find the riverbank. "She had not felt wet at all down in the river, but up panting on the bank she was soaking, her hair was streaming and her hands were wet, water fell down from her armpits and between her legs, down her forehead and into her eyes . . . and she vomited up the slimy, muddy water she had swallowed from the bases of the weeds and water grasses. She stank, her nose choked with her own evil smell."

Crying—more wet added to the water she was immersed in—she opened her eyes and saw someone washing her face gently. And she knew she had vomited up the poison. The doctor was comforting her, telling her not to be embarrassed, but happy that she had rid herself of the rank material in her stomach. They would make her clean and comfortable and she would begin to feel better.

"But you must have patience," the doctor said. "You have been very sick. Very sick," and, he continued, they were doing "all that it is possible for us to do. The rest you must do for yourself. No one, not the most skillful physician in the world can make you live if you will not." And he added, looking steadily at her: "You have a strong healthy body, and from what I can gather, you have had a rich and colorful life. There must be some reason why you want to go on, isn't there?"

Aline wondered as he talked of "how much he knew." And dutifully, as he continued to urge her to help them keep her alive—"There must be wonderful things in a life like yours"—she tried as hard as she could to remember those things. But again, she felt herself drifting into the strange world between conscious thought and sleep. And now she saw herself on a wooded hill with a faint light shining through large-massed wisteria trees. She sat down quietly inside this scene, and almost immediately, she remembered, she began to feel remarkably peaceful. She sensed she was "alone in the world," in a web woven only by herself. This was her life, hers alone. She could live it or abandon it, as she decided.

Aline described this, too, in her novel, and her suicide attempt did indeed represent a turning point for her. For the rest of her life, she would remember the hospital visions as the beginning of her ability to resume responsibility for the quality of her life. She could look to no one, not even Thomas Wolfe, to fill that pack on her back. "No one else could breathe her breath," she wrote in *The Journey Down;* "it was only her pulse that beat in her wrists, her own mind that thought her own thoughts."

Whether or not Tom came to visit Aline in the hospital is uncertain, but she left there knowing she had been given another chance at life. She believed she would eventually heal, but she also knew there would be many moments of regression. Predictably, to prepare for these times, she went to work. Her hands would not be idle. They would work as hard and be as devoted to their commitments as they had ever been before.

She did many projects back to back, and sometimes overlapping. Two more plays for Elmer Rice, and one on Broadway starring Eva Le Gallienne and Ethel Barrymore. She was working with friends and was thereby doubly enriched. But while she enjoyed these assignments very much, the one that truly helped her to overcome the persistent throb of loss was another job with Herman Shumlin, who was introducing a new playwright to the American theater—Lillian Hellman. The play was called *The Children's Hour*, and it dealt with lesbianism, radical material for the stage in those years. Yet, despite her devotion to this project, Aline would still feel emotionally flattened on too many days, as if she had been ironed into a two-dimensional cutout of the artist Aline Bernstein.

"There were obviously days when she just couldn't work," Mr. Shumlin remembers, angry not at Aline, but at the "scoundrel" who had caused her such protracted suffering. It was then that Aline hired Sointu Syrjala as her assistant, to help her get through the bad days. Even so, by the time the show opened in November, she was exhausted. In spite of her fatigue, however, she continued to look for assignments. Added to her more personal reasons for wanting to work was the fact that money was still tight for the Bernsteins. Their standard of living remained high in the still depressed economy, and if they chose to live this way, every family member must make his contribution. Once, in a note to Tom—for she still wrote him—she spoke of being "broke," and the word infuriated him. "Being broke in the understanding of most of us does not mean apartments at the Gotham Hotel and homes in Westchester County and trips to California," he sneered, referring to Aline's mention of a possible visit to California to investigate designing for the movies. Actually, Wolfe's anger stemmed from his anxiety over the approaching publication of his second novel. At Maxwell Perkins's insistence, he had cut his original manuscript into two parts, leaving the story of his love affair with Aline for a later volume. But even cutting and revising only the first part had been a long and arduous task. He felt spent, and he was also extremely nervous about the public's reaction to his second book.

Aline had little time to brood over Tom's surly mood, for abruptly, while she was out in California, tragedy ripped through her slowly rebuilding life. Edla's husband, Jack, dropped dead, cutting off a scant year of marriage.

Mrs. Loeb remembers an incident connected with this event which seemed to her symbolic of the family's attitude toward life. Having rushed over to Edla's apartment when she got the news, she offered to make some additional phone calls for them. The telephone was in the apartment's single bedroom, and when she went inside, incredibly, there was Jack Benjamin lying on the bed, waiting to be carried to the mortuary. No sheets attempted to hide death's face. "He was simply lying there, waiting to be disposed of," Mrs. Loeb recalls with a trace of a smile. "Something in that whole family was so basic, so fundamental . . . they took it for granted he should be in his bed until he was put underground—and that anyone who needed to use the telephone would just sit down there beside him and make their calls!"

Aline decided it would be better for Edla to fly out to California than for Aline to fly home. A change in scene would give her daughter time to "prepare herself for the hard dull pain of everyday life." Aline was staying in a hotel cottage in Carmel, and had already fallen in love with the grandeur of the Big Sur mountains. She had not been able to help writing Tom about it, encouraging him to plan a trip there someday soon, so that he could spend some time writing among the "mighty hills and wooded valleys like a cathedral."

She hoped that the serenity of the surroundings would help her child emerge from her deep stunned sadness. "She is so quiet and full of dignity," Aline wrote home, after Edla joined her, "but it would break your heart to see her tragic face; it is almost more than I can bear."

They stayed in Carmel through Christmas, for Aline felt the holiday season at home would accentuate Edla's loss. It seemed strange to see Christmas decorations on streets that blazed under a scorching sun. "I have to remind myself," Aline commented, "that after all, Christ was born in an even warmer climate than this."

The California weather was the least of the adjustments Aline had to make to West Coast life. Before Edla's arrival she had gone to Los Angeles to arrange for movie work. The mission was successful, but hardly pleasing. The industry was wonderful technically, she wrote Thomas Beer from the tranquillity of Carmel, "but horrible in many ways too. . . . It's rather menacing to think the whole country's taste is influenced by a few ignorant, avaricious, low men. And you can't beat them down either."

Despite her misgivings, Aline signed a contract to design the costumes for a movie that would be made in the spring, based on Rider Haggard's novel *She,* and starring her good friend Helen Gahagan Douglas. Helen and Melvyn Douglas had met Aline in New York, and visited her whenever their work brought them back there. Miss Gahagan, who years later would go on to a political career, possessed a very different intellect from that of most film stars, and Aline felt lucky to have such a congenial ally at the start of her own film career.

Of the costumes Aline designed for the film's supernatural theme,

Miss Gahagan says: "Her clothes for me were simply superb. They were almost breathtakingly creative, and yet absolutely perfect technically —but then, that was Aline's genius."

At last, after a brief visit to San Francisco, because "My father used to love the place, and so I needed to see it," Aline and Edla came home. But happy as she was to be there, it was difficult for Aline to feel satisfied when the news from abroad was so increasingly grim. It was terrifying to read the stories in the newspapers, and even more so in the letters she and Theo received from relatives in Europe. It was unmistakable that Adolf Hitler's ambitions were ominous and extended far beyond the boundaries of Germany. Concern about recovering from the Depression had perhaps made Americans too blind to what was happening in the rest of the world. But now, in 1935, fear was spreading and only those who were determined to ignore reality could avoid being touched by it.

Rather than envying the ability to rationalize difficult truth, Aline had only contempt for those who did so. Seeing Ethel off on a buying trip aboard the new ocean liner the *Normandie,* she was disgusted with the opulence which, she felt, pandered to the passengers' most Philistine tastes. "No matter what the slogan says," she protested, "fifty thousand Frenchmen *can* be wrong. . . . It's the most hideous and vulgar display of the world's goods my eyes have ever lit on, and come the revolution, I burn it up first thing."

All in all, Aline found herself irritable and far less patient with other people's behavior than she'd been in the past. Sham and artifice and grandiosity angered her quickly. Life was hard and short, and people must bring meaning to it. Beauty could be made by the artist, but humanity must be nurtured in the soul. Particularly when there was so frighteningly little humanity in the world at large.

As more time passed and life around her still seemed so often unlovely—"Has no one found a way to live?"—she discovered herself turning to a happier past, remembering with great tenderness the very earliest days of her life. And as she had once done for Tom, she began to commit these memories to paper. The more she wrote, the more determined she became to reclaim her experiences so that they might perhaps appear one day as stories under her own name.

In early March, when she was out in California again, working on the film for Helen Gahagan, she received a prepublication copy of Tom's book *Of Time and the River.* He had sent it to her through Maxwell

Perkins and taken off for Europe. Her reactions were mixed. She was, however ruefully, excited that Tom wanted her to have his book, but she grew apprehensive when she read a passage at the end of the novel which he had marked for her. In it, the autobiographical protagonist, Eugene, first sights Esther, the fictionalized Aline. Describing his initial glimpse of her from shipboard, the passage begins: "He turned and saw her then, and so finding her was lost, and so losing self was found." In the margin of the page, Tom had written simply: "My dear!"

Taken in conjunction with the statement in the author's introduction that "This novel is the second in a series of six, of which the first four have now been written, and the first two published," Aline was alarmingly certain that the next book in the series would continue the story of Esther Jack in far too much detail for her family's peace of mind. At the end of March, she decided to write to Perkins and tell him her fears. Her daughter had recently suffered a terrible blow, she wrote, and should be protected from further pain. "It's an age-old discussion, this business of who or what is to be sacrificed for a work of art," she said, but with all the pain in the world that can't be avoided, she had to fight to prevent what could be. Especially when it concerns "my people." She added that she could understand why it might be difficult for Perkins to believe her fierce loyalty toward her family, but he must accept the fact that the Bernstein family was "an uncommon one." Their life together had followed a unique and unfading design. They had shared everything, "not only our affections and pleasures, but our possessions and sorrows," while at the same time granting each other "the right to lead a life apart in the world." They did this, she said, not out of false innocence or illusion, but because they had always loved and respected each other. They understood, and more importantly, accepted, all aspects of "each other's faults and beauties." Tom should not be allowed to sully such people by his characterizations of them, nor in his distorted revelations of his life with Aline. He "cannot, he must not, I will not allow him to betray me."

Perkins responded with calm politeness, great brevity, and very little that was comforting. As Aline wrote to Thomas Beer: "he claims his duty lies with his firm and with T.W. . . . So much for human nature! We live in a vale of tears."

Aline also wrote to Tom in Europe, but this letter stressed his not appropriating material for his work which rightfully belonged to her. At the same time, she warmly congratulated him on the new novel. To her surprise, she received an answer almost immediately, which ignored the question of who owned the stories of her life, but expressed his joy that she had liked his book. Indeed, he confessed to having wept at her praise. He had tried, in the writing of that book, to produce a work that would be "worthy of me and of you." To receive her approval "makes a great music in me."

The reviews of the novel were extraordinary. Even those critics who took issue with Wolfe's lack of discipline called him an author of enormous power and richness. But the more reviews Aline read, the more she worried about Tom's next novel, which the critics were already speculating about. Therefore, in early June she arranged to see Mr. Perkins in his office. The meeting was tense, and it was then that Perkins admitted having once told Tom that his relationship with Aline must inevitably end. The confession made Aline tremble with rage, and she was far too agitated to continue the meeting. When the editor tried to shake her hand in farewell, she thrust her hands behind her back and hissed, "I consider you my enemy."

She regretted her rudeness almost immediately and wrote to apologize, but her resentment of Maxwell Perkins continued. Only later, after Perkins himself had known the sting of Tom's rejection, would Wolfe forge a bond between the two. In her letter of apology, she could not avoid further words of anger and scorn. It was unspeakably sad, she wrote, that a love of such caliber as hers for Tom should become such an evil thing. "The only evil in it came from his own jealousy, certain qualities in his temperament, and, added to that, your sinfully conventional point of view."

Later in the month, Aline read that Tom had returned from Europe. The press greeted him like a conquering hero, and as she read his jubilant interview and studied his grinning photograph, pride welled up in her at the realization that the success they had dreamed of together had at last arrived. How wonderful it would have been to be there on the dock to meet him. She could not help fantasizing as she sat drinking her morning coffee, inventing a scene in which while the reporters flocked around him, she stood demurely to one side, watching his face all flushed and excited as he answered their questions. And then, as he beckoned to her, she would walk quickly to his side to accept a public tribute.

Actually, it was Perkins who had waited for Tom on the dock and one of his principal reasons for doing so was to tell Tom about Aline's demands. Perkins was sure Tom would get terribly upset at the news, but instead he waved it away and spoke of Aline only with affection. After several rounds of drinks, he even insisted on taking his editor on a nostalgic visit to Eighth Street. "There, Max," he said, "there is the place where I lived in the attic and wrote *Look Homeward, Angel!*" Their inhibitions dulled by drink, the two climbed up the fire escape and through the attic window into the long, low room that had held so much love and promise. And Tom marveled to the point of tears at "all the strangeness and the glory and the power of life."

His nostalgia did not impel him to get in touch with Aline, but she continued to write both to Perkins and to him. Her entreaties to Tom took on a new ring of conviction, for the notes she was making about her childhood seemed clearly to be the beginning of another book. "I have written my own story about Nana and Daddy and the actors in New York," she explains. "I am working to make it better and I ask you to let me keep it. I will not tell it so successfully as you could, but it is my own, and my own words fit it well."

He did not answer her, and her anxiety increased, as did her determination to resolve the issue. A plan began to take shape in her mind. She would arrange an accidental meeting, one that neither Perkins nor Tom could deny her, as they might if she asked for an appointment. And so one day, she dressed carefully in the kind of print dress Tom had always admired and came into the city from Armonk. In late afternoon she went to the Chatham bar in the hope that the two would come in for their customary meeting over cocktails. A wide-brimmed hat kept her face in shadow as she sat at a little corner table that faced the clock. She had barely touched the drink she'd ordered when they came into the room and were ushered to a table by the fawning captain. Her throat closed with feeling, so tightly that she knew she would not be able to speak. She would have to wait until the wave of emotion subsided before she approached them. Perhaps, she thought, they would notice her, and then she would not have to make the first difficult move. Indeed, from the moment the two men sat down, Tom had been glancing over at her, as if the dress and hat touched some subliminal awareness. But now Perkins looked toward her in a random glance around the room, and she knew by the expression on his face that he had instantly recognized her. He leaned across the table and whispered to Tom, who wheeled around as if he'd been struck. Tilting her head from under her hat, she stared at him, meeting his eyes. Wolfe jumped up from his chair and strode across the room to her. Voice husky, he told her she looked beautiful, and the emotion she heard, and saw in his face as well, made tears spring to her eyes.

They were both too moved to stay in a public place, and at Perkins's suggestion, they decided to return to Scribner's offices, where they could talk privately. Despite the intensity of her feeling, Aline began to reiterate her arguments and demands even while they were walking there, and as Tom listened, he felt again the nagging urge that had been plaguing him for some time. Now that he was earning considerable sums of money, he would have liked to pay Aline back for all she had done for him; to try and even the score between them. He told her this as they sat in Perkins's office, interrupting her own earnest pleading. Aline answered quickly. Neither her life story nor her love was for sale. Whatever she had done for Thomas Wolfe had been done in "the fullness of our love and my faith. Let me keep that truth, Tom," she finished quietly.

But Wolfe was caught up in his need to settle the past. Nervously waving her demurral aside, he ran out of the room to find Perkins, who had left them alone together. He wanted to find out from Max what percentage of his royalties could be set aside to free him of his haunting sense of indebtedness.

Some biographers of Thomas Wolfe report that when he and Perkins returned to the office, they found Aline about to swallow the contents of a vial of pills. Terrified, Tom knocked the bottle out of her hand and scooped her up in his arms as she lapsed into unconsciousness. Perkins hurriedly summoned a doctor who had offices in the Scribner building, and the doctor was able to determine from the label on the bottle that no pills were missing. He was certain she had not yet swallowed any pills, that she had simply fainted.

Despite the vividness of this anecdote, Aline's own papers suggest that the bottle was in her hand because she was going through her purse to find a handkerchief. The tension of the meeting was indeed making her feel faint. But the time was over when the turmoil she knew through Thomas Wolfe would overpower her desire for life—even without him.

When she regained consciousness, Tom wanted to see her home, but she refused, wishing only to be alone and to grow calm again. She took a cab to Armonk, for once not regretting the extravagance. To her astonishment, Tom followed her to Westchester. She was barely inside her bedroom when he appeared at the Dutch door that opened directly on to the garden. The shock of seeing his flushed face and huge body almost made her faint again. "He called me a lecherous old woman and cursed me that he could not get me out of his soul," she wrote, still horror-struck, to Bella after Tom finally left hours later. "This all sounds like a dream, but Bella, it is the God's truth. . . . He came in and we sat up all night, and he told me he could not have any relations with any woman but me, and that I was so bad that he could not stand it. . . . Crazy! . . . Well, I finally got him to go away, and that is the end. His next book I'm sure will be all my stuff, and I may as well give it to him."

The air of resignation in her letter to Bella quite accurately reflected Aline's mood after that night. Let Tom do what he would. "Nobody can ever be degraded but by himself," she decided. The false starts, the tentative decisions, had at last come together to form a new vision of the life remaining to her, built on her visions in the hospital. "What I have of my own, the heart and core of myself, must neither be beaten, nor modified, nor even magnified by any other human being." It was a vow, as sacred as though made in church, one that would allow her "to be finally free of this corrosion."

As the months passed, she was able to respond to Tom and even visit him occasionally, as the loving friend he had long professed he wanted her to be. "Your welfare and happiness and success," she wrote in one note, "are always the dearest things in the world to me, the same as those of my own children." The statement seems an almost calculated concession to reality. She was a woman of fifty-five with a grown family, he was a man in his mid thirties, famous and sought after by scores of free young women.

One September day, she left his new apartment at 48th Street and First Avenue and then walked crosstown and up to Central Park. It was a fine day for a walk, and the colors of the trees picked up the colors of the loosely wrapped bolt of cloth she held in her arms. She had brought the fabric to show Tom, for she was planning to make it into curtains for his living room.

Reaching the park, she moved between the playing children and the young mothers wheeling their baby carriages. Suddenly she paused. A face and voice had come into her mind. They belonged to Robert Henri.

"Never let the fact that things are not made for you, that conditions are not as they should be, stop you," he had often told her. No, he would continue firmly, you must "go on anyway. . . . Everything depends on those who go on anyway."

Briskly, she turned toward the gates and headed for home.

# Part Five

## 1934-1955

# 21

She had known Thomas Wolfe in his "beauty and horror," and now, released from need and passion, she could concentrate on the beauty when she played back scenes of their life together. To say she no longer missed him would have been untrue. In her own words, she could no more help missing him than she could help the color of her eyes. But she was concentrating on the present and the future, and the central figures of these landscapes were once again her family. The bond that had always held the Bernsteins together now lightened almost visibly. Although they still maintained their separate lives, family projects increasingly absorbed them. One friend recalls seeing them in heated argument over what color to stain the floor of a downstairs porch in Armonk. They had indicated their preferred colors on sample tiles, and all talking at once, they got down on their hands and knees in different corners of the room to demonstrate the wisdom of their choices.

"I don't remember who won," the friend says, "undoubtedly Aline, but what I do remember is how extraordinary their involvement was with the house and with each other."

Most people observed a particular closeness between Aline and Theo in those days. On weekends they would stride arm in arm through the park in the city or around the Armonk reservoir in the country, as they used to when they took their Sunday-afternoon walks as a young couple. It would be romantic to claim that their union was unscarred by the events of the past several years, but it is true that no one ever detected any sense of "making do" in Aline's homecoming or any heroic martyrdom in Theo's welcome to her.

Aline accepted just one design assignment during the fall season of 1935, and that one only because it was an architectural challenge. For a play called *Night in the House,* by Rodney Ackland, she transformed the stage of the Booth Theater into a two-story, three-room section of a house. The ingenuity and practicality of the set won unanimous high praise from the Broadway critics, who stressed how "remarkable" its "varied effects were upon the dramatic narrative."

But she chose to turn down other work for a while, even though good offers were relatively scarce. Americans, even New Yorkers, were seeking less expensive forms of entertainment than the theater, and producers were having a difficult time finding investors for their shows. Across the country, actors, playwrights and craftsmen, along with people in the other arts, were swelling the ranks of the unemployed. Although Aline, as Mrs. Theodore Bernstein, did not have to be concerned about survival, many of her friends and colleagues did, and she worried on their behalf. Not only did they need money, she'd fret to Theo; they needed audiences, whether for their paintings or their plays, because an artist without an audience is never wholly fulfilled. Continuing to be an ardent advocate of Franklin Roosevelt, she greeted with enthusiasm his declaration that the Depression was hurting the artist as much as the farmer and businessman. In August 1935, legislation was enacted to help alleviate this problem. Under the Works Progress Administration, a Four-Arts project was established which would give work to artists, writers, musicians and actors. Within the first six months, 40,000 people were on the payroll in these divisions, and the programs continued to grow rapidly. In the Federal Art Project alone, some four to five thousand people would be employed annually, enabling artists like Stuart Davis, Jack Levine, Arshile Gorky, de Kooning and Tamayo to survive. By the time the program was curtailed in 1939, more than 48,000 oils and watercolors had been sent out on permanent loan to schools, libraries and hospitals, while 1,300 murals decorated post offices and other public buildings. The graphic arts, sculpture, ceramics and model buildings were similarly supported, while an archives program called the Index of American Design hired nearly five hundred artists to search out the American past for articles used in daily life, and create a permanent visual record of American decorative and folk arts. On completion, the Index was stored in the National Gallery in Washington, and it has served as a vast reservoir of "carefully painted and drawn reproductions of Americana."

Aline volunteered her services to the arts programs, at one time supervising an ambitious display of historical costumes that was mounted in Macy's department store. She was grateful for the chance to participate in an undertaking that was helping so many people she cared about. Until now she had felt helpless to do anything to make their lot easier. The best she'd been able to do was lend them whatever extra money she managed to put aside from her share of family expenses, or to peddle the work of her artist friends to colleagues of Theo's who had hung on to their fortunes.

"Why not, Theo?" she demanded when he complained about her conducting such business at a dinner party. "Look," she said impatiently, "they're getting incredible bargains, and somehow they all seem to have dollars still floating around like dust in a sunbeam!"

Perhaps the program that excited Aline most of all was the theater project, directed by Hallie Flanagan, a woman whom she already knew quite well. Mrs. Flanagan had come to her new job from her post as head of the acclaimed Experimental Theater at Vassar College, which she had founded, and she brought with her a moral and artistic vigor that quickly carried the Federal Theatre Project beyond its original function of giving unemployed actors work. Mrs. Flanagan believed history would judge her productions: "Our job is to see that the enterprises in which we are engaged are worth the effort."

The Federal Theatre Project would employ ten thousand people and operate theaters in forty states. It published a nationally distributed theater magazine, conducted a research bureau that made its resources available to schools and community theaters, and played to audiences totaling millions. In keeping with the artistic climate of the time, the project invented the "Living Newspaper," a cinematic and journalistic type of production that dealt with such subjects as housing and strikes and flood control. It was in the Federal Theatre that Orson Welles was first introduced to audiences, and Sinclair Lewis appeared in the New

York production of the adaptation of his novel *It Can't Happen Here.*
Admission to such plays was often free, and rarely was there a charge
over thirty cents.

Part of Mrs. Flanagan's design was to have regional theater centers
and directors throughout the country. While certain plays were presented simultaneously in perhaps twenty theaters, other productions
would reflect the needs and tastes of a particular city or state. She had
asked Elmer Rice to serve as the director in New York, and this of
course made Aline's participation even more enjoyable. But even after
Rice left the Project, she continued to donate her time and skills to Mrs.
Flanagan, whom she had come to admire more and more.

Many contemporary playwrights were committed to the union of
art and social conscience, as Robert Henri and his friends had once
been, and, years later, Aline would explain to students how so many
of the plays of the thirties reflected this marriage. Plays like *Waiting
for Lefty,* by Clifford Odets, and *Bury the Dead,* by Irwin Shaw,
would mirror real life for an audience, and this sometimes resulted
in a play's being attacked as "leftist" or "politically slanted." Aline
was contemptuous of such reasoning. She believed instead that the
ferment of the times was creating the kind of energy the artist is
fed by. As Irwin Shaw would later reminisce about the theater of
the thirties, it was uncommonly exciting just because "We all
thought of what we wanted to express, and what had to be said,
rather than about success."

Even with her volunteer activities to supplement her professional
assignments, Aline still had more free time than she was accustomed to.
And for a while, she relished it. She considered taking courses at the Art
Students League, but when she went there to visit, the students made
her feel too "ancient," and she decided simply to paint more on her
own. So she would happily arrange still lifes of fruits and flowers from
her garden in Armonk and place her easel in the morning sun to capture certain shadows on the vase or bowl. She bought a loom and took
up weaving, and Ethel would sometimes join her in the long, cool
workroom on weekends. They would rarely speak to each other, but
would concentrate on the hypnotic motions of the loom and the sound
of the shuttle moving back and forth. And Aline took up needlework
again, embroidering blouses for Ethel and Edla and for the cook to wear
to church on Sunday. It was a time to be quiet and to move slowly, and
she savored the calm new rhythm. She felt, she said, "a fine, inner

peace," one that "I would not have thought possible a few years ago." In a letter to a friend, she wrote: "There are certain things I would never have known, never would have felt, if I had not been through what I knew these past years." Then her letter seemed to break into a smile as, philosophy aside, she added: "But please, don't try it on that account!"

She was even resting more now, propping herself up in bed to do her work, happily indulging in atypical disorder. "I wish you could see my bed," she wrote another friend. "I have a drawing board, a T-square and triangle, a lot of pencils, thumb tacks, erasers, tracing paper and some books on architecture. You know how I've always loved to use my instruments," she continued. "You put a triangle against a T-square, and you have a gorgeously uncontrovertible fact." Still, she confessed, invariably she pushed "all this serious stuff" away, and reached for a bag of chintz, spilling the scraps with abandon all over her bed as she began sewing on a patchwork quilt that "who around here needs, for Christ's sake?!"

*From Death to Morning*, a collection of short stories by Tom, was published in November 1935. Once again, the reviews were enthusiastic. And only a month later, the *Saturday Review of Literature* serialized a small book of his which Scribner's would publish the following year. It was called *The Story of a Novel* and described the agony involved in becoming a writer.

As Aline read the magazine she grew reflective. Tom had given Maxwell Perkins abundant credit for his own success, and she felt a stab of jealousy that Perkins had received the public acknowledgment she had never known. But she also thought that the words of gratitude had an ominous ring. She better than anyone knew how abruptly Tom could retreat from dependency. How, if frightened and angry, he could "embark on the mighty stride of changes, his cruel and relentless disentanglements from all that bound him." She did not welcome the prospect of Maxwell Perkins encountering such treatment; now that she had become more reasonable, she bore him no malice.

And Aline knew there were already strains in Tom's connection with Scribner's. She had not heard from him since they'd exchanged notes on his birthday, but on a recent December weekend, he'd called to demand frantically that she put some money of his into the Gotham safe until the banks opened on Monday morning. He had decided to withdraw his accruing royalties from Scribner's, who had been keeping his money for him. He wanted a regular bank account, he told Aline, safe from Scribner's "prying" eyes.

Watching him lope down the street after they'd put the money away, his expensive new coat flapping and stained as always, Aline was flooded with memories. This was not a new sensation. More and more of late, she had found herself trying to understand the complexity of their alliance. Indeed, so compelling was the urge to do this that she had put aside writing about her childhood and instead was trying to commit the truth of Tom and herself to paper. "I think the story will be interesting," she wrote to Bella. "Anyway, it is interesting to me."

Best of all she loved to write in Armonk, at her desk facing the garden. The orchard trees around the house were heavy with plums and cherries, and when she left her writing she would gather up the fruit to make into preserves for her celebrated weekend brunches. Sometimes at these parties, when the sun seemed more tempting than the admiration of her guests, she'd go up to the sun porch, take off her clothes and lie naked under the enveloping warmth. It tickled her to imagine what her guests would say if they knew where she had gone, particularly those guests who were neighbors, and considerably more proper than her artist and theater friends who had come up from the city. Happily, though, everyone seemed to mix well together in her house, and certainly Aline had no trouble finding things to talk about with these neighbors. For one thing, she'd joined the Westchester Garden Club, and took her membership very seriously. "I wear my best white shoes and my best lady's hat to our meetings," she reported to other friends, "and I ask good questions, and everybody loves me."

She entered all the club's contests, and when she'd win a prize, she glowed with pleasure. Once she won first prize, and sported the big blue ribbon for days, even on her evening clothes. She had entered the "most original" display, representing the show's largest and smallest entries. In identical copper pots, one as large as a bathtub, the other barely bigger than a thimble, she'd arranged flowers from her garden. It had taken Teddy and Theo and the gardener to carry the big pot to the show. "Wasn't it worth it, boys?" she bubbled on the way home, and of course, to a man, they agreed that it was.

In the fall of 1936, she once more felt at the height of her designing powers, but work was still scarce. She did do another play by Lillian Hellman for Herman Shumlin, called *Days to Come,* but a singularly poor cast helped close it within a week. "You know," she sighed to Theo

310

when she read the notices, "I think it is bad enough sometimes to be an actor, but to be a bad actor is simply unforgivable." With so much of Broadway shuttered, she again looked to Hollywood for work, frustrated that she could not make use of her talent. "I read every day about the big-shots they've hired," she'd grumble. "I just know I'm so much better than any of them. . . . I think they're fools not to let me do something really distinguished in color designing. . . . Well," she'd say then, "it's not for me to complain, although I find I'm able to complain with the rest of them."

Actually, professional worries were the least disturbing of her concerns. She was persistently distressed these days by Teddy's health. He had been suffering from episodes of obscure inflammations and near-hemorrhaging nosebleeds. When he returned from a trip to Europe with Ethel, Aline had had to arrange for an ambulance to meet him at the dock so that he could be taken to Mount Sinai Hospital to stop the bleeding that had persisted for the last three days of the voyage. Much of the time Aline could forget that Teddy's heart was none too good, but when he was this ill, the knowledge of his cardiac condition overwhelmed her with apprehension. "I am a wreck tonight," she wrote to a friend, trying to pass the time till morning, "but I will be all right when Teddy is home and well again."

But even when Teddy came home and was apparently feeling well, her mood could still turn bleak when she read the relentless signs of danger from abroad. "It just looks worse each day," she'd moan. "This is the first time in my life that I really despair of humanity—how can great masses of people allow and countenance the horrors?"

Writing to Bella, her perennial confidante, who was spending much of her time in Hollywood, Aline reported: "I saw a copy of *Life* magazine a few weeks ago with pictures of the ladies high up in the Hitler entourage. They were dressed in evening clothes, and I cannot tell you how it infuriated me." And she added, with grim satisfaction: "I took my scissors and jabbed them through and through. Did you see the pictures, Bella?" she finished, as though her friend were sitting across the room rather than across the country. "How can they eat and sleep and dress that way, the bastards."

Feeling so impassioned about the world's injustice and, in particular, about the plight of Europe's Jews, Aline was acutely shaken by a visit from Tom one winter evening in early 1937. She had by now accepted that "he hates us all like poison," and as she reflected on their relation-

311

ship in her writing, she could no longer avoid confronting that "twist in him" which was his anti-Semitism. But she had not expected to be hurt by it again.

However, she reported in an early-morning letter to Bella Spewack that near midnight the previous evening, Tom had stormed into the Gotham Hotel demanding to see her. He was so drunk he could barely stand, and the deskman, anxious to avoid a scene, summoned Aline to the lobby. As soon as she stepped off the elevator, "he started the most awful row about the Jews." Shrilly he "denounced the entire race . . . they should be wiped off the face of the earth." Suddenly the shouting stopped as he angrily peered down at her. Aline had remained silent all this time, hoping to quiet him, but her silence seemed to have inflamed him more. As if he could not stop until he had struck a response from her, he waved his hands wildly in the air and, teetering precariously, began to yell: "Three cheers for Hitler! Three cheers for Hitler!"

The porter and the desk clerk, who had been discreetly looking elsewhere, wheeled around to face them. And, Aline reported to Bella, it was as if a geyser of rage and humiliation erupted inside her.

"Bella . . . do you know what I did? I landed out and punched Tom in the nose!" To her astonishment, because he was so drunk, he tumbled to the floor. But she did not feel triumphant as she stood over his sprawled body, nor when she asked the men to put him out of the building.

"It was the most sickening experience of my life, so far," she wrote, as dawn brightened outside her window. "I think everyone who admires him so much should know about the Jew attitude. . . . I have always protected him so far as I could, because of that certain greatness I have felt about him, but this was finally too much. . . . It was a sample of what must be happening all over the world, only fortunately I was so placed that I could strike out."

Perhaps because the world did seem in such upheaval, Aline, as 1937 began, threw her energies into a new interest that united her love of fine design and her respect for the transitions and traditions of history. During the last several years she'd often discussed the idea of a costume museum with Lee Simonson and Irene Lewisohn. It was a dream they all planned to make real sometime in the future, and now, suddenly, Aline felt the time had come. She communicated her urgency to her friends. After a flurry of planning meetings, Aline found a loft on West

Forty-sixth Street, and as soon as the lease was signed, the Costume Museum officially existed. From that moment on, she devoted every spare moment to the project. She collected materials and clothing from friends, from antique stores, from people she wrote to all over the world, so that the collection she was assembling would present a historical and aesthetic record of the evolution of dress.

Part of Aline's reason for wanting to open her museum at this time was her feeling that its existence in New York would benefit people like Ethel, who earned their living in the world of high fashion. It was evident that Paris could not serve as the fashion center for designers much longer and that New York was the logical substitute. A costume museum would be a valuable resource. She presented this argument and many others in a fund-raising position paper, along with projected plans for the museum's development. There would be a library of books on the apparel of a particular period, and also on "the paintings, sculpture, ceramics, and tapestries of that time," so that the broadest cultural awareness of an era could be gained. There would be workrooms where costumes could be studied and sketched and patterns cut. And there would also, of course, be revolving exhibitions, "related to historic events, timely events, art events, trade interests, or merely to the display of beautiful things to delight the eye."

"I do nothing but sit at my instrument and write, then go out and bother people about the Museum," she told her friends. "I am just crazy about it. . . . I must get some movie fortunes interested." But at other times, she was apologetic about her "obsession . . . I feel like a wretch when there is so much suffering all over the world." Still, "it is my nature to be caught in these things . . . somebody must do the fancy work."

Much of the work could hardly be labeled fancy. She spent hours on her hands and knees poring through crates grown filthy with the years' accumulated grime. After such an afternoon, she felt like an anthropologist on a dig, for she never knew, when she ripped open a packing case or pushed deep into a rotting barrel, what treasures she would find. Early in her collecting there were two such treasures which made her breathless when she held them in her hands. One was a jaunty troubadour's suit which she recognized as her father's. She herself had sewn the buttons on the vest one Sunday afternoon in Mamie's boardinghouse. She closed her eyes, and could see her father in his shirtsleeves, teasing her about taking so much time with her fancy stitches.

She had barely had time to absorb this find, when there was another. In a heap of old Shakespearean costumes she found a black suit, clearly worn by a Hamlet of long ago. Stitched into the crimson lining was the name "John Wilkes Booth."

Besides undiminished efforts for the museum, 1938 was also to bring the publication of Aline's second book. She had completed the story about Tom and herself, submitted it to Alfred and Blanche Knopf, and it was scheduled to be published in the spring. If she felt any concern over how her family would react when the book came out, Aline gave no sign of it, although she did sometimes express her worry about Tom's reaction. In any case, what was really important was that she could now legitimately think of herself as a writer, and make writing a part of her life. And indeed, she began to write all the time. Articles about the theater and memories of her childhood appeared under her name in the *Atlantic Monthly* and *Harper's Bazaar* and *Theatre Arts* magazine. "How I wish I had begun to write earlier in my life," she'd sometimes sigh as she studied the pages.

So great was her pleasure in her new mode of expression that even the latest literary news about Tom failed to upset her. He had finally made the break with Scribner's, after a long and painful series of attempts. She'd heard that a weary Maxwell Perkins had said at last: "If you have to leave, Tom, go ahead and leave, but for heaven's sake, don't talk about it anymore."

In his search for a new publisher, Tom had been given to drunken calls made from phone booths, plaintively announcing: "This is Thomas Wolfe. Would you like to publish my books?" He had finally settled with Harper & Brothers, and under the guidance of a new editor, Edward Aswell, he was once again writing about Esther Jack.

"I'm going to have a book written about me," Eva Le Gallienne remembers Aline saying with more pride than concern. There were several reasons for her calm. She believed enough time had passed to soften Tom's resentments of the Bernstein family; she did not believe Tom wanted or needed to hurt her anymore; and her own version of their union would be published first.

*The Journey Down* received the sort of reviews the most seasoned writer could hope for. "Aline Bernstein's sensual and sensitive impressions are breathtaking . . . deep down things which are usually found only in people's eyes are written indelibly and in exquisite pain on her pages." Mail poured into the Gotham from literary friends who were amazed at her latent gift for writing. Lewis Mumford wrote her: "You have all the instincts of a writer—above all the ability to reveal yourself without standing between the material and the reader." And perhaps most gratifying to Aline because of her lifelong love for poetry, May Sarton wrote: "I was up all night reading your book. It is a beautiful piece of work, with the intensity, texture and peculiar sustained excitement of a poem."

Maintaining their composure, the Bernstein family gave no indication of being anything but proud of Aline's latest success. As for Tom, she heard nothing directly, but mutual friends brought back reports of his being genuinely pleased at her achievement. Although he complained mildly that she had painted herself too innocently, he bragged about her ability (and his own early recognition of it) to express profound sentiments in prose as pure and simple as a child's. At times like these, she was told, he tended to get deeply sentimental about their past, describing gentle scenes in Ambleside and confessing to a love for Aline Bernstein that had never dimmed.

When she heard these stories, Aline thought about calling Tom, especially since she was also hearing that he did not look or feel very well. His skin was sallow, people said: he had grown quite heavy, and he talked about feeling "old." But she did not call him, preferring to maintain her equilibrium, knowing in her heart that if he needed her, he would let her know.

Only a few weeks later, he did call her, from Vancouver. He'd turned in his manuscript to Aswell, and left for a vacation in the Pacific Northwest. But he had begun to feel ill, and now he lay in a hotel room, feverish and frightened. He had chills, he told her anxiously, and his head was throbbing with unbearable pain. He needed help. He was going to die, all by himself. It was awful to be alone in a strange city when you were so sick. Aline did her best to comfort and calm him. "Try to feel my hand on your brow, Tom. . . . Remember how I used to be able to take away your headache? . . . It will go away now. . . . I promise." When he seemed less upset, she urged him to try to get some sleep; he could call her again if he needed to. And in the morning, he must promise to see a doctor. She hung up the phone and lay sleepless against her pillows; he would probably go on calling her for the rest of her life whenever he was frightened or sick or drunk.

Tom did not call again that evening, nor did he see a physician in the morning. Later she was to find out the full details of his progressive

315

illness. From Vancouver he had moved on to Seattle, where he'd fallen desperately ill with pneumonia. After being hospitalized for many weeks, suffering from severe headaches and frequent periods of delirium, he was moved to Johns Hopkins Hospital in Baltimore, just as his father had been years before. Suspecting a brain tumor, the doctors performed an exploratory operation, which revealed that his brain was riddled with tubercles. Evidently the pneumonia had opened up an old tuberculosis lesion on his lung, and tubercle bacilli had entered his bloodstream and been carried to the brain. No surgical procedure was possible. He was simply sewn up again. His head swathed in bandages, he was returned to his room to await what his family, who had been summoned to his side, could only hope would be a mercifully swift death.

It was Maxwell Perkins who broke the news to Aline, for despite his break with Scribner's, Tom had clung to the editor's friendship. And it was Perkins who gently urged Aline not to go to Baltimore to see Tom. "Julia is here, and we don't know what she would do if she sees you," he said. "I really think it's better for Tom if you don't come." Aline did not argue. She trusted Perkins's opinion, and above all, she wanted Tom to be peaceful.

Thomas Wolfe died at six-thirty in the morning of September 15, 1938, less than three weeks before his thirty-eighth birthday. It was Edward Aswell who brought Aline the heartbreaking gift of knowing that the last words Aswell heard Tom speak were of her. In fevered confusion, he had tried to lift himself in the bed to peer around the room. Searching every corner, his eyes black against the white bandages, he had whispered, "Where's Aline. . . . I want Aline. . . . I want my Jew."

"I told him you were coming, and he smiled, and lay down again," Aswell reported.

Aline went out to her garden and looked over the hills. The irony of Tom's dying before her had not escaped her. She had no answer for this twist of fate any more than she had for the one that had brought them together. She could only feel that during the span that bridged their beginning and this ending, she had made his life less lonely, less tormented. She would hold on to that thought as she lived out her own life, in a world forever diminished.

# 22

There are those who would say that Aline felt a new kind of peace after Tom's death. As if, despite her grief, she had finally been purged of all vestiges of yearning for what could never be. So Tom's photograph stayed by her bedside. "Look at Tom," she'd say to visitors, escorting them to her bedroom. "Isn't that a marvelous picture of Tom?" She had all his letters wrapped up in a huge bundle, and put them under her worktable, where she could see their bulk. And she proudly proclaimed his genius to people who out of innocence or curiosity mentioned his name.

But she also went on working with growing power. Within weeks of Tom's death, she was engaged to do another Lillian Hellman play, *The Little Foxes,* starring the volatile young actress Tallulah Bankhead. Aline was immediately drawn to Miss Bankhead and proved uniquely able to handle her extravagant swings of mood. "Let me talk to her," she'd say during a stormy rehearsal, and she would take the actress off to a corner and soothe her until the scene could continue. Perhaps because she was so responsive to Tallulah, Aline's costumes for *The*

*Little Foxes* were extraordinarily effective, revealing through the utmost subtlety in cut and color the developing themes of female strength and foreshadowings of evil.

The play opened in February 1939, to excellent reviews for everyone involved. For Aline, this meant more offers for new work, but her heart was elsewhere now. She who had never bothered to preserve a rendering of her drawings, or keep a scrapbook of her designs, thought night and day about "my museum." Not that she felt proprietary toward it. When, later, colleagues would suggest putting up a plaque to commemorate Aline's role in the museum's inception, she turned the idea down flatly. "I did it because I wanted to," she'd say impatiently. "What kind of philanthropy is that?"

Money was a little easier for the Bernsteins now, and so they could encourage Aline's interest in this nonpaying project. Her share of household expenses was absorbed without complaint, and they agreeably pitched in for the fund-raising parties that threw their homes open to the public. "Our house was like Grand Central Station—only with carpeting," she reported after a weekend of entertaining. And she added gratefully: "It was an awful chore, but the kind of chore that my whole family does not seem to mind."

Between parties, she'd run around the city, pocketbook stuffed with "little tracts" to hand out to businessmen in their offices or to friends she spotted in restaurants. Her principal goal this winter and spring of 1939 was to find a new home for the museum, since it had already outgrown its original loft. One day, as she was packing up her things to go out on some more "pestering visits," she received a phone call from Nelson Rockefeller, whom she knew only slightly. It was Ethel who was close to the Rockefellers through her work at Bergdorf's. Indeed, only recently, Nelson's mother, the distinguished philanthropist and collector Abby Aldrich Rockefeller, had come to the store to ask Ethel for advice, explaining that she felt she should cut a more fashionable figure now that her sons were all becoming prominent. "I don't want you to make me into a Jean Harlow," she said shyly. "Only just see if you can make me more presentable."

Now, shortly after telephoning her, Nelson Rockefeller was passing plans for the extension of Rockefeller Center across his desk to Aline, and casually offering her a suite of rooms for the museum. "I pinched myself under the table," Aline would soon exult to Theo, "and I wished my papa was there to see Mr. Rockefeller handing me land on a silver tray!"

But the visit was not over yet. Nelson Rockefeller also handed Aline one hundred thousand dollars in negotiable securities so bulky they couldn't find an envelope large enough to hold them. Finally, she stuffed them into a brown paper bag, and clutching the parcel to her chest, she rode the bumpy Sixth Avenue elevated train down to Wall Street to turn the stocks over to her husband's care.

How odd it sometimes seemed to find herself on such an ascending curve when the world was caught in such a downward spiral. Hitler's occupation of Austria and Czechoslovakia and the Munich Pact were dreadful indicators of what the new year would bring. She'd lie in her bed at night, chilled with apprehension. "You cannot unleash man's most dreadful passions and have no scars," she'd say. "You can't murder and torture and hate and curse, without a rebound, even if it's someone else's fault. . . . It's like a hurricane that blows three times around the earth."

And there was other trouble; less cataclysmic but closer to home. Hallie Flanagan's efforts and achievements were being, in Aline's opinion, outrageously undermined. For a variety of reasons—the possibility of war, competition from professional theaters, declining enthusiasm for the New Deal and a more aggressive conservative element in government—major cuts had been made in WPA appropriations, and still more were promised. The final blow to the Theatre Project had been struck the summer before when the newly created House Un-American Activities Committee began to investigate its possible "left-wing tendencies." In January 1939, they made public their conclusion that "a rather large number of the employees of the Federal Theatre Project are either members of . . . or are sympathetic with the Communist Party." Despite denials and protests by the theatrical community, Congress announced it would cut off all appropriations for the Federal Theatre Project as of June 30 that year. The decision enraged Aline: she considered it grossly unfair to the program and to Hallie Flanagan, and a terrible blow to America's cultural life.

Then, in late spring, Tom's story about her girlhood visit to Richard Mansfield was published in the *Atlantic Monthly.* As Aline first read the borrowed tale, which began with the young narrator saying: "You would have adored Daddy. He was so wild and beautiful . . ." she was not angry. In fact, she thought, it was almost as if Tom had left her a legacy by commemorating her experience in print. But soon this response seemed naïvely romantic. Almost immediately after the story appeared, Harper's brought out Tom's novel *The Web and the Rock.*

It was the first of the two novels Edward Aswell had edited for publication after Tom's death, and the reading public was very curious about it. Wolfe's break with Perkins and his premature death had encouraged speculation about the writing he'd left behind. Publication of *The Web and the Rock* evoked what one critic sourly called great flurries of "melodramatic excitement," and Aline could not pick up a newspaper or magazine without reading about Thomas Wolfe and "Esther Jack."

Aline herself put off reading the novel when Aswell sent her a copy. It sat on her night table like Pandora's box, tempting and frightening, daring her to confront Tom's version of their love affair. When she finally began to read it, she was swiftly caught up in feelings of such intensity that from time to time she'd have to put the book aside and rest. But, she later told a friend, "so much of the book made me angry that I finally stopped being anguished."

Actually, her anger was directed more toward Tom's treatment of her family than of herself. Although Esther Jack is sometimes dealt with cruelly, overall she is described with an adoring pen. As Paschal Reeves would later write about Wolfe's attempt to "fictionalize the most important relationship in his adult life . . . Surely the ghosts of many women, from Helen of Troy to Jennie Gerhardt, must have curtsied to Esther Jack."

But the Bernsteins gave no hint of serious distress at Tom's characterizations, and perhaps as a result of their equanimity, Aline was soon back to savoring the immediate moment and life's familiar pleasures. It was an attitude she continued to proselytize to friends. When Bella and Sam Spewack bought a country home in Pennsylvania, Aline quickly scribbled a welcoming poem:

> Welcome to your home, dear Sam and Bella,
> May you always have a well-filled cellar,
> May you always have a groaning table,
> With meat and bread and vegetable. . . .

And the poem skipped along with wishes for a lovely garden, and good plumbing, and dry walls, and productive typewriters, and added also that other ingredient for Aline's concept of the good life:

> May only those come to your door,
> Who never, under any circumstances,
> Could be a bore. . . .

In this spirit, she took time out from museum work and her writing to do one more play for Herman Shumlin, *The Male Animal,* by James Thurber and Elliott Nugent. As world affairs worsened, it was important to help people laugh. Indeed, laughter and loving had never seemed so crucial. "We must all cling together and treasure each other," Aline would say repeatedly. "If we are able to do that," then perhaps "man cannot go entirely bad."

In the middle of the year, Harper's published Tom's last novel, *You Can't Go Home Again.* In this book, the love affair between Eugene and Esther bitterly declines. Memories of that trajectory burned Aline's mind as she read the narrative. Then, to her astonishment and aggravating her discomfort, she began to receive letters from readers, mostly women, who had been greatly moved by the story of the love affair. Having learned the open secret of Esther Jack's identity, they asked Aline to give them some deeper, more intimate understanding of her involvement with Thomas Wolfe. She did her best to circumvent these intrusions on her privacy, but as she did so, she felt again the desire to tell more of her story herself. Long before she ever met Thomas Wolfe, the themes of her life had been taking shape, and she wanted to present them to readers in her own words. She turned back to her typewriter with increased commitment, to continue recalling and recreating the childhood of *An Actor's Daughter.*

The memoir was published by the Knopfs the following spring, to reviews that were uniformly favorable. "The inhabitants of this childhood glisten with reality," the *Herald Tribune*'s critic wrote in a full-page review. "The reader could dress them, order dinner for them, choose a wine. . . . The reader is given the best of all literary illusions —intimacy." Still others reviewers praised her for bringing back an era that had become as "remote as Carthage. . . . This New York so recently vanished . . . has buried its sights and sounds too deep for excavation . . . but it is given life and dimension by this sort of personal, affectionate account."

In response to such praise, Aline dimpled and said, "I feel there is nothing I could not do well." All the parts of herself, she continued with matter-of-fact pleasure, while they had always functioned well, now "have come together like an orchestra."

This feeling of renewal and heightened energy stood Aline in good stead when war finally struck and took hold. She and Ethel immediately joined the Red Cross, and wearing their uniforms, went several nights a week to meetings, where they rolled bandages for surgical dressings. "Oh, Bella, will it ever end?" she wrote her friend after one such meeting. "Can you believe," she asks incredulously, "that I sat beside one woman whose four sons are in active service?"

Often, at these sessions, Aline would look across the circle of women at her sister's gray hair and lined face, and nostalgia clutched her throat so tightly it brought tears to her eyes. In her mind were pictures of Ethel and herself as clear-eyed young women starting out their life together. She could see them taking their place in circles of other women in the kitchens of Henry Street tenements, sewing on costumes for the settlement house pageants. The sadness of time gone would grip her at these moments, but it would invariably pass into a grateful sense of how tightly loyalty and love had bound them together through the years.

Besides her work at the Red Cross, Aline formed a committee called the Scenic Artists War Group, which provided relief organizations with the advice and services of the various crafts in her union. Now, too, instead of giving fund-raising parties for her museum, she entertained for war-related causes. She threw open the doors of the house in Armonk and gave picnics on its lawns, and frequently a weekend round of parties would yield several thousand dollars. For days after the crowds left, she'd tell friends, the whole family was "too tired even to rest. . . . Everywhere we sat or lay down, it hurt."

But her fatigue would always pass quickly, and despite a recurring problem with arthritis, which, Edla says, "she did her damnedest to ignore," and her weight being up—"How can anyone expect me to diet in this kitchen?"—Aline in her sixties was an uncommonly vigorous and attractive woman. She did, of course, make light of her female charms now. "No one's made any improper advances to me all winter," she'd sigh mockingly. "The nearest approach was when Nelson Rockefeller took my hand and said he wished I knew his mother better!" Or she'd declare to a friend who was weeping over a turbulent love affair: "Oh, my . . . Thank God I'm fat and grey and almost sixty-five. I'm far more interested in my new potato-pancake maker than some fellow's manly progress." The comparison sent her into peals of laughter, and although her friend was at first irritated by Aline's sudden lapse in sympathy, she was soon cheerfully distracted by the pancakes Aline insisted on whipping up for lunch.

That day, this friend recalls, Teddy had been in the kitchen at lunchtime, and indeed it continued to be Teddy, of all the family members, who most shared Aline's dedication to relishing life. Whether it was exulting over the best potato pancakes in the city ("absolutely nonpareil, Ma") or devising elaborate practical jokes, they played off each other's capacity for fun. One prank of Teddy's brightened the winter of 1942 for Aline as she avidly followed its progress, pressing her son for more details every night. Down at the Loeb-Bernstein office, it was customary to have a betting pool on various college football teams around the country. Teddy had decided to invent a team, from an equally fictitious teachers' college in the Midwest, and every week he faithfully called in the scores to the *New York Times* and other city papers. He carefully mapped out a progression of success so impressive that his team looked increasingly promising to the sportswriters. As their interest was piqued, Teddy, in his ostensible role as the college's publicity representative, provided the newspapers with background stories on the players' personal lives. It took a full football season before the hoax was ultimately disclosed by Walter Winchell.

In 1943, as Aline divided her time between writing and designing— "There are two more books I would love to write, but I love to design too, and I know I am so good at it"—and also went on with her war efforts and her work for the museum, still another door opened in her life. Walking through it seemed to promise a singularly concrete way of connecting with other people, of communicating the beliefs she held dear. She began teaching design at Vassar College. Hallie Flanagan, now dean of Smith College, had introduced Aline to the new director of Vassar's experimental theater, Mary Virginia Heinlein, and the women had become instant friends. When Miss Heinlein urged Aline to teach costume design on a part-time basis and also to serve as a production consultant, Aline felt particularly taken with the idea.

She would say later that the teaching at Vassar was one of the richest experiences of her life. Getting off the train each week in Poughkeepsie and walking through the campus gates were invariably moments of immense satisfaction. She would take the last train home at night, so tired it felt as though she'd "left half of myself behind." But it was worth it. "I feel more than ever that I can give young people something for their lives," she said to her family, in defense of having taken on still more work. Even, she added, if what she gave them was only "a sense of their own importance in the scheme of life."

She had "an electrifying effect on everyone—her classes and ourselves," a Vassar colleague remembers. As for Aline, the affection was totally returned. The girls, with "their fine strong faces," touched her deeply. She wrote to Maxwell Perkins, who through the years had become a respected friend: "It gives me a pang to think of what they all have in store for themselves, such wallops as they are going to have to take, and nothing can save them." And the drama faculty's relative lack of sophistication delighted her. Their innocent enthusiasm about the theater was captivating after the "phonies" who seemed to be steadily infiltrating the profession. "I would not like to stay at Vassar forever," Aline explained, "but a little bit of it at a time is very fine. . . . It sets one up after the bastards one can encounter in show business." And, she added, it was so important to teach young people to "keep their own self straight" and "their skirts out of the mire."

Indeed, whether she was standing over a cutting board in a classroom or hopping up on stage to explain a lighting effect, the focus of Aline's teaching was, always, to begin and end with "fine intention." One must have "habits of decency and honesty and high thinking," no matter what you designed. No matter if your enterprise was Ibsen or vaudeville, there is nothing "highbrow" about high thinking. "Make a piece of truth in the theater," she'd conclude earnestly, "and you will make something beautiful."

An additional pleasure in her teaching was that Theo was able to share the Vassar experience with her. He loved to chat with the English professors about Shakespeare and attend lectures given by visiting scholars. Over a dinner at the faculty club, or at a party in some professor's home, Aline would beam proudly at her husband's holding his own in esoteric Shakespearean discussions. And her colleagues at Vassar found her obvious delight in Theo's participation touching in a couple married for so long a time.

It was during her first year of teaching at Vassar that Aline learned that Maxwell Perkins, as executor of Thomas Wolfe's estate, had sold Wolfe's collection of unpublished work and original manuscripts to William Wisdom, a private collector. Included in this collection were almost all Aline's letters to Tom. The news was shocking to her at first. Although she could not exactly recall the contents, she knew there was a great deal in the letters she would not want strangers to read. Nonetheless, as she thought about Tom's effects being preserved in a permanent collection, the idea of her letters being public seemed less frightening, and she even began to consider contributing her own letters from Tom. She had always intended to will the correspondence to Harvard after her death, but now, with Perkins's encouragement, she entertained the idea of turning it over to Wisdom so that his collection would be as complete as possible. Besides, Wisdom had announced his intention of donating the collection to a major library, and Harvard was his likeliest choice.

That Harvard be the ultimate destination of the collection was stipulated by Aline when she wrote to Wisdom offering him the letters. She explained how painful a step it was for her to take. "I loved him a great deal . . . and it is difficult to reach a balance between feeling and common sense when feeling runs so high as it did with us, but I am trying to take the sensible view of this."

That, despite her offer, Wisdom was still considering other recipients for the collection irritated Aline. Harvard had meant a great deal to Tom, and she felt he would want his papers to be there. She told Wisdom this several times, leading him to complain to Max Perkins that she was an insufferable "busybody" who "needs to have her hand in everything." Meanwhile, Aline continued to complain to Perkins about Wisdom's ineptitude. "I know I'm right about him, Max," she'd say impatiently, quoting a line from Samuel Goldwyn: "Sometimes I'm right, but I'm never wrong." Why couldn't she just forget about this sale, she'd demand irritably. Why couldn't she "just wrap the letters all up in a parcel and take them up to Harvard myself?"

Perkins managed to convince her that the collection should be in one piece, and that Aline's letters from Tom were so important a part of the whole that they should not be housed separately. Having temporarily mollified her, he turned back to Wisdom, urging him to complete the transaction. Finally, the negotiations were completed, and Aline wrote Wisdom that the purchase price should be sent to the Federation of Jewish Charities, to help the plight of Jews around the world. "Personal profit from the sale of such letters would be impossible for me," she explained simply.

Only to Max did she admit a small element of mischief in her decision. After all, one had to enjoy the irony of money from Thomas Wolfe going to help the Jews.

If her composure had been at all shaken by these forays into her past, it was even more affected when Scribner's published a volume of Thomas Wolfe's letters to his mother. Max sent her a copy and she quickly wrote to thank him, but she could not resist letting him know there was "No use trying to think I'm not going to have a fit."

But by the time she had finished reading Tom's letters to Julia, his letters to Aline herself were gone. The space under her worktable was occupied by a cheerful basket holding certain tools of her life as she lived it now. Even though she had recently suffered two severe falls and injured herself quite badly—"What is it makes me do all these things? It can't be just chance"—the basket was soon filled to overflowing.

# 23

"I go to bed instead of staying up all night as I used to do. I drink nothing and do not smoke, and soon my wings will be coming out and I will have to have them clipped in order to wear my clothes."

So Aline summed herself up in the mid 1940s in a letter to Mabel Wolfe, Tom's sister, whom she had remained in touch with through the years. In fact, in spite of her jesting tone, Aline's life was quite abundantly rich. "She used to wake up early in the morning," Peggy Murphy remembers fondly, "and as soon as she heard me in the kitchen, she'd call to ask me what it was like out, and what she should wear. And then, there she'd be, in a minute, ready to start her day. . . . It was marvelous to see her work, either in her studio, or when the people from the museum would come for meetings, or even when she was planning one of her parties. And of course," Peggy finishes with a sigh, "the phone was always ringing. Oh, she was an extraordinary person . . . so full of life. Why, she was never tired, I swear. In all the years I worked for her, I never once, when she was well, heard her say she was tired."

It sometimes seemed to Aline that her vision could scarcely hold the pictures it had accumulated. It was as if her life were a window, and when she looked through it she could see all the experiences that "had pulled and twisted and molded her." As she embraced each day, remembered tastes and tears and joys drifted in front of her "like branches that swing in the early spring breezes."

Not that she spent much time on reflection: as Peggy indicates, she was very busy. She could afford to be selective about her assignments now, but she complained when she wasn't bringing in a substantial income. No less than before did she want to "pay my own way." Unfortunately, there were too few plays in the commercial theater that afforded aesthetic satisfaction along with good wages.

One play that did meet these criteria was *Harriet,* the biographical study of Harriet Beecher Stowe. The production would star Aline's dear friend Helen Hayes, and it was to be directed by a young man she admired, Elia Kazan, a graduate, like Tom Wolfe, of Baker's workshop. Aline's sense of history had deepened through her work with the museum and she took the assignment even more seriously than usual. However, it was not easy to achieve the results she wanted, because the city was plagued by war shortages and materials were scarce. Miss Hayes remembers that "it was a revelation to watch this woman create an authentic wardrobe for me and the whole cast, with not one piece of material that was really right for it. She used upholstery material, curtain material, white muslin that she dyed herself—she must have worn her shoe leather off going around the city finding things."

Aline's optimism and refusal to compromise inspired, as it generally did, all the people who worked with her. As Miss Hayes recalls with a smile: "I love to think how cunning she was not to let people know she was determined to have things her way. She was so soft and loving and gentle and easygoing, and yet she'd sweep everyone up in her authority of how things should be done."

Another favorite assignment of this period, though quite different in tone, was for the newly formed Ballet Society, which evolved into the New York City Ballet. Their first production was to be a ballet based on a poem by Colette, *The Spellbound Child,* with music by Maurice Ravel. It was a fantasy, filled with animals who spoke and furniture that came to life. Aline relished the chance to be whimsical, to extend reality extravagantly. As if her imagination itself were dancing, she put together electric-blue bats and lavender dragonflies, costumed cups and saucers to complement each other when they whirled in each other's arms. "Oh, there is nothing better than making enchantment," she'd sigh happily when she stood in the wings and watched the rapt faces of children in the audience.

Aline had always enjoyed children, and there was a particular reason for her present interest in them. Edla had recently married a young man named Peter Cusick, and now she was pregnant, a fact that entranced Aline. Everything about her daughter's pregnancy seemed to fascinate her. "Do you know they can listen to the little heartbeat with a stethoscope?" she'd report incredulously, or she would say in bemused apology, "Ethel is crocheting and knitting like mad, but all I seem to be able to do for the kid is just think about it."

And when the baby, a boy, was born, she was even more ecstatic. A quick visit to Edla, and she was at the hospital nursery, Theo and Teddy at her side, "looking at the kid through the glass," and declaring that he was "objectively, unquestionably beautiful." Not that he needed to be to win her affection; as she said to Theo, "he is Edla's baby, and so he will take his place."

Just before Michael was born, the family celebrated another milestone. In this year of 1944, Teddy would turn forty, surely a cause for celebration when one remembered his fragile childhood. To celebrate, Aline gave a party in Armonk, inviting some twenty-six of the family's closest friends. "It was superb," Aline reported to Bella, who hadn't been able to attend. "We had a huge casserole of chicken in cream, two tongues cold with jelly, a vast ham, a dish of cold curried eggs (yummy, made by Mrs. Edla Cusick), two dishes of stuffed eggs in aspic, a salad of new potatoes and baby string-beans mixed with cucumbers in sour cream, sliced tomatoes, pickles and birthday cake baked in an old heart-shaped copper. We were in the kitchen for two days, and it was worth it." And she added teasingly: "Now, Bella, do you think we are gross? You wouldn't have thought so if you were there because it was all so pretty and full of good feeling."

Good feeling generally ran high in the family now. The only tension that ever crept into their meetings was political in origin. The 1944 elections were upon them, and although many other Democrats were weighing their loyalty to Roosevelt against his precedent-shattering decision to run for a fourth term, Aline remained faithful. She was afraid that Teddy would feel pressured to shift to the Wall Street bias, to share his father's staunch Republican convictions. Thus, when he announced he was voting for Roosevelt again, Aline said with maternal pride that he "showed much strength of character." Actually, it intrigued her that many other families were splitting their vote. "I think this is a very heartening thing . . . that people are at last independent enough of the old restrictions to vote as they think," And she'd preach the need for such independence at the various rallies she attended with her sculptor friend Jo Davidson. It was not uncommon for Theo to leave his office and see her with Jo at a rally on Wall Street, or find her leading a parade down the center of White Plains when he went to town on an errand. Her local activities, in the resistantly Republican towns, usually brought her home in irritated despair. "My God," she'd say, "Dewey's picture is covering Westchester. . . . Well, it just beats me that folks are so wrong and so complicated."

But if the political scene distressed her, one aspect of her professional life continued to bring immense satisfaction. The Costume Museum was going to be absorbed by the Metropolitan Museum of Art. Aline had worked on the merger for a long time, doing everything from running planning meetings "with the quality" to acting as the project's "press officer." "I'd never want to write these for a living," she said one evening, as she passed a batch of publicity releases around for her family to read, "but I think I did a good job, don't you? It was fun, and I made them good and fancy."

It was a proud move for Aline. To think that after a lifetime of studying in museums she had a genuine connection with one of the very greatest. Her pride contained no awe, however. Stella Blum, currently director of the Costume Museum and in 1944 a young woman starting her career, remembers how Aline livened up board meetings by bringing "a bag of goodies to them. . . . She'd hang up her coat, and we'd all wait for her to open her shopping bag and distribute Danish pastries, or some rich butter cookies that she made herself."

"After all," Mrs. Blum remembers Aline explaining, "working and eating are both part of the fun of life, so why not combine them?"

At dusk, walking home from the museum through Central Park, Aline would feel sweetly nostalgic as she drank in all the familiar sights, and played them back against some of the amazing new ones. Her walk was a little briefer than it would have been a while ago, for the family had at last moved from the Gotham Hotel to a real apartment on West Sixty-fourth Street, close to this beloved stretch of open land. Indeed, one of the reasons Aline had chosen the apartment was that her bedroom windows faced the park; she'd waken to the patterned reflections of its trees playing across her walls. "I am so contented with the physical aspects of my life, that it almost seems a sin," she'd say with the guileless delight of a child.

It was a fine apartment to write in, and she was doing a lot of that now, working on a new novel as well as continuing to do articles about design. A favorite project was *The Martha Washington Doll Book* for young children, which she had written and also illustrated. It told the story of the history of furniture and dress, and it contained cutout dolls of Martha Washington so that young readers could do some designing of their own. Aline told the children how to trace the outlines of the dresses she had drawn and then fill them in with colors of their choosing. "You can even paste on your dress some silk or fine cotton, if thin enough," she wrote in a tone that is never patronizing, even when she admonishes her readers to "be sure and keep the outline precise so that it will fit the figure."

"Have you seen my dolly book?" she'd ask her friends proudly. And if she didn't, Theo was sure to bring it out for inspection. It was understandable that he would enjoy this child-related achievement of Aline's, for rarely had any man taken to the role of grandfather so happily as he. "He is our own dollink baby," Aline reported after a weekend visit from Michael; "both grandma and especially grandpa came in for plenty of hugs and kisses. . . . Young Cusick is clearly a kind and affectionate little gentleman . . . and growing teeth to boot."

The *Doll Book* was published in 1946, and the following year brought the publication of what was to be Aline's final novel, *Miss Conden.* Although the story is not as recognizably autobiographical as *The Journey Down,* the theme of *Miss Conden* borrows from life in ways that would be difficult to ignore. As the novel unfolds, a lovely young woman becomes involved in an extramarital relationship which leads to great physical and emotional pain. At the novel's conclusion, it is only the husband's remarkable capacity for compassion and forgiveness that saves the woman from complete personal tragedy.

The reviews for *Miss Conden* were again excellent, and most of them praised the author's combination of talents. George Freedly began a long review by saying: "If Aline Bernstein will continue to design for the theater, then I can forgive her for being so brilliant a writer that she keeps on practicing her newer profession," while for the *New York Times,* Florence Crowther wrote: "With the same artistry and passionate love for fine things, textures, color tones and satiny woods, and the same urgency for rightness . . . which she has displayed in the theater as a designer, Mrs. Bernstein has dressed the stage for her story."

If Aline felt a certain coming to conclusion with this story of extramarital love, it was underscored by the sudden death of Maxwell Perkins later that year. As she wrote to Mabel Wolfe after the funeral: "I believe that no one in the world knew how things were with Tom and me but Max." That she still thought about how it had been with Tom was obvious to anyone who saw her regularly. Wolfe's picture had stayed on her table, and often, in the middle of a conversation, she would look over at it and say, matter-of-factly, "We loved each other with the best that was in us." And then, with the barest pause, she would pick up the threads of talk again.

Often now, her conversation concerned the Ninety-second Street YMHA. She had added this institution to her other interests because she felt that in the postwar climate, people needed an oasis like the "Y." Many Americans had realized that despite the end of the war, their life would never be simple or peaceful again. It was therefore necessary, she believed, to develop resources for personal tranquillity. The "Y," with its music and poetry programs, was such a place, and as John Malcolm Brinnin, then director of the Poetry Center, remembers: "She was resolutely generous toward us. She believed in our intentions and was determined to aid them." In particular, the "Y"'s poetry programs fed Aline's spirit. But when she wanted to hear music played in its "most perfect" atmosphere, she would leave New York and travel to Stockbridge, Massachusetts, for the summer music festivals at Tanglewood. Usually, Teddy went with her. They stayed in the large house of old friends who understood that their guests would be out of the house early in the morning to attend rehearsals, and would not give up one evening of music for the most interesting party.

Perhaps only Teddy truly understood the joy Aline found in fine music, even when her hearing became much worse. Indeed, her loss hardly mattered. "Sound as such disappears," she'd explain, but she would feel instead "an enormous internal reaction, a loosening and crackling, a breaking up of informed feeling and knowledge." And it seemed to her that this knowledge must be as old as all the centuries, for surely the sentiments that gripped her were "too great to have been accumulated just in my own lifetime."

There was never a better place to experience these sentiments than at Tanglewood, with the music rising over the green lawns and blending into the fresh, sweet-smelling air. When, in years to come, Aline thought about the music festival, it was the summer of 1948 that especially stood out. There were several concerts that season which featured young performers. "The thousands of young people filling the lawns and music shed, the young musicians who were being given the opportunity to perform with some of music's greatest masters . . . The two young pianists, and the clear-eyed chorus who formed youthful union with the glorious creations of artists long gone from life," would, when she looked back on them, seem to symbolize her own beginnings and endings.

In February 1949, Edla gave birth to her second child, a daughter, named Edla Frankau. "She is a raving beauty," Aline reported, "golden hair and great dark eyes, people stop on the street to look at her in her carriage." But that joy was soon quite terribly dimmed. Only a few weeks after the baby's birth, on March 11, Teddy suddenly died. Standing next to his father in the Loeb-Bernstein office, reading the Dow Jones ticker, Teddy Bernstein suddenly fell to the floor. Even as Theo knelt beside him, desperately calling his name, taking his son's hand in his own, he knew that Teddy was dead. The sword of Damocles had finally descended.

The office went into nightmare action: physicians and the police were called, Peter Cusick summoned. While Peter tried to find Aline, Carl Loeb telephoned the news to Helen Walker, Ethel's assistant at Bergdorf's, asking Mrs. Walker to tell-Ethel. He felt he needed to be with Theo, but he also knew that this was not information to give to Ethel over the phone.

"It was lunchtime," Mrs. Walker remembers, "and I called around to several restaurants to find Ethel, but I couldn't locate her, and so I waited downstairs at the entrance to the store to meet her when she arrived back." She offered some pretext to get Ethel upstairs to Mr. Goodman's office, and there they told her that Teddy was very ill. And Ethel, born to stoicism, looked at Mrs. Walker and said in a flat voice, "Well, tell me the rest of it."

"And I said, 'I don't have to,'" Mrs. Walker recalls sadly, "and so of course she knew that he had died." After a few moments of silence, the younger woman asked whether she should accompany Ethel "to see Aline," and Ethel nodded acceptance of the help she rarely asked for, but which every member of the family knew they would need now.

That day Aline had gone to Edla's apartment to take her daughter and Michael out to lunch, aware that her grandson was not always happy about his new sister. Coming back to the Cusick apartment after the treat, during which grandmother had made it clear to Michael that his position in her heart was secure, Edla heard the phone ringing and went into the bedroom to answer it. "It was my husband, telling me my brother had died, dropped dead in the office in front of father. And I came in to tell mother, and she was looking out the window, very pensively. I didn't know how else to say it except to say that Teddy had died . . . and she stood there . . . and didn't seem to move a muscle at the message . . . and she said, very clearly, 'Yes, I know.' "

People remember Aline's quietness during this period. Some would call it passive; others, resigned; still others, accepting. And indeed, with grief etched into every line of her face, she suffered this blow with relative calm. The rest of the family did the same. There was an enormous funeral, although Ethel disapproved of the pageantry. But Teddy had great numbers of friends, and of course the family did, and Aline felt a sense of rightness about the scale of this final ceremony. However, although the casket was open, no member of the family went up to view it. And when the rabbi who had spoken briefly at the service called the apartment to arrange a visit of consolation, Aline brushed him off impatiently. "I'll call you if I want you to visit me," she said. "I've lost Teddy now and I must get to work." Peggy Murphy, who was standing near the phone at the time, says she knew what Aline meant even if the rabbi was confused. She knew that it was in her employer's nature to move on from grief, even though the grief would always cast a shadow behind her.

"They picked up and went on with their lives right away," Peggy says, "but their lives were never the same. Mr. Bernstein became an old man overnight, and Mrs. Bernstein would get this faraway look on her face and I'd know that it was Teddy who was in her mind, but they never said anything sad about it." And then Peggy remembers, tears misting her eyes, the only time she did hear the Bernsteins express their loss. "One night," she says, "months after Teddy's passing, they were sitting together in the living room reading, and Mrs. Bernstein looked over at her husband and said suddenly, 'We miss Teddy, don't we?' And Mr. Bernstein looked to her and said, just as quietly as herself, 'We will always.' "

To certain close friends, Aline did speak of her pain. "It never leaves me for a moment," she said to Terry Helburn. "It swamps me, and I hardly know what to do." In a letter to Mary Virginia Heinlein, she apologized for being "so sad and tearful" over a lunch at Vassar, "but sometimes this grief breaks through all the guards I try to put up against it. . . . Sometimes my will is not strong enough, and down I go." People told her the violent stage of grief would pass, and she had to hope that they knew whereof they spoke. "I guess they must," she said, "otherwise the world could not go on." And she ended the letter, typically, by expressing her impatience with her lapsed ability to see her life in broad perspective. "I hate to be so concerned with myself. I must get over that." In a similar letter to Bella, she wrote: "I do not want to be a sad and tragic old girl. I want to go on with life in a way that I have lived, although of course," she adds, "with such monstrous changes." And she concluded: "No one will ever know how Teddy and I supplemented each other, his constant loving care and attention to us. Well, God only knows what it is all about."

The family spent a quiet summer in Armonk, beginning with the Decoration Day weekend, a particularly painful time because of the annual local parade Teddy and she had always marched in. "Of course I could not make the parade this time," she told a friend who had come to visit, explaining that instead, "I went down to the end of our land near the lake, where there is the lovely pine forest, and just sat there."

An even more difficult day to get through was Teddy's birthday, but to Aline's surprise, a contingent of his friends drove up from the city to be with her. "It almost broke me down," she said later, "but they were so kind, and that is something to be cherished."

For a few days in midsummer, she and Theo went to Stockbridge. As the music of a Brahms concerto swept over her, she looked at her husband and saw tears streaming down his face. They reached for each other's hands, and she thought how right she had been to decline Terry Helburn's invitation to travel with her to Europe. Inside the narrowed circle of their lives, Theo and she had moved closer to one another. For the first time in their complex lives together, he would admit distress when she was away from home too long. Thus she had written to Terry that she could not leave him alone this summer: "Peggy says he moons around all the time when I'm not here, and he is so wonderful and so kind and sweet with everyone in spite of his grief . . . he needs to share it with me."

By summer's end the Bernstein family had come to a decision. They would sell the house in Armonk. "It was too sad and empty for them,"

Peggy says. "It was so awfully lonely without Teddy," while Aline would explain simply: "I have accepted the fact that the house must be sold, that this part of my life is over. . . . I am doing my best to come to a place in life that if it can never be bright and happy, can be bearable and not too hard on my friends."

In her preparation to move on, Aline began to "clean up and throw away" a great many effects from her past. It was time to disengage. She burned at least five hundred drawings that had piled up through the years and destroyed most of the original manuscripts of her writing. Letters, photographs, bits of memorabilia, were thrown away or burned, not in any great dramatic ceremony, but in quiet, often private gestures of farewell. She commented very little on what she was doing, except to tell Edla that "I'm doing what you would have to do after my death," and even this was said more with an air of being pleased with her own efficiency than morbidly.

Life moves on . . . one decision leads to another . . . even in descent.

If they could leave Armonk, they could leave the apartment as well. They had not lived in it for very long, but the building was beginning to change. The landlord was threatening to convert to self-service elevators and hinting at breaking up large apartments like their own into several smaller ones to reap a higher income. But most of all, it was the apartment's memories she wanted to leave. An apartment that contained "Teddy's room" would make it difficult for her to work in her own. And as she had told the rabbi, what she wanted most to do now was to work.

"The change will do us good," she told her sister and her husband as she showed them around the new apartment she had in mind, at Seventy-eighth Street and Park Avenue. Despite its elegant address, she found it gracious and unpretentious, and as she told friends: "Theo, Ethel and I have concluded being our age, we wanted as much comfort as we can manage."

It was from this apartment that she arranged yet another disengagement. She sat down at her desk one morning and wrote a letter of resignation to Mary Virginia Heinlein at Vassar. Miss Heinlein suspected that although Aline still spoke of adoring to "be around the young ones," being around young people was too painful for her now. In the letter, Aline gave as her reason the desire to throw herself into harder, more concrete work than teaching. She ends on a sad and pensive note: "My small amount of work at the College has been a precious part of my life, and I wish it could go on."

For now, though, she would return full force to the theater. "I have had a good time seeing all the old faces," she writes to Bella, who was on her way to Europe. "At the costumer's and the wigmaker's, the sewing girls are all so glad to see me and so kind. I have felt my old creative spirit returning, and I know you will be happy about that. . . . I want to work all the time; it is the best medicine. I know that for sure." After sending her love to Bella's husband, Sam, she wistfully concluded: "Take a good look for me in Paris, look at everything, and give it my love also."

Aline was grateful to be offered an assignment she could become absorbed in. *The Little Foxes* had been put to music, and producer Cheryl Crawford would open it in October 1949 as an opera called *Regina*, with a score by Marc Blitzstein. Her work for the production would win Aline the coveted Antoinette Perry "Tony" award, and on the night of the award presentations, the Bernstein family sat in the audience, knowing full well what determination to survive had brought Aline here. She had remained faithful as well to her belief that personal sorrow must be kept separate from professional responsibility. Indeed, she would say later that the "Tony" award pleased her most of all by proving she had still been able to do this.

While Aline had certainly thrown herself into work with the desperate energy of someone fighting to survive, it is also true that Teddy's death heightened her sensitivity to the nuances of experience. Whether it was the expression on a person's face or the mood potential of particular colors, she was, a friend remembers, like "a fine recording device." Pictures of yesterday as well as possible stories yet to be told flowed out of almost everything she observed. A pot of jam in a grocer's window on Madison Avenue could become a pub in Ambleside or tea on an English train. Once, when she let her mind play with something she had seen, she wrote a story about it that soon charmed readers of *The New Yorker* magazine.

It began when she arranged a surprise visit to the library of J. P. Morgan for her writer friend George O'Neill. O'Neill was a devotee of Keats, and Mr. Morgan owned the original manuscript of *Endymion*. As she looked around the impressive room, Aline was struck by a small box, "wrapped in Christmas paper and tied with tinsel ribbon," sitting on Morgan's desk. There was a little card attached to the box with ribbons and a spray of holly, and Aline picked it up to read the message

337

lettered in a childish scrawl: "Merry Christmas, Mr. Morgan." She was immediately intrigued by the question of what anyone, especially a child, would think of giving J. P. Morgan for a Christmas present, and that night she went to her typewriter and wrote "The Mystery of the Little Box."

That the story involved a child gave it particular significance for Aline. The innocence of childhood seemed increasingly precious to her now. Thus, when she thought about memorializing Teddy in some way, she decided to establish a fund in his name at the YMHA to sponsor new plays and playwrights for children's theater. As soon as the idea came into her head, it seemed exactly the proper commemoration of her son's gentle spirit. Her announcement of the "Theodore Bernstein Memorial Fund" asked: "Will someone write a play for children with some gaiety, some sense of what is still beautiful, some lift of the spirit, yet keeping the dramatic quality of plot, story, and interest?"

In 1950, Aline became seventy. She was working on *The Happy Time* for Richard Rodgers and Oscar Hammerstein, and the producers gave her an elaborate birthday party in her most natural environment— backstage at a Broadway theater. People from every branch of the theater—craftsmen, actors, directors—were invited to celebrate the birthday of their invincibly youthful colleague. She beamed at the champagne toasts, and her rosy skin glowed. Only the hearing aid she had finally given in to indicated that the years had diminished her in any way. The "warmth and sweetness" that defined her for people like Richard Rodgers embraced everyone at the party. "Being with Aline," says Mr. Rodgers, "one always received an immediate and lasting impression of joy and kindness."

She made many new friends in these years who shared Richard Rodgers's sentiments. Frances Steloff, owner of the Gotham Book Mart and organizer of the James Joyce Society, remembers feeling when she first met Aline, that "she was like a sunburst . . . radiating gentleness and beauty. . . . I wanted to be her friend so I could experience her more often."

Hence Aline became an enthusiastic member of the Joyce Society, and frequently participated in its programs. In a talk entitled "An Encounter with Joyce," she described Thomas Wolfe's meeting Joyce on a sightseeing bus. The society stimulated her interest in Joyce, and she found inordinate pleasure now in reading his work aloud, savoring each phrase as she rolled it around her tongue. But she enjoyed no less language of a quite different sort—the boisterous "gab" of her buddies in the union. Many people remember (with an affection they might not have felt at the time) being awakened around midnight by a phone call from Aline. Over the sounds of a jukebox and shouts of male laughter, she would breathlessly entreat them to repeat a joke they'd told her so that she could share it with her pals over their after-meeting rounds of beer.

Her vitality seemed undimmed, although she continued to suffer occasional falls and had recurring headaches and some blurring of vision. She went on looking for more work, but so much that was being produced these days displeased her through being either too "highbrow" or in ugly bad taste. She'd mumble irritable criticisms to her companions when she went to opening nights, forcing herself to stay put for the entire performance. One night a reporter from the *Herald Tribune* overheard an exchange between Aline and another woman in the audience and printed it in the morning newspaper. The woman had been sitting in front of Aline and had forgotten to remove her high feather hat throughout the entire first act. When the curtain fell, she begged Aline's forgiveness. "Don't worry about it," Aline snapped. "I'm only sorry it isn't larger."

She managed to find four productions to work on that pleased her during the 1950–51 season, although they did not turn out to be commercially successful. The one that did a little better than the others was Arthur Miller's adaptation of Ibsen's *An Enemy of the People*. That Aline found the combination of classic and contemporary writing inspiring was confirmed by the reviews. Even the normally sardonic Wolcott Gibbs praised her highly, while marveling at "a career that goes back almost to the shelling of Fort Sumter."

Gibbs's tone was affectionate, but it was certainly true that no member of the Bernstein family took to the idea of retirement easily. Theo, although well into his seventies and never restored to full vitality after Teddy's death, still went regularly to his office. And Ethel, despite a recent siege with a broken hip, gave no hint to ambitious younger employees that she was ready to step down. So deeply entrenched was her reign that Andrew Goodman delighted in telling the story of a dream he'd had when he'd taken over the European buying duties because of Ethel's injury. In the dream he showed his purchases to her, and in her contempt for his choices, she savagely attacked him with her cane.

Their one concession to age was to take more vacations. After a few summers of living in hotels and rented cottages on Long Island, they bought a house of their own in East Hampton. It was not as grand as the one in Armonk, but it did allow them to watch and smell and hear the sea and to have a long stretch of quiet beach to walk on. For some time Aline had been worried about Theo. He seemed fragile and wan. So it was good to see the color in his face when they'd return to the cottage at the end of a long walk. But when they were back in the city, he began to look ill again and to show signs of decline. Always a good sleeper, he now would roam around the apartment at night. Often he and Aline would meet each other in the kitchen, where both had gone for a glass of warm milk laced with honey, hoping it would help them get back to sleep. One evening in 1952, he complained to her of a terrible headache, and there was a stricken look on his face. Soothingly she helped him back to bed, where, later that night, he suffered a stroke.

Ethel flew home from Europe when she was notified, because initially the doctors did not know how severely Theo had been damaged or if he would recover at all. He did, in fact, recover consciousness in less than a week, but there was permanent damage to his speech, and his memory was elusive, which caused him intense distress.

Immediately the house was mobilized about him. Nurses were hired around the clock and given specific instructions by Aline to treat Theo with unwavering dignity. If they didn't, if they gave any indication of professionally patronizing care, they were dismissed.

"Oh, those girls came and went," Peggy Murphy recalls. "Mrs. Bernstein put up with not a minute of what she thought was bad treatment."

"You must remember, Peggy," Aline would explain, "Popsie could die tomorrow, so we have to let him live the best way he can and wants to today." She became embittered when friends stopped visiting after their initial calls of concern. "People are afraid of illness," she said contemptuously, and began to create a life for Theo to offset this. She established a routine which included his being driven around Central Park before picking up Ethel at Bergdorf's to take her home for dinner. She cut back a great deal on her own social life, and now, again, Ethel was her principal companion. To make their time at home more productive, Aline commissioned an artist whose work she admired to come to the apartment and give the sisters lessons in the art of painting flowers. At seventy-two and sixty-six, the two women became students again. Wearing their smocks, they sat in front of their easels, listening carefully to their teacher.

Aline did entertain, though, even more than before, now that she went out less often. Not just for her own amusement, but because she wanted Theo to remain engaged with their life. No matter what the purpose of the party—to raise money or to welcome friends—Theo was always present. Dressed impeccably, he sat in his favorite chair in the living room, his eyes, friends recall with some awe, following his wife wherever she moved. From time to time Aline would smile, or walk over to pat his hand, or address some comment to him as if she knew he was the only person in the room who could truly understand what she was saying.

"She protected him passionately," a friend remembers, recalling her own rare exposure to Aline Bernstein's anger. "I had told Theo I'd be there at lunchtime," the friend explains, "but I became detained, and decided to grab a sandwich and come later in the afternoon. I called and told a maid, but I suppose she wasn't able to make the message clear to Theo. When I came to the apartment, Aline was waiting for me, and was furious. 'Promises are important to him now . . .' she said. 'He has little enough happening in the day . . . he must not be disappointed. . . . You are never to break your word to him again if you wish to remain in our lives.' " And the friend says rather wonderingly: "I would never have thought Aline Bernstein's voice could sound so cold."

Not yet realizing her own deteriorating condition, Aline only knew that injuries and discomfort befell her more frequently than before. In the spring of 1952, she wrote to Mary Virginia Heinlein that she was in the hospital, recovering "from a fall and back injury, a case of phlebitis and general debility. This has been a tough winter for the family." She reported that Theo's progress was very slow and bemoaned having "to be away from him now." Perhaps recalling the treasured days that she had once shared with her friend, Aline ends her note: "I miss my life terribly. . . . I feel gone with the wind."

Not quite gone yet, though, she'd declare soon, when, up and around again, she was looking for work. She took on a couple of small assignments just to keep her hand in. The pay wasn't much, she reported, "but it's better than a kick in the eye."

In 1953, a chance came along that she knew immediately had been worth having waited for. She was asked to help stage *The World of Sholem Aleichem* at the Barbizon Plaza Theater, bringing to sophisticated modern audiences a glimpse of a folklore and humor many of them had never known. To Aline, of course, the accents and gestures of the people on stage were lovingly familiar, a factor most critics took note of when they praised her costumes. Surely, they said, Mrs. Bernstein's "memories of the old days on the Lower East Side" made her able to "costume so sensitively and perfectly now."

She would, she said, do "at least one more show," before seriously thinking about retiring. But one night, while dining with a friend, she kept rubbing her eye, apologizing because something seemed to be wedged in it. It was a sensation that persisted, and a few days later, Peggy Murphy remembers, she came into the kitchen looking bewildered. "Peggy," she said, "I think I've got something awful coming on me . . . would you help me to my room?"

Ethel summoned their physician, and after a brief examination, he determined that Aline had suffered a small stroke. Worse, he was certain she would do so again, each time experiencing progressive damage.

"She'd be sitting with people, and she'd get a little twitching in her body," Peggy remembers of the next few months. And true to the doctor's prediction, each episode made her more infirm, until at last she suffered widespread permanent paralysis. And so it was that the Bernstein family now had only one member who was living a semblance of its old rich life. "My aunt took over completely," Edla recalls, "supervising nurses as well as the domestic staff before she went to work, ordered the food, kept the cook and the nurse from attacking each other over their spheres of influence. . . . She'd start to work at nine-thirty in the morning shaking like a leaf!"

When Ethel Frankau closed the door of the apartment, she usually left her sister and brother-in-law side by side in their wheelchairs in the library, reading a book or watching television. "I will never forget the sight of them alongside each other in those chairs," a friend recalls, echoing the memories of numerous other men and women—Alfred Knopf or Dorothy Gish or Helen Hayes—those people who visited Aline during the months of her protracted illness.

"She was never without people," Peggy says contentedly, and for the most part Aline seems to have enjoyed the visiting break in her day. But she would only greet her friends in the library or her bedroom. She rarely entered those rooms which had once held her liveliest engagements with life, the living and dining rooms.

Most of the time Aline seemed to her guests the serene, stoical person they had always known. But sometimes, without warning, a dark mood would descend and she would be bitter and self-pitying.

"God, I wish I were really dead," she'd rage. "What a fool way this is for a person to live." And Alfred Knopf remembers her saying, in a quieter but tortured voice: "Alfred, can you believe it was only a little while ago when we were that glorious family?"

Mostly, however, she let only Peggy and Ethel and Edla see her frustration. Only they knew her anguish at being administered to by nurses around the clock. "Look," she once said to Ethel, who came in while she was having a sponge bath. "Look how my life is being lived by strange women." But because she did generally mask her suffering in front of other people, they continued to come and see her, bringing her presents of food although eating was another of life's pleasures that no longer mattered to her. If she did eat anything, it tended to be sweets. Jam or cookies or candy. One friend remembers being gratified because Aline had become very animated about the huge bag of chocolate miniatures she'd brought her. "She kept pulling the wrappers off the candy, dropping them on the covers, and popping the whole piece into her mouth." And then, the friend remembers with a smile, Peter Cusick's mother appeared unexpectedly. Mrs. Cusick was a very proper woman and it was obvious to Aline's friend if not apparent to Aline that the woman was horrified to see Aline's nightgown slipping from her bosom as she lustily devoured the chocolates in a bed now littered with candy wrappers.

Always, when the visitors left, she would wheel herself into Theo's room, and wait with him for Ethel to return from the store, for Theo was no longer strong enough to accompany the chauffeur when he went to Bergdorf's to fetch her.

"She and Mr. Bernstein drew very close, so close," Peggy says and offers an illustrative anecdote. Peggy had felt that Aline could be a bit more mobile than she was and that it would be good for her to get out of the chair, even for a few minutes. One morning she began to urge Aline to try and stand up, but Aline only sighed and smiled and gently pushed Peggy's hand from her arm. "Look, Peggy," she said, waving her hand toward Theo, who was watching her from his chair. "Leave it this way, Peggy . . . Pop can't talk, and I can't walk. Let's just leave it that way."

As the months passed, Aline Bernstein seemed to fade into a shimmering reflection of herself. Her appetite for food and drink hardly existed, and her ability to sustain interest in even the most cherished company was obviously reduced.

One morning as she sat in front of her window and watched the traffic of people on the street already tinged with fall, she turned to her sister and whispered, "Ethel, when will I be free?"

Freedom comes in many shapes to someone like Aline Bernstein. To a person whose capacity for life was almost beyond measure, when that capacity is so severely shrunken, freedom must surely have lain in not having to confront at all the skimpy framework of experience that was all the life left to her. Her mind, so filled with detail and image, did not want to be dulled by pain or medicine, did not want its excitements sullied by self-pity and bitterness. And so it was that those who cherished her breathed a sigh of loving relief when in early September she fell into a semi-coma, and on September 7, 1955, those eyes which had taken in so much closed forever.

"The funeral was a grand party," Peggy says proudly. "For two days people overflowed the funeral parlor. . . . Miss Frankau hated it, but Mrs. Bernstein would have loved it." Then, with an irreverence her employer would have cherished, she remembers that "they flattened her hair just terrible, and put on way too much jewelry . . . but she was still beautiful."

They all came . . . friends from Henry Street and from the Metropolitan Museum; friends from the theater and the worlds of art and literature; her union buddies and her students from Vassar. They poured through the impersonal funeral home and exchanged stories about the person they knew in a thousand different ways, whose life had touched theirs across the multiple neighborhoods of the city she had finally said goodbye to. As they left the funeral parlor, more than one person looked around the city streets and said, "New York will never be the same with Aline gone. . . ."

Ethel Frankau lived on, caring for her brother-in-law, Theodore Bernstein, until his death three years later in 1958. At that time she moved to a smaller apartment with Peggy Murphy, continuing to work at Bergdorf's until the day of her own death at eighty-five in 1971.

# Selected Bibliography

*Primary Sources*

Bernstein, Aline. *Three Blue Suits*. New York: Equinox Cooperative Press, 1935.

Bernstein, Aline. *The Journey Down*. New York: Alfred A. Knopf, 1938.

Bernstein, Aline. *An Actor's Daughter*. New York: Alfred A. Knopf, 1941.

Bernstein, Aline. *Miss Conden*. New York: Alfred A. Knopf, 1947.

Helburn, Theresa. *A Wayward Quest*. Boston: Little Brown and Co., 1960.

Henri, Robert. *The Art Spirit*. Philadelphia: J. B. Lippincott Co., 1923.

Wolfe, Thomas. *Look Homeward, Angel*. New York: Charles Scribner's Sons, 1929.

Wolfe, Thomas. *Of Time and the River*. New York: Charles Scribner's Sons, 1935.

Wolfe, Thomas. *The Web and the Rock*. New York: Harper and Brothers, 1939.

Wolfe, Thomas. *You Can't Go Home Again*. New York: Harper and Brothers, 1940.

*Biographical and Critical Sources*

Barton, Michael. "Aline Bernstein: A History and Evaluation." Diss., Indiana University, 1971.

Braider, Donald. *George Bellows and the Ashcan School of Painting*. New York: Doubleday, 1971.

Crowley, Alice Lewisohn. *The Neighborhood Playhouse: Leaves From a Theatre Scrapbook*. New York: Theatre Arts Books, 1959.

Homer, William Innes. *Robert Henri and His Circle*. Ithaca: Cornell University Press, 1968.

Hughes, Glenn. *A History of the American Theatre, 1700–1950*. New York: Samuel French, 1951.

Kennedy, Richard S. *The Window of Memory: The Literary Career of Thomas Wolfe*. Chapel Hill: University of North Carolina Press, 1962.

Kennedy, Richard S., and Reeves, Paschal. *The Notebooks of Thomas Wolfe*. Chapel Hill: University of North Carolina Press, 1970.

Mielziner, Jo. *Designing for the Theatre*. New York: Harcourt, Brace and Co., 1965.

Nowell, Elizabeth. *Thomas Wolfe: A Biography*. Garden City, N.Y.: Doubleday, 1960.

Pollock, Thomas Clark, and Cargill, Oscar. *Thomas Wolfe at Washington Square*. New York: New York University Press, 1954.

Stowell, Donald, Jr. "The Costuming in America: The Ideas and Practices of Robert Edmond Jones, Norman Bel Geddes, Lee Simonson and Aline Bernstein, 1915–1935." Diss., University of Texas at Austin, 1972.

Walser, Richard, ed. *The Enigma of Thomas Wolfe*. Cambridge: Harvard University Press, 1953.

# Index

Bernstein *(cont.)*
nery hull, 229; dies, 344; discovers joys of reading, 33–34; drinking, 290–291; drinks Nana's sleeping potion, 25–26; early married life, 49–51; early months of affair with Wolfe, 137–148; efforts to stop Wolfe's third novel, 298–300; and Federal Art Project, 307; followed to Armonk by Wolfe, 301–302; in garden club, 310; gets Watson's promise of help with education, 37–38; gives Wolfe's letters to purchaser of collected papers, 324–325; gives Wolfe subsidized stay in Europe, 149–150; at Gloucester, 85; goes to live with Aunt Gert, 43–44; goes to live with Nana, 40; and Henry Street Settlement House, 58–63; joins union, 172–173; marries Theo, 48–49; meets Thomas Mann, 291–292; meets Wolfe, 111–120; move to Nana's house, 25–26; and Neighborhood Playhouse, 65–66, 87–89; on the road with father and family, 27–31; opts for life in theater, 29–30; psychoanalysis, 91–92; purported affair with Bellows, 70; quarrels with Wolfe, 220–223; rents loft, 143–145; return from Europe, 121–124; second meeting with Wolfe, 126–130; second trip to Europe with Wolfe, 196–198; and seeking publisher for first Wolfe novel, 213–214, 217–220; spasms of dieting, 90–91; suffers series of strokes, 342; summer at Ambleside with Wolfe, 151–160; takes to drink after Wolfe leaves, 264–265; teaches design at Vassar, 323–324; and Teddy's illness, 74–75, 77; tensions between Wolfe and, 204–209; third meeting with Wolfe, 131–134; thrown out by Julia, 277–278; trip to Europe without Wolfe, 222–226; visit to friends on Jersey Shore, 38; visit to Richard Mansfield, 16–17; war work, 321–322; and Wolfe's drinking bout at Plaza Hotel, 282–283; and Wolfe's threat to write to Teddy, 280; works with Simonson at Theatre Guild, 82–83; writes about affair with Wolfe, 284–285
Bernstein, Edla (daughter), 35, 46, 123; birth, 52; on childhood, 61–62; engagement announced, 288–289; European trip with Ethel, 177; remarries, 329; widowed, 295–296
Bernstein, Theodore (Theo) (husband): 170, 187, 188, 216, and Aline's affairs, 71–72, 138, 145; buys land in Armonk, 122; compassion at end of Aline's affair with Wolfe, 279; heart attack, 286; joins

new Loeb firm, 276; marries Aline, 48–49; and opening of *Dybbuk*, 141, 142; as Shakespeare scholar, 69; suffers stroke, 340
Bernstein, Theodore Jr. (Teddy) (son), 61, 170; begins banking career, 122–123; birth, 51–52; dies, 333–335; football team practical joke, 323; 40th birthday, 329; health deteriorates, 311; illness, 74–75, 77; joins new Loeb firm, 276
Bernstein (Theodore) Memorial Fund, 338
Bernstein ménage: and Aline's affair with Wolfe, 163–164; and building of house in Armonk, 199–200; involvement at Neighborhood Playhouse, 88; in Park Avenue apartment, 241–242; political disagreements, 235–236; and preparation of Armonk house, 231–232; sells Armonk house, 335–336; at start of Depression, 247–248; sublets apartment and moves to Armonk, 261–263
Birmingham, Stephen, 55–56
Blitzstein, Marc, 337
Blum, Stella, 330
Boni and Liveright, 213
Boyd, Ernest, 219
Boyd, Madeleine, 219, 235, 277
Brinnin, Malcolm, 332
Brotherhood of Painters, Decorators and Paperhangers Local 829 AFL, 172
*Bury the Dead* (Shaw), 308

*Caesar and Cleopatra* (Shaw), 86, 92
Calder, Alexander, at Aline's party, 248–253
*Camille* (Dumas), 269
Cane, Florence, 267
Cane, Melville, 69, 84, 266–267, 292–293; and Wolfe's first novel, 217–218
*Caprice* (Sil-Vara), 236
Carnovsky, Morris, 167
Carroll, Albert, 184
*Cherry Orchard, The,* (Chekhov), 229
*Children's Hour, The* (Hellman), 295
Civic Repertory Co., 203–204, 216, 229, 284
Cooper, Violet Kemble, 87
Costume Museum, 312–314, 318–319; absorbed by Metropolitan Museum, 330
Costume workshop, 79–80
Cowley, Malcolm, 105
Crane, Stephen, 84
Crawford, Cheryl, 337
*Critic, The* (Sheridan), 93
Crowther, Florence, 331
Curtiss, Mina, 110, 118, 119, 131, 256

349

350

*Welcome to Our City* (Wolfe), 93, 104, 107
Welles, Orson, 307
Wertheimer, Maurice, 247
Westchester Garden Club, 310
*We the People* (Rice), 284, 288
*White Wings* (Barry), 167
Wilson, Edmund, 105
Wisdom, William, buys Wolfe's papers, 324–325
Wolfe, Ben, 101, 102
Wolfe, Fred, 101
Wolfe, Julia, 98–99, 100, 103, 276, 316; throws Aline out, 277–278
Wolfe, Mabel, 100, 214, 276, 327
Wolfe, Thomas, 81, 93, 94; "accidental" meeting with Aline, 300–301; affair with Aline begins, 135–136; affair with Aline ends, 256–259; on Aline, 70–71; Aline's letters on food to, 19; at Aline's party, 248–253; on Aline's sketches, 89; Aline's trip to Europe without, 222–226; anti-Semitism, 162–163, 170, 179, 221, 311, 312; applies for Guggenheim fellowship, 246–247, 253–254, 256; and arguments over Aline's disciplined attention to her craft, 24; on Bellows, 70; at Chapel Hill, 101–102; dies, 315–316; drinking bout at Plaza Hotel, 282–283; and drunken brawl in Munich, 233–235; drunken scene in Gotham Hotel, 312; early months of affair with Aline, 137–148; early years, 97–101; in Europe, 107–108; excerpt from first novel published, 239–240; fan letters on first novel, 243–244; first novel accepted by Perkins of Scribner's, 235, 237; follows Aline to Armonk, 301–302; at Harvard, 103–104; leaves Scribner's for Harper & Brothers, 314; letter on Aline's book, 286–287; meets Aline, 111–120; and new studio, 200–201; in New York, 105–107; quarrels with Aline, 220–223; returns from Europe, 179–180; second meeting with Aline, 126–130; second trip to Europe with Aline, 196–198; and seeking publisher for first novel, 213–214, 217–220; stay in Europe to write, 169–170, 171, 174–176; story based on Aline's visit with Mansfield, 16–17, 319; strains in connections with Scribner's, 309–310; subsidized stay in Europe, 149–150; summer at Ambleside with Aline, 151–160; tensions between Aline and, 204–209; third meeting with Aline, 131–134; threatens to write to Teddy, 280; visited by Ethel in London, 270
Wolfe, William Oliver, 98, 99, 100, 101, 104
Woodsend, Harry, 199
Woollcott, Alexander, 140, 191, 249
Works Progress Administration, 306
*World of Sholem Aleichem, The,* 341
*Would-Be Gentleman, The* (Molière), 229
Wright, Russell, 57, 86, 90, 230
Wylie, Elinor, 189

YMHA, 92d Street, 332
*You Can't Go Home Again* (Wolfe), 188, 321